Sustainable Football

This book provides a comprehensive, up-to-date overview of the different environmental strategies adopted in the football world to foster sustainability.

The authors lay out useful insights, both for scholars and practitioners, to improve good governance in football organisations by empowering environmental organisational and operational actions. As well as examining practical methods of implementing green initiatives, the book discusses their added value from different perspectives including football fans, football managers and policymakers. By identifying the most important green actions for the dissemination of environmentally friendly behaviours at both individual and organisational levels, the book demonstrates how football organisations can use operational and organisational methods to develop an environmental sustainability strategy. The book contributes to developing the role of the football world by covering different facets of sustainability such as the circular economy, climate change, green marketing, fan engagement and more.

It will be a valuable resource for scholars and students of environmental management, sustainable business and corporate social responsibility, as well as professionals working in the football industry.

Luca Marrucci is a research fellow at the Institute of Management at Sant'Anna School of Advanced Studies where he is also part of the research group on Sport Sustainability. His research interests range from corporate environmental management, through sustainable consumption and production, to resource efficiency and circular economy. He is currently working in several European and national projects. He is also involved in teaching courses at the University of Siena and he is Adjunct Professor at the Institute Lorenzo de' Medici of Florence.

Tiberio Daddi is Associate Professor in Management at Sant'Anna School of Advanced Studies where he coordinates the research group on Sport Sustainability Management. His research interests range from corporate environmental management to sustainable consumption and production, from environmental footprint, performance and LCA to circular economy. He is project manager of relevant international projects funded mainly by the

European Commission, he has been involved as a European project evalua-
tor, and he is a partner of Spin Off company of the SSSA. He has authored
numerous scientific publications in international journals relating to the relevant research area. He teaches in the International PhD in Management, the
Master's in Environmental Management and Control of the SSSA, and the
Executive Master's in Circular Economy Management at the Luiss Business
School of Rome.

Fabio Iraldo currently holds academic positions as Full Professor of Management at Sant'Anna School of Advanced Studies, where he co-ordinates a
research group within the Institute of Management, and as Research Director at GREEN, formerly IEFE – "Centre for Geography, Resources, Environment, Energy and Networks", a research centre at Bocconi University
in Milan. Fabio is the leader of the sustainability management area at the
Institute of Management. He is responsible for teaching courses in Sustainability Management in several postgraduate MSCs and business schools (SDA-
Bocconi, SIAF). Among his main research activities, there are pilot projects
and studies carried out on behalf of national and EU institutions. He is the
author of more than 100 articles, many of which were published in international scientific reviews with Impact Factor.

Routledge Research in Sustainability and Business

For more information about this series, please visit: www.routledge.com/Routledge-Research-in-Sustainability-and-Business/book-series/RRSB

Sustainable Football

Environmental Management in Practice

Luca Marrucci, Tiberio Daddi, and Fabio Iraldo

Routledge
Taylor & Francis Group

LONDON AND NEW YORK

Designed cover image: Henrique Macedo

First published 2023
by Routledge
4 Park Square, Milton Park, Abingdon, Oxon OX14 4RN

and by Routledge
605 Third Avenue, New York, NY 10158

Routledge is an imprint of the Taylor & Francis Group, an informa business

British Library Cataloguing-in-Publication Data
A catalogue record for this book is available from the British Library

ISBN: 978-1-032-13238-9 (hbk)
ISBN: 978-1-032-13236-5 (pbk)
ISBN: 978-1-003-22827-1 (ebk)

DOI: 10.4324/9781003228271

Typeset in Bembo
by codeMantra

Contents

1 Perspective on environmental management in the frame of sport social responsibility

1.1 Environmental sustainability in sport social responsibility

Environmental conditions derived from unsustainable consumption and production patterns have led to the need to change society's behaviours and to adopt new solutions to combine economic success with the preservation of natural resources and social responsibility (Mebratu, 1998). With environmental issues becoming more and more current, and the awareness of citizens around the world informed by events such as fires in the Amazon and Australia and floods in different parts of the world, the question of environmental sustainability is becoming more and more central in different sectors of society.

The sport world is not excluded from all these issues. In fact, since 2007, the EC claimed that

> the practice of sport, sport facilities and sport events all have a significant impact on the environment. It is important to promote environmentally sound management, fit to address inter alia green procurement, greenhouse gas emissions, energy efficiency, waste disposal and the treatment of soil and water. European sport organisations and sport event organisers should adopt environmental objectives in order to make their activities environmentally sustainable (EC, 2007).

This underlines the need for moving towards a sustainable dimension of sport in consideration of the fact that sport's impacts on the environment are certainly significant. In this situation, the sport world cannot ignore the impacts produced on the environment but must also work for a sustainable future by using its great power of influence on public opinion to implement a real cultural revolution based on the solidity of values which are specific to sport. Therefore, it would be able to act on the behaviour of the sport organisations themselves, evoking frequently a virtuous alliance between sport and the environment.

In a context like this, it is necessary to start thinking about opening a new era, the era of sustainable sport, with priorities and objectives such

DOI: 10.4324/9781003228271-1

as reduction of CO_2 and other GHG emissions, energy efficiency and use of renewable sources of energy, sustainable transport, rational use of natural resources and limitation of waste, production and recycling of materials, use of products biodegradable, protection and promotion of biodiversity, etc.

Football is one of the most played and loved sports in the world. The passion for this sport keeps countless generations glued to the screen. The world of football has long turned its attention to numerous social issues such as racism, inclusion, diversity, etc., however only recently have football organisations started focusing on their environmental impact. Nevertheless, before starting to analyse possible strategies to foster the transition towards a more sustainable football, it is important to revisit the evolution path of the corporate social responsibility concept in the football world.

As recognised by Smith (2009), sport has always represented a preferential tool through which to achieve social benefits. The ability to aggregate large numbers of people, promote healthier lifestyles, increase people's well-being and be a source of inspiration for millions of young people around the world, constitute peculiarities that identify the world of sport as one of the most significant social phenomena able to influence the behaviours of millions of people.

The use of football or of sport in general as a preferential vehicle for social and cultural growth has been repeatedly recognised by various international organisations (Giulianotti, 2011). In 1978, UNESCO recognised multiple "qualities" in sport and in particular physical education as a "fundamental right for all". The United Nations (UN) considers sport as the fulcrum of a civil society; that, through it, increases its dynamic of positive transformation in the fields of education, health, development, peace, gender equality and social integration. Therefore, the UN General Assembly, with resolution 67/296, established the International Day of Sport for Development and Peace. It is celebrated every year and all over the world on 6 April (starting date of the first Olympic Games of the modern era, held in Athens on 6 April 1986). Both the UN and UNESCO, through their behaviour, have recognised in sport a tool capable of promoting social integration and economic development in different geographical, cultural and political contexts as well as to spread the ideals and fundamental values of peace, fraternity, solidarity, non-violence, tolerance and justice. The UN (2015) has given sport full recognition in the 2030 Agenda as the way forward for the sustainable development of nations. In fact, in the Declaration of the Agenda, paragraph 37, it is recognised:

> the growing contribution of sport to the realization of development and peace in its promotion of tolerance and respect and the contribution it makes to strengthening the capacities of women and young people, of individuals and communities, as well as health, education and social inclusion goals.

The UN also supports the role of sport in achieving the Sustainable Development Goals (SDGs). In addition to the UN, the European Union (EU) has also given much importance to the role of sport in the frame of social responsibility. Both have repeatedly expressed their desire to cooperate with the most influential clubs in the world, for the realisation of projects for humanitarian purposes.

Considering the uniqueness with which football influences everyday life, the emotions of people or the radical bond, historical and cultural value in force between the clubs and the territories to which they belong, it is not surprising that corporate social responsibility has forcefully become part of the daily life of football clubs. The role that football plays in the community, and the importance for the football industry to be present in this area, have led to the exploration of different horizons that lead football to have an increasingly important role on a social level. In fact, as for all corporate organisations, even for football clubs, it is becoming increasingly essential to set the cornerstones of their work, distinguishing their reasons for being, the pillars of the clubs' beliefs, the objectives to be achieved and the responsibilities to be faced.

As proved by Godfrey (2009), "Corporate Social Responsibility (CSR) may be good for sport and sport organizations and sport may be good for CSR." In fact, participation by sport organisations in CSR and related activities contributes to broadening the CSR concept and increasing its legitimacy in society. Sport, thanks to its highly visible, well-regarded and well-known set of social actors, could foster a new management approach for private sector companies which, most of the times, are not interested in contributing to creating and sustaining a higher quality of life in the society. Moreover, as suggested by Levermore (2010), the employment of CSR in sport organisations has allowed for development initiatives to extend to communities where traditional development schemes tend not to reach, especially youth communities.

The determinants and the reason for adopting CSR strategies in sport organisations can be both internal and external. Babiak and Wolfe (2009) investigate the drivers of socially responsible activities promoted by professional sport teams. The authors showed that external drivers of CSR, in particular key constituents, the interconnectedness of the field, and pressures from the league were more important determinants of CSR initiatives than the internal resources available to deliver CSR efforts (i.e., attention, media access, celebrity players, coaches, facilities). However, CSR initiatives stemming from external pressures usually cannot be sustained in the long run as they are largely not in accordance with an organisation's internal values and inherent core competencies. At the same time, if CSR initiatives are too linked with internal drivers, they may often neglect important societal needs. The authors concluded their research suggesting that the optimal CSR condition for sport organisations is one where both high external and internal determinants exist, maximising both the internal resources and the external stakeholder benefits for greater societal gain.

Anagnostopoulos et al. (2014) focused their attention on process-related issues. Specifically, the authors explored the decision-making process used in relation to CSR-related programmes. Their findings reveal that decision-making consists of four simultaneous micro-social processes ("harmonising", "safeguarding", "manoeuvring" and "transcending") that form the platform upon which the managers in sport organisations make decisions. According to Anagnostopoulos et al. (2014), *harmonising* is the process that explains those conditions which affect managerial decision-making in sport organisations. This process entails a variable degree of dependence such as the available resources, both financial and human, these organisations might have; the existence or otherwise of specified requirements that facilitate or constrain their engagement on CSR-related programmes; and the need for flexibility that allows these organisations to adjust themselves to new situations and conditions. *Safeguarding* is the micro-social process that explains the set of reasons which leads managers to make the decisions they do regarding CSR-related programmes. *Manoeuvring* is the modus operandi managers employ to deal with the factors that constrict harmonising and safeguarding. This process comprises the tactical action that is required to tackle the challenges and constraints the managers are faced with when making decisions. *Transcending* is the micro-social process that spurs foundations' managers' decision-making as a result of the large scope for further CSR-oriented involvement. This process seems to occur because of the high degree of passion these managers have for their jobs. The authors concluded claiming that these four micro-social processes together represent *assessable transcendence*, i.e., a process that is fortified by passion, contingent on trust, sustained by communication and substantiated by factual performance enables CSR formulation and implementation in this organisational context.

Walker and Parent (2010) suggested that many ways exist in which the sport industry is addressing CSR. The authors classified social involvement into three distinct categories: corporate social responsibility, corporate social responsiveness, and corporate citizenship. Corporate social responsibility is viewed as a "subset of corporate obligations dealing with a company's voluntary and discretionary relationships with its societal and community stakeholders to minimize or eliminate harmful effects and maximize long run benefits to society" (Matten and Moon, 2004). Contrarily, corporate social responsiveness can be presented "as a way to manage and respond to societal and stakeholder demands" (Epstein, 1987). Lastly, corporate citizenship (CC) has a twofold definition. According to Matten and Crane (2005), there are two sides of the corporate citizenship concept: the limited view and the equivalent view. The first one sees corporate citizenship merely as synonymous of CSR and it can be used interchangeably with CSR. The equivalent view suggests that the business itself is part of public culture and can expand its impact wherever business operations exist. Thus, corporate citizenship can be considered as an extension of the CSR concept. In fact, while CSR is seen more as an external orientation and a moral obligation (Matten and Crane, 2005), CC can be regarded as a cultural, legal, global and embedded dimension of social involvement.

Starting from these various forms of social involvement, Walker and Parent (2010) analysed sport organisations' websites in order to frame the most common social involvement practices. The authors concluded that social involvement varies considerably in the sport industry and this variation can be partially explained by geographical reach, stakeholder influences and business operations of the organisations. Sport teams and leagues were those linked to the community, quality of life and education. Contrarily, multinational organisations are more likely to adopt corporate citizenship activities than those operating in more localised context. The authors suggested that the magnitude and scope of the social involvement tends to reflect the profile and size of the organisation. However, as suggested by Walters and Tacon (2010), the starting point of every CSR activity should be stakeholder management. In particular, it is important to understand stakeholder definition and salience, sport clubs' actions and responses, and stakeholder actions and responses.

Despite all the positive intentions of sport organisations, CSR in sport is faced with several key issues. Giulianotti (2015) identified three main concerns that affect different areas of CSR activity and sport-based interventions. The first issue is related to the extent to which CSR and sport-based interventions have tangible social impacts and benefits. In fact, monitoring and evaluation strategies of CSR activities are still very controversial as proved by Kihl et al. (2014). A second concern centres on the politics and accountability of CSR. In particular, the main concern is on the extent to which user groups are fully consulted on their needs and engaged in the planning, delivery and evaluation of CSR projects. The last issue is connected with reputational risk. In fact, organisations which pick up negative headlines in their main areas of activity will always attract significant degrees of public scepticism or critical comment if they engage in CSR activity which is associated with a wider marketing makeover. Regardless of the CSR activity adopted by a critical organisation, they will always have to face the risk that this activity may be perceived as a smokescreen for covering its harmful operations.

However, Nyadzayo et al. (2016) demonstrated the positive role played by CSR in building relationship quality in the context of sports organisations. In fact, their study provided evidence of a direct impact of CSR activities on relationship quality. Moreover, the authors recognised that relationship quality, in turn, drives customer loyalty. Importantly, relationship quality is found to fully mediate the relationship between CSR and customer loyalty.

The importance of customer loyalty has been also pointed out by Scheinbaum and Lacey (2015). The authors proved that event social responsibility leads to fan attachment to an event, event word-of-mouth and sponsorship patronage. Fan attachment increases consumer promotion of an event to others and mediates the relationship between event social responsibility and the extent to which attendees share favourable word of mouth about the sponsored event. The results of the study also confirmed the strong link between event social responsibility and attendees' support for sponsors, via patronage of their products. For corporate sponsors, the results offer evidence for how sponsorship of community-based events provides an opportunity for a company to demonstrate good corporate citizenship while increasing patronage intent of attendees at a professional sporting event.

As proved by Inoue et al. (2017), the relationship between perceived CSR and behavioural loyalty is positively mediated by customers/supporters' involvement. However, when the effect of involvement on behavioural loyalty was mediated by commitment, the indirect effect of perceived CSR turned negative. These findings indicate that the contribution of CSR initiatives to behavioural loyalty is not as robust as past research suggests, and is also contingent upon specific psychological states activated by consumers' perceptions of such initiatives.

CSR and sport, often in combination with each other, are being increasingly voiced as vehicles that can assist various forms of social and economic development (Levermore, 2011). For this reason, professional sport teams are increasingly creating charitable foundations engaging in activities that target community development agendas. Initially, most scholars thought that the development of foundations within the sport industry was driven by both organisational (internal) and market (external) reasons (Minefee et al., 2015). However, sport organisations' role in the community goes beyond organised sport and the passion shown by fans and employees alike, the media attention and the applicability of the context in itself to provide momentum for a variety of CSR initiatives. Kolyperas et al. (2016) proved that in-house structure could not ensure the viable scalability of CSR. Considering the increasing importance of CSR activities promoted by sport organisations, foundations set up made sure that misalignment of interests between personnel looking after the community side and their counterparts responsible for the business side of operations could be overcome. In this way, sport organisations are able to eliminate potential conflicts of interest between the two entities. Another reason to create charitable foundations is strictly economic. In fact, funding bodies, such as local authorities, governmental organisations and third-party agents (including sponsors), were more inclined to link with non-profit formats than commercialised businesses.

The need to create charitable foundations was also determined by the increase in CSR activities. In fact, as explained by Rowe et al. (2019), there is a wide selection of possible CSR actions. The authors identified 14 specific categories of community activities based on their nature ad focus.

Considering the breadth of community-oriented practice activities captured, the authors grouped the identified activity subtypes into meaningful categories. Three overarching categories were formed as higher order themes: a) giving (identified in 37% of all initiatives), where a team used

Table 1.1 Type of activities underpinning community-oriented practice initiatives by Rowe et al. (2019).

Initiative type	% cases where evident	Description
Lend team brand or image to an organisation/cause	100%	Allow a non-profit organisation/cause to use relationship with the team and team brand to support a specific agenda or message.
Build awareness, promote a cause or advocate	85%	Take steps to assist a non-profit organisation or cause to promote their message (no associated financial arrangement or outcomes) and/or advocate for a specific cause.
Develop resources, messages and/or content	33%	Develop resources, such as course content, to be used to engage with the members of the community.
Disseminate or deliver resources	33%	Engage with members of the community to deliver or disseminate particular resources.
Player appearances	20%	One or more players/past players, coaches or cheerleaders making an appearance at an event/venue or acting as an ambassador for a cause/initiative.
Give away goods	19%	Providing goods and services, including clothing and merchandise or health-testing services.
Aid or facilitate fundraising for an organisation/cause	12%	Provide active or passive support to a non-profit organisation/cause in efforts to raise funds (not drawing on team/organisation or foundation funds).
Provide award or recognition	10%	Publicly provide an award or recognise the efforts of an individual, group or organisation.
Donate to, or sponsor, an organisation/cause	8%	Donations made using team/organisation or foundation funds to a third-party, non-profit organisation, cause or individual. May also form financial component of an "award" or "grant".
Provide facilities	7%	Provide access to a facility (typically team/foundation owned).
Volunteering and giving promotion	7%	Encourage members of the public and organisation staff to donate their time, goods and/or services to helping others.
Give away tickets	4%	Provision of tickets at any level (general admission to corporate function) at no cost to recipient.
Provide grants or facilitate provision	3%	Providing grants to non-profit organisations or individuals seeking support using team, organisation, foundation funds, or drawing on partner funds.
Facilitate or provide scholarship	1%	Provide funds via team/organisation, foundation or partner funds to support study endeavours.

existing team or organisation resources as part of the initiative; b) activating (identified in 88% of all initiatives), where a team encouraged community stakeholders to take action to address identified issues; and c) capacity building (identified in 34% of all initiatives), where a team sought to develop skills and capacities through the development and delivery of programming (see Table 1.2).

According to Rowe et al. (2019) sport organisations primarily targeted health and education agendas. However, differences were observed across regions and with regard to the target agenda, demonstrating differences within practices across regions.

So, sport has the power to change society, and the CSR activities through which social change occurs have the potential to enhance the organisation's performance and competitiveness (Trendafiova et al., 2017). Moreover, developing actions to benefit others and demonstrating concern about challenges facing a community would allow sport organisations to increase credibility, enhance reputation and create a company culture that is inclusive of a community (Miragaia et al., 2015). In fact, as suggested by Trendafilova and Babiak (2013), responsible initiatives may be based both on defensive factors (e.g., risk management to manage social legitimacy) or value-adding factors (e.g., enhancing market demand from customers and fans).

Table 1.2 Categories of community-oriented practice activities by Rowe et al. (2019).

Broad category	Associated initiatives	Description
GIVING (37%; used existing team or organisation resources as part of the initiative)	Donations, grants, giveaways, tickets, player appearances, provision of facilities.	Activities in this category involve a team drawing on its own resources (human, financial or physical), or those of its partner organisations or foundations, to support community development outcomes.
ACTIVATING (88%; supported, rewarded and encouraged action)	Fundraising, building awareness/promoting causes, awards and recognition, encourage volunteering or donations, lend brand or image.	This type of action involves teams encouraging community stakeholders to take action to address identified issues by raising awareness, encouraging donations and volunteering, and allowing non-profit organisations and causes to draw on their association with the team to raise awareness and encourage action.
CAPACITY BUILDING (34%; developing skills and capacities through programming)	Developing and disseminating resources.	This category encapsulates what SFD scholars and practitioners might refer to as "programmes", which target specific issues and work with particular individuals or groups to provide education, training, advice and resources to assist in developing skills and capacity of individuals and groups in the community.

Among all sports, football has a pivotal role in the diffusion of CSR activities due to its large popularity all over the world. In fact, as proved by Francois et al. (2019), football demonstrates a more international outlook in CSR activities than other sports. Most major clubs and national leagues have been thoroughly investigated by scholars analysing CSR engagement and motivation.

Hamil and Morrow (2011) focused on Scottish Premier League clubs arguing that these clubs are well positioned to act as vehicles to deliver CSR because of their community embeddedness and the strength of their stakeholder relationships. The authors suggested that Scottish clubs are driven by a) the normative expectations of executives or stakeholders, b) a response to wider social agendas, or c) potential economic benefit. These findings were confirmed also by Reiche (2013) who analysed the German Bundesliga. The author identified societal CSR drivers such as re-establishing local roots and serving as a model for society as well as economic motives such as strengthening customer retention and capturing sponsors' interest. Anagnostopoulos and Shilbury (2013) interviewed the charitable foundation managers of the top two divisions of English football. The authors found a paradoxical context in which CSR managers make strategic decisions in an endeavour to harmonise multiple environmental and institutional "recipes". Managers are confident that they have the capability to do so, yet realise that this capability is the result of a heavy reliance on external and/or internal resources. Ráthonyi-Ódor et al. (2020) reviewed the CSR activities carried out by teams playing in the Premier League and the Primera División. Even though some clubs share detailed statistical information about their actions and even publish their future plans, in the case of most clubs, the accessible information is rather superficial and lacks any exact descriptions. Blumrodt et. (2012) observed the CSR values adopted by sport clubs in the French first football division. The authors recognised that CSR is synonymous with organisations' social and ethical commitment, but at the same time claimed the need to integrate CSR within clubs' management strategies.

As explained above, geographical differences between CSR strategies emerge also in the football industry. In fact, as proved by Jäger and Fifka (2020), English club representatives focus on community issues, while their German counterparts take a more holistic approach. Moreover, the organizational integration of CSR differs, as English clubs rely on financially independent charities, while German clubs carry out most of the activities themselves. However, despite these differences, Alonso and O'Shea (2012) demonstrated the significance of the sport organisation as a support network or *"social anchor"*. Thus, considering the success of CSR activities and the environmental crisis that we are facing, it is not surprising that sports, but in particular football, are moving towards a more sustainable approach. In fact, more recently, environmental sustainability has become part of the main CSR strategies of football clubs (Fifka and Jaeger, 2020).

Most studies mainly analysed the environmental sustainability of mega football events centring their attention almost always on logistics and transportation (Dolles and Söderman, 2010). Sofotasiou et al. (2015) point out the climatic challenge faced by Qatar 2022 FIFA World Cup. The authors focused in particular on maintaining thermal comfort conditions within the football arenas due to the critical temperature of the region, estimating that a load of 115 MW/h per game at least should be consumed in order to provide both indoor and outdoor thermal comfort conditions.

As we will see in depth in the next chapters, one of the most impactful aspects connected to football sustainability is mobility. Thus, it is no wonder the literature is rich with studies on this topic related to both grassroots and professional football. Moreover, Jalil et al. (2019) proved that the awareness level of event organisers influences the sustainability of an event and provide evidence that encapsulates the importance of event management and event logistics to the public. Triantafyllidis et al. (2018) compared the quantity of CO_2 emissions generated from spectators' transportation to collegiate sporting events at an on-campus university stadium and at an off-campus stadium. The authors found significant differences between the two stadium locations regarding the spectators' choice of transportation mode and distance travelled.

However, Liu and Schwarz (2020), focusing on the Chinese context, recognised that "environmental initiatives", are not yet considered one of the most important CSR activities. In addition, focusing exclusively on mega sport events means having a limited view of the football industry. In fact, among the many sporting activities, football is the most popular and most practiced sport in the entire globe. It is practiced all over the world, especially in Europe, Central and South America, Asia and Africa. However, professional football in terms of numbers of people are just a small part. Amateur and youth football represent a deeply widespread and rooted sport (at national level, about one in fifty-eight Italians is registered with a football club).

It is time to extend the boundaries of the analysis recognising that football, with all its different nuances (e.g., events, professional, grassroots, etc.), is an important reality in our society. Fighting climate change and promoting sustainability must be a priority for every football organisation as social campaigns on inclusion, diversity and racism have been in the past. Managing the environmental sustainability of football is not just an issue for professional football or mega events, but it something that daily affects our lives. When we go the stadium to see our favourite team, when we play for our local club, when we go playing futsal with our friends, when we bring our children to the training, etc., in all these cases we can play a role in reducing the environmental impact of football. Nevertheless, football organisations cannot pass the buck only to individuals, they should be the example, they should drive the transition towards a more sustainable football. The first step of this process is starting to consider environmental management as a strategic approach and not just as a CSR activity. It is time to bring environmental activities to a next level integrating them directly in the business strategy of the organisation and not considering them as an occasional initiative.

1.2 Environmental management as a strategic approach

Safeguarding the ecosystem and minimising the impact of the environment have in recent years taken on increasing importance in the eyes of business management. They have over time become crucial components in the development of new corporate strategies not only in the football world, but in every industry and sector.

Even though the level of commitment given by organisations to environmental issues has been extremely diversified, it now appears certain that the awareness of the importance of green aspects has caused organisations to internalise environmental protection within their own strategies. It has become increasingly common for the top management of an organisation to start being concerned about the effects on the environment of their industrial and commercial operations.

Before focusing specifically on the football industry, it is important to understand the path that has led to the inclusion of the "environment" among the decisional variables of organisations. The main cause of the attention on environmental issues amongst organisations can undoubtedly be found in the substantial, and very worrying, deterioration of environmental conditions which has marked the last two decades. It is generally recognised that the development of the linkages between organisations and the environment through an increasing commitment to environmental issues is a process that is mainly caused by the exponential worsening of the environmental situation. It can be easily conceived that without a concrete escalation of the problem, organisations would definitely not have started considering the concerns highlighted exclusively by a few society groups with an extremely high environmental sensitiveness and awareness.

However, the deterioration of the environmental conditions cannot be the only reason for the diffusion of green strategies. In fact, unfortunately, the past is rich with environmental disasters which did not have an immediate impact on the ecological conscience of organisations. In recent years, our society has registered a general increase in the sensitivity towards the environment. A growing public awareness has given a decisive push in putting environmental protection at the top of the list of priorities for our society. In fact, as proved by Boiral and Paillè (2012) "the birth and the evolution of a true environmental conscience represent the most significant change in the socio-cultural system and in this context, can be seen as the main driving force of the transformation".

In addition to these two reasons, there is also an economic driver which contributes to boosting the internalisation of the environmental aspects within organisations' strategies, i.e., the possibility of obtaining an economic advantage. Testa et al. (2020) demonstrated that the competitiveness of green products and services has grown thanks to the wide spread of green consumption practices evidenced by consumers' tendency to show their environmental awareness through their purchasing choices. Organisations with environmentally friendly production of services and products have gained a competitive advantage from this shift in the market which has also fostered other organisations moving towards this new green direction.

These changes have been supported by policymakers. New regulations and innovative tools have been released by public authorities in order to increase the effect of incentives already caused by the changes in society, thus accelerating the transition towards a more sustainable world. All these changes have allowed the admission of the essential role of environmental matters from the organisations' perspective.

It is well known that the translation of the concept of sustainable development on a real-life basis can trace one of its key determining factors to the progressive crackdown on environmental legislation (Iraldo et al., 2011). This crackdown has, thus, encouraged the management of many organisations to take into account environmental aspects when determining their strategies, the need to consider environmental sustainability as an essential component of their targets and the adoption of innovative measures in their activities.

However, organisations are also influenced in the adoption of green strategies by external factors such as the context in which organisations operate. The context is determined by the extent to which green transformation variables have been implemented and can be identified in the changes in the external macro environment. These aspects may influence in different ways and timeframes the decision of organisations to adopt green strategies. It is possible to identify four types of contexts.

The *stable context* is typical of less developed countries, in particular Third World countries and Eastern European countries. Environmental regulations are practically absent even though the problems linked to managing the natural environment are very serious. The lack of interest by institutions can be explained by the total absence of changes in the societal and economic system. A lack of public awareness about environmental problems and consequentially an insufficient power to influence political decisions in putting ecology matters on the legislators' agendas characterised these countries.

The *reactive context* characterised most of the industrial sectors in Western countries in the last decades of the second millennium. In this context, active mobilisation for a solution to environmental problems was limited to small groups of people (environmental groups, residents of areas with high ecological risks, employees of dangerous factories, etc.), whilst the rest of public opinion was totally removed from any visible involvement on the environmental front. In addition to this, consumers showed very little interest in products that were environmentally friendly and environmental legislation evolves very slowly.

In the *anticipative context*, public opinion is very interested in environmental problems and quite often intervenes to ensure that stricter regulations are brought in. It is apparent how this context is characterised by the presence of the first element which marked the transition of the environmental question from obligation to opportunity: anticipation of regulations. Lack of ecological involvement by consumers, however, persists which basically means that the economic–competitive system remains static. A particularly significant example of the anticipative context is provided by the European Common Market where decisions concerning environmental regulations are taken at community level, thus avoiding any interference by single national organisations.

The transformation of the significance of the environmental question, thus, comes to an end and becomes a source of opportunity for competitiveness. The *proactive context* can only be found in specific sectors of the market, although some are gaining in significance.

Even though the approach to the environmental question is realistically not at all homogenous either for all sectors, until now the basic determinant of an organisation's behaviour towards environmental matters remains the context in which it can be found. In fact, organisations which have the perception of having plenty of time to adapt to environmental regulations are less willing to anticipate legislation. It also makes no sense for those organisations to adopt a strategy and a marketing policy based fully on the environmental quality of products in a context that is not proactive.

Thus, the business models of organisations can be classified according to the features of the context where they are established. The *adaptive business* (stable and reactive context) whose actions carried out for environmental protection are only induced by a command–and–control policy by policymakers. The *responsive business* (anticipative approach) which is, despite the presence of environmental regulations, characterised by the innovative way it pursues its goals. At the same time, its actions are not voluntary or systematic like those of the strategies of an active business. The *active business* (proactive context) considers the environment to be a competitive challenge which can allow it to identify new areas of profit and social consensus.

Business models can be also classified according to the managerial methods adopted to manage environmental aspects. In fact, most of the organisations located in a stable and responsive context adopt a *passive model*. It is characterised by a strong resistance to change. Organisations see environmental problems as a cost and not as an opportunity and they limit themselves to containing the impact on the environment to the extent to which it is imposed from the outside. The *adaptive model* is typical of organisations which comply with regulations and, at the same time, react to stimuli from society by putting innovative behaviours into place. Lastly, the *proactive model* concerns organisations that have understood the opportunity offered by the environmental question in terms of ecoefficiency and savings within the organisations' boundaries, but above all economic prospects across the market.

Starting from these types of business models, it is possible to also classify the related strategies. In a stable and reactive context, passive organisations would adopt a *follower strategy* which consists of a strict observance of all legislative standards or even the failure to observe them if this behavior would be less costly. Adaptive organisations would be based on a *market-oriented strategy* where everything is dominated by the market. Organisations will prompt improvement of the environmental quality of the business only if this increases profits or reduces costs. Contrarily, the strategy which sees the environment as a key factor (proactive) foresees the integration of the environmental variables in the organisational strategy at all levels.

Naturally, what has been described here is simply a rather generic reference framework, but it provides a pretty good idea of the situation on environmental topics. It can be applied to all industrial and commercial activities, and thus, also to the football industry. Integrating environmental management within organisations' daily activities would allow them to embrace a proactive approach looking at environmental issues not as a problem, but as an opportunity.

A systematic approach to environmental management can provide organisations useful insights and information to build long-term success and create opportunities to contribute to sustainable development:

- Protecting the environment by preventing or mitigating negative environmental impacts;
- Mitigating the potential negative effect of environmental conditions on the organisation;
- Supporting the organisation in fulfilling its compliance obligations;
- Improving environmental performance;
- Controlling or influencing the way in which the organisation's products and services are designed, manufactured, distributed, consumed and disposed of using a life cycle perspective that can avoid the involuntary shifting of environmental aspects to another stage of the life cycle;
- Achieving financial and operational benefits that may arise from the implementation of valid alternatives for the environment that can strengthen the organisation's market position;
- Communicating environmental information to relevant stakeholders.

The next chapters of this book will provide useful support to the football industry in the fight against climate change, in the transition towards a circular economy and in the adoption of a proactive strategy and approach. The book mixes theoretical and practical approaches in order to facilitate the comprehension of the main environmental issues, but simultaneously providing support the adoption and the implementation of environmentally sustainable activities. For this reason, within the next chapters, case studies will be presented and set in their relative theoretical framework.

References

Alonso, A.D., O'Shea, M., (2012). "You only get back what you put in": Perceptions of professional sport organizations as community anchors. *Community Dev.*, 43(5), 656–676. doi:10.1080/15575330.2011.645048

Anagnostopoulos, C., Shilbury, D., (2013). Implementing corporate social responsibility in English football: Towards multi-theoretical integration. *Sport Bus. Manag.: Int. J.*, 3(4), 268–284. doi:10.1108/SBM-05-2013-0009

Anagnostopoulos, C., Byers, T., Shilbury, D., (2014). Corporate social responsibility in professional team sport organisations: towards a theory of decision-making. *Eur. Sport Manag. Q.*, 14(3), 259–281. doi:10.1080/16184742.2014.897736

Babiak, K., Wolfe, R., (2009). Determinants of Corporate Social Responsibility in Professional Sport: Internal and External Factors. *J. Sport Manag.*, 23(6), 717–742. doi:10.1123/jsm.23.6.717

Blumrodt, J., Bryson, D., Flanagan, J., (2012). European football teams' CSR engagement impacts on customer-based brand equity. *J. Consum. Mark.*, 29(7), 482–493. doi:10.1108/SBM-04-2011-0050

Boiral O., Paille P., (2012). Organizational Citizenship Behaviour for the environment: measurement and validation. *J. Bus. Ethics,* 109, 431–445. doi.org/10.1007/s10551-011-1138-9

Dolles, H., Söderman, S., (2010). Addressing ecology and sustainability in mega-sporting events: The 2006 football World Cup in Germany. *J. Manag. Organ.*, 16(4), 587–600. doi:10.5172/jmo.2010.16.4.587

EC (European Commission) (2007). White Paper on Sport. COM(2007) 391 final.

Epstein, E.M., (1987). The Corporate Social Policy Process: Beyond Business Ethics, Corporate Social Responsibility, and Corporate Social Responsiveness. *Calif. Manag. Rev.*, 29(3), 99–114. Doi:10.2307/41165254

Fifka, M.S., Jaeger, J., (2020). CSR in professional European football: an integrative framework. *Soccer Soc.*, 21(1), 61–78. doi:10.1080/14660970.2018.1487840

François, A., Bayle, E., Gond, J.-P., (2019). A multilevel analysis of implicit and explicit CSR in French and UK professional sport. *Eur. Sport Manag. Q.*, 19(1), 15–37. doi:10.1080/16184742.2018.1518468

Giulianotti, R., (2009). The sport, development and peace sector: A model of four social policy domains. *J. Soc. Policy*, 40(4), 757–776. doi:10.1017/S0047279410000930

Giulianotti, R., (2015). Corporate social responsibility in sport: critical issues and future possibilities, *Corporate Governance*, 15(2), 243–248. doi:10.1108/CG-10-2014-0120

Godfrey, P.C., (2009). Corporate Social Responsibility in Sport: An Overview and Key Issues. *J. Sport Manag.*, 23, 698–716. doi:10.1123/jsm.23.6.698

Hamil, S., Morrow, S., (2011). Corporate social responsibility in the scottish premier league: Context and motivation. *Eur. Sport Manag. Q.*, 11(2), 143–170. doi:10.1080/16184742.2011.559136

Inoue, Y., Funk, D.C., McDonald, H., (2017). Predicting behavioral loyalty through corporate social responsibility: The mediating role of involvement and commitment. *J. Bus. Res.*, 75, 46–56. doi:10.1016/j.jbusres.2017.02.005

Iraldo, F., Testa, F., Melis, M., Frey, M., (2011). A literature review on the links between environmental regulation and competitiveness. *Environ. Policy Gov.*, 21, 210–222. doi:10.1002/eet.568

Jäger, J., Fifka, M., (2020). A comparative study of corporate social responsibility in English and German professional football. *Soccer Soc.*, 21(7), 802–820. doi:10.1080/14660970.2020.1749052

Jalil E.E.A., Hui L.S., Ning K.E., Fai L.K., (2019). Event logistics in sustainability of football matches. *Int. J. Sup. Chain. Mgt.*, 8(19), 924–931.

Kihl, L., Babiak, K., Tainsky, S., (2014). Evaluating the implementation of a professional sport team's corporate community involvement initiative. *J. Sport Manag.*, 28(3), 324–337. doi:10.1123/jsm.2012–0258

Kolyperas D, Anagnostopoulos C., Chadwick S., Sparks L., (2016). Applying a communicating vessels framework to csr value co-creation: Empirical evidence from professional team sport organizations. *J. Sport Manag.*, 30(6), 702–719. doi:10.1123/jsm.2016–0032

Levermore, R., (2010). CSR for Development Through Sport: examining its potential and limitations. *Third World Q.*, 31(2), 223–241. doi:10.1080/0143659100371 1967

Levermore, R., (2011). The paucity of, and dilemma in, evaluating corporate social responsibility for development through sport. *Third World Q.*, 32(3), 551–569. doi:10.1080/01436597.2011.573945

Liu, D., Schwarz, E.C., (2020). Assessing the community beliefs about the corporate social responsibility practices of professional football clubs in China. *Soccer Soc.*, 21(5), 584–601. doi:10.1080/14660970.2019.1704270

Matten, D., Moon, J., (2004). Corporate Social Responsibility. *J. Bus. Ethics*, 54, 323–337. doi:10.1007/s10551-004-1822-0

Matten, D., Crane, A., (2005). Corporate citizenship: Toward and extended theoretical conceptualization. *Acad. Manag. Rev.*, 30, 166–179. doi:10.2307/201 59101

Mebratu, D., (1998). Sustainability and sustainable development: Historical and conceptual review. *Environ. Impact Assess. Rev.*, 18(6), 493–520. doi:10.1016/S0195–9255(98)00019-5

Minefee, I., Neuman, E.J., Isserman, N., Leblebici, H., (2015). Corporate foundations and their governance: Unexplored territory in the corporate social responsibility agenda. *Ann. Soc. Responsib.*, 1(1), 57–75. doi:10.1108/ASR-12–2014–0005

Miragaia, D.A.M., Martins, C.I.N., Kluka, D.A., Havens, A., (2015). Corporate social responsibility, social entrepreneurship and sport programs to develop social capital at community level. *Int. Rev. Public Nonprofit Mark.*, 12(2), 141–154. doi:10.1007/s12208-015-0131-x

Nyadzayo, M.W., Leckie, C., McDonald, H., (2016). CSR, relationship quality, loyalty and psychological connection in sports. *Mark. Intell. Plan.*, 34(6), 883–898. doi:10.1108/MIP-08–2015–0148

Ráthonyi-Ódor, K., Bába, É.B., Müller, A., Bács, Z., Ráthonyi, G., (2020). How successful are the teams of the european football elite off the field? CSR activities of the premier league and the primera division. *Int. J. Environ. Res. Public Health*, 17(20), 7534, 1–32. doi:10.3390/ijerph17207534

Reiche, D., (2013). Drivers behind corporate social responsibility in the professional football sector: A case study of the German Bundesliga. *Soccer Soc.*, 15(4), 472–502. doi:10.1080/14660970.2013.842877

Rowe, K., Karg, A., Sherry, E., (2019). Community-oriented practice: Examining corporate social responsibility and development activities in professional sport. *Sport Manag. Rev.*, 22(3), 363–378. doi:10.1016/j.smr.2018.05.001

Scheinbaum, A.C., Lacey, R., (2015). Event social responsibility: A note to improve outcomes for sponsors and events. *J. Bus. Res.*, 68(9), 1982–1986. doi:10.1016/j.jbusres.2015.01.017

Smith, A., (2009). Theorising the Relationship between Major Sport Events and Social Sustainability. *J. Sport Tour.*, 14(2–3), 109–120. doi:10.1080/14775080902965033

Sofotasiou, P., Hughes, B.R., Calautit, J.K., (2015). Qatar 2022: Facing the FIFA World Cup climatic and legacy challenges. *Sustain. Cities Soc.*, 14(1), 16–30. doi:10.1016/j.scs.2014.07.007

Testa, F., Iovino, R., Iraldo, F., (2020). The circular economy and consumer behaviour: The mediating role of information seeking in buying circular packaging. *Bus. Strategy Environ.*, 29(8), 3435–3448. doi:10.1002/bse.2587

Trendafilova, S., Babiak, K., (2013). Understanding strategic corporate environmental responsibility in professional sport. *Int. J. Sport Manag. Mark.*, 13(1–2), 1–26. doi:10.1504/IJSMM.2013.055199

Trendafiova, S., Ziakas, V., Sparvero, E., (2017). Linking corporate social responsibility in sport with community development: an added source of community value. *Sport Soc.*, 20(7), 938–956. doi:10.1080/17430437.2016.1221935

Triantafyllidis, S., Ries, R., Kaplanidou, K., (2018). Carbon Dioxide Emissions of Spectators' Transportation in Collegiate Sporting Events: Comparing On-Campus and Off-Campus Stadium Locations. *Sustainability*, 10(1), 241. doi:10.3390/su10010241

United Nations, (2015). Transforming our World: The 2030 Agenda for Sustainable Development.

Walker M., Parent, M.M., (2010). Toward an integrated framework of corporate social responsibility, responsiveness, and citizenship in sport. *Sport Manage. Rev.*, 13(3), 198–213. doi:10.1016/j.smr.2010.03.003

Walters, G., Tacon, R., (2010). Corporate social responsibility in sport: Stakeholder management in the UK football industry. *J. Manag. Organ.*, 16(4), 566–586. doi:10.5172/jmo.2010.16.4.566

2 Environmental sustainability in football

2.1 State of the art of the diffusion of environmental sustainability among football organisations

CSR has also obtained a pivotal role in the football world. Starting from the social context, football organisations have expanded their attention towards environmental issues. Aware of the environmental issues the world is facing, football has started to increase its commitment and efforts towards sustainability. Despite the importance of the topic of environmental sustainability, the academic literature has mainly focused on the concept of CSR. Even though some football organisations have already adopted environmental practices to reduce the impact of their activities (Todaro et al., 2022), the contribution on green sustainability in the football world is still scant.

First of all, it is necessary to keep in mind that the relationship of football to environmental sustainability management is relatively unknown (Daddi et al., 2021b). Despite the increasing recognition of the growing role of football in regard to environmental sustainability, it remains unclear what role football organisations have with regard to environmental action and what is currently being done. Moreover, as demonstrated by Raimo et al. (2021) who focused on 80 football clubs that qualified for the UEFA Champions League and UEFA Europa League group stages for the 2019–2020 season, football clubs still disclose relatively little information about sustainability issues. Casper et al. (2012), focusing on Australian football subdivisions, recognised that although environmental concern is high, there is disconnect between concern and action perhaps due to a lack of communication, cost concerns and a lack of knowledge about sustainability initiatives. However, this does not mean that football clubs do not face environmental issues. Pedersen and Rosati (2019) studied organisational tensions and the relationship to CSR in the football sector. Focusing on Danish football clubs organised in the Danish Football Association, the authors concluded that clubs primarily face tensions linked to football/non-football activities and elite/non-elite discussions. Moreover, the results demonstrate a significant, positive relationship between the level of organisational tensions and the clubs' engagement in social and environmental activities.

DOI: 10.4324/9781003228271-2

Casper et al. (2021) investigated pro-environmental sustainability behaviours in relation to political affiliation in the framework of US college sport sustainability efforts. The authors identified that Democrats reported significantly higher pro-environmental values and norms. Despite the internal political dynamic, what is extremely important about this study is that sustainability programme engagement, sponsored initiatives awareness and influence of initiatives on behaviour were politically neutral.

However, the literature on environmental sustainability in the sport sector can be divided into two main areas of research: event management and organisations management.

EVENT MANAGEMENT

One of the first big football events where environmental concerns have been addressed was the World Cup 2006 held in Germany (Dolles and Söderman, 2010). In doing so, the German Organizing Committee did not have the objective of creating a short-term vision, but rather of making a long-term and lasting contribution to the improvement of environmental protection in hosting a mega sporting event. Four main areas, i.e., water, waste, energy, and transportation, were covered by the Organizing Committee, which also added climate protection as the fifth area of action and was recognised as a cross sectorial task.

Still on FIFA World Cup, but related to the 2014 competition hosted by Brazil, Vinciguerra et al. (2015) focused on the application of sustainability concepts during the works to reform and make adequate the Maracanã Stadium, addressing the recommendations of the LEED certification. Centring their attention mainly on waste management, the authors suggested a series of action aimed at reducing the environmental impacts of construction processes such as reusing the bentonite mud from the drilling process of cutting roots. In fact, after slurry settling, the construction allocated the material to a licensed ceramics factory where bricks and tiles were produced that were used in the construction of the building site of the Maracanã, reusing the material in the construction itself. Another sustainable action taken on the construction of the Maracanã was the removal of the lawn and topsoil. The topsoil is the first soil layer, usually between 15 and 20 cm deep, where the largest part of organic matter (nutrients) in the soil is concentrated. This soil is ideal for reuse in landscaping and agriculture. The topsoil removed from the Maracanã was referred to a company specialising in planting and used in the reforestation of rainforest species. The authors concluded by recognising that it was perceived that the implementation of a sustainability certification could help reduce the loss and waste of materials in the construction site, provide environmental awareness to stakeholders and establish strategies and actions to minimise waste in the construction site as well as its correct final disposal.

One of biggest problems related to large-scale soccer stadiums realised specifically for mega events is their management in the events after life

(Daddi et al., 2021a). This is the case with the Jeju World Cup Stadium located in South Korea and realised on the occasion of the 2002 FIFA World Cup (Park et al., 2016). Although the government of the stadium have made significant efforts toward creating profits from the stadium, it has proved to be too difficult for several administrations to cover its full operational, maintenance and conservation costs. The municipality who owns the stadium provided thus an independent renewable electricity generation system for the operation of the stadium in order to obtain relatively low values for the cost of energy.

Category	Visitor total Ecological Footprint (gha/day)	Visitor Ecological Footprint at home location per day[a] (gha/day)	Visitor additional Ecological Footprint (gha/day)
Food and drink	1,413 (0.0194 gha/visitor)	266 (0.0036 gha/visitor)	1,147 (0.0157 gha/visitor)
Drinks (alcoholic)	502	26	477
Drinks (non-alcoholic)	81	9	72
Meat and meat products	654	88	566
Cereals	35	19	16
Fruit and vegetables	20	27	–7
Oils, fats and spreads	60	10	50
Milk and dairy products	55	75	–20
Sugar and confectionary	6	11	–4
Other	Negligible	2	–2
Transport (ex. air)[b]	1,670 (0.0229 gha/visitor)	111 (0.0015 gha/visitor)	1,559 (0.0214 gha/visitor)
Car	1,139	101	1,038
Rail	325	2	3,234
Coach	164	0.4	164
Private hire bus	41	0.5	41
Local bus (park and ride)	0.05	3	–3
Other modes (inc. walking, taxi, motorbike)	Negligible	4.3	–4
Infrastructure[c]			
Stadium	0.10	–	–
Total	3,083 (0.0422 gha/visitor)	377 (0.0052 gha/visitor)	2,706 (0.0371 gha/visitor)
Waste[d]	151 (0.0021 gha/visitor)	–	–

Note: [a]Based on levels of consumption for an average UK resident per day.
[b]All transport calculations have excluded air travel to enable comparisons to be made.
[c]The Ecological Footprint of infrastructure for an average UK resident is not directly comparable as it includes the impact of housing and other general infrastructure including offices, schools, etc.
[d]The Ecological Footprint for event waste is not directly comparable with that of an average UK resident as it includes other household waste such as furniture and garden waste.

Figure 2.1 Ecological footprint of 2004 FA Cup Final by Collins and Flynn (2008).

Measuring the environmental sustainability of a major sporting event is one of most recent and innovative branches of studies on green football. Collins and Flynn (2008) measured the ecological footprint of the 2004 FA Cup Final. Even though ecological footprint estimated the environmental impact of people, Measuring the ecological footprint of a major sporting event such as the FA Cup Final represented a novel application of the tool. In fact, the findings of this research provided detailed information on visitor consumption patterns at a major sporting event.

In this case study the ecological footprint was also used to calculate the additional ecological impact generated by the event. This was calculated by estimating visitor resource consumption at their home location (per day) and subtracting this from their total consumption at the event for each of the footprint component areas. The additional footprint generated by visitors attending the event was 2,706 gha (0.0371 gha/visitor)[1]. The additional ecological footprint was calculated for the transport and food and drink components only, as comparable data were not available for capital investments (that is, stadium infrastructure) and waste at the visitors' home locations. If the total ecological footprint of an average visitor at the event is compared with that estimated at their home location for the same duration (that is, one day), the total impact of the event is found to be eight times greater. This significant difference is not surprising, as visitors attending the FA Cup Final will consume resources in different ways from their normal practices.

Visitor travel to the event had the most significant impact, although also visitor food and drink consumption also had a significant impact. However, the study did include in its analysis the impact of the event venue, as it was the main fixed asset that the majority of visitors would use during the event. Thus, the analysis focused exclusively on the indirect impact of the event, i.e., those activities on which the organisation of the event do not have direct control over, such as supporters' mobility and consumption. However, understanding visitor consumption and its environmental impact potentially can assist decision makers and those managing events to plan and organise them in such a way as to limit their impact. For his reason, the authors suggested some insights aimed to reduce the environmental impact of the three main impactful area, i.e., visitor travel, food and drink, and waste.

As regards visitors travel, the authors indicated that replacing car with coach or rail would allow a reduction of 22.5% of the total ecological footprint and around 40% of the specific impact of transport. Reducing the impact of visitor food and drink consumption can be pursued by simply replace all beef products with chicken (–14% of total ecological footprint and –30% of food ecological footprint). However, the best solution, (–16% of total ecological footprint and –35% of food ecological footprint) would be the adoption of organic food and drink. Contrarily, increasing consumption of locally produced food and drink would leave both the ecological footprints almost unaltered. Nevertheless, this may be due to the fact that only a small proportion of the total food and drink consumed by visitors at the event was imported.

Moreover, the energy required for food transportation is relatively small compared to that used for its production and processing. Lastly, regarding the impact of event-related waste the authors claimed that a 30% increased recycling rate of paper and card, glass (plastic) and food waste would reduce the waste ecological footprint by 5%.

Toffano Pereira et al. (2019) expanded the analysis to the Premier League clubs assessing their carbon footprint using the patterns of their domestic travel in the 2016–2017 season as a proxy for analysis. The study shows that, within the 2016–2017 season, the EPL clubs produced circa 1,134 tonnes of CO_{2-eq} as a result of their travel, where transportation accounts for 61% of the carbon footprint. Given the disproportionally high share of air travel in the total carbon footprint of Premier League club travel, this transportation mode represents a major mitigation opportunity. The authors suggested playing games at "neutral" stadia located midway for extremely distanced clubs since this strategy has the potential to reduce the carbon footprint of clubs. In fact, even though in the case of a neutral stadium the carbon footprint of hotels tends to increase since both clubs will play away from home, the reduction in carbon footprint of transportation is considerable and this option can be considered feasible. Toffano Pereira et al. (2019) also suggested working on procurement policies and practices. In particular, as regards the air travel services requested by the clubs for away games, biofuel-driven flights should be considered. The same also holds true when devising carbon mitigation strategies for hotel accommodation. The football clubs should strive to stay in hotels that have implemented sound greenhouse gas (GHG) emission reduction measures.

Considering the importance of supporters' mobility, other studies centre their attention on this topic. In particular, Jalil et al. (2019) proved that the awareness level of event organisers influences the sustainability of an event and provide evidence that encapsulates event management and event logistics importance to the public. Triantafyllidis et al. (2018) investigated the carbon dioxide emissions of spectators' transportation in collegiate sporting events comparing on-campus and off-campus stadium locations. Transportation modes and distances travelled by spectators largely influenced CO_2 emissions. The authors showed that there are differences in environmental impact among the transportation modes chosen by spectators. Public transportation, e.g. bus or metro, is the favoured mode in a high-density area, and has less impact on the environment. However, spectators did not utilise carpooling for the on-campus events as much as spectators of the off-campus events, i.e., many drove alone or used public transportation. Spectators of the off-campus events chose to carpool or use a bus. Many on-campus event spectators preferred to use vehicles, even for short distances. This may indicate that spectators of the on-campus football events (CFE) did not consider the environment when choosing their transportation mode or it may just be more convenient to take the car. At the off-campus events, findings showed that both carpool and bus modes impact CO_2 emissions significantly. Spectators who took the bus generated significantly less CO_2 emissions compared to spectators who carpooled. Off-campus events should aim to promote alternative ways for spectators to attend the event that will generate little to no CO_2 emissions. On-campus event spectators traveling greater than 80 miles primarily used cars, and there are opportunities to introduce bus and carpooling modes for longer travel distances. Moreover, off-campus events have a relatively expensive parking fee for cars. If sporting events' parking has a high cost, spectators may be more likely to use public transportation if available and carpool. The authors suggested that both event locations should promote transportation alternatives with low to no associated carbon emissions, e.g., bus and eco-friendly modes compared to car/scooter and carpool modes, parking policies should be reviewed, e.g., on-campus events providing free parking on campus, and lastly, recognising that the location of an event in an area that is urban, dense and served by public transportation will not necessarily reduce the aggregate impact of spectator's travel to and from the event without other policies and incentives.

Still on supporters' mobility, using an extensive geographic sample of ticketing data from Tennessee's home games during the 2015–2018 seasons, Cooper (2020) estimated the carbon footprint for each game, each contributing polluter and each season. The total season footprint over the four years was estimated to be 154,717,114 kg CO_{2-eq}, but most importantly, another time transportation was found to be the most impactful sector as shown in Table 2.1.

According to the author, in addition to promoting environmentally friendly ways of travel to their supporters, football clubs should educate their fanbase on the very fact that there is a carbon footprint associated with their game attendance. If fans do not even know how their actions contribute to glocal environmental problems, they cannot make intentionally sustainable choices. Educating the public about how personal activity affects ecological sustainability is an important first step in encouraging better environmental habits and promoting responsible resource use and consumption.

On air emission, but focusing on volatile organic compounds (VOCs), Dutta et al. (2016) warned about large-scale assemblies of people in a confined space which can exert significant impacts on the local air chemistry due to human emissions of volatile organics. In addition to VOCs emitted directly from human bodies, the authors indicated waste disposal and discharge

Table 2.1 Average carbon footprint by emission sector by Cooper (2020)

	Hotels	Waste	Food	Stadium	Travel
			kg CO_{2-eq}		
Total	7,521,038	2,800,636	18,806,449	37,460,413	88,128,578
Average per season	1,880,260	700,159	4,701,612	9,365,103	22,032,145

of food waste as other related indirect sources. The need to strengthen the attention on waste management is not only, thus, a question related to environmental well-being, but also to human well-being. In fact, unique spatiotemporal variations in VOCs species within a confined space can have unforeseen impacts on the local atmosphere and lead to acute human exposure to harmful pollutants.

ORGANISATIONS MANAGEMENT

The second branch of studies on environmental sustainability in sport have studied how football organisations have improved the performance of their stadiums and infrastructures. For instance, as proved by Kellison and Hong (2015), owners and quasi-owners of football facilities such as stadia, training centres, etc., reviewing green facility proposals considered the input of several groups, including the design firms, the media, political leaders, environmental activists and local citizens. According to the authors, the primary incentives for owners and quasi-owners to adopt sustainable designs were economic savings over the life of the facility, perception-management opportunities and demonstration of their innovativeness. Thus, the adoption and diffusion of pro-environmental stadium design will still face some barriers in the decision-making process.

Some studies, instead of focusing on mega events, analysed the environmental efforts of single clubs or of national leagues. Rathonyi-Odor et al. (2020) investigated the nature of CSR activities carried out by teams playing in the Premier League and the Primera División in the 2018–2019 season, and how these CSR actions serve environmental protection and society, manifesting the concept of sustainable development. The authors examined the available reports regarding all the 40 teams, focusing on information about their CSR related to six main areas:

1. The use of land and landscape (e.g. conserving biodiversity, protecting the ecosystem, largely modifying an entire region);
2. Clean energy (e.g. applying renewable energy, avoiding climate change, reducing carbon footprint);
3. Energy efficiency (e.g. using clean technology, LED lighting, energy saving, movement sensors, voltage optimisation equipment);
4. Water management (e.g., rainwater-collection system);
5. Waste management (e.g., prioritising the 4R principles: reduce, reuse, recycle, repair);
6. Environmental impact of activities deriving from sport (e.g. transport, food, office work).

Land use and landscape were the topics less considered by the clubs. The clubs report on regeneration and land alteration projects in order to create their training centres based on environmental protection values. Other activities are tree planting with the purpose of providing better air quality, the reduction of pesticides and other chemicals, and how to handle protected species in the area.

As for clean energy, establishing solar panel systems, installing air source heat pumps and using solar energy to heat water are common ways of reducing their carbon footprint. Energy efficiency appears to be emphasised at all clubs, in most cases through LED lighting (inc. floodlights), optimisation of the air conditioning system, and high-efficiency building services systems with intelligent controls.

For water efficiency, the most often mentioned operations are rainwater and greywater collection used for irrigation, dirty water recycled and used for irrigation, waterless urinals, and low-flow fittings and fixtures in order to reduce their demand for municipal drinking water.

All clubs took steps in waste management to contribute to environmental sustainability (including food waste used for anaerobic digestion; composted organic waste; creating battery recycling points; and sending plastic, cardboard, wood, paper and aluminium for recycling). In addition, more than one club pointed out that they are reducing single-use plastic.

Lastly, Liverpool is certified ISO 50001, Manchester United is ISO 14001, while Manchester City is LEED-gold. Real Madrid, Celta Vigo and Athletic Bilbao all have a well-known certification (LEED, ISO). FC Barcelona is the first sports complex in the centre of a major city that has obtained the German DGNB pre-certification, a system for evaluating and certifying sustainability, which considers the environmental, economic and cultural aspects of the buildings. Real Betis has officially joined the Climate Neutral Now initiative of the UN Climate Change, committing to take action to reduce its greenhouse gas emissions.

In connection with the environmental effects of activities related to sport organisations, we highlighted three areas: transport, food and office work. Clubs rarely go green in the office (e.g. using recycled paper, separate waste collection, energy saving lighting, using personal cups instead of plastic ones). Real Madrid is one of the few teams involved in ecological action related to their office work. They are doing their best to inform their workers on this subject; workers can drink filtered water instead of tap water, and employees have been asked to reduce their plastic bottle use. Clubs mention among their actions that in their operations creating sustainable transportation is important both for the clubs and their staff and for the supporters. They try to raise supporters' awareness about using public transport, riding bikes and walking. None of the clubs mentioned environmentally friendly action in connection with eating.

The authors conclude that Arsenal and Real Madrid can serve as examples for the other members of the sports sector due to their high commitment to environmental topics. However, the quantity and detail of the information shared by clubs is rather varied. Some clubs introduce their CSR activities in full detail. They share detailed statistical information about their actions, while some of the clubs even publish their future plans. However, according to Rathonyi-Odor et al. (2020), in the case of most clubs, the accessible information is rather superficial and lacks any exact descriptions.

Bunds et al. (2019) conducted a case study of SC Freiburg's carbon-neutral stadium construction process. The authors showed that environmental concerns were included through a political process that incorporated the interests of a diverse stakeholders. In particular, the city and the club worked together to manage different environmental issues:

- Energy: energy was designed to satisfy the city and residents. Thus, the club proposed solar panels that integrate into the grid, supplying power for the rest of the city when available and providing the club with credits to purchase renewable energy when necessary.
- Heat: the club proposed that heat to warm the pitch and buildings would be provided by a local factory that creates steam which can be capped and sent via pipe to heat the pitch and stadium.
- Grass: around 20 hectares of grass will be planted as compensation for the lost grass in the area of the new stadium.
- Wind: the city and the club commissioned a number of analyses to ensure the stadium would not block the wind necessary for glider and motorised flying.

The authors concluded that a new stadium is sustainable when the material public's interests (mainly environmental in nature, but also economic and social) are reconciled in the stadium as a matter of fact.

It is not rare to find environmental practices born in the context of other industrial sectors that are converted to the football world. This is the case with recovering heat from wastewater discharged from showers to preheat the incoming cold water. Incentivised by its carbon cost-effectiveness, wastewater heat exchangers have been selected and incorporated in a newly constructed Sports Pavilion at the University of Brighton in the UK. Ip et al. (2018) performed a life cycle analysis aimed at evaluating the environmental and financial sustainability of a vertical waste heat recovery device, with comparison to the normal use of a PVC-U pipe. The results indicated that the seasonal thermal effectiveness was over 50% enabling significant energy savings through heat recovery that led to short carbon payback time of less than two years to compensate for the additional greenhouse gas emissions associated with the wastewater heat exchangers. However, the life cycle cost of the wastewater heat exchangers is much higher than using the PVC-U pipe, even with significant heat recovered under heavy usage, highlighting the need to adopt more economic configurations, such as combining wastewater through fewer units, in order to maximise the return on investment and improve the financial viability.

Despite the contributions collected on environmental sustainability in the football world, wide room for improvement is still present in this sector. This has two main causes: 1) a problem related to the "environmental governance" of football events and 2) a problem related to the "operational management" of environmental aspects during the events. However, before starting to understand possible strategies to overcome these issues, it is important to understand the main environmental problem in this area for football organisations, i.e., climate change and the huge and avoidable production of GHG emissions.

The attention posed by the main actors of the football world on sustainability is constantly rising. Recently, UEFA unveiled a sustainability strategy "Strength through Unity" focusing on human rights and the environment. Through its new strategy, which will run until 2030, UEFA wants to inspire, activate and accelerate collective action to respect human rights and the environment within the context of European football. It is worth noting that the guidelines on sustainable football produced by the LIFE TACKLE project coordinated by the authors were cited within this strategy.

Aware that environmental issues represent a potential risk for football, UEFA defined a specific strategy. In accordance with the Environmental Commitment approved in 2021, UEFA is determined to be part of the solution to preserve and regenerate the environment and leverage the power of football to raise awareness and catalyse action. Along the way, it measures progress on how it prevents, minimises and remediates the impact of football on the environment. UEFA identifies four main policies: circular economy, climate and advocacy, event sustainability and infrastructure sustainability.

Regarding the circular economy, UEFA catalyses circular economy solutions together with partners and stadiums/event venues, with a particular focus on product packaging, plastics, single-use items, food loss and waste. Furthermore, it integrates circularity criteria in the UEFA Stadium Infrastructure Regulations as well as in UEFA campus facility management. The organisation also creates and continuously updates a repository of best practices targeting football, capturing innovations and lessons learned across member associations, leagues and clubs.

Regarding climate and advocacy, UEFA transitions from a reliance on compensation to a focus on reducing emissions from its carbon footprint. Furthermore, it leverages the global popularity of UEFA's elite competitions to communicate about the urgency of climate action. Alongside, a repository of best practices in football solutions targeting environmental protection will be created, capturing innovations and lessons learned. Lastly, UEFA continues efforts to minimise its internal organisational footprint.

The creation of the UEFA sustainable event management system (SEMS) will enable the measurement and benchmarking of event sustainability in football and provide end-to-end traceability of UEFA's impacts across its events. In the further implementation of the system, UEFA will collaborate closely with member associations, leagues and clubs. This will result in a process of continuous improvement around areas such as carbon footprint measurement, sustainable procurement and waste management. Lastly, this will lead to further cooperation and innovation with host cities, partners and other football stakeholders to shape a sustainable legacy for events.

Lastly, in relation to infrastructure sustainability, UEFA produces a Guide to Sustainable Stadiums, which integrates best practices in a wide range of areas (e.g., pitch treatment, energy, water, materials, electricity, mobility). Furthermore, UEFA integrates sustainability criteria into its Stadium Infrastructure Regulations as part of the UEFA club licensing system.

Moreover, UEFA integrated LIFE TACKLE's "Guidelines for the environmental management of football events" through an official letter sent by Michele Uva, Director of Football & Social Responsibility (FSR) at UEFA, to the Secretary Generals of its 55 member Federations on 1 March 2021. In this letter, UEFA expressed its full commitment to the LIFE TACKLE project and strongly encouraged National Football Associations (NFAs) to adopt the Guidelines at their governance and operational levels.

LIFE TACKLE is one of the several EU-funded projects on environmental sustainability in football. The project aims to promote actions for the environmental management of football matches and the environmental awareness of fans. In addition to LIFE TACKLE, there are also other examples of EU-funded projects which represent an interesting way for football organisations to receive support both technical and economic to improve their environmental performance, efforts and commitment.

ERASMUS+ SPORT GOALS aims to improve the environmental governance in football organisations. In particular, it focuses on women's and youth football teams with the aim of improving the environmental impact of their clubs and football matches. GOALS aims to increase their environmental awareness and promote the adoption of more environmentally friendly behaviours. The project also intends to strengthen cooperation between institutions and sport organisations boosting the adoption and the implementation of environmental governance actions. ERASMUS+ SPORT GREENCOACH instead addresses grassroots sport organisations and aims to improve their environmental impacts by incorporating monitoring and benchmarking activities and sustainability as a cross-cutting element in their daily management. It also aims at promoting healthy lifestyles at individual and community levels, especially among young athletes.

Making the sport sector more sustainable and greener is also the main idea behind the ERASMUS+ SPORT GreenSportsHub. The project aims to test the potential of the sports sector as a high-profile and news agenda-driving industry, to be a channel for the societal behavioural change needed to make the European Green Deal a reality by focusing on good governance so that leaders have the knowledge and skills to place environmental sustainability at the heart of their strategy.

Lastly, the Horizon2020 GREENFOOT develops and performs a community-based financing concept for renovating stadiums, practice facilities and related buildings according to energy efficiency and renewable energy standards. The concept consists of crowdfunding methods comprising creative investment packages and associated financial contracts that attract fans and community members to invest in the energy transition.

2.2 The challenge of climate change for football organisations

Climate change has been recognised as a major problem since the First World Climate Conference in 1979. This scientific meeting illustrated how climate change could affect human activities, issuing a statement calling for world governments "to predict and prevent possible climatic changes of anthropogenic origins with possible negative repercussions on the well-being of humanity". Nevertheless, more than 40 years have passed by, but we are still dealing with this issue. Moreover, the situation seems to be even worse.

Recent extreme weather events and natural disasters have shown that climate change can cause serious economic and social impacts. In recent years there has been a succession of catastrophic events and consequent economic losses that have been progressively classified as the most damaging compared to those that occurred in previous years, following now an incremental damage trend. According to the Sixth Assessment Report of the Intergovernmental Panel on Climate Change (IPCC, 2021) "human influence on the climate system is clear and recent anthropogenic greenhouse gas emissions are the highest in history. Recent climate changes have had widespread impacts on human and natural systems".

Since the contribution of human activities to climate change has been recognised, political, social and economic actors are called upon to seek alternative models of production and consumption in order to mitigate this negative externality. This objective implies, on the one hand, the reduction of GHG emissions which influence the speed and extent of change. On the other hand, the implementation of adaptation measures to environmental and socio-economic impacts. These two types of response to climate change in terms of mitigation and adaptation actions are complementary. Climate change mitigation therefore refers to human intervention to reduce the sources of greenhouse gas emissions or improve their absorption. Adaptation, on the other hand, refers to the process of adapting to current or future climatic conditions and its effects in order to moderate and avoid damage or exploit advantageous opportunities.

The risks of climate change can be expressed as a combination of the probability of occurrence of both dangerous events and other phenomena related to climate change and the impacts caused by them. Thus, mitigation aims to reduce the likelihood of occurrence, while adaptation aims to manage impacts. On the one hand, mitigation actions reduce the pressure of climate change on natural and human systems thus allowing more time to adapt. On the other hand, adaptation limits the negative effects of climate change although it does not prevent them all. It may seem that these are two alternative strategies, but they are two complementary strategies for managing climate risk. In fact, despite mitigation efforts, the climate will continue to change, so adaptation measures are needed. But as adaptation will not be able to avoid all negative impacts, mitigation is key to limiting changes in the climate system. Adaptation can be understood as direct damage prevention, while mitigation as indirect prevention. Without mitigation, adaptation for some natural systems would be impossible, while for most human systems it would involve very high social and economic costs. Both strategies include technological, institutional and behavioural options that can be encouraged with the introduction of economic and political tools. However, the ability to mitigate and adapt depends on socio-economic and environmental circumstances and the availability of information and technology. Consequently, climate change poses a major challenge, both in the present and in the future, particularly for the decision-making process.

The scale of the climate change impacts could be even greater than that of globalisation and information technology and could cause an economic revolution. Therefore, all organisations need to combat climate change by implementing both mitigation and adaptation measures as complementary strategies to address the risks of climate change. The direct and indirect impacts of climate change on organisations are many and concern not only the regulatory sphere (e.g., those related to the introduction of carbon regulatory policies both internationally and nationally), the market sphere, (e.g., changes in the demand for products and services), but also the sphere related to the physical impacts that affect the environment in which organisations operate. However, this latter sphere can represent a great challenge for organisations, leading to a reconsideration of the relationship they have with their natural environment, which has been considered predominantly stable in most of the world. In fact, the organisation-environment relationship has so far been considered from a pollution perspective, therefore in terms of the impact of the economic world on the environment (inside-out). Now this view needs to be reconsidered in terms of how the climate can affect organisations and the surrounding environment (outside-in). All organisations, including those in the football world, must contribute to the achievement of the Paris Agreement goal of maintaining a temperature rise below 2°C above preindustrial levels and pursuing further efforts to limit the increase in temperature to 1.5°C.

Given the importance of the phenomenon, the importance of cooperation between the public and private sectors is being reconsidered towards a joint effort to improve the resilience of local communities. Football organisations, in addition to reducing their vulnerability through adaptation measures, could press civil society and institutions to take anticipatory measures to address the physical impacts of climate change. In fact, once the phenomenon of climate change is recognised, organizations can reduce their emissions by improving their activities. These changes could also bring not only economic but also reputational benefits. Thus, on the one hand, organisations have to adapt themselves to physical climate-induced changes. On the other hand, in doing so, they develop adaptability and resources that can be shared with other stakeholders to avoid or reduce both direct impact and further indirect impact of climate change. To support sustainable development and efforts to build a Green Economy, organisations' contribution to climate change adaptation is essential.

In fact, the risks for local communities are also the risks for organisations because the communities provide fundamental resources to the organisations themselves. Moreover, organisations are also strictly linked to ecosystems since they provide natural goods and services (i.e., ecosystem services) such as flood protection, water supply, etc. which have an important economic value for the organisations (Li et al., 2017). Communities, which include suppliers, employees, fans, people who live in the areas where organisations are located, and other stakeholders, help determine the ability of organisations to operate and thrive. Therefore, the success of organisations also depends on the prosperity of local communities and ecosystem services. Consequently, the adaptation of organisations to climate change can be very beneficial for local communities and ecosystem services.

Therefore, organisations should consider improving the climate change resilience of the community in which they operate as a strategic imperative that goes beyond the scope of CSR. Furthermore, the possession of resilient resources is an important competitive opportunity under the pressure of global warming. Considering the increase in the frequency and intensity of current and future meteorological and climatic events, the development of European and international policies on the reduction of GHG emissions and the growing attention of the population towards these issues which are also cause of changes in the market demand, the fight against climate change should be strategically important at every organisational level in every organisation.

Over the last decade, climatic variability compromised the organisation of some international sporting events (Dingle and Mallen, 2020), with economic consequences and extensive damage to the structures put in place for the development of the events. In many cases, these climatic and meteorological events caused significant delays (e.g., Australian Open in 2014) or even the cancellation of important events sports (e.g., the Swiss Para Alpine Skiing World Cup in 2017).

Extreme weather events that change the climatic conditions may frequently have negative repercussions, both direct (e.g., by damaging physically the infrastructures which host the event) and indirect (e.g., profit loss or additional costs). In this context, according to Berkhout (2012), the organising bodies play a central role in response to the challenge posed by climatic changes. From a management point of view, as well as the activities related to agriculture or tourism, sport can be considered a climate-dependent productive activity. Thus, the quality of the product/service offered (i.e., sporting event, competitive performance) can be compromised, but it can also acquire added value, depending on the climatic conditions and environments in which this takes place. Vulnerability, resilience and adaptation strategies of the organising bodies of a sporting event understood as a climate-dependent productive activity depend not only on the economic resources available, but also on the level of knowledge and awareness on the environment and on climate change. The organising bodies will be called to develop new management strategies and to implement effective adaptation measures.

Dingle and Stewart (2018) investigated the issues that climate change poses for major Australian sport stadia and the organisations that manage them, and any organisational responses to such issues. The results revealed four primary climate change issues: organisational uncertainty, greater management complexity, cost risks associated with water and energy resources, and waste outputs. The authors demonstrated that while most physical impacts are manageable, the primacy of commercial and operational imperatives determine organisational responses ahead of government climate policy, and any direct climate "signal" to adapt.

A recurring problem, widely emphasised by the organisers of outdoor events in stadia, is related to the procurement of water. The reduction of rainfall in conjunction with a high evaporation level, in fact, made it more and more difficult to maintain optimal conditions of the turf for carrying out the sport activities. This, thus, requires an increasing supply of external water, with a consequent increase in the cost of water and the implementation of new plants and infrastructures, negatively impacting the sustainability of the sport event. A second element that connects the organisation of sporting events and climate change is clearly the increase of temperatures, which is closely connected with energy supply problems. With a view to mitigating climate change, consumption optimisation and strategies of energy efficiency are key issues for the reduction of greenhouse gas emissions (i.e., CO_2, CH_4, N_2O, etc.) and the containment of their effects on global warming. On the other hand, from an economic point of view, these management strategies are also useful to offset the additional direct costs induced by climate change itself. Unfortunately, to date, the use of renewable energy has not reached significant coverage.

The reduction of greenhouse gas emissions is directly connected with the containment of the increase of the annual global average temperature. However, in the evaluation of the impacts related to sport events, more attention should be placed on the temperature conditions in relation to the season and the venue of the sporting event itself. In fact, sports activities, that are carried out in the winter season, face various problems linked to the increase of temperature. In the case of winter sport activities, in general, it is easy to imagine that an increase in the temperature can compromise the existence itself of the snowpack. This may favour snow melting and forcing organising bodies to use artificial snow generation systems or the transport of natural snow from other sites, as happened in Vancouver in the 2010.

A third element to consider is linked to government policies for the medium to long term. A global government strategy is currently limited to the stipulation of agreements that are not strictly binding which, however, risk destabilising the economic strategies of organising bodies. Government management policies for the medium and long term are still too general and the introduction of a badly defined carbon tax creates a climate of uncertainty which slows down possible investments. Another element that must be taken into consideration concerns the management of waste in the context of the sporting event. Waste management fits into the context of climate change as the disposal of solid waste during sporting events contributes to greenhouse gas emissions. Waste management should implement closed-loop recycling systems at major infrastructures hosting major sporting events and should be encouraged by government bodies.

Climate change also threatens winter sports (Morrison and Pickering, 2013). Natural snow suitable for winter sports will continue to decline in the long term up to medium altitudes. The duration of the snow cover in late winter will thus decrease by weeks, as well as, albeit to a lesser extent, at the beginning of the season. Although the central months of the winter tourist season will be less affected by the phenomenon, the situation is critical. In this context, the climatological conditions for the production of artificial snow are also changing. The number and duration of potential snow periods (i.e., the periods in which artificial snow can be produced) will be reduced (Damm et al., 2014).

The increase in temperature and humidity conditions has an impact not only on the economic and logistical aspects of the sport world, but also on the health and safety of athletes, both professional and amateur. However, practicing physical activity in conditions of high temperatures and humidity can cause thermal stress in athletes, with more or less serious consequences such as thermal oedema, cramps, heat syncope, heart attack. Since physical exercise in environments characterised by high temperatures and humidity can have negative consequences on health, it is legitimate to ask what the impacts of global warming may be on the health of athletes engaged in outdoor sports. The increase in temperature will not only have effects on pathologies related to thermal stress, but also on the safety of athletes. In fact, the increase in temperature will also lead to an increase in rainfall. Moreover, an increase in humidity in the outdoor playing field determines also an increase in the likelihood of injury for athletes. In the winter season, the increase in rainfall can favour the formation of ice, with similar consequences for winter sports. In conclusion, the impacts of climate change on sports activities, both at a professional and amateur level, must also be assessed in relation to the safety, well-being and health of athletes.

The nature of the football sector is a recipe for a high carbon footprint, and when you take into consideration football fans (indirect carbon emissions), the impact will probably be several magnitudes bigger. However, sport in general, but especially football is not only influenced by climate change but it is also an opportunity to implement effective measures to combat it.

For that reason, the sustainability of football matches and stadiums has also been gaining more and more interest. UN Climate Change invites sports organisations and their stakeholders to join a new climate action for sport movement. This initiative aims to support and guide sports actors in achieving global climate change goals. UN Climate Change claims that sports organisations can achieve this by taking responsibility for their climate footprint, which in turn will incentivise climate action beyond the sports sector, and therefore help global ambition step up in the face of the threat posed by climate change. According to the official website of UNFCC, uniting behind a set of principles, sports organisations and their communities have created an initiative by collaborating in order to position their sector on the path of the low carbon economy that global leaders agreed on in Paris: the Sports for Climate Action Initiative. Participants in the Sports for Climate Action Initiative commit to adhere to a set of five principles and incorporate them into strategies, policies and procedures, and mainstream them within the sports community, thus setting the stage for a wider dissemination of the message and long-term success. The Principles of Sports for Climate Action Initiative will serve to mainstream climate action and will outline actions that, at a minimum, meet fundamental responsibilities in the areas of environmental sustainability and combatting climate change (UNFCC, 2020). The participants in the Sports for Climate Action Initiative will commit to adhere to the following five principles:

- Principle 1: Undertake systematic efforts to promote greater environmental responsibility;
- Principle 2: Reduce overall climate impact;
- Principle 3: Educate for climate action;
- Principle 4: Promote sustainable and responsible consumption;
- Principle 5: Advocate for climate action through communication.

Football has accepted this invitation and several top clubs from the most important leagues of the world signed the Climate Pact, e.g., LA Galaxy, Forest Green Rovers F.C., VfL Wolfsburg, Juventus, Real Betis Balompié, Arsenal, Liverpool FC, Tottenham Hotspur Football Club, Paris Saint-Germain, etc. In addition, UEFA signed in December 2020 the Climate Pact with European Commission. UEFA's president on that occasion stated: "By reaching a Europe-wide audience of millions, football has the potential to dramatically shift mindsets on climate change – a critical first step to getting everyone involved in creating a climate-neutral economy". In addition, effective governance (including environmental governance) is a key element in ensuring that football authorities function properly. Following the Good Governance in Sport of the European Commission, UEFA started a good governance reform in 2017, member associations have been required to align their governance structures to UEFA provisions. However, while some National Football Associations (NFAs) have initiated a reform process, many still not have significantly improved their governance standards. In this framework several initiatives have been adopted in recent years, such as UEFA announced that it will plant 600,000 trees across the 12 host countries of EURO 2020, some football clubs, e.g. Real Betis Balompié, Liverpool, etc., have decided to be "climate neutral" i.e., to calculate their carbon emissions and to offset them by buying carbon credits, Juventus from season 2020–2021 will plant 200 trees for every goal scored, etc. As for mega events, Tokyo 2020 set the sustainability concept of the Olympic Games as "Be better, together – For the planet and the people". Sustainability is also at the heart of the FIFA World Cup Qatar 2022. The FIFA World Cup 2022 Sustainability Strategy will enable the delivery of a tournament that sets new benchmarks for social, human, economic and environmental development.

The changing climate is therefore already affecting some sports and forward-looking organisations are already taking mitigation actions. The first concerns the analysis of risks, that is, to include the estimate of the possible losses caused by the suspension of matches and the impacts that consequently fall on the athletes. Only after becoming aware of the vulnerabilities of an organisation, it is possible to find adaptation strategies.

2.3 Risk perception of environmental impacts

According to World Economic Forum (2021), extreme weather events, natural disasters and the failure of mitigation and adaptation to climate change are among the top five most important risks that threaten humanity. All these risks are in turn connected to other risks such as the water crisis and migration. In addition to these, in the top ten positions, we find other urgent environmental challenges such as the acceleration of biodiversity loss and the collapse of ecosystems as well as natural disasters caused by anthropogenic activities.

As shown in Figure 2.2, environmental risks are the most relevant both in terms of impact and likelihood. Surprisingly, even in years conditioned by the COVID-19 pandemic, the World Economic Forum ranked environmental risks as four of the top five by likelihood with "infectious diseases" as fourth. As with COVID-19, climate change impacts are likely to play out disproportionately across countries, exacerbated by long-existing inequalities. Unfortunately, unlike COVID-19, there is no vaccine for environmental degradation. Failure to act would inevitably lead to catastrophic physical impacts and severe economic harm that would require costly policy responses.

In recent years, environmental risks and all the other risks related to them, including extreme weather events, climate change and water-related crises, have become increasingly important in the general landscape of risks to humanity, both in terms of impact and of probability. The risks associated with climate change indiscriminately affect civil society, institutions, organisations of various kinds and even the financial markets. As regards the last two actors, the risks are represented not only by climatic events and the impacts connected to them, but also by the regulations to mitigate greenhouse gas emissions, the social mutations and the variations in demand. Exposure to these risks can represent a driver for defining a response strategy to climate change (Kolk and Pinkse, 2008).

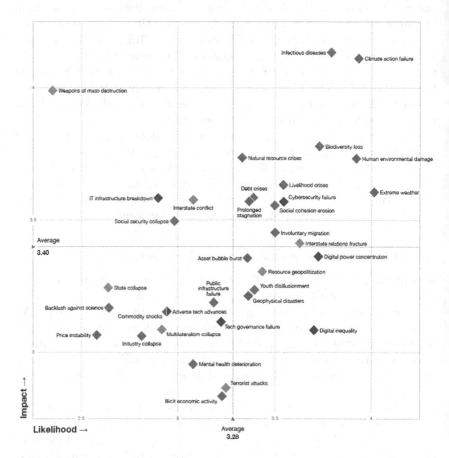

Figure 2.2 Global risk landscape by World Economic Forum (2021)

Identifying risks related to climate change is often considered one of the first steps in defining and implementing climate change response strategies (Weinhofer and Busch, 2013). A risk is often defined in terms of the combination of the consequences of an event (including a change in circumstances) and the likelihood of the event occurring (ISO, 2018). If the expected consequences are positive, then it is an opportunity. However, in practice, risk often refers to the event or its consequences. From this perspective, the main risks associated with climate change identified in the literature are regulatory and legal risk, physical risk, reputational risk, economic and financial risk, innovative and technological risk and changes in consumer needs.

Several studies (Gasbarro et al., 2018; Aguinaldo et al., 2019; Daddi et al., 2020) have shown that risks and opportunities related to climate change arise from a combination of impacts associated with three main drivers:

- Physical changes related to the climate, both direct and indirect;
- Climate-related regulatory changes;
- The change in market demand conditions.

Below, we report an overview of the various climate risk classifications done by Gasbarro and Iraldo (2020).

2.3.1 Regulatory and legal risk

The evolution of the international and national regulatory framework has a profound impact on society and the economy. The legal risk can be related to legislation, regulation or the limitation of emissions from products or processes. In practice, they are regulations aimed at reducing the contribution of human activities to climate change, such as regulations concerning CO_2 emissions. Regulations can have a profound impact on the growth and profit of organisations, as well as entire industries. So far, the discussion among policymakers, practitioners and scholars has focused mainly on the legislation aimed at limiting GHG emissions as an additional cost if the transition is not properly managed by organisations. However, with the definition and implementation of regulations aimed at limiting the rise in temperatures to below 2°C, it is reasonable to expect a reduction in the quantities of coal, oil and gas burned for the production of electricity. Furthermore, if you think about the Energy Strategy of the European Union at 2050, the EU has set a target of reducing GHG emissions by 80–95% compared to 1990 levels. To achieve these goals, major investments are needed in new low-carbon technologies, renewable energy, energy efficiency and grid infrastructure. It is clear that these policies and interventions will have a profound impact on organisations that consume large amounts of energy, but at the same time they can represent a great opportunity for the introduction of alternative solutions and technologies. The evolution of the regulatory framework can be considered a risk or an opportunity, but this depends on the type of sector or simply on the perception of the individual organisation. The world of football is not immune to these changes. In fact, considering both the consumption of electricity, mainly caused by the lighting of the stadiums during night matches, and the consumption of fuel energy such as gas for heating and fuel for transport, it is easy to think of a substantial increase in procurement costs of these resources. The transition to green energy will then not only be a question of environmental sustainability, but also an economic challenge that could impact the already weak corporate balance sheets of many football clubs.

The evolution of the regulatory framework may also concern the use of natural resources as a result of the physical impacts of climate change from the perspective of adaptation strategies. For instance, the legislation may introduce restrictions on the withdrawal of water as a consequence of drought phenomena. This limitation may cause strong impacts on several actors, such as civil society for the industrial, agricultural, tourism sectors and even the football world. A normative act related to water withdrawal restriction may strongly hamper football clubs. In fact, as already explained, the reduction of rainfall in conjunction with a higher level of evaporation has made it increasingly difficult to maintain the optimal conditions of the turf for sports activities. This situation already required a growing supply of external water resources, with a consequent increase in the cost of water and the implementation of new facilities and infrastructures, negatively impacting the sustainability of the sporting event. The introduction of a restriction could lead to the definitive collapse of an already precarious system.

This last regulatory aspect could be new for organisations and is closely linked to the physical consequences of climate change on natural systems and therefore on ecosystem services. In fact, the need for adaptation policies together with mitigation ones was recently highlighted in the international agreements signed in Paris in December 2015.

The legal risk is also linked to the eventuality of the obligation to compensate or refund a subject for the involvement in environmental offenses and/or for damage caused by negligent behaviour. It can result from regulatory non-compliance due to negligence of suppliers or distributors. This may cause the application of administrative and/or pecuniary sanctions. It can concern, for example, the exceeding of emission limits, as well as the non-compliance of products following climatic events or pollution following extreme climatic events.

2.3.2 Physical risk

The occurrence of gradual climate change and associated extreme hydrogeological, meteorological and climatological events can have a profound impact on natural, socio-economic and health systems. With a growing world population and a consequent increase in the demand for food, in a context of scarce water, energy and natural resources, climate change is a risk multiplier. Thus, aggravating the scarcity of resources and placing further stress on socio-economic systems.

With regard to organisations, some sectors have been identified as the most sensitive to climate change: sectors that depend on specific internal conditions of temperature and seasonality such as agriculture, tourism, etc.; sectors with infrastructures located in sensitive areas (such as coasts and floodplains) and those with assets with a very long life; sectors dependent on climate-sensitive inputs such as the food industry; sectors that depend on large-scale infrastructure such as energy, auto and transport.

Physical risk related to climate change can have numerous consequences for organisations, such as operational continuity, damage to plants and warehouses, damage to infrastructures, market risk, innovative and technological risk, financial risk, reputational risk, the legal risk, well-being and safety of athletes, etc.

2.3.3 Reputational risk

Whole sectors or organisations for which brand loyalty is an important component of the value chain can be exposed to reputational risk if they persist in the use of products, processes or practices with a negative impact on the climate. For example, in the case of the "Dieselgate" scandal, the discovery of the exceeding of the legal limits of emissions of Volkswagen cars led to a reduction in sales, a downward change in stocks on the stock exchange and negative reputational impacts. Reputational risks concern the trust of institutions, consumers and even employees in the organisation. Conversely, implementing an adaptation strategy or accepting responsibility for climate change can lead an organisation to improve its relationships with stakeholders as well as improve its reputation.

2.3.4 Economic and financial risk

Financial risk is related to the possible loss of financial stability both in terms of balance sheet and in terms of listing on the markets. This risk could be a consequence of physical risks or it could be caused by a high emission profile of the organisation, taxed or even only negatively evaluated by the market and by the shareholders. In the case of physical risks, there may be the need to obtain financings for the repair of damage caused by climatic events, or to run into additional insurance costs to cover physical risks. With regard to emission performance, financial risk also occurs when investors consider environmental and sustainability performance in their assessments and investment decisions. In fact, it appears that the financial markets are starting to incorporate climate change in order to determine the risk rates for organisations. Recently, in addition of the interest on emission performance, investors have start to pay attention also on physical risks of organisations.

2.3.5 Innovative and technological risk

On the one hand, the innovative and technological risk relating to climate change concerns the development of innovation and technologies aimed at reducing GHG emissions from products, services and processes. On the other hand, it concerns the development of innovation and technologies aimed at improving the resilience of organisations to physical risks and the management of extreme events. Crucial factors of this risk linked to low carbon technology innovation are the speed, the diffusion and their success, together with the degree of transformation and rethinking of the current methods of production and provision of services. In fact, in a world with carbon emissions limits, new markets are created, such as that relating to renewable energy, products with a low carbon footprint, green building, new financial services, etc. An important competitive element in the age of climate change is the possession of assets that are resilient to physical impacts and efficient from the point of view of the use of natural resources. In fact, these assets could determine a competitive advantage. For instance, an increase in water temperature could lead to an increase in algae with consequences on the use of water for production processes and for the distribution of drinking water for civil uses. In this case, investing in water treatment systems that take into account the increase in temperature could represent an improvement in efficiency, a reduction in costs and a competitive advantage over competitors.

2.3.6 Changes in consumer needs and in the supply chain

The demand for goods and services could be influenced not only by the mitigation objectives that direct it towards low carbon products and services, but also by the physical impacts of climate change. Indeed, physical changes related to the climate could affect the demand for some products and services, representing both an opportunity and a risk for different sectors. For example, the increase in average summer temperatures leads to an increase in the demand for drinking water, putting pressure on supply companies as well as sources of the natural resource.

The risk in the supply chain is connected to vulnerability determined by the geographical distribution and by the other variables that characterise the suppliers. The increase in the effects of climate change could lead to an increase in the procurement costs of raw materials and energy, as well as the interruption of the supply and alteration of the quality of the products. The greater the complexity of the supply chain, the greater the risk and the likelihood that climate change will affect the stability of the supply chain.

Note

1 The unit of measurement of the ecological footprint is the global hectare (gha) which corresponds to one hectare of productive space with productivity equal to the world average calculated for biologically productive lands and waters.

References

Aguinaldo, M.E.C., Daddi, T., Hamza, M., Gasbarro, F., (2019). Climate change perspectives and adaptation strategies of business enterprises: a case study from Italy. *Int. J. Sustain. Dev. World Ecol.*, 26(2), 129–140. doi:10.1080/13504509.2018.1528571

Berkhout, F., (2012). Adaptation to climate change by organizations. *Wiley Interdiscip. Rev. Clim. Change.* 3(1), 91–106. doi:10.1002/wcc.154

Bunds, K.S., McLeod, C.M., Barrett, M., Newman, J.I., Koenigstorfer, J., (2019). The object-oriented politics of stadium sustainability: A case study of SC Freiburg. *Sustain.*, 11(23), 6712. doi:10.3390/su11236712

Casper, J.M., McCullough, B.P., Smith, D.M.K., (2021). Pro-environmental sustainability and political affiliation: An examination of usa college sport sustainability efforts. *Int. J. Environ. Res. Public Health*, 18(11), 584. doi:10.3390/ijerph18115840

Casper, J., Pfahl, M., McSherry, M., (2012). Athletics department awareness and action regarding the environment: A study of NCAA athletics department sustainability practices. *J. Sport Manag.*, 26(1), 11–29. doi:10.1123/jsm.26.1.11

Collins, A., Flynn, A., (2008). Measuring the environmental sustainability of a major sporting event: A case study of the FA Cup Final. *Tour. Econ.*, 14(4), 751–768. doi:10.5367/000000008786440120

Cooper, J.A., (2020). Making orange green? A critical carbon footprinting of Tennessee football gameday tourism. *J. Sport Tour.*, 24(1), 31–51. doi:10.1080/147750 85.2020.1726802

Daddi, T., Bleischwitz, R., Todaro, N.M., Gusmerotti, N.M., De Giacomo, M.R., (2020). The influence of institutional pressures on climate mitigation and adaptation strategies. *J. Clean. Prod.*, 244, 118879. doi:10.1016/j.jclepro.2019.118879

Daddi, T., Rizzi, F., Pretner, G., Todaro, N., Annunziata, E., Frey, M., Iraldo, F., (2021a). Environmental management of sport events: a focus on European professional football. *Sport, Business and Management: An International Journal.* 12(2), 208–232. doi:10.1108/SBM-05-2020-0046

Daddi, T., Todaro, N. M., Iraldo, F., Frey, M., (2021b). Institutional pressures on the adoption of environmental practices: a focus on European professional football. *Journal of Environmental Planning and Management*, article in press. doi:10.1080/096 40568.2021.1927679

Damm, A., Köberl, J., Prettenthaler, F., (2014). Does artificial snow production pay under future climate conditions?-A case study for a vulnerable ski area in Austria. *Tourism Management.* 43, 8–21. doi:10.1016/j.tourman.2014.01.009

Dingle G.W., Stewart, B., (2018). Playing the climate game: climate change impacts, resilience and adaptation in the climate-dependent sport sector. *Manag. Sport Leis.*, 23(4–6), 293–314. doi:10.1080/23750472.2018.1527715

Dingle G.W., Mallen C. (2020). Sport and Environmental Sustainability: Research and Strategic Management. London: Routledge Ed.

Dolles, H., Söderman, S., (2010). Addressing ecology and sustainability in mega-sporting events: The 2006 football World Cup in Germany. *J. Manag. Organ.*, 16(4), 587–600. doi:10.5172/jmo.2010.16.4.587

Dutta, T., Kim, K.-H., Uchimiya, M., Kumar, P., Das, S., Bhattacharya, S.S., Szulejko, J., (2016). The micro-environmental impact of volatile organic compound emissions from large-scale assemblies of people in a confined space. *Environ. Res.*, 151, 304–312. doi:10.1016/j.envres.2016.08.009

Gasbarro, F., Iraldo, F., Daddi, T., (2017). The drivers of multinational enterprises' climate change strategies: A quantitative study on climate-related risks and opportunities. *J. Clean. Prod.*, 160, 8–26. doi:10.1016/j.jclepro.2017.03.018

Gasbarro, F., Iraldo, F., (2020). Managing the risk of climate change: business approaches and strategies. FrancoAngeli. ISBN:9788891789983

Ip, K., She, K., Adeyeye, K., (2018). Life-cycle impacts of shower water waste heat recovery: case study of an installation at a university sport facility in the UK. *Environ. Sci. Pollut. Res.*, 25(20), 19247–19258. doi:10.1007/s11356-017-0409-0

IPCC, (2021). IPCC, 2021: Summary for Policymakers. In: *Climate Change 2021: The Physical Science Basis. Contribution of Working Group I to the Sixth Assessment Report of the Intergovernmental Panel on Climate Change* [MassonDelmotte, V., P. Zhai, A. Pirani, S.L. Connors, C. Péan, S. Berger, N. Caud, Y. Chen, L. Goldfarb, M. Gomis, M. Huang, K. Leitzell, E. Lonnoy, J.B.R. Matthews, T.K. Maycock, T. Waterfield, O. Yelekçi, R. Yu and B. Zhou (eds.)]. Cambridge University Press. In Press.

ISO, (2018). ISO 31000:2018 Risk management – Principles and guidelines.

Jalil, E.E.A., Hui, L.S., Ning, K.E., Fai, L.K., (2019). Event logistics in sustainability of football matches. *Int. J. Supply Chain Manag.*, 8(1), 924–931.

Kellison, T.B., Hong, S., (2015). The adoption and diffusion of pro-environmental stadium design. *Eur. Sport Manag. Q.*, 15(2), 249–269. doi:10.1080/16184742.201 4.995690

Kolk, A., Pinkse, J., (2008). Market Strategies for Climate Change. *Eur. Manag. J.*, 22(3), 304–314. doi:10.1016/j.emj.2004.04.011

Li F., Liu X., Zhang X., Zhao D., Liu H., (2017). Urban ecological infrastructure: an integrated network for ecosystem services and sustainable urban systems. *J. Clean. Prod.*, 163, S12–S18. doi:10.1016/j.jclepro.2016.02.079

Morrison, C., Pickering, C.M., (2013). Perceptions of climate change impacts, adaptation and limits to adaption in the Australian Alps: The ski-tourism industry and key stakeholders. *J. Sustain. Tour.*, 21(2), 173–191. doi:10.1080/09669582.201 2.681789

Park, E., Kwon, S.J., del Pobil, A.P., (2016). For a green stadium: Economic feasibility of sustainable renewable electricity generation at the Jeju World Cup venue. *Sustain.*, 8(10), 969. doi:10.3390/su8100969

Pedersen, E.R.G., Rosati, F., (2019). Organisational tensions and the relationship to CSR in the football sector. *Eur. Sport Manag. Q.*, 19(1), 38–57. doi:10.1080/16184 742.2018.1546754

Raimo, N., Vitolla, F., Nicolò, G., Tartaglia Polcini, P., (2021). CSR disclosure as a legitimation strategy: evidence from the football industry. *Meas. Bus. Excell.*, article in press. doi:10.1108/MBE-11-2020-0149

Ráthonyi-Ódor, K., Bába, É.B., Müller, A., Bács, Z., Ráthonyi, G., (2020). How successful are the teams of the european football elite off the field? Csr activities of the premier league and the primera division. *Int. J. Environ. Res. Public Health*, 17(20), 7534, 1–32. doi:10.3390/ijerph17207534

Todaro, N. M., McCullough, B., Daddi, T., (2022). Stimulating the adoption of green practices by professional football organisations: a focus on stakeholders' pressures and expected benefits. *Sport Management Review*, article in press. doi:10.1080 /14413523.2022.2046971

Tóffano Pereira, R.P., Filimonau, V., Ribeiro, G.M., (2019). Score a goal for climate: Assessing the carbon footprint of travel patterns of the English Premier League clubs. *J. Clean. Prod.*, 227, 167–177. doi:10.1016/j.jclepro.2019.04.138

Triantafyllidis, S., Ries, R.J., (Kiki) Kaplanidou, K., (2018). Carbon Dioxide Emissions of spectators' transportation in collegiate sporting events: Comparing on-campus and off-campus stadium locations. *Sustain.*, 10(1), 241. doi:10.3390/su10010241

UNFCC, (2020). Sports for Climate Action Framework. https://unfccc.int/sites/default/files/resource/Sports_for_Climate_Action_Declaration_and_Framework.pdf

Vinciguerra, M., Figueiredo, E.P., Drummond, F., Zaeyen, C., Moreno, Í., Malafaia, B., (2015). Waste management in the reform and adequacy of the Maracanã Stadium for the FIFA Football World Cup 2014. *Key Eng. Mater.*, 634, 97–112. doi:10.4028/www.scientific.net/KEM.634.97

Weinhofer, G., Busch, T., (2013). Corporate Strategies for Managing Climate Risks. *Bus. Strategy Environ.*, 22(2), 121–144. doi.org/10.1002/bse.1744

World Economic Forum, (2021). The Global Risks Report 2021. 16th Edition. ISBN:978-2-940631-24-7 http://www3.weforum.org/docs/WEF_The_Global_Risks_Report_2021.pdf

3 Organisational and operational environmental management in football

Focusing both on all the phases of the sport event life cycle (i.e., conception, organisation, staging and closure) and on all the phases of an organisation's life cycle (i.e., procurement, production, distribution of the services/products, etc.), in this section we aim to show the best practices that will help both football events' key actors and organisations to improve their environmental management. This would also help to guide the diffusion of best practices in the related football leagues and stadiums. The main aspect of the approach adopted in this chapter is its focus both on the governance and operational aspects of the organisations involved in the environmental management of a football event, of a stadium and of the organisation's daily working life. The first section (section 3.1) covers the best practices in the field of governance. In this section the roles of the different stakeholders (National Football Associations, event organisers, suppliers, etc.) are defined to assure an effective environmental management structure. Moreover, the governance section will outline all the best practices linked to the planning and monitoring of improvement actions, the training and internal-external communication needs, as well as performance monitoring, reporting and a periodical review of the governance system and its achievements. The second section of the guidelines will be dedicated to the operational best practices. In this part of the guidelines the best practices will cover the major phases and tasks in the organisation of a football event (context of the event, event, procurement, mobility and logistics). The last section will be specifically dedicated to stadium management. Stadium management is a broad concept used to define an integrated and systematic process to support and improve the effectiveness of the primary activities and key services provided within the stadium, before, during and after a sport event. Accordingly, stadium management envisions a wide array of very diverse activities, ranging from the management and maintenance of buildings, facilities and infrastructures to the provision and monitoring of key primary services (such as water and energy).

DOI: 10.4324/9781003228271-3

3.1 Practices on the governance of football organisations and events

This section on governance collects all the actions and strategies that must be adopted and developed at the organisational and decisional level, i.e., practices relating to the overall organisation of the event such as the appointment of an environmental manager, the adoption of an environmental management system, the development of a specific sustainability strategy etc. whereas the operational practices are more directly connected with the event phase.

In general terms, *governance* refers to the broad framework of regulations, systems, roles, and procedures that enable an entity or organisation to function and achieve its objectives. Given such a wide domain, a more specific definition of the term is difficult to formulate. However, for the sake of the present section, governance is understood as a set of voluntary self-regulatory tools that leaders or managers implement to direct and manage one or more specific aspects related to the functioning of an organisation, event or activity. More precisely, governance:

- Defines the vision, mission and values of an organisation;
- Defines organisational structures and design;
- Assigns roles and responsibilities to directors and employees in compliance with existing regulatory frameworks;
- Shapes decision-making processes and control mechanisms;
- Safeguards the equitable treatment of shareholders;
- Ensures transparency and accountability with respect to stakeholders.

In these terms, governance appears as a primary function in the organisation of sport events and, most importantly, a crucial leverage for steering sport events towards sustainability. Greening sport events indeed requires altering existing governance mechanisms as well as introducing new self-regulatory and managerial tools within existing governance frameworks. Voluntary self-regulation aids sport organisations to codify mechanisms and tools supporting the overall organisation of sport events in a more environmentally responsible and transparent manner. Accordingly, sport organisations are increasingly undertaking efforts to establish comprehensive self-regulatory frameworks within which inscribing and monitoring activities from an environmental perspective. Besides providing a coherent regulatory structure to environmental management efforts, self-regulation helps communicating such efforts to external stakeholders by means of consistent reporting initiatives and, ultimately, establishing a permanent dialogue and interface between stakeholders and the organisation.

An effective framework for environmental governance should account for a wide array of organisational, strategic and operational dimensions. Such dimensions are well explicated by the so-called Deming cycle, also known as the "Plan-Do-Check-Act" (PDCA) management method, which underlies the majority of certifiable management systems (such as, for instance, ISO 20121 management standard for sustainable events or ISO14001 and EMAS Regulation management standards to implement and certify an Environmental Management System). According to the PDCA management method, continuous performance improvement is achieved through the following steps:

1. Planning improvement objectives;
2. Implementing improvement actions (e.g., training, operational control, etc.);
3. Assessing the results (e.g., internal or external audits);
4. Reviewing the management process in order to set new coherent objectives.

The practices on the governance of football events presented in this paragraph are interpreted as means to operationalise the above-mentioned four steps of the PDCA management method. From this perspective, the practices are categorised according to six operational dimensions of governance: a) assigning roles and responsibilities; b) planning; c) auditing and monitoring; d) certifiable management systems; e) reporting and communicating; f) managing stakeholders' relationships.

The primary task of environmental governance is defining roles and assigning environmental responsibilities within the organisation or organising committee. Usually, this is accomplished by appointing an environmental manager or a sustainability committee. Assigning environmental responsibilities implies clarifying how decisions about green aspects will be managed within the organisation. On the one hand, environmental responsibilities may be allocated to a specific organisational unit or function in order to concentrate decision-making with regard to environmental issues within a unique decisional centre. On the other hand, an environmental manger may be appointed within each organisational or operational unit in order to decentralise decision-making.

This particularly applies to environmentally sound large sporting events, since many of the tasks of an event organiser affect aspects of the environment. Ecological issues can only be adequately considered, however, when the environment has a staunch supporter on the organising committee. Each organisational unit should have someone responsible for the consideration and integration of environmental demands, and someone should also be appointed with overall responsibility for environmental issues. Moreover, in the case of large events it is advisable to establish an environment department in the organising committee. Environmental staff can be successful only when they are provided with sufficient financial and personnel resources and when they are involved in all important decisions.

The environmental manager should be placed in the organisational chart of a sport organisation in a position that can allow him/her to report directly to the top management and that can interact adequately with all departments involved by environmental issues (purchasing, operations, etc.).

Sometimes a sport and football organisation could decide to appoint an Environmental Committee to discuss about the different issues. An example is given by the Governance Sustainability Committee established by Juventus FC. In particular to ensure that the process has a systematic structure and a unified and shared approach to sustainability, the President of Juventus asked all corporate departments to contribute to the identification of a contact person for all sustainability issues.

This led to the establishment of the Sustainability Committee: an independent body formed by the representatives of all corporate departments that has the task of promoting the principles and values of sustainability within the Club. In line with Juventus' approach, each member of the Committee is responsible for applying sustainability to the business of his/her department and in turn, to represent the department within the Committee when defining the strategic objectives and KPIs.

Under this point of view, Juventus FC represents a good example of sustainability governance. In fact, besides establishing a central Governance Sustainability Committee, Juventus FC decided to appoint a sustainability officer in order to foster a systemic, pervasive and shared governance on environmental issues. Regardless of such organisational considerations, the allocation of environmental responsibilities should be matched by the allocation of resources, both human, financial and capital. In this sense, top managers need to empower environmental managers, or the environmental department, in order to effectively push environmental governance within their sport organisations.

Once roles and responsibilities are defined, the next step for an effective governance is planning objectives and the means to achieve them. Planning implies breaking down objectives into activities to be performed and identifying the specific actions that need to be implemented, as well as resources that need to be activated in order to successfully achieve such objectives. Integrating environmental concerns in pre-event planning contributes to ensuring that environmental principles are effectively incorporated in every relevant aspect of the event management and are accounted for in the budgeting process. Planning with regard to environmental management aspects contributes to increasing stakeholders' (such as the workforce, contractors, suppliers and all departmental units) awareness about environmental issues and about their specific environmental responsibilities.

Effective planning makes use of workflow management tools in order to coordinate activities and instruct the workforce about environmental aspects associated with each relevant activity. Accordingly, workflow management plans should account for the main activities to be carried out before and during event-time, such as food preparation, waste management, energy management, event promotion and materials, logistics, mobility and transport. To further detail the environmental aspects of each activity, checklists can be used to keep track of environmental aspects alongside workflow activities and assure that all actions are met and environmental aspects monitored.

The checklist can be broken down into categories including: a) Water b) Venue, c) Transport, d) Energy, e) Waste Management, f) Equipment, Supplies and Products, g) Event Promotion and Materials, h) Catering, and i) Training/Awareness. The use of checklists can be used also to ensure a workflow assurance. Workflow assurance is a way to assure key event-time sustainability processes from beginning to end by means of emphasis on the strategic decisions on key processes.

Waste constitutes a major environmental externality for most stadium management activities; accordingly, adopting a waste management plan emerges as a best practice to contribute to preventing and reducing waste production, while improving recycling and recovery rates, well in advance of sport events. Waste management plans aim to plan in advance waste reduction objectives, actions to achieve them and to further detail specific quantitative milestones, in order to allow event organisers to set up all the necessary infrastructures. Early planning allows the event organiser to set up all the necessary infrastructure to ensure proper waste management. Waste management plans allow sharing and agreeing waste reduction objectives among all relevant actors that are expected to play a role, such as municipalities, local waste companies and treatment plants, etc.

It is evident that waste management requires the active engagement of several actors: municipality, government, waste local operators, local waste facilities and treatment plants, the construction companies. The basis of the waste management programme at all venues can be a two-way bin system which divides recyclable (paper, plastic cups and PET bottles, metal and glass) and non-recyclable waste (e.g., non-recyclable packaging). They should be bespoke bins with coloured wheelie bins used in all the relevant areas. Graphical and text messages (signage) to assist supporters in avoiding bin contamination should be put near the bins. As part of planning activities with regard to waste management, the recovery of recyclable materials should represent a fundamental step in each event's workflow management plan. Recycling and recovery initiatives allow reducing environmental impact of all waste producing activities, while simultaneously reducing the cost associated with waste collection and disposal.

As in the case of waste, greenhouse gas (GHG) emissions are among the most detrimental environmental externalities associated with a wide array of activities carried out during the organisation of sport events, especially the most carbon-intensive and energy-intensive activities (such as heating, cooling, mobility and transportation). Emissions of climate-altering GHG, especially carbon dioxide, contribute to worsening global warming, which is a major cause of environmental degradation and a major threat to sustainability of modern lifestyles. To reduce the impact of sport events on global climate, organising committees should plan and put in place GHG emissions offsetting activities. A carbon offset is a reduction in emissions of carbon dioxide or greenhouse gases made in order to compensate for or to offset an emission made elsewhere

Carbon offsets are measured in tonnes of carbon dioxide-equivalent ($CO_{2\text{-}eq}$). One tonne of carbon offset represents the reduction of one tonne of carbon dioxide or its equivalent in other greenhouse gases. There are two markets for carbon offsets. In the voluntary market, individuals, companies or governments purchase carbon offsets to mitigate their own greenhouse gas emissions from transportation, electricity use and other sources.

Apart the offsetting activities of the hosting organisations, this option could also be offered to the attendees of the sport or football events. Especially in the case of air transport to and from the event location the host or the licensee could inform attendees on possible ways of CO_2 offsetting and encourage them to use this opportunity.

Similar activities aim to compensate carbon emissions associated with a specific sport event by funding GHG saving or carbon dioxide reduction initiatives implemented somewhere else. Offsetting initiatives may envision participating in voluntary carbon emission allowances markets, purchasing renewable energy credits or funding tree plantations.

Adopting carbon offsetting initiatives implies measuring and monitoring GHG emissions associated with each activity, in order to estimate the amount of CO_2 event organisers need to compensate. This implies creating a so-called GHG inventory, which constitutes a relevant aspect in the auditing and monitoring dimension of environmental governance. Indeed, a GHG inventory is a crucial management tool for identifying the activities that are most impactful in terms of GHG emissions, with the aim of structuring a coherent and effective reduction strategy. As set forth by the standard ISO 14064, GHG inventories may have diverse scopes. GHG inventories may exclusively focus on emissions generated by activities that are directly owned or controlled by the organisation or event organiser. Broader GHG inventories may include indirect emissions associated with purchased energy consumption. Finally, wider GHG inventories may even include all indirect activities associated with the value chain of the reporting organisation, such as, in the case of sport events, emissions associated with spectators travelling to the stadium.

Besides accounting for GHG emissions in dedicated inventories, organising committees should constantly monitor the overall environmental profile of activities according to a wider set of environmental indicators, especially for decision-making purposes. Developing baseline information on operations is crucial for tracking the progress of environmental improvement initiatives, as well as for establishing updated data repositories for decision-making purposes, for identifying improvement opportunities and setting objectives. Tracking environmental performance not only helps quantify these improvements, but can also help operations staff understand where there are opportunities for increased efficiency and potential cost savings. Thus, developing a system of environmental indicators to collect and monitor environmental improvements can be of fundamental importance.

Environmental data are collected and assessed by means of environmental auditing. Audits allow gathering information on-site on the performance of activities with regard to specific environmental aspects. Audits that are most commonly performed are energy audits and waste audits. Energy audits aim to develop thorough knowledge on the current energy consumption profile of a building or group of buildings, in order to identify efficiency improvement opportunities. In particular, the energy audit is a useful tool to:

- Provide thorough knowledge of the current energy consumption profile of a building or group of buildings;
- Identify and quantify energy savings opportunities in terms of cost-benefit;
- Report results.

The main goal is to have a clear picture of the energy performance and consumption of the sites in order to identify and plan the most effective changes to:

- Improve energy efficiency;
- Reduce costs for energy supplies;
- Improve environmental sustainability in the choice and use of sources.

Connected to energy management, there is specific management system that foresaw energy audits. ISO 50001 grounds its management structure on the paradigm of continuous improvement, supporting organisations to systematically control and reduce energy consumption in their daily activities. In particular, ISO 50001 sets forth procedural requirements for identifying and setting data-informed energy efficiency objectives, measuring results of energy conservation initiatives and setting new challenging objectives.

Similarly, waste audits analyse facilities' waste streams, gathering information on typologies of waste materials produced, estimating the amount of recyclable or compostable materials, and how much of each category is currently recovered for recycling. Waste audits record the sources, composition, weight, volume, seasonal variation and destinations of the materials that the venue generates.

Once environmental data are collected, environmental impact assessment (EIA) methodologies provide a solid and reliable scientific ground for keeping track of sport events' environmental profile according to a multi-indicator approach. First of all, EIA requires an initial analysis of the context aimed at identifying which environmental impacts could be generated by the event and thus, determining some requirements for the final approval. Therefore, an EIA will often include indicators such as carbon footprint, air pollution, impact on human health, land use and impact on biodiversity in order to provide an understanding of the environmental footprint of the event as complete as possible. As in the case of GHG inventories, EIA should embrace as wide a scope as possible, including activities regardless of the organising committee's level of influence. Similarly, EIA methodology should account for all environmental impacts regardless of the organiser's level of influence. This means that the assessment includes stakeholders' activities, as well as those of event partners: teams, staff, volunteers, the media and broadcasters, VIPs and spectators, clubs, constructors, etc.

The wider the scope of the EIA, the more informed and accurate will be the environmental cost benefit analysis the organiser will be able to carry out. Environmental cost benefit analysis supports decision makers in planning environmental improvement initiatives based on the economic availability of the organiser, expected results and cost of the initiative.

Besides supporting organisers in managing events' environmental, sustainability and energy performance, management systems help organising committees in making their environmental protection efforts visible to external stakeholders, such as spectators, local communities, suppliers, through certification. Environmental and sustainability management indeed help organisations improve their reputation in the eyes of stakeholders and in establishing a trustful relationship with clients and suppliers.

Similarly, environmental reporting and communication initiatives are crucial tools for maintaining solid and transparent relationships with external stakeholders and for valorising environmental protection and sustainability efforts. Sustainability reporting initiatives are adopted by organising committees during large sport events to spread awareness about the sustainability strategy underlying the organisation of the event, gain attention and commitment to their sustainability objectives from external stakeholders and, after the conclusion of the event, to report results of all the sustainability initiatives and inspire future event planners.

Sustainability reporting in relation to major events plays three main roles:

1. During the conception and planning phase, it helps with setting targets and strategies to reach them, it obliges organising committees to consult with their main stakeholders and to commit to the achievement of specific targets and objectives;
2. After the event conclusion, it works as a legacy document where all the actions and strategies adopted are reported along with their results: it becomes a useful document for future event planners;
3. In both cases it is a communication vehicle aimed at spreading information on the sustainability strategy of the event and on its impacts on the local economy, society and environment so it can also prove useful in relations management with local authorities, NGOs, group of citizens, etc.

A good sustainability report should follow the principles set out below. These are drawn from The Global Reporting G4 Sustainability Reporting Guidelines (Global Reporting Initiative, 2013):

Principles for defining report content

• Stakeholder inclusiveness – Identify your stakeholders and explain how you have taken into account their reasonable expectations and interests.

- Context – Present your performance in context. The underlying question of sustainability reporting is how your organisation affects (or plans to affect) economic, environmental and social conditions both within your sector or sport and at different geographical levels (local, regional, national, etc.).
- Materiality – There are many topics that could be reported, and it is important to focus on those that may reasonably be considered important for reflecting your sustainability impacts and/or could influence decisions by stakeholders. Materiality is the threshold at which aspects become sufficiently important that they should be reported.
- Completeness – The report needs to cover material aspects and their boundaries such that readers can gain a fair appreciation of your significant sustainability impacts and achievements over the given reporting period.

Principles for defining report quality

- Balance – The overall presentation of the report should provide an unbiased picture of both positive and negative aspects to enable a reasonable assessment of your performance to be made.
- Comparability – By presenting information in a consistent manner, you should be able to assess your performance against previous reporting cycles and other similar organisations or events.
- Accuracy – Information should be sufficiently detailed and factually correct for readers to assess performance.
- Timeliness – Reporting intervals should be reasonable, and the information contained should be as up to date as possible.
- Clarity – Information should be accessible and understandable to those reading the report. (It is reasonable to expect readers to have a general understanding of your organisation and its context, but try to minimise technical jargon requiring specialist knowledge to understand.)
- Reliability – Processes for gathering, collating and analysing information for use in the report should be capable of being examined to establish the quality and relevance of the information. This is an important part of gaining stakeholder confidence in the veracity of your reporting.

One of the most important things to do is to figure out which aspects of sustainability it needs to prioritise. It is easy to say that everything is important, and of course that is true. However, there are always some topics or issues that are particularly important for a specific event to address as a priority, because they relate to the main areas of impact, while others may be interesting and worthy but not directly relevant.

Having defined the scope, the next step should be to establish some objectives and targets in the form of an action plan. An objective is something that you plan to do or achieve. It should be relevant to your vision and purpose and related to the priority themes you have identified.

Targets are important because people like to see tangible things that you are working towards. However, these need to be realistic. If you pitch too high you risk falling short, and conversely, targets that are too easy will fail the credibility test. To get the balance right, it is worth testing draft targets with a sample of different stakeholders to gauge their reaction.

Monitoring is about checking that you are on track towards meeting your targets. Here you can set what are called key performance indicators (KPIs). If, say, your target is a 20% water reduction in a year, your KPI could be the amount of water reduction achieved within six months. If the figures show you have managed only 5% after six months, you can see you are falling behind on your target. In that case, you could decide to implement more water conservation measures to get back on track, or identify the factors preventing you from meeting the target and decide if the target needs recalibrating. It is not always practical to have KPIs for every target; some are either done or not done. However, you can set deadlines, so if something is over time that should flag up a warning.

A further opportunity for fostering environmental protection, while improving organisational reputation and stakeholder relationships, is provided by environmental awareness raising campaigns. Major sport events are indeed a great vehicle for conveying environmentally friendly messages, giving visibility to organisations' environmental efforts and for raising audience's awareness about sustainability issues. To be effective, awareness raising initiatives should aim to engage the public by means of awards or initiatives (e.g., involving athletes, providing free tickets, etc.) that ensure a broad participation and resonance of the initiative.

As previously stated, engaging stakeholders constitutes a fundamental aspect of environmental governance and strategy, which can be realised by means of very diverse initiatives and methods. Stakeholder engagement with regard to an organisation's environmental and sustainability strategy aims to gain commitment and support from relevant stakeholders for the realisation of said objectives, as well as gain feedback and advice on environmental performance targets and means to achieve them. Several methods may be adopted for engaging stakeholders, depending on the context, types of stakeholders and objectives. For instance, surveys, focus groups, mailing lists, workshops or multi-stakeholder consultations are methods that organisers can adopt at an early stage of environmental planning in order to understand stakeholders' needs and demands and plan their environmental strategy accordingly.

As a subsequent step to stakeholder engagement, developing relevant partnerships is a further crucial aspect of an effective environmental strategy that should be managed at the governance level. In the context of sport events, relevant actors may include international sport organisations (such as FIFA, UEFA, etc.), NFAs and other national sport organisations. For the sake of implementing an effective environmental strategy, it is fundamental to partner with local authorities, such as municipalities hosting the event, in order to coordinate environmental initiatives, such sorted waste collection. Similarly, private and public transportation companies are fundamental partners to address concerns about improving the sustainability of mobility solutions to and from the event.

Furthermore, partnering with private companies allows organisers to gain sponsorships for the event, which could help with funding the most ambitious environmental improvement initiatives. Indeed, partnerships can lead to significant economic benefits, and the visibility that a major event can grant to a private sponsor can be profitable. Most importantly, sponsorships are also important opportunities for cooperating and generating new ideas on how to improvement the sustainability of the event. To this aim, event organisers should engage sponsors in productive idea sharing, networking and cooperation.

3.1.1 Procurement

Green Procurement (GP) may be defined as a process whereby organisations seek to procure goods, services and works with a reduced environmental impact throughout their life cycle when compared to goods, services and works with the same primary function that would otherwise be procured.

At the European level, the GP approach has been endorsed in a number of EU policies and strategies concerning public procurement and recognising its potential to encourage a more sustainable use of natural resources and establish behavioural changes for sustainable consumption and production. Major studies aimed at identifying those products that have the greatest environmental impact throughout their life cycle single out three areas as having the greatest impact: food and drink, private transport and housing. Together, they are responsible for 70 to 80% of the environmental impact of consumption, and account for some 60% of consumption expenditure. The food and drink area, in particular, causes 20 to 30% of the various environmental impacts of private consumption, and this increases to more than 50% for eutrophication. In such a context, GP can be a major driver for innovation, providing industry with real incentives for developing green products and services and stimulating the markets towards more sustainable solutions.

Stadium managers should adopt a Green Procurement system aimed at orienting the behaviour of all the main stadium's suppliers toward the use of eco-compatible materials, the minimisation of resource consumption and the reduction of the environmental impact of their products and services. At the same time, stadiums' managers should try to also influence their key partners, sponsors and necessary contractors (i.e., necessary contractors that cannot be substituted such as the local waste operator or the local recycling facilities) towards the adoption and implementation of green criteria in their daily operations and in the selection of their own suppliers.

Green Procurement in stadium management can affect overall adverse environmental impacts in the three main detected relevant categories: private transport, housing and food and drink. In relation to private transport, stadium managers can conclude ad hoc agreement with local transport companies to push supporters' preferred public transport means. In terms of housing, the easiest equivalence can be made with the stadium's infrastructure and its adoption of green building criteria: this is something that stadium managers can address in a very limited way since, apart from some renovation intervention and the instalment of renewables sources of energy, there is little they can do to modify a pre-existing building. And, in any case, renovation and renewables instalments are costly interventions that not all stadiums can afford.

Some smart solutions on these aspects are described in the chapter dedicated to stadium management, however, there are some procurement choices that can help in addressing this issue as well.

In fact, if the instalment of renewables is not feasible or, in any case, not sufficient to cover the whole amount of energy required to ensure a stadium's functioning, one solution could be the purchase of certified green energy, i.e., energy produced by renewables sources and fed into the electric grid.

Ideally, the total amount of green energy to purchase should equal the effective energy consumption of the stadium, with the amount of energy already generated by renewables deducted, if any. However, certified green energy can be more expensive to purchase and thus, the effective coverage of the whole amount of energy consumption would not be always possible: in this case, a partial purchase of green energy would be preferable than nothing.

In certain cases, there could also be a pre-existing long-term contract of energy provision with a certain contractor that does not foresee the possibility of buying green energy. A smart solution to this impasse could be the purchase of an equivalent amount of certified green energy to fed into the concerned national grid, as a sort of "compensation for equivalent". This is not, for sure, the preferable solution, however, it can work for overcoming previous energy provision contracts that did not foresee the purchase of certified green energy.

During the 2006 Football World Cup, since direct supply of football stadiums was not possible – operators had long-term contracts with their respective suppliers – a "substitution solution" was developed. The energy sponsor fed 13 million kWh of electricity into the German supply network before the World Cup began. This electricity was wholly generated in a Swiss hydropower plant, part of which is recognised as a new plant in accordance with "OK power" criteria. The increased cost was borne by the energy sponsor. The utility EnBW (Energie Baden-Württemberg) provided certificated green electricity (OK power) in its capacity as "national supplier". It was not possible, however, to supply stadiums directly with green electricity, since stadium operators already had contracts with their respective energy suppliers.

Engie provides 100% renewable energy for Roland-Garros. Since 2015, Engie's offer provides 100% renewable green energy for stadiums, including the CNE, Jean-Bouin and Roland-Garros stadiums. This collaboration guarantees a three-year supply of electricity from 100% renewable sources, mainly hydropower and solar power.

The football arenas in Frankfurt, Wolfsburg and Leverkusen switched to eco-electricity suppliers permanently in 2011, while the stadiums in Augsburg and Bochum already had renewable energy systems before. The stadiums in Bordeaux, Saint-Etienne and Toulouse purchased certified renewable electricity.

In relation to drink and food, there are several green criteria that can be useful to prevent food waste and food-related waste, i.e., food packaging waste. First of all, stadium managers might think about elaborating food packaging guidelines to distribute among their caterers and food and beverage providers and subcontractors and concessionaries (e.g., kiosks and food trucks next to the stadium's entrance). Catering operations account for approximately 80% of waste during an event, and therefore it is paramount that both the packaging and food waste are planned and managed throughout the entire process. Rio 2016 has developed a Packaging Guide to advise the suppliers on their commitments and best practices. This guide explains the types of packages that are available as well as the Rio 2016 requirements. One of the commitments is to reduce the packaging during the Games and increase the use of recyclable packaging, made with recycled contents and/or, in some cases, biodegradable and compostable.

For the London 2012 Games all caterers were asked to use packaging according to the Packaging Guidelines, which stated that all food packaging for the Games would be compostable or recyclable and using a single waste stream where possible. Compostable packaging included plates, cutlery, hot drinks containers and lids, cold drinks containers and paper food containers. Recyclable packaging including salad containers and commercial cold drinks bottles.

During the South Africa 2010 World's Cup waste production was reduced by serving takeaway food with minimum packaging and recyclable materials in the stadiums and fan-parks. Paper towel was used as a form of packaging. Recyclable packaging was used by Budweiser and Coca-Cola.

In general, food packaging should be minimised and avoided at all when possible: one solution, could be the adoption of reusable and washable tableware. When disposable tableware is necessary however, these guidelines should suggest which type of food packaging materials should be avoided (e.g., plastics) and which should be preferred. However, it is difficult to use reusable cutlery and plates so disposable tableware is usually preferred. However, dirty plastic tableware has to be disposed of with unsorted waste whereas dirty paper tableware can go in the organic fraction (only for certain types of paper). In order to prevent high production of unsorted waste during events, some criteria on the usable tableware can be inserted in the tenders and contracts prepared with the catering service providers. In particular, also taking into consideration the local segregate waste collection rules, the usage of biodegradable and compostable tableware could be imposed, or a more general ban on the usage of plastic tableware and packaging can be applied. The usage of compostable tableware presents the advantage of making all the used tableware disposable in the organic fraction together with food waste. This also makes the separation operation even easier and faster for caterers. This would be particularly useful when adopted in municipalities that collect organic waste as a separate waste fraction and have easy access to composting plants.

In order to prevent waste production from catering services during EXPO Milano 2015, suggestions were put forward to use plates, cups, cutlery, etc. made of such materials that could be washable on site and reusable, as well as to provide water and beverages on tap. A fundamental criterion adopted to maximise recovery consisted of the request, whenever washable and reusable tableware had not been provided for, to employ compostable and biodegradable (EN 13432 certified) disposable items, thereby simplifying the set of recommendations for visitors/clients regarding the correct sorting of waste produced by consumption activities within catering areas. At the end of July 2015, a thorough verification was carried out at all 168 food outlets on the site in order to check the actual compliance with the provision and identify corrective actions whenever necessary. It turned out that only 57% of the used tableware was compostable, 4% was reusable and 37% was mixed. Therefore, even though the prevalent use of compostable disposable items was certainly a positive achievement, which definitely supported the effectiveness of actions carried out, the share of non- compostable disposable items was still significant, especially in specific cases such as cutlery and ice cream cups. All considered, there was a certain amount of confusion concerning compostable and non-compostable materials. Furthermore, both visitors and staff encountered several difficulties in visually making out the difference between compostable and non-compostable polymers. Such issues could be solved if, for example, there were a unique, international colour-coding for the different types of packaging materials, and in particular to make a distinction between compostable and non-compostable ones: colours are more readily understandable than the various certifying labels.

Nevertheless, compostable packaging is not always the best solution. The San Francisco Giants found that while compostable food containers worked for their system, compostable plastic cups were not the right solution for them. When the Giants offered compostable cups in their ballpark, fans were confused and did not consistently compost them, so the cups ended up contaminating the recycling stream. The Giants changed their service ware options so all of their drinkware was recyclable, while the food packaging remained compostable. This simplified procedures and messaging and helped the team to achieve a diversion rate of nearly 90%.

In order to maximise separate waste collection at the stadium and in its vicinity, a proper waste management plan should be adopted by stadium managers and some procurement solutions should also be considered. Cleaning is the first stage and precedes all the other stages of waste management. The efficiency of cleaning services and segregated waste collection depends on harmonious and precise cooperation between the cleaning services provider (a cleaning company), transport and the waste processing operator. Cleaning services include dry and wet cleaning of different surfaces, the collection of discarded waste (waste left on tables), washing of sanitary equipment and other equipment and places. The selection of the right waste and cleaning service providers can make a big difference in terms of waste management. Timing selection and engagement of this subject is also of utmost importance. The environmental function should be consulted for the selection of this key service provider. Furthermore, the cleaning service can also cause great environmental damage if it uses the wrong type of detergents and cleaning procedures. This should ensure the inclusion of ad hoc green criteria, e.g., on detergents and cleaning procedures, and the necessary alignment with waste management procedures aimed at maximising waste production and separate waste collection. If these objectives are set in the bids' offers and constitute a selection criterion, the provider will be more committed to achieve them and could also be considered liable if they are not met at certain level.

In addition, waste bin selection can seriously affect the success of the waste management plan: it may seem a secondary issue, but it can actually make a huge difference. In fact, bins should be strategically positioned in accordance with the expected different types of waste stream production (e.g., paper container next to stationery and organic bins next to food and beverage providers) and they should be all the same type and reproduce the same infographics and colours in order to be easily detected and distinguished by the public. These precautions can strongly affect supporters' behaviour and influence the final separate waste collection percentages.

Waste has to be separated in a way that it can be treated separately by the municipal or private waste disposal facilities. Special consideration has to be given to hazardous wastes (e.g., energy-saving lamps, pharmaceuticals), electrical appliances as well as toners and colour ink cartridges. These wastes need to be separated, collected and disposed of appropriately.

The selection of the right type of bin for separate waste collection along with the provision of clear information on it (which types of materials can be collected in that specific bin) is fundamental for reaching ambitious separate waste collection targets. Colour-coding and infographics should be clear and similar to the ones used in the local context (e.g., colour codes used by the municipality that hosts the event) to avoid confusion. The same type of bins and signals should be used for all the event's sites. To improve operations flexibility, bins should be designed in a way that allows their destination to be easily changed (e.g., use removable and interchangeable adhesives to signal waste fractions). Waste stations should be carefully located: in every station, there should be one bin for each waste fraction (according to the specific destination of the area).

To identify the best solution in terms of bins selection from a functional point of view, organisations shall apply the following criteria:

a. Functionality of bins to reach the set selective waste collection objectives; bins should be modulated into three to five compartments for the different streams of recoverable materials: paper and cardboard, plastic and metal packaging, organic matter, glass and residual dry matter;
b. Maximal reduction of occupied space (130 litre per bin and 1–2 m^2 taken up at each collection point);
c. Prevention of any overflowing (total volume calculated according to the degree of filling and emptying frequency throughout the day);
d. Prevention concerning safety (stability, surfaces and edges, rigid bins for glass and organic matter) and security (allowing for a rapid content inspection);
e. Use of bin surfaces for educational pictogram notices on environmental themes and for providing precise indications on waste sorting in different languages;
f.   Positioning of collection points for maximum waste interception (proximity to potential large waste producers, including catering facilities and food and beverage points of sale, as well as most popular areas for visitors, such as gates and rest areas).

Finally, waste should be prevented in the first place: this means that some green criteria could be set as waste prevention measures. For instance, on the occasion of football matches, it is quite common to distribute merchandise and promotional materials as well as choreography-aimed items: these are often disposable products that end up in the unsorted waste fraction. The insertion and adoption of green criteria in the selection of all these types of products could effectively prevent the generation of a significant amount of waste.

Advertising and the dissemination of information also involves distribution promotional objects. If used, it is better to utilise useful objects. It is possible, moreover, to adopt promotional gadgets which are more respectful of the environment through their technology (e.g., rather than battery calculator, prefer a solar calculator), their composition (for objects made of wood, prefer wood from managed forests sustainably such as FSC, PEFC[1]; products using recycled materials; etc.) or their manufacturing process. Products can also be interesting due to the questions they elicit and the answers they bring (e.g., games of awakening and awareness on the environment for example), or messages they convey (textiles certified as European Ecolabel or from fair trade, foods derived from organic farming, etc.) and so on.

Given the large amount of waste generated by the supporters' choreography at the end of football matches, there is the opportunity to reduce the environmental impact of the choreography by using accessories made of recycled and recyclable plastics (recycled LDPE). Recycled polyethylene is mainly obtained from processing the waste of industrial products (e.g., plastic bags for the food sector) made of low-density polyethylene (LDPE), followed by adding a portion of virgin material in the mix. LDPE is a thermoplastic polymer made from the monomer ethylene and belonging to the polyolefins group. The regenerated polyethylene utilised in the manufacturing of the flags is both recycled and recyclable, after disposing of it in the appropriate waste stream. Price and performance of choreography items made of recycled materials are equally comparable to choreography items made of virgin materials.

These abovementioned measures could be collected in Green Procurement Guidelines that should serve as an internal document for all the main stadium's direct purchases and that could also be distributed among all the stadium's suppliers, contractors, partners and sponsors in order to align all these key subjects with the stadium's approach to green provision of its main goods and services.

In the elaboration of such guidelines, the following aspects should be taken into consideration. At the general level, the inclusion of environmental criteria may relate to all stages of the procurement process, from supplier selection, technical specification, evaluation of suppliers, awarding of contracts, auditing and improving supplier performance and ongoing contract management. Whilst different partners, contractors and sponsors may have different procurement terminology, the procedures and stages in procurement cycles are often similar:

1. Definition of the object of the contract (subject matter) – Environmental criteria may be incorporated into the object of various types of contracts in different ways. For example, in supply contracts, ecological criteria for the goods supplied may be expressly indicated (e.g., recycled paper for printers and photo copiers);
2. Candidate selection (selection criteria) – The candidate selection criteria in the call for bids may contain environmental aspects regarding the technical capabilities of the candidates. In this case, candidates are selected on the basis of the evidence they are able to provide to demonstrate their capacity to carry out their activities in an environmentally sound manner, e.g., evidence of the regular environmental training of their staff, or of specific environmental management measures which they routinely apply. A certified environmental management system (such as EMAS or ISO 14001) – if covering and attesting environmental management capacities as laid down in the selection criteria – shall be recognised as evidence of compliance;
3. Definition of technical specifications and contract performance clauses – Environmental criteria may affect the definition of the technical specifications of the contracts in two ways:
   a) as technical standards – e.g., raw material characteristics, quality levels, production methods, etc. as contained in technical laws or

regulations or industry standards – incorporated by requiring: I) the use of certain raw or basic materials having low environmental impact; II) specific production processes (e.g., organic foods in food services); III) eco-labels in product specifications.

b) as functional and performance requisites including environmental components (e.g., energy consumption within use). Contract performance clauses may be included in the call for bids that specify the method of executing works in order to ensure environmental protection. Clauses may address, for example: materials delivery methods; environmental training of personnel; means of transportation; reduction in energy and water consumption during execution of work;

4. Inclusion of award criteria – Environmental criteria can be incorporated in the assessment of the bids' quality as specific award criteria leading to the final choice of the supplier. For example, the possession of environmental certifications or any other pertinent environmentally friendly feature may constitute a distinctive rewarding "plus" for those contracts whose proper management of environmental aspects is important.

The suggestion is to integrate the environmental criteria in those phases of the contract-awarding process being more effective in terms of environmental performance, e.g., via technical specifications criteria instead of award criteria, whenever possible and feasible.

3.2 Practices on the operational management of football events

The previous section analysed good practices on football events governance, i.e., how the organising entity should structure itself in order to ensure proper environmental management during the event phase. In the following section, we are going to analyse all the operational activities that have to be taken into consideration for the event phase dividing them per environmental aspect.

3.2.1 Water consumption

Football events, and the running of a stadium more generally are resource-intensive. Water, energy, light and heating have to be provided for the basic functions of the stadium. Such resources are generally used in large quantities; hence, any practice promoting their reuse or maximising the efficiency of how they are employed may have a greatly positive environmental impact. In the case of the Australian team Melbourne Cricket Club, in order to achieve its goal of better water management, the Club invested in the implementation of a water treatment plant that transforms sewage water into Class A recycled water. The recycled water is employed to irrigate the lawns surrounding the stadium and within toilet facilities. This practice allowed a reduction in the costs related to water consumption as well as a reduction in water usage by 50%, thus improving the sustainability of resource consumption of the stadium.

As far as water efficiency is concerned, diverse typologies of water conservation systems are frequently adopted to reduce the amount of water consumed for activities like turf irrigation, which do not require the use of potable water. Conservation systems may simply envision installing water-efficient plumbing fixtures for monitoring water flows through drip irrigation techniques, while more complex systems may include water recovery systems via drainage of land and ditches. Solutions for reducing stadiums' reliance on external water supplies include adopting storm water management systems or rainwater recovery systems. Similar techniques may require installing modular rainwater tanks on the top of stadiums' roof surfaces, drainage pipes that connect collector tanks to storage tanks, and filtering systems for ensuring water quality, as well as hydraulic and sanitary safety. Besides reducing water consumption, similar practices are particularly useful for avoiding water shortages during interruptions of public water supplies.

The Mercedes-Benz Stadium uses 47% less water than the standard due to water-efficient fixtures and conservation infrastructure that also allows rainwater to be used for irrigation. Green Point Stadium, Cape Town reduced potable water use by 10% through water-saving technologies in the stadium design, the roof was designed to collect rainwater, and the landscaping around the stadium included water-wise plants and water-efficient irrigation systems (drip irrigation). In addition, low-flow showerheads and aerated taps were also used. In Moses Mabhida Stadium, water metering was conducted for the stadium, in addition to the water-wise fittings and rainwater harvesting into a 700 cubic metre underground storage facility, and intelligent irrigation, resulting in 74% reduction of potable water. Similarly, the Maracanã Stadium in Rio has an array of 18 massive rainwater harvesting tanks. Each tank can store as much as 6,000 litres of water and can be interconnected with other tanks to fulfil the water volume requirements for any domestic, commercial or industrial application. The rainwater tanks are fed from the roof (an area of 32,000 m²), which has been engineered to collect large amounts of rainwater for use in the stadium's water systems, reducing its reliance on externally supplied water by 40%. The modular rainwater tanks supply water to irrigate the pitch, as well as for use in the 292 toilets and restrooms. The restroom facilities are also equipped with ecological flushing systems and intelligent faucets. Rainwater is soft and therefore it does not produce any limescale deposits. To harvest rainwater, the drainage pipes from the existing roof surfaces are connected to the rainwater storage tank via the low-maintenance rainwater filter. Filtering the rainwater ensures that the water quality can be preserved for long periods of time so that high-quality water is immediately available on demand.

Day after day there is a high consumption of water in flushing, baths, clothes washing and diverse washes. Since these operations do not require the use of potable water, the recovery of rainwater for these operations is increasingly seen as a key point in strategies to combat water scarcity. The compact stormwater systems allow the treatment and storage of rainwater and grey water, in order to allow their reuse in conditions of total efficiency and hydraulic-sanitary safety. Rainwater and grey water after treatment can be reused in the following uses:

•   Washing of floors and/or stadium benches after each game or at cleaning times;
•   Discharge of flushing;
•   Irrigation of turf area.

To complement, it will be of interest to use:

•   Flow reducers on all faucets and showers in the stadium;
•   Install shuffling with double discharges;
•   Flow reducer in compressors used for cleaning the stadium.

Besides the use of rainwater, several simple and easily replicable solutions may be adopted for reducing water consumption, also in relation with activities that require the use of potable water. For instance, installing low-flow showerheads and aerated taps in locker rooms and gyms, adopting ecological flushing systems with double discharges option and self-closing taps in the toilets, water-free dry urinals across the stadium areas, etc. In addition to being easy to implement in already existing facilities, these practices also offer great opportunities for reducing the amount of water consumed in routine stadium management activities. Indeed, more than 40% of the total amount of expensive potable water consumed in stadiums is associated with the use of toilets and urinals.

Ever since it was built, the Volkswagen arena in Wolfsburg has had over 230 water-free urinals in spectator zones. Due to the overwhelmingly positive experiences of this action, they changed over to dry urinals in other areas of the arena (including the business sector, executive boxes, administrative areas and changing rooms). Furthermore, those above-mentioned areas should have also been fitted with water-saving devices (some with sensors). For Volkswagen Arena, in financial terms we are looking at savings of €4,200 per annum after investment costs of €30,000. The investment should therefore pay for itself after seven years.

The Hamburg stadium has renovated its urinal flushing system outside the stadium. The central urinal flushing system was replaced by 16 separate steering units and 26 lighting groups. This enables individual toilets to be used and cleaned on their own. Previously, 25 lighting groups and 14 urinal flushing groups could only be activated simultaneously by means of a switching command, which entailed water consumption of 6 m^3 per hour during usage and cleaning. Hamburg stadium estimates to save at least 2,500 m^3 of fresh water, 2,500 m^3 of wastewater and 8,120 kwh of electricity per year.

The installation of faucet aerators (mixture of air and water) in areas such as public bathrooms, pantries, office bathrooms and maintenance areas enables organisations to reduce water consumption, avoid water scarcity and successively reduce associated costs. After the selection of the faucet aerator by the procurement department, the maintenance team can gradually install the faucet aerators in the different areas. One of the advantages of this practice is that water saving is a widely popular subject, with many solutions and opportunities to choose from in the market. Another factor that makes this practice easy to apply is the fact that internal resources can be used, such as a maintenance team, to carry out the installation of faucet aerators, without the need for an external contractor. The application of faucet aerators saved 20–25% of the water previously consumed.

3.2.2 Waste production

Sport nowadays is capable of attracting large numbers of spectators, fans, as well as presence of media. Stadiums and other sports venues can easily have capacities to welcome a large city with a population of 50,000 to 90,000 people. Although different in every country in terms of popularity, sports events taking places in these sports venues can easily turn into a fully functional town, with many facilities available – food and beverage providers, restaurants and other hospitality providers, sanitary facilities, commerce and other commercial activities. These characteristics can easily apply to various popular sports across the planet – hockey, basketball, tennis, American football, rugby and especially football – which is considered the most popular sport across the world and is especially popular in Europe. Once we add to these other activates, such as mobility and energy consumption for instance, one can easily consider a stadium as a living large town for a day. It's well known that an average European Union citizen generates 1.3 kg of waste per day (Eurostat, 2018[2]). Multiply that by up to 100,000 people involved in a large-scale football game, such as a Euro Cup game, for example, and we have something that should not be easily ignored.

This is why material flows and environmental management in general must be observed and adjusted or improved in order to meet certain sustainability criteria. Although a football match lasts 90 minutes, a football game must be considered more than a one-day activity, including the planning of the event in the three days before the match; the arrival of the teams, media, fans, pre- and post-game activities, departure from the stadium during the match day; all the post-match activities such as collection and disposal of waste. This further means that a sport event is not only what happens on the pitch, although being the most important part of a game. We are talking about the immediate impacts around the stadium, the stands, commercial stadium facilities, transportation hubs and more. And then, once the day is over, the following morning it could easily seem like nothing happened. Where did all the people go, what happened to their waste, all the resources needed for organising the game?

As mentioned before, football events can easily be considered as a living large town for a day. Therefore, the waste generated in the stadium can easily be aggregated to that generated in households and commerce. In football events, food waste represents an important kind of waste, thus, a system of separate waste collection has to be set up both in the common areas open to the public and in the technical areas reserved to staff and service providers.

The choice of the different waste fraction to collect separately should be taken considering:

• The local waste management regular practices (which are the fractions that are normally collected separately in that municipality) and the local waste facilities;
• The type of waste that is normally produced in every specific venue's areas (e.g., food waste in restaurants and kiosks in the immediate vicinity of the stadium before the matches, special waste in the infirmary, etc.).

In order to set up an efficient waste management collection system during football events, it is necessary to engage different actors like the event organisers, venue and stadium authorities, site owners and host cities, hospitality services and licensed souvenir providers, commercial partners, concessions stand operators, cleaning service providers, waste management operators, hotels, sponsors, other partners and organisations, etc. The bottom line is that the stadium needs to develop a separate collection scheme similar (if not same) to the one deployed by the local authority in order to facilitate the collection and treatment afterwards. There are cases where a certain local or regional authority had good separate collection performance, but these good results are missing in football games. Football games, given the number of people attending them and the amount of waste, can easily improve the overall local waste management performance.

More recently, some football organisations, like the Johan Cruijff ArenA, have started installing containerised anaerobic digesters using bacteria to break down organic waste and converting it into green energy. Thus, organic waste will be no longer trucked off with other waste to be processed in another part of the country, but will treat directly near the stadium and help power the stadium. However, this approach is not always possible due to spatial and odour issues. Thus, each football organisation should evaluate the best solutions interacting also with the local waste company and the municipality.

In addition, ad hoc training to waste and cleaning service providers' staff and to all the persons that will work on the event sites and somehow will produce waste is needed to ensure maximum waste recycling rates, prevent waste to landfill, exploit the event to educate spectators and raise awareness over waste management issues. During the six months of the EXPO Milano 2015, an average of 70% separate waste collection rate was maintained. Five different waste fractions were separated by both staff and visitors: paper, plastic and aluminium, glass, organic and unsorted waste. Additionally, special and hazardous waste produced by staff during regular work and maintenance operations was collected separately on request by the interested pavilion. The amount of waste prevented and the amount of materials recovered were registered through CONAI's Environmental Meter: a system developed by the Italian packaging consortium for measuring how many resources can be recovered through an efficient separate waste collection system. According to CONAI's Environmental Meter, selective waste collection and the transferral of resources for recycling allowed savings of 306 tonnes of CO_2, 4.7 million kWh of electricity and over 50,517 m^3 of water. The Meter was indeed created to quantify the avoided impact in comparison with unsorted waste landfilling, based on a model measuring the phases of collection, transportation, pre-treatment and recovery of waste. Based on LCA (life cycle assessment) methodologies, it was implemented with data provided by the local waste management company and by the plants the different materials were sent to. Quantities of material collected and sent to be recycled also allowed the obtaining of secondary products. Here are some examples for each material: 244,196 fleece sweaters from PET plastic; 2,552 benches from other mixed plastic; 59,022 wrenches from steel packaging; 2,855 mocha pots from aluminium; 2,545 wardrobes from wooden boxes; over 6 million shoe boxes from paper and cardboard packaging; almost 1,500,000 bottles from glass; 193 t compost from organic waste.

Generally, there are two separate areas for waste processing:

• Front of house (FOH): spectator areas and general access areas where competition spectators and guests are located;
• Back of house (BOH): service (technical) areas, where work is performed to prepare, manage and hold the competitions.

To make the separate waste collection easily understandable in spectator areas, a two-flow waste collection system should be organised in the FOH for spectators:

RECYCLABLE – plastic bottles, glass bottles (only in hospitality areas), film-based packaging, aluminium and tin cans, glass and broken glass, clean paper;

GENERAL WASTE – food and drink remnants, soiled paper wrapping and dirty napkins, hygiene-related items, teabags, other waste that is considered non-recyclable.

In particular, a two-flow separate waste collection system should be introduced in all the general access stadium areas, including, but not limited to, territories around stadiums, stadium entrances/exits, areas close to food and beverage selling points and merchandise concessions, hospitality areas, any other places with open access for spectators.

A good practice is the development of short operative waste management guides aimed at explaining how the waste has to be managed, what are the collection procedures and which equipment to use (different types of bins, bags, temporary waste storage points, etc.). Fractions to be separated must be on a clear on which materials and objects can go into a specific waste fraction, for example:

- Organic waste from kitchens and grass clippings for composting or anaerobic digestion which results in compost and/or energy for further use;
- Recyclables, resulting from consumption of plastic bottles, aluminium and tin cans, glass bottles in some cases, or from catering services during the match, like film-based packaging; paper from commerce and offices falls under this category, too;
- General waste, including various non-recyclable single-use items, or simply material not suitable for recycling.

These guides must be distributed to all the subjects that are going to work on the event sites in a timely manner: they must have time to understand the procedures, ask for help in managing particular situation and familiarise themselves with terms and equipment. Waste management guides can be prepared for every stadium.

Separate waste collection may be hampered by two factors. For security reasons, football organisations may be forced to reduce the number of bins present within the stadium perimeters thus avoiding the possibility to correctly separate the waste. Moreover, most of the time, the bins are located near bars and kiosks, while supporters mainly buy food and beverages there, they consume them at their seats. So, when they have finished, they just leave the waste in the stands. A possible solution is to provide bags of different colours to the stewards which can be used to manually collect the waste during the match.

With regard to waste management, efforts should be undertaken to implement practices aiming to facilitate separate waste collection, increase the amount of waste that is recycled rather than sent to landfills and, most importantly, reduce waste generation at the source. Concerning waste collection, stadia may face restrictions on the number and type of bins that can be located across stadium areas, because of safety and security concerns. Therefore, separate waste collection and sorting is often carried out by cleaning service companies that take care of collecting waste produced by supporters and spectators after game time. Crews of pickers that walk the rows of the stadium collecting plastic bottles and large trash items using a two-bag technique could be adopted. Pickers would walk the rows placing plastic bottles into clear plastic bags while putting the larger non-recyclable items such as trays, cups, paper/plastic litter material into black plastic bags. As the bags are filled, pickers would tie off the bags and leave them for collection crew to handle. As the pickers finish the initial "pick" and bags are removed, a secondary crew could follow the pickers with leaf blowers pushing litter down rows to aisles where it is bagged for disposal.

Once collected and sorted, compostable waste materials (such as food waste and worn-out grass turf from the pitch) can be converted into reusable compost. Waste conversion and composting allows the diverting of considerable amount of waste from landfills, as well as reducing costs associated with waste disposal, by producing compost that can be used for gardening and farming. Similarly, other materials like cooking oil utilised for food preparation could be recovered and recycled for producing biofuels. For instance, Geoffroy Guichard stadium's (in Saint-Etienne, France) lighting system runs on biodiesel produced from recycled cooking oil previously utilised in the stadium. The practice has recovered and recycled more than 20,000 gallons of cooking oil into 18,600 gallons of biodiesel. Both the recycling and then the use of biodiesel allowed the reduction of the amount of waste sent to landfills and the amount of carbon emitted. However, similar initiatives imply installing machinery, such as compactors and organic dehydrators, and having adequate infrastructures for treating waste on-site under safe conditions.

Football events of any kind attract a large audience and since such events last at least two hours, food and refreshments are nearly inevitable – especially refreshments, from water and soft drinks to alcohol. These refreshments usually come in single-use plastic packaging – cups or bottles, usually due to security reasons. But at the same time, these are the easiest for distribution and they don't require any additional logistics – washing up, return, storage, etc. However, due to these characteristics, such packaging material becomes a big concern as it makes up a large share of waste in stadiums and sporting venues.

Numerous solutions exist worldwide, which combine deposit schemes, reuse principles, etc. The Brazilian Football Confederation, in collaboration with the Ministry of Environment, established the Green Cup, which is a competition for teams from the north and midwestern regions of the country in which the competition is based on the completion of a set of actions that foster environmental awareness through activities such as recycling materials. Part of the efforts made by the Green Cup resulted in an innovative exchange machine in which fans, before and after match events, could exchange PET bottles for tickets. The exchange machine allowed fans to collect and send in a total of 2 tonnes of plastic bottles to four different cooperatives affiliated to the national recyclable waste pickers' movement.

Nevertheless, following the waste hierarchy, prevention is always better than recycling. Thus, avoiding the production of waste should be the main strategy to reduce the environmental impact. The USTA Billie Jean King national tennis centre, an American stadium complex and home of the US Open Grand Slam tennis tournament, has some green initiatives in place including installations of water refill stations to encourage people to use refillable water bottles and cut down on single-use bottles. The same practice exists at Fiddler Amphitheatre in Colorado. The Fiddler's Green operations team installed new water refill stations to support guests who want to fill their own reusable water bottles. EXPO Milano 2015 also saw 24 water refill stations installed all over the Exposition Site.

A key waste-avoiding measure is the implementation of a reusable cup system. The key areas are the drinks counters in public viewing areas. The advantages of a reusable cup system are plain for all to see. Provided there is an adequate collection and cleaning system, one cup can be used several times at one tournament. The use of reusable cups is also an important environmental signal to fans.

The Danish experience, as a part of Copenhagen's current Resource and Waste Management Plan, reports on the city administration's partnership with event organisers to test reusable cups to replace single-use plastic cups. The concept is adding an extra step of logistics to event management since reusable cups must be returned washed after use. However, it adds several benefits including lower CO_2 emissions, higher user satisfaction, less cleaning and a potential economic benefit. A user evaluation conducted at the two-day festival in Copenhagen shows that 98% of the participants would like festivals in general to replace single-use cups with reusable cups.

Spectators at the French Open, held at the Roland-Garros stadium, are given Ecocup reusable cups to cut out single-use cups, a simple strategy that has also led to economic savings. The objective of this particular practice is to propose a decision support tool to select the best mode of packaging to serve drinks according to the environmental, economic and logistical constraints of each event organiser or to understand the conditions to be met to reduce environmental impacts.

A life cycle assessment (LCA) was conducted in Denmark in the frame of the FORCE project to compare a number of scenarios with either reusable cups or single-use cups. The overall conclusion from using reusable cups instead of single-use cups based on experiences from a festival in Copenhagen shows that reusable cups need only three use cycles before becoming an environmental benefit. The study compares single-use cups made of PET at a weight of 12.5g. The reusable cups are made from PP and weighing 41 g. Former studies confirm this conclusion. The results show that if an event with 50,000 servings replaces single-use plastic cups with reusable cups it can save 2,000 kg CO_2. Overall, the LCA shows that the environmental footprint is 60% lower with reusable cups compared to single-use cups.

Some clubs also use cups made of bio-plastics to replace single-use plastic cups with more sustainable solutions. However, these solutions differ and the environmental sustainability depends a lot on the characteristics of the cups, their origin, the afterlife, disposal options, etc. But replacing cups used at events is usually proven to be an easily replicable practice. However, most of the time the choice to adopt bio-plastic cups is part of a bigger strategy. In fact, there are sport clubs that have certain measures and practices in place as a part of an overall strategy or a programme. Such as the Philadelphia Eagles of the American National Football League that started the programme "Go Green" in 2003 in order to be more environmentally responsible. In particular, among others, they focused on two event management-related practices and improvements.

The club installed a bio-digester that decomposes pre-consumer food waste and can handle up to 150 kg daily. For a successful and efficient usage of this installation, both fans and employees play an active role as they are encouraged to use proper containers during each match event. Since the installation, the digester has digested more than 6.7 tonnes of food waste. The practice adopted by Philadelphia Eagles allowed the reduction of the costs associated with the collection and disposal of waste. However, the initial costs of acquiring and installing such a technology and necessary equipment hinder and affect the practice's replicability potential.

Modern sporting events, especially the most popular ones across the world such as football, the Olympics and other popular sports regionally (hockey, basketball, handball …) not only attract millions of spectators, stadium goers and those in front of TVs combined, but also require modern coverage. This implies a whole set of electronic and electrical equipment in order to provide the best experience to those attending or watching the event. It is rather easy as the technology continuously improves. However, the continuous improvement also leads to perceived and planned obsolescence or simply outdated equipment.

There are several different approaches to this issue – leasing, proper WEEE management (including collection and treatment), donations, etc. Over a year before the London 2012 Olympic Games, the London Organising Committee for the Olympic and Paralympic Games (LOCOG) approached selected leasing companies to buy technological equipment at the outset and then rent it back to LOCOG for the duration of the Games. The outcomes of this project were:

- Computing equipment: 60% of laptops, computers and servers (some 16,500 items) were, by the time a contractual agreement had been made with suppliers, earmarked to go back to schools. It was initially planned that these assets would be offered to schools only within six London boroughs. A decision was later taken to widen the geographical scope of recipients such that children across the whole of the UK could benefit from the Games legacy.
- Televisions: televisions were procured using a "buyback" condition with an independent resale organisation and a "preparation for reuse" requirement on the supplier (Panasonic). Once the Games were over, televisions would be taken back by the supplier for reconditioning to a standard where the original warranty was valid. Some 8,168 televisions were reused in this way, diverting over 160 t of potential waste from landfill.

These significantly reduced the amount of time and resources LOCOG had to employ in order to meet its target of reusing or recycling.

Through the "Tokyo 2020 Medal Project: Towards An Innovative Future For All", gold, silver and bronze medals for use at the Tokyo 2020 Games were manufactured from metal materials recovered and extracted from used consumer electronic appliances such as used mobile phones, so-called "urban mines", donated by people across Japan. This project which is supported by people's efforts was a good demonstration of ways to build a more sustainable society using resources more efficiently. Scientific surveys suggest that the estimated remaining amount of gold and silver-containing resources stored aboveground is in the ratio 7:3 compared to that underground. The demand for metal materials from the above-ground resources called "urban mines", i.e., consumer electronics such as mobile phones, is increasing every year. There are 68 times more gold and 5.6 times more silver in cell phones, in terms of content ratio, compared to underground mines. Utilisation of urban mines is promoted globally as they contain far more minerals than the underground resources (mines).

Over a span of two years, with more than 90% of Japan's local authorities participating, the Tokyo 2020 Medal Project collected 78,985 tonnes of electronic devices — including 6.21 million cell phones — from across Japan to produce the 5,000 Olympic medals that were awarded in Tokyo. The gold, silver, and bronze elements of the devices were obtained through smelting, a process that involves heating and melting to extract a base metal. This meant that the final goals of 30.3 kg of gold, 4,100kg of silver and 2,700kg of bronze were reached.

3.2.3 Material consumption

Whatever sport we talk about, a game requires different equipment. Depending on the sport it could be rackets, balls, shoes, technical equipment, clothes, etc. Most of this equipment is durable and can be reused; however strict standards for high-level games require a continuous replacement of those. This is why donation or an exchange of sports equipment is a common practice where lower-level clubs or junior clubs can benefit from perfectly functional equipment. And then there is an important added value of such a practice – it prevents the equipment from becoming waste. The best thing about this practice is that it can be used not only in football, but also in other sports. The renewal of the stock of materials (e.g., nets, poles, tatamis, etc.) is a good opportunity to avoid the generation of waste by equipping structures that do not have the financial capacity to invest in new equipment.

If a certain sport implies wearing uniforms, employers should consider setting up a proactive return–of–uniform policy for when individuals leave their employment. This will increase the supply of uniforms for reuse and save on purchasing new uniforms. Longer duration of the uniforms implies the postponing of new purchases and amortising the investment over a longer period. Both practices can be linked with the circularity concept of durability; consequently, increasing the lifetime and reducing the environmental footprint of uniforms and sports equipment.

However, professional football clubs may be conditioned by their technical sponsorship. In fact, the company which provides the technical equipment will most likely every year change the look and the style of the T-shirts and of all the other sportwear. Donation may be also hampered by specific terms and conditions of the merchandising contract. Thus, it might be more useful and strategic to work on reducing the impact of the production of sportswear and merchandising.

Speaking of the circularity concept of durability, the example of temporary structures and installations could easily fall under this reuse principle. Large sport events usually use a large number of temporary structures and installations, such as tents, containers, barriers, stands, that are built within and aside venues for operational needs. Smart design choices also allow efficient use of existing materials, including modular structures, to reduce the amount of customised manufacture. For the Qatar 2022 World Cup, the Ras Abu Aboud stadium was designed by Fenwick Iribarren Architects and will consist of a series of containers placed inside a steel supporting structure. This will allow the system to be quickly assembled, disassembled and then reassembled in a new position after the conclusion of the event. The containers will be suitably modified to contain various key elements of the stadium, such as stairs, bathrooms and small kiosks. The stadium will be located on a 450,000 square metre site on the waterfront just south-east of Doha and will have a seating capacity of 40,000.

These temporary facilities include tents for catering and medical aid, restaurant and sanitary facilities, media centres and offices, terraces and stands. Temporary facilities are always very important, since most activities – such as catering, shows, games and exhibitions – take place in the area surrounding the actual sporting event. Even a complete sports facility can be erected as a temporary construction. Low-waste and resource-saving construction methods are therefore of particular importance in this area.

For instance, Rio's 2016 headquarters were a temporary modular structure whose expansion followed the head count growth, allowing the reduction of underutilised space and eliminating unnecessary materials and energy use. Preassembled steel structures arrived ready to use on-site and came together through a simple mechanism of assembly consisting of slots. With this method, construction work was three times faster than usual, with minimal disposal of rubble. Up to 80% of the modular material will be reused in future installations.

For the 2006 World Cup's TV presenter studios, the substructure of the 48 studios was built as a frame, and the studios themselves were erected as a superstructure in a modular system. Individual elements were suitable for reuse, which would not have been possible with conventional studios. For example, walls and roofs comprised sandwich elements from container construction, which could be reused after the World Cup.

Still in the field of football uniforms and clothing but passing from a focus on durability to a focus on reuse and recycling we can mention the possibility of using recycled plastic from ocean to realise football clothing. "Ocean Plastic" is a programme which aims to reduce the amount of plastic in the sea beds through the realisation of highly performing clothes. It is possible to reduce the amount of waste in the oceans and at the same time prevent the accumulation of plastics. The most important economic benefit deriving from this initiative is the possibility of redesigning the sportswear through innovative materials and then making a business out of it. Adidas, in 2018, started an initiative with regard to the creation of the third-away shirt of the Italian football club, Juventus FC, made of 100% recycled polyester containing the Ocean Plastic material.

Supporters' choreographies during football matches (e.g., flags, banners, etc.) imply a large consumption of materials, mainly plastics. By purchasing and utilising choreographic materials (specifically flags) made from recycled plastics, instead of virgin material, football organisations can reduce their environmental impacts. For example, on the occasion of the Serie A SPAL–Bologna match played on 25 January 2020, SPAL supporters utilised 6,000 white and blue flags (the colours of the SPAL team) made of recycled polyethylene. The club identified a supplier of choreography materials (flags) made of recycled plastics (recycled polyethylene). Six thousand flags (3,000 blue and 3,000 white) were ordered and purchased by SPAL for the match and distributed to the fanbase. The environmental benefit of the activity was assessed by performing an LCA on the flags made of recycled polyethylene, especially focusing on the reduction of greenhouse gases (specifically CO_2). Recycled polyethylene is mainly obtained from processing waste of industrial products (e.g., plastic bags for the food sector) made of low-density polyethylene (LDPE), followed by adding a portion of virgin material in the mix. LDPE is a thermoplastic polymer made from the monomer ethylene and belonging to the polyolefins group.

The size of each flag was 40 cm x 60 cm, weighting 39 g with the thickness of 009 μm, which corresponded to a total of 234 kg of recycled polyethylene for the 6,000 flags. Producing 1 kg of recycled polyethylene corresponds to emission of 0.79 kg of CO_2, against emissions of 2.78 kg of CO_2 for producing 1 kg of virgin polyethylene. Accordingly, each 1 kg of recycled polyethylene corresponds to savings of 2 kg of CO_{2-eq}. Therefore, the analysis showed that use of the 6,000 flags made of recycled polyethylene resulted in a saving of 936 kg CO_{2eq}, which can be compared to the emissions produced by heating a 60 m^2 apartment for 23 days.

3.2.4 Food and beverage consumption

All stadiums distribute meals before and during football matches within the stadium's perimeter and outside the gate. In addition to the classic bar and kiosks located between the stands of the stadium where it is possible to buy mainly snacks and drinks, all the professional clubs have a specific area dedicated to catering services. In fact, several people are regularly hosted by professional clubs in an area where they have free access to food and beverages. Moreover, we need to consider also all the kiosks located outside the stadium, where supporters can buy food and drinks too.

Several sport and football organisations have adopted food choice to reduce the environmental impact of this activity. The choice is to sensitise both supporters and players towards a more sustainable lifestyle. In fact, being vegan for the team means not only avoiding any kind of organic food or derivate but also contributing to the reduction of the negative impact towards the environment and animal welfare during livestock farming. Adopting a vegan or vegetarian diet could be the "single biggest way" to reduce your environmental impact on earth. Researchers at the University of Oxford found that cutting meat and dairy products from your diet could reduce an individual's carbon footprint from food by up to 73%. Meanwhile, if everyone stopped eating these foods, they found that global farmland use could be reduced by 75%, an area equivalent to the size of the US, China, Australia and the EU combined. Not only would this result in a significant drop in greenhouse gas emissions, but it would also free up wild land lost to agriculture, one of the primary causes for mass wildlife extinction. The study, published in the journal *Science*, is one of the most comprehensive analyses to date into the detrimental effects farming can have on the environment and included data on nearly 40,000 farms in 119 countries. The University of Oxford study reveals that meat and dairy production is responsible for 60% of agriculture's greenhouse gas emissions, while the products themselves provide just 18% of calories and 37% of protein levels around the world. Similarly, organic farming avoids the use of industrial fertilisers and pesticides. This means soil and groundwater remain unharmed by chemicals. Because organic farming uses mineral fertilisers from natural manure, energy which would otherwise be used in the production of industrial fertiliser is saved. Additional options suggested by the International Olympic Committee (IOC) are:

- Food sourcing to include local products;
- Food waste to be reduced by donation to charity and other NGOs;
- Finished product packaging and disposable tableware to be reduced;
- Vegan and vegetarian offer to be increased;
- Use of compostable tableware and reusable cups;
- Offer seasonal menus in order to reduce road miles and the energy needed for fresh produce production;
- Use certified organic food

In 2017, Forest Green Rovers was officially recognised as the world's first vegan football club. Back in 2015 they replaced their menu with fresh, vegan food. They have made a big impact on fans, players and other clubs, reaching an audience of billions since they officially became a vegan club. They decided to become a vegan club because of the huge environmental and animal welfare impact of livestock farming, as well as to improve player performance and give fans healthier, tastier match day food. Freshly made vegan food is much healthier than processed meats, with far less risk of heart disease. Vegan food is becoming the diet of choice for athletes like Sergio Aguero, Lionel Messi, etc. because of the boost it gives to their performance.

However, some fans may be reluctant to consume vegetarian or vegan food. Football organisations may adopt two leverages to nudge green food: 1) working on awareness raising by adding green claims on the environmental benefits of vegetarian and vegan food and 2) adopting pricing options by increasing the cost of food that includes meat and decreasing the cost of vegetarian and vegan food.

3.2.5 Energy consumption

Modern stadiums can be considered artificial cities, taking into consideration the number of people visiting one during an event. They have their own commercial zones, catering options and much more. Energy is an essential element for each stadium's functionality. However, there are still cases where generators play an important role. Generators consume a baseline of fuel even if they are not employed at capacity, and the "fuel consumed" versus "power generated" relationship is not linear. Efficiency is therefore largely determined by load. A good rule of thumb is that around 70–80% load is perfect (optimum). Going downwards, anything between 80% and 50% load is still good (reductions in efficiency are marginal), but as the load goes down from 50% to 25% efficiency reduces. The "danger zone" is below 25% with low efficiency. Below 10% one needs to really start thinking about better ways to manage power.

For example, create fuel cost savings by using a number of generators in sequence that operate only in times of peak demand, rather than running one large generator continually. Share generators across the site, for example power for toilets, multiple catering outlets and field lighting could all be driven from one source.

In addition, the plan of the energy use by creating an energy use map for your whole event could be considered a good practice, for example through the following activities:

- Know demand peaks and troughs and what levels they will reach;
- Know where energy is consumed: stage, lighting, campsite, catering, heating;
- Specify energy requirements correctly by understanding what power is needed and working with the supplier to create efficient solutions.

Grass needs four components to grow: light, water, heat and nutrition. Some large stadiums experience issues in growing natural grass due to the fact that sunlight cannot reach the whole grass pitch. The reasons can be related to local climate conditions (i.e., in Northern Europe, winter's hours of sunlight are limited so grass doesn't grow naturally), or to the shape of the stadium that might prevent sunlight from reaching some parts of the pitch.

So far, solutions that use artificial lights have been both financially and environmentally costly. Assuming that a stadium in average European weather conditions is equipped with 72 high pressure sodium light bulbs of 1,000 W each, that consume up to 3,000 MWh, it is estimated that the yearly costs (for electricity only) amount to €300,000. In terms of environmental costs, this solution emits up to 1,000 tonnes of CO_2.

Second Sun has developed an innovative solution based on a reflector system that can reduce the need for artificial light using natural sunlight. Their sustainable system for natural grass growth is based on intelligent and automated mirrors that redirect the natural sunlight on to any area of the pitch where the grass needs it inside a sports stadium. This will provide the necessary Photosynthetic Active Radiation (PAR) light to promote the photosynthesis inside the grass plant. In this way, this system can substitute the usage of UV lamps installed for grass growth: this means much lower energy consumption and CO_2 emissions, while keeping the pitch in the high-quality condition needed. The Second Sun System can be installed in the existing structure of the stadium and the mirrors automatically deploy and retract from underneath the stadium's roof when needed. These reflectors can be easily installed and moved around the stadium and project the sunlight on to the desired areas of the pitch where sunlight is needed. The system is designed and built with advanced automation and an intelligent control technology. In contrast to artificial light rigs, there will be no inconvenience to the groundsmen transporting the system in and out of the stadium nor storing it when not in use.

By deploying this solution, the savings for sports stadiums are substantial both from a financial and sustainable perspective since the need for supplementary artificial growth lightning is significantly reduced or eliminated. Depending on the country, this system cannot fully substitute artificial light in winter, but can substantially reduce the need to use it throughout the year. The yearly consumption of a stadium is estimated to decrease to 2,250 MWh, with yearly costs (for electricity only) decreasing to €225,000. In terms of environmental costs, emissions would decrease to up to 750 tonnes of CO_2.

The use of LED lighting systems to stimulate grass growth as a less energy-consuming alternative to HPS (high pressure sodium light bulbs) systems was tested in many European countries. However, LED trials in Germany, Ireland and France revealed that it was not possible to create the same quality of growth during winter with less total energy input than with an HPS system. In individual situations it even occurred that the LED systems with infrared required more energy input to create the same amount of light output (mmol) and heat (°C) as HPS systems. For instance, research showed that "the influence of warmth has been often underestimated as a growing factor. Although the light is creating photosynthesis, the temperature is crucial for the process and should always be in balance with the light. In most climate regions the minimum temperature is not achieved naturally during the winter season; it requires an additional heat-source to allow growth"(Dusenge et al., 2019) While with HPS up to 50% of the energy reaches the plant as radiation heat, the energy-heat (convection) from LED does not reach the plant. Therefore, although LED lights are more energy-efficient than HPS, they are not the best solution for promoting optimal quality pitch.

As previously noted, optimising the use of resources along all primary processes and activities is a fundamental function of stadium management. However, optimisation goals must guarantee that key services are effectively provided and that spectators' needs and expectations are met, especially in terms of comfort, accessibility and safety. Balancing efficiency and customers' satisfaction requires stadium managers to understand resource consumption parameters associated with each key service and monitor how such indicators fluctuate during peak hours and slack hours (for instance, during and before/after game time) in order to identify optimisation opportunities based on the differentiation of key services. This is especially relevant for energy-intensive primary services, such as lighting and heating, whose energy requirements made up large part of stadiums' energy consumption, as well as energy bills.

To improve energy efficiency, adopting an integrated building management system is a necessary step for collecting data on energy consumption associated with services like heating, conditioning and lighting provided throughout the stadium. Energy management tools allow monitoring real-time operational data in order to elaborate modular energy efficiency schemes based on data collected. Innovative management systems include cloud-based solutions for controlling services through a unique centralised in-cloud hub, considerably reducing time and personnel efforts. Similar tools support stadium managers to monitor energy needs and efficiently distribute energy throughout the venues during peak times, avoiding service interruptions due to electrical overloads and controlling energy consumption associated with lighting, heating and conditioning systems.

In the stadium of Dresden, a timing analysis for events provided optimised control commands for building services management, including lighting modes, switching on/off of heat consumers, cooling systems and ventilation and air conditioning equipment. In Mercedes Benz Arena in Shanghai, the arena's operations team focused its efforts on how to maximise energy efficiency throughout the venue, which included installing a cloud-based energy management system that monitors real-time operational diagnostics, allowing the team to adjust energy schemes based on collected data. For example, the arena's HVAC and lighting systems are now linked up to one computer program, allowing staff to adjust settings throughout the day, without much effort. The operations team of the stadium can set energy efficiency schemes throughout the venue and adjust these schemes through a centralised cloud hub location, minimising the time and personnel needed to monitor the systems. Additionally, Mercedes-Benz Arena invested in 12 air curtain machines in its West Hall to improve indoor air quality and maximise energy efficiency to help stabilise temperatures within the venue. Twickenham Stadium (rugby) commissioned a stadium-wide energy management system to help cope with energy distribution during peak times. It's based on 250 new monitoring points. The improved Wi-Fi connectivity allows for power monitoring (e.g., quality, voltage, current and power factors at the ground, etc.) to maintain optimal energy usage.

Heating is often one of the most energy-intensive and expensive services provided within stadia. However, several solutions can be adopted to improve energy efficiency associated with heating, therefore reducing energy costs and limiting climate-altering emissions, without undertaking expensive renovation works. First, heating modulation and control programs could be adopted to set precise time programming and modularly regulate temperatures in different areas of the stadium (such as locker rooms, offices, gyms, etc.), according to the specific needs of athletes, supporters and staff.

Other smart solutions for optimising energy consumption in relation to heating services may envision installing hydraulic balancing valves in the heat supply lines across the stadium. Hydraulic balancing valves control the flow rate of hot water, evenly distributing heat to the different radiators according the specific output demand. The purpose of hydraulic balancing valves is to correctly regulate the correct amount of heat in every area of the stadium based on the required heat output in the pipeline network, therefore avoiding overheating areas located closer to the heating centre while inadequately supplying areas that are unfavourably located. This simple measure simultaneously allows improving the comfort of the building, by avoiding excess or inadequate heating, while reducing waste of energy and avoidable CO_2 emissions in the atmosphere. In the stadium of Sinsheim, an analysis of the distribution and usage of heating in the stadium was carried out, and it demonstrated that a reduction in the flow temperatures could be implemented which would lead to savings in heating oil and pellet use of around 10–15%. The reduction in heating requirements is around 160,000 kwh/year and have consequently brought about a drop in CO_2 emissions by approximately 43,000 kg CO_2 / year.

Lighting constitutes a relevant energy-intensive activity in stadium management. Around 20% of the electricity used in stadiums is accounted for by lighting. However, it offers several smart and economically efficient opportunities for improvement based on the adoption of energy-saving and cost-efficient technologies. First, the adoption of energy-saving light bulbs, such as LED or fluorescent lights, as a replacement to more energy-intensive incandescent or halogen light bulbs, is set to produce relevant energy savings. Besides adopting LED lights, which are considered particularly efficient in the case of field lighting, efficiency could be improved by adopting a modular regulation system for floodlights, which allow regulating the intensity of floodlighting according to a specific time or demand, in order to avoid lighting the pitch at full capacity when not necessary. Installing presence detectors or timers in the locker rooms, washrooms and other places to prevent the lighting of different spaces from being lit during periods of inactivity could be a useful and simple solution.

In preparation for the FIFA 2010 in South Africa, LED technology was substituted for fluorescent tubes on the emergency lighting circuit and reduced the electricity load. This translated into energy saving of 56% or 2,119,482 kWh per annum (i.e., 21,120 tons of CO_{2-eq} over their lifetime). Replacing old stadium floodlights with energy-efficient floodlights reduced the total electricity load from 315.7 kW to 126 kW. This translates into an energy saving of 12,096 kWh per annum, i.e., 151 tonnes of CO_{2-eq} over their 15-year lifetime.

Efficiencies associated with better light management can be conspicuous. For instance, as a result of improving floodlights' energy performance, the Berlin stadium opted for reducing transformer voltage, from 420 to 400 volts. The costs of €3,900 generated by this action are offset by energy savings of €10,000 per year, as well as indirectly extending the equipment lifespan, and reducing CO_2 emissions by approximately 46,000 kg per year.

Environmentally proactive stadiums can decide to move beyond energy efficiency and directly generate green energy, such as solar energy. Sports facilities frequently offer sufficient space for installing photovoltaic panels – whether on roofs or in the immediate vicinity of the stadium. It is important to notice that photovoltaic plants are not only of interest for new buildings, but they can also be retrofitted to existing sports facilities. The energy generated is usually not directly supplied to the sports facility, but is fed into the power supply network. Installing solar or wind power plants allow reducing energy costs, while reducing climate-altering emissions.

Since the summer of 2005 the Stade de Suisse in Bern operates the largest solar plant integrated into the roof of a football stadium anywhere in the world. For this it was awarded the EUROSOLAR Environment Prize and the Swiss Solar Prize. The roof modules together form an area of 8,000 square metres. In its first year of operation around 800,000 kWh of electricity were produced; this is equivalent to the average annual consumption of around 250 households. In its final form the roof will accommodate 12,000 square metres of modules and produce an annual total of 1.2 million kWh of electricity.

Even though stadium roofs are generally open and relatively fragile structures, the later installation of photovoltaic plants is nevertheless possible. It is demonstrated by the example of Kaiserslautern stadium, where installation of the largest photovoltaic plant that has ever been installed on the roof of a German football stadium began in 2006. In all, around 5,000 modules are being installed. They cover an area of 6,000 square metres and, fitted close together, they would more than cover a football field. In its ultimate configuration the plant will have an output of up to 800 kWh and generate up to 720,000 kWh of electricity each year – enough to supply 200 households with electricity for a whole year.

In August 2010, NASCAR's Pocono Raceway in Long Pond, Pennsylvania became the largest solar-powered sports facility in the world. Pocono installed a 25-acre, 3-megawatt array in a former parking lot adjacent to the track. It consists of 40,000 American-made photovoltaic modules and is large enough to be seen from outer space. The solar array, which offsets more than 3,100 metric tonnes of CO_2 annually, provides enough power to operate the entire raceway and 1,000 homes nearby (the raceway sells the energy it doesn't use to local utilities).

The New Lawn, home of the English Football Club Forest Green Rovers, is a stadium that is characterised by an ultimate energy management thanks to the installation of solar and wind panels. Regarding the environmental benefits, solar and wind panels guarantee 100% renewable energy and generate 65% of the total power. Only solar panels make 20% of the total energy. Regarding the economic benefits, the use of solar and wind power allows reducing the costs related to the energy consumption. Philadelphia Eagles is an American National Football League club that in 2003 started the programme "Go Green" in order to be more environmentally responsible. In particular, among others, they focused on green energy. The club implemented in the stadium 11,108 solar panels and 14 wind turbines that power completely all the operations. Regarding the environmental benefits, the Eagles' stadium runs completely on sustainable energy. This reduced electricity consumption by more than 50%.

In Bordeaux, a pergola composed of 60,000 photovoltaic panels provides shade for 7,000 parking spaces and electricity for 5,000 households. That parking area is shared between the exhibition park and the stadium and is one of the largest photovoltaic plants in France.

3.2.6 Communication

Communicating new measures and practices to game goers, who usually span over several different age groups, cultural backgrounds, genders, etc. is always a challenge as it is an essential step towards a successful implementation. Fans and spectators need to recognise and acknowledge where environmental measures are taking place in stadiums and how they themselves can contribute. Experience shows that it is essential to define the precise location of posters and stickers as early as possible.

Examples are plenty and they include modern means of communicating objectives and reasons behind the implementation of a certain measure and can be found in different forms, including passive-aggressive messages, acknowledging people's efforts, offering alternatives and many more. For instance, stickers and posters featuring the Green Goal logo attracted attention to areas where environmental measures were taking place, such as the installation of water-saving valves in toilets and the use of reusable cups to reduce waste at the Women's Football World Cup Germany 2011. In other areas, the involvement of fans was acknowledged with posters like the one which read "Did you travel here by public transport? If so, thank you for supporting the FIFA Women's World Cup 2011 Environment Campaign!" Eye-catching stickers and posters were often positioned in busy areas, so it can be safely assumed that a large proportion of fans were reached.

The replicability potential is very high in case of this measure, as it can be adapted to local or national communication patterns or sense of humour and can be highly customised in order to reach as many attendees at stadium events as possible.

Whatever good practice a stadium or a football club decides to implement, communicating these practices and bringing it closer to the game goers is as important as the practice itself. Because the practice makes sense only if exploited by the people attending the event. Most major events involve several volunteer active participations during the event: volunteers usually provide information to spectators and are trained on some basic topics (security and safety, general organisation, public transport station locations, etc.). Engaging volunteers in spreading the event's environmental objectives and asking for their help in sharing on the most environmentally friendly behaviour can make the difference.

Advertising and information dissemination in stadiums may involve promotional objects that may come in physical or digital formats. Although digital communication should be preferred, some physical banners and other accessories still exist. The material of these advertising banners is mostly made of PVC (polyvinyl chloride), with physical characteristics of durability, flexibility and low flammability. In order to not sending banners to landfills, event organisers should donate banners to employees or entities and institutions that are interested in the reuse of this material or can reuse them in their own facilities (e.g., segregation of benches for safety and protection of fans, protection of spaces susceptible to infiltration and in the operation and management of the stadium as protection of turnstiles).

Lastly, to promote the adoption of environmental practices and foster sustainability of sport events, National Football Associations (NFAs) and other sport organisations could establish sustainability awards or prizes in order to engage football clubs, stadium managers, as well as other relevant stakeholders (such as suppliers, contractors and supporters). Sustainability competitions could be organised at the national level: committees could be appointed by NFAs to monitor sport events and evaluate environmental performance based on environmental criteria like sustainable food, green procurement criteria, waste management and carbon footprint. Similar initiatives could help engaging diverse stakeholders and foster a collective and proactive commitment to environmental performance, leveraging the expectations of reputational gains.

3.2.7 Sustainability of infrastructures

Sustainability of infrastructures is a broad concept used to define an integrated and systematic process to support and improve the effectiveness of the primary activities and key services provided within the stadium, before, during and after a sport event. Accordingly, stadium management envisions a wide array of very diverse activities, ranging from the management and maintenance of buildings, facilities and infrastructures to the provision and monitoring of key primary services (such as water and energy).

Effective stadium management is crucial for ensuring the functionality, safety and comfort of sports events, and, consequently, satisfy spectators' demand for safe entertainment and further attract people to attend stadia. From this perspective, activities such as the ordinary and extraordinary maintenance of infrastructures (such as buildings, parking spaces, electricity and water supply systems) emerge as a core function of stadium management. Similarly, the provision of adequate equipment, cleaning and security services are further aspects of stadium management.

At the same time, stadium management plays a crucial role in the business model of sport events to ensure the economic sustainability of events. Stadium management envisions tools and methods for evaluating the performance of the services provided, setting improvement objectives and ensuring that established goals are met. Assessing services performance by monitoring key indicators is indeed a crucial function of stadium management, aimed at quantifying the effectiveness and efficiency of operations, reducing waste of resources and planning optimisation strategies.

Altogether, stadium management refers to a set of transversal and interdisciplinary support services that, once integrated within a coherent management system, are essential to the functionality of sport events in stadia. As a result, stadium management emerges as a very complex activity, which requires shared efforts from diverse actors (from stadiums' employees to contractors) and affects multiple stakeholders (such as supporters, athletes and local communities). Nevertheless, stadium management is the primary responsibility of the stadium manager, who is appointed to supervise and coordinate each aspect of this challenging task.

In recent years, environmental concerns have been increasingly integrated in stadium management practice, due to increasing pressures from regulators and civil society for more sustainable sport events. Being a transversal and overarching activity that supervises most of the services provided within stadia throughout all the phases of an event life cycle, stadium management provides several important opportunities for "greening" sport events.

First, stadium management is responsible for setting up and maintaining basic infrastructures of the stadium. Accordingly, "green building" principles could be applied to reduce the overall environmental impact of the stadium's infrastructures throughout their life cycle (from design to construction, from maintenance to renovation). Such principles focus on improving resource efficiency of buildings, by adopting greener technologies and more sustainable materials, and by deploying environmentally responsible practices. More specifically, green building principles pursue the improvement of the following aspects: a) sustainable materials and materials efficiency; b) energy efficiency; c) water efficiency; d) waste reduction and waste recycling.

Solutions for improving the sustainability of materials, and materials efficiency, concern the adoption of technologies or processes that allow reducing resource consumption and environmental impacts deriving from the maintenance of stadiums' infrastructures.

From this point of view, since stadiums' managers always have to substitute a significant number of damaged seats after each match, it would be the case to look for seats made from recycled materials instead of virgin plastic ones. Currently, most seats are made from plastic and tend to be not very resistant thus supporters easily break them during matches.

Revet Recycling, an Italian company specialised in the recycling of plastics, has launched the initiative "Re-sit down and jump for goal!" aimed at realising stadiums' seats in recycled plastic. They created seats partially realised from recycled plastic (30–40%). The recycled material is named "plasmix" and is realised from plastic containers (flacons, bottles, caps, lids, etc.) recovered and recycled thanks to the separate waste collection system of Tuscany, Italy. The realisation of this innovative seat is the result of an ambitious R&D project carried out by Revet in cooperation with Omsi, a company leader in the production of stadium seats. The main challenge was to find the proper combination of recycled and virgin plastic materials in order to ensure the fulfilment of FIFA's flameproof seat requirements. Eventually, the final prototype has passed both the mechanical and flameproof checks and is ready to enter the market.

Traditional seats are made by 1.75 kg virgin polypropylene, while the seat made with recycled plastics has 0.7 kg of recycled plastics and 1.05 kg of virgin polypropylene. According to these data the adoption of a recycled seat in a stadium causes a reduction of the carbon footprint of 1 seat from 5.34 to 3.47 $CO_{2-eq.}$ (-35%) and a reduction of water footprint from 1.65 to 0.98 m^3water (-41%).

Further solutions for materials efficiency and sustainability may involve the use of recycled materials, or other low-impact materials, in the construction of facilities such as temporary stands or tents. Temporary facilities are indeed frequently required at large events; they are built for a specific event and then dismantled or removed on its conclusion. These temporary facilities may include tents for catering and medical aid, restaurant and sanitary facilities, media centres and offices, terraces and stands. Low-waste and resource-saving construction methods are therefore of particular importance in this area: the construction of sports facilities indeed involves considerable emissions of greenhouse gases and airborne pollutants as well as the use of land and resources. To prevent or reduce environmental impact, temporary facilities may be built using modular, durable and reusable materials in order to extend their life cycle, while the use of consumable materials should be limited as much as possible to prevent waste generation. As an alternative, temporary structures may be rented. Similarly, the use of facilities produced using recycled materials is a simple and smart solution for reducing material consumption and waste at the source.

During the 2006 FIFA World Cup the International Broadcasting Centre (IBC) was the central "powerhouse" for television broadcasting to a billion people. The IBC was built using recycling-favourable construction methods and regenerative raw materials. Ceiling beams and carrier profiles were made of solid wood, and walls of glued multilayered coniferous wood. A total of 966 tonnes of wood – 40 lorry loads – were used to build the IBC. At the end of the World Cup the greater part of the material was not waste but rather recyclable material. The wooden elements of the studios, for instance, were later used in the construction of 60 houses.

The use of environmentally friendly products in maintenance, cleaning and renovation of facilities and structures is set to considerably improve stadiums' environmental performance. Simple and economically efficient solutions for greening the above-mentioned activities may envision the use of products certified according to reliable environmental certification schemes (such as the EU Ecolabel), and abandon products with the worst or unclear environmental performance. Similar environmental criteria can be applied for procuring environmentally friendly products that can be commonly used in a wide array of activities, even the simplest ones. For instance, environmentally friendly paints can be adopted for the maintenance of stadiums' infrastructures and buildings, greener cleaning products may be adopted for cleaning seats and terraces, and even EU Ecolabel sanitary products (such as sanitary paper and napkins) may be provided in the stadiums' toilets.

3.2.8 Pitch management

Furthermore, in the case of stadiums hosting football events, the pitch requires considerable maintenance due to intense wear and tear during matches and to the quality standards required by football clubs, NFAs and UEFA. Accordingly, diverse options could be envisioned to reduce environmental impacts and material consumption associated with turf treatment and maintenance. In this regard, stadiums like the New Lawn, home of the English Football Club Forest Green Rovers, have opted for adopting organic pitches, which eliminate the use of fertilisers, pesticides and other detrimental chemical substances.

The club promoted a set of sustainability initiatives that have allowed it to substantially reduce its ecological footprint, becoming in 2018 the world's first UN certified carbon-neutral football club. These initiatives include a particular choice in terms of turf treatment. In particular, it is characterised by an "organic" pitch, which basically means artificial pesticides and fertilisers are not used, and a solar-powered mow-bot that goes around and treats the pitch 24/7. The club's organic playing surface, spread using Scottish seaweed, is thought to be the first of its kind in the world. Their process for growing an organic pitch avoiding the use of chemicals includes:

• 90 tonnes of sand injected into the pitch to improve drainage;
• Fraise mowing which removes the grass leaf but allows mature roots to remain and provide a "nursery" for new grass seed;

- Another 90 tonnes of top sand;
- 15 bags of grass seed containing six different types of rye-grass;
- 3 tonnes of organic fertiliser with seaweed, magnesium and soil improver;
- Watered with 800 litres of compost tea;
- Added 20 litres of coconut wetting agent which helps water flow evenly to all parts of the soil profile and prevents over/under-watering.

These practices avoid the negative environmental impacts deriving from pesticides and fertilisers used for natural grass. The choice of having an organic pitch along with the daily monitoring thanks to the mow-bot allows the club to avoid the use of chemicals or other detrimental substances that can impact the quality and the duration of the turf.

In 2011, the University of Colorado Boulder implemented a pesticide-free, organic fertiliser management system for all campus turf, including most sports and recreation fields. As part of this programme, CU–Boulder invested roughly $30,000 to install seven 250-gallon brewing tanks across campus to make compost tea, a biologically active organic liquid fertiliser. A total of 70 pounds (10 pounds per tank) of premium vermicompost (compost from worm bins) is brewed to yield 1,750 gallons of compost tea, which is then applied over roughly 70 acres through the campus-wide sprinkler system. The overall pesticide reduction programme cut the university's use of herbicides on turf areas by 93% by the end of 2012 (compared with 2009). The benefits of using this organic fertiliser and pest management system on campus sports fields include improved drainage, higher oxygen levels and less compaction, leading to faster turf recovery after intensive use.

Alternative pitches include artificial ones. Today artificial turf is becoming popular again in the European football leagues. An artificial bespoke pitch ensures good athletic performance and lower levels of water and fertiliser consumption. For instance, artificial turf surely promotes significant water savings. A pitch requires on average 20,000 litres of water a day to keep it in "prime condition". Research in the US showed that each full-sized rectangular artificial turf field saves between 1.8 million to 3.7 million litres of water each year, as the need for irrigation is totally eradicated.

In addition to this, natural grass fields require frequent maintenance, including mowing and fertilising (for non-organic grass), the use of lighting rigs for stimulating grass growth (depending on the region or month of the year), and periodic reseeding. Chemicals such as fertilisers and herbicides, which produce greenhouse gas (GHG) emissions when manufactured, are used for growing and maintaining non-organic turf grass. The use of fertilisers and pesticides leads to contaminated run-off that is also potentially harmful to the environment, and though some herbicides and fungicides are still needed for artificial surfaces, they are in lower quantities than those needed for natural grass.

However, artificial turf also poses some environmental concerns in terms of chemical leaching, stemming from the infill material that is typically derived from scrap tires. Tire rubber crumb contains a range of microplastic contaminants and heavy metals that can volatilise into the air and/or leach into the percolating rainwater, thereby posing a potential risk to the environment and human health. On the other hand, natural grass reduces surface temperatures and has the ability to store atmospheric CO_2 in the soil as organic carbon. Synthetic pitches, on the contrary, can reach temperatures of 70°C on a hot day, up to 40% hotter than a natural field. This is not only uncomfortable for players but can also contribute to the urban heat island effect, increasing local air temperature by up to 4°C.

Lastly, if well maintained, a grass pitch is theoretically self-renewing, and even if the surface is replaced, the waste is still biodegradable. Synthetic pitches on the other hand pose a problem at end of their life span in terms of waste disposal. Technological developments are however increasing the life span of artificial turf and recycling technology is also being developed that has the potential to recycle 99% of pitch materials.

The main issue relating to artificial turf is its end-of-life disposal. Different companies have worked on the development of a system for recycling it. Smart solutions for improving material efficiency include recycling worn-out artificial turf by means of a mechanical process that separates waste from recyclable materials (such as grass fibres, sand and rubber) which are then used for producing new plastic materials. Re-Match turf recycling has, the first in the world to do so, developed a separation process that makes it possible to clean and recycle 99% of the old artificial turf. The separation is a mechanical process. The used artificial turf runs through several separation steps, where both air and sieving are used to separate. In addition, Re-Match uses separation tables and gravity to separate the individual components and remove waste. Re-Match's advanced separation technology is tested thoroughly for the cleanliness of the end product and the efficiency of the process. Once the Re-Match process is complete, we have 99% clean products. These are ready for use in production and installation of new artificial turf – completing the life cycle – a cradle-to-cradle solution.

In the high-tech and patented plant, the turf is downsized, dried, separated and cleaned – without using water. The result is four clean materials (sand and rubber, grass fibre and backing) without creating additional waste products The 99% clean sand and rubber, grass fibre and backing is of the highest quality, and regularly quality tested by an external institution.

The granulated grass fibres are used within a host of other industries and recycled by either compounding or pelletising, ready to be used in the production of new plastic products. The infill (sand and rubber) is either reused in new turfs or in other applications – such as field/landscape/sporting applications. Re-Match has received an ETV (Environmental Technology Verification) certification.

With regard to costs, a grass pitch is much cheaper to install as it costs up to £100,000 per pitch compared to £400,000 to £800,000 for installing an artificial pitch. However, despite the high initial costs, an artificial surface provides increased revenue by giving a speedier return on the initially larger investment. Estimates suggested costs savings of £100,000 a year on turf repairs. Artificial surfaces have less regular maintenance costs, while natural turf has generally quite high costs for equipment, fertilisers, chemicals and water. When the capital and operating costs of artificial and natural turf are compared to actual usage over a 12-year life span, calculations show that artificial turf per game costs are approximately 65% cheaper than natural grass.

Higher income could also be achieved by opening the stadium up for more outside events without any negative effects on the condition of the pitch. For instance, one of the most appealing features of artificial turf is its durability. A standard natural grass sports field can accommodate approximately 360 games per year while a lit artificial turf field has the capability of accommodating approximately 2,080 games per year during primetime hours. This works out to an approximate 6:1 ratio.

Natural grass and artificial turf each have their advantages and limitations. The choice of one over the other must be contextualised and different factors should be taken into account (e.g., its component parts, the context of its climate, whether it's designed for professional use or for communities, etc.). A well-managed artificial pitch may be an appropriate choice where the alternative is a fertilised, water-intensive, pesticide-heavy professional pitch. On the other hand, a poorly maintained synthetic pitch is not only a poor environmental choice, but also a poor playing surface. It's about choosing the right pitch for the right location and use.

Pitch monitoring systems can be used to increase the quality of the surface but also to optimise efficiency of resources such as the lighting system. The system collects data that provides 24/7 accurate insight to help the organisation get the best possible control over their sports playing surface. A sensor permanently installed on the roof provides continuous data. Mobile sensors collect all information on the grass and in the soil whenever the playing surface is not in use.

3.2.9 Biodiversity

Although it may not always seem a predominant issue, biodiversity conservation should be a key element in any environmentally responsible approach to sports event management. Environmental management should be preserving green areas sited in the proximity to the stadium and, most importantly, protecting the biodiversity of the natural environment where the stadium is located. Stadium management activities should be designed taking into consideration the specific needs and characteristics of local fauna and flora that could be affected by stadium activities in order to avoid causing harm to biodiversity. To this aim, so-called differentiated management should be applied, according to which operations are designed and scheduled according to the quality of local green areas. Differentiated management aims to rethink the maintenance of green spaces, particularly by promoting the development of fauna and flora biodiversity and optimising the maintenance and use of phytosanitary products. The differentiated management of green spaces is divided into four classes inducing an intervention adapted to ecological issues: Ornamental, Classic, Semi-natural, Natural. Whoever is in charge of green spaces should plan the training of the employees in the differentiated management and determine a plan of maintenance to be adapted. Using a service provider is possible to integrate the requirements when renewing contracts. It is important leave in all green areas a "wild" area of a few square metres without treatment to promote the development of biodiversity. It is possible to apply the principles of an ecological management reference system for green spaces, because there are different labels and standards for providing green space managers with indicators specific to ecological management.

3.2.10 Mobility and logistics

All football events bring together people from different locations. In the case of mega football events, citizens from all countries are attracted to one specific location. Thus, their carbon footprint can be considerably high due to the international transportation, especially travel via airplanes, to the locations hosting the event.

A new role that should be included in the organisational chart of football organisations is the mobility manager. An important professional for organisations that have many employees, to reduce the environmental impact of home-work trips and organise sustainable mobility. The mobility manager can be classified as a figure specialised in managing the demand for mobility and promoting sustainable mobility in the context of home-work travel for employees. However, in the context of football, its role may also include other travel such as talent scouts, staff, players and so on.

In fact, the mobility of football organisations is for sure one of the most important aspects from an environmental point of view. Starting from the car fleet of the organisations which include not only the cars owned by the organisations, but also the cars that some sponsors may provide to players and staff members, the club bus and so on.

For example, FIFA's 2006 Green Goal Programme aimed to organise the most environmentally friendly event by tackling the issues revolving around water and energy usage as well as transportation. During any sporting event, transport has a significant impact on the carbon footprint of the overall event. For the Sydney Olympics the organisers succeeded in providing local, public means of transportation to and from the venues of the event, however at a greater scale, they did not have any impact on how the international and national spectators and fans arrived in Sydney.

It is therefore very important to implement practices to increase the use of public transport. At any major sporting event, transport is generally one of the chief contributors of environmentally harmful emissions. Firstly, it is important to convince as many fans as possible to reach the host venue of the event with the means of public transportation that has the least impact on the environment (e.g., rail, buses, bikes, walking, etc.). The methods to put into action this best practice include the presence of discounts on public transportation to and from the venue of the event as well as the availability of one or more means of public transportation with high frequency, which serve the public from before the beginning of the event to after the end of the event. This best practice allows lowering the CO_2 footprint of an event as well as helping generate higher profits for local transport companies. It is easily replicable, but a key challenge involved in this best practice is the need for connection stations and services between the venues of the event.

Additional measures can be adopted in order to foster public transport preference over private cars:

- Discounts on public transport tickets on match/event days;
- Higher frequency of the lines connecting venues to key city points (e.g., stations);
- Longer period of service of public transport (e.g., extension to one hour after the end of the event);
- Include the price of public transport in event ticketing;
- Adjusting the timing of the event to avoid peak travel times.

It is possible to set up a shuttle system (at stations and at airports), bike rentals, a system of car sharing to reach the event avoiding the use of individual cars. The licensee or the host of the meeting/event can organise and promote a special mobility service for attendees to support environmentally responsible travel to the meeting/event and mobility on the spot. This can be: (bicycle) taxi services or shuttle services (preferably with alternative drive or electric mobility), the organisation of carpools, bicycle rentals/organisation, etc.

On the average for World Cup games and cities, during the FIFA Men's World Cup Germany 2006 around 57% of visitors used public transport for travel to and from stadiums (including park and ride). A further 6% made their way on foot, around 11% travelled by coach. Travel by environmentally favourable means of transport therefore accounted for a total share of 74%. Only 23% of visitors to stadiums travelled there by car. The reasons for the success of public transport were, above all, the good connections of stadiums to the public transport network, the quality of services (for example, their frequency), few parking spaces at stadiums and, especially, the "CombiTicket", which was introduced for the first time at a World Cup championship and entitled ticket holders to travel free of charge on match days on the entire public transport network of host cities. Germany will host UEFA EURO 2024 and it has already started working on sustainability topics. Since fans' movements can hardly be influenced directly by event organisers, the focus must be on deploying attractive services to favour the use of ecologically beneficial modes of transport. Alongside the classic CombiTicket, long-distance travel by other means (such as long-distance coaches) will be made cheaper by offering an expanded ticket. On purchasing a ticket for a match, fans will be offered the Combi-Ticket Plus easily and cheaply. The model will have various levels: Level 1 covers cheap rail travel on routes between the host cities for the entire duration of UEFA EURO 2024. Level 2 offers cheap long-distance rail travel throughout the Deutsche Bahn network. Level 3 includes complete free use of the entire public transportation network for the full duration of the tournament.

Roland-Garros runs a promotional campaign to educate spectators on environmentally friendly transport options. The Roland-Garros carpooling website reduces the number of cars travelling to the event. The tournament has also developed a transportation "eco-calculator" that helps spectators choose the most environmentally friendly way of getting to the event. Roland Garros initiatives between 2010 and 2016 had a direct and measurable impact: 11.1% increase in spectators using public transport, 21% decrease in spectators using a personal car and 2.7% increase in spectators walking or cycling.

The transportation between venues of the sporting event can be transformed into a more environmentally sustainable service by operating environmentally friendly vehicle fleets. This best practice aims to transform all vehicles employed during the staging of a sporting event, especially VIP and staff vehicles, into environmentally friendly transportation. For example, the Tokyo 2020 organisers are planning to use fuel-cell vehicles and hybrid vehicles to reduce the impact that VIP and staff transportation as well as fans' mobility from the venues will have on the event's carbon footprint. The organisation of environmentally friendly vehicles requires planning during the preparatory phase of the event as well as during the actual staging of the event. Overall, it requires strong cooperation between the event organisers and the sponsors, which are usually the main providers of VIP transportation. This service offers varied opportunities to do something for the environment, for example through the use of low-fuel vehicles with high exhaust standards or alternative engines and the use of hybrid and gas-run vehicles. The use of light free-flowing oil noticeably reduces fuel consumption. Special training for drivers offers great potential for fuel savings of between 10% and 25%. Since vehicles are generally provided by sponsors, corresponding arrangements should be included in contracts. Driver-only journeys should be avoided. The use of minibuses instead of cars can reduce the number of necessary journeys

Related to mobility another issue is the impact of freight movements. Sport involves much specialised equipment and athletes, and teams often need to transport their kit around the world. Freight is not limited just to sports equipment; sports events also require vast quantities of goods and materials that have to be transported to and from venues, and this can add substantially to the carbon footprint. The impacts of freight are similar to those of transporting people, just different in scale and the types of vehicles used. Logistics managers therefore need to consider the environmental impacts of different transport modes and routes, and the social and economic impacts on host communities where large numbers of truck movements in and out of venues can cause localised disruption, noise and air pollution. Measures to reduce the impact of freight logistics for events may include:

- Location of distribution warehouses to allow the best route to venues to minimise impact on communities and optimise travel times;
- Optimal loading of vehicles to avoid wasted journeys;
- Operating a "quiet night-time delivery" policy;
- Selecting freight suppliers that operate modern low-emission fleets and compensate their carbon emissions;
- Where practical, using rail and river options instead of road transport; and
- For overseas freight, favouring sea freight over air freight, to significantly reduce carbon emissions.

In the case of touring teams and mobile events, the challenge is to achieve a balance of optimising what has to be transported each time and what can be used locally at the different stages of the tour. What might be saved on freight could be lost through waste from using local materials and equipment on a one-off basis.

The operation of the Tokyo 2020 Olympic Games requires the transportation of a large amount of people, materials, goods and waste. Transportation contractors and waste disposal contractors are encouraged to reduce CO_2 emissions through distribution by using low-pollution and fuel-efficient vehicles and practicing eco-driving such as the reduction of sudden acceleration and braking and the reduction of engine idling. For transport of materials and waste, in particular, they will aim to reduce CO_2 emissions by securing efficient transport routes according to transport plans developed in advance, and implementing efficient transport according to the state of road congestion. For food procurement, they will seek to reduce CO_2 emissions associated with logistics by selecting food in season and produced in neighbouring regions wherever possible, with consideration given to quality and costs.

The Stade de Nice was given an eco-design based on a life cycle approach, with the objective of limiting the environmental impact of the construction and use of the stadium. The stadium's structure is made up of 4,000 m^3 of wood, which stores carbon and contains little embodied energy compared with other materials. Local materials were used to reduce the impact of transporting building materials.

Often it is hard to plan which transportation solutions are the most efficient and environmentally friendly. The transport sector is a major producer of greenhouse gases. However, with more than 3.5 million sport events each year reducing GHG emissions related to travelling is a real challenge. Therefore, a suitable best practice can be the implementation of transportation software. It helps public authorities to find viable solutions for the transportation of goods that are environmentally friendly, allows the reduction of human fatigue and is economically efficient. The Optimouv software tool is able to calculate the best routes to employ to reduce the travel distance to sporting events, further minimising the carbon footprint of the sports sector.

Another important best practice to abate the CO_2 produced by the mobility involved in a sporting event is to communicate to the fans and supporters attending the event the climate-compatible ways in which they can travel to and from the event. Supporters' mobility to and from a sporting event venue may require international transportation, meaning that the CO_2 footprint of the event will grow even larger. Since it is often difficult to find all the necessary information about the means of transport to a sport facility, in order to allow fans to travel environmentally friendly transportation it is very useful for them to receive, together with the programme or invitation to the event, a document with all the practical information on how to reach the event location with soft mobility to promote environmentally friendly transportation. This simple best practice helps minimise the sport sector's carbon footprint with a very easily replicable method. The organising team should be in charge of providing the necessary information on transportation means to all fans. Attendees should as a priority be informed about climate-compatible travelling to and from the event. Train connections, bus schedules, information about the availability of public transport, distances between station and event location, etc. should be described in detail.

During an event, fans' mobility to and from sporting venues also occurs through the use of private cars. Initiatives aiming at diffusing the practice of carpooling enables to maximise the efficiency of private cars so that more than one person travels in a car. This practice prevents the need for others to use their private cars and therefore it reduces the total number of private cars employed. It is recommended that electronic platforms are used to advertise the carpooling system. Overall, carpooling is a more environmentally friendly and sustainable way to travel, as sharing journeys reduces pollution, traffic congestion and the need for parking spaces. It is also a means to divide the travel expenses and therefore it gives an economic benefit to the participants of the carpool. FC Porto created a specific portal "Dragons to Ride" to help its supporters to move to support the team by facilitating carpooling. Carpooling is a more environmentally friendly and sustainable way to travel as sharing journeys reduces air pollution, carbon emissions, and, in terms of car traffic logistics, reduces the traffic congestion on the roads and the need for parking spaces. Carpooling usually means to divide the travel expenses in equal parts between all the occupants of the vehicle (driver and passengers). By having more people using one vehicle, carpooling reduces each person's travel costs such as: fuel costs, tolls, the stress of driving and the cost of vehicle repairs.

The use of bikes and/or electrical scooters during the staging of an event is another best practice which can allow for a more environmentally friendly movement of fans. A system of electric bikes and/or scooters allows fans to rent an electric bike or a scooter to reach a venue of the sporting event or to move from one venue to another. This means of transport is environmentally friendly and also reduces traffic congestion. This best practice is highly replicable and is compatible with other mobility best practices (e.g., carpooling initiatives). It can be applied during the staging and breaking out of the event. The main actors responsible for the implementation of this best practice are the event organisers. Bicycle-sharing or electrical scooter systems are services in which bicycles or electrical scooters are made available for shared use to individuals on a short-term basis for a price or free. A bike or scooter system allows people to borrow a bike from a "station" and return in at another "station" belonging to the same system. Stations are special bike racks that lock the bike, and only release it by computer control. The user enters payment information, and the computer unlocks a bike. The user returns the bike by placing it in the station, which locks it in place. For many systems, smartphone mapping apps show nearby bikes and open stations.

However, most of the stadiums do not have any infrastructure to welcome cyclists. Moreover, one negative occurrence, quite notorious in fact, is bike theft. This discourages many cyclists from cycling to mass events, such as concerts, sport events and similar. Temporary bike parking could turn permanent if an agreement is reached and a cooperation between concert organisers and sport event organisers is achieved. Such an opportunity would surely be well perceived by the visitors and cyclists as it would save them time when returning home, as they would not only avoid traffic jams but also cramped trams, metros and buses. The only additional effort that the event organiser would need to provide is staff that would make the bike park secure. The launch of a secured bike park should include extensive media coverage and the participation of celebrities and/or athletes as testimonials would increase customers' knowledge and awareness. While building and installing a permanent secured bike park could result in certain costs, transforming an existing temporary bike park into a secured one would only require providing and ensuring the required security and staff.

Lastly, flights are one of the most significant impacts connected to football organisations' mobility. For this reason, football organisations should start taking into account adopting sustainable aviation fuel (SAF) for their flights. SAF is an alternative fuel produced from sustainable feedstocks and is very similar in its chemistry to traditional fossil jet fuel. Using SAF results in a reduction in carbon emissions compared to the traditional jet fuel it replaces over the life cycle of the fuel. Jet fuel packs a lot of energy for its weight and it is this energy density that has really enabled commercial flight. Today, there are not any other viable options for transporting groups of people quickly over very long distances, so everybody is dependent on this type of fuel in aviation. SAF gives an impressive reduction of up to 80% in carbon emissions over the life cycle of the fuel compared to traditional jet fuel it replaces, depending on the sustainable feedstock used, production method and the supply chain to the airport. However, SAF is currently more costly than traditional fossil jet fuel. For this reason, the best solution to reduce the impacts is to choose, where possible, trains and other more sustainable mobility options.

Notes

1 FSC: Forest Stewardship Council; PEFC: Programme for the Endorsement of Forest Certification schemes.
2 https://ec.europa.eu/eurostat/statistics-explained/index.php?title=Municipal_waste_statistics

References

Dusenge, M.E., Duarte, A.G., Way, D.A., (2019). Plant carbon metabolism and climate change: elevated CO2 and temperature impacts on photosynthesis, photorespiration and respiration. *New Phytologist*, 221(1), 32–49. doi:10.1111/nph.15283
Global Reporting Initiative, (2013). The Global Reporting G4 Sustainability Reporting Guidelines. Amsterdam, The Netherlands.

4 Environmental certifications for football organisations

4.1 Introduction to environmental certifications for football organisations

Environmental certifications can be divided into two main areas: certifications relating to organisations and certifications relating to products and services. Although it is a completely self-explanatory subdivision, it should be emphasised that, in the past, certifications relating to organisations (and therefore of their management systems and/or their activities and production processes) always applied to the activities that are under their management control.

This does not imply that a life cycle assessment (LCA) will be required, but the organisation will have to carefully consider the phases of the product or service that can be controlled or influenced. It is also important to note that a certified organisation must focus on all production of goods or provision of services and cannot only be concerned with a specific product or service line present in a wider range offered to the market. Therefore, in the world of football, this certification could not be issued exclusively for the first team or for the youth sector, but should cover all the relevant activities connected with the organisation.

Product certification, on the other hand, focuses its attention precisely on a single product line (understood as a manufactured good or service) normally considering its entire life cycle, understood as the set of activities that are carried out in order to produce the good or service and from the cradle (extraction of raw materials) to the grave (management of waste that will be produced in the end use or their recovery). In this sense, an environmental certification relating to the product differs from the certification of organisations because it can also concern only a single life cycle of a specific line of products/services, within the range offered to the company. This has two important consequences.

On the one hand, an organisation can certify a product and continue to produce others without complying with certification requirements. On the other hand, the criteria must be respected for all phases of the life cycle of the product/service to which the certification refers, regardless of whether or not these are under the direct management control of the applicant organisation.

DOI: 10.4324/9781003228271-4

Another important element of environmental certifications is the standardisation, accreditation and verification system that underlies their implementation. In order to be able to endorse with a credible recognition the environmental excellence demonstrated by the applicant organisations (for their activities/processes or for their products), all the certification schemes described in the following pages felt the need to guarantee their users, and more generally the community, about the reliability of the commitments undertaken and the concreteness of the results achieved (in terms of achieving the set improvement objectives, compliance with performance requirements, correct measurement and transparency of relevant environmental information, etc.).

In a globalised world characterised by relationships based on instant exchanges of information, computerised communication channels, rapid decisions necessarily based on such information, the authoritativeness of the schemes and the certainty, transparency, homogeneity and rigour in their application is a guarantee of seriousness and possible feedback to stakeholders and the market, especially in commercial relations. For this reason, the certifications analysed in the following paragraphs, albeit in a different way and with the level of incisiveness varying according to the source from which they originate, all leverage on: 1) standardisation systems (i.e., definition of certification requirements and rules for its release and maintenance); 2) possibility of using independent third parties to request a compliance check; and 3) on some form of accreditation of these subjects. Voluntary standardisation, as will be seen, also operates through a mutual recognition system which (at least with reference to some certification schemes) serves the purpose of further consolidating the guarantees provided.

Even though to date there are no studies which specifically investigate the effect of environmental management system on football organisations, the academic literature has strongly analysed the effectiveness of certified environmental management systems in the improving of environmental performance and reputation of organisations in different sectors.

Both practitioners and academics have investigated the effects of environmental management system (EMS) adoption on organisational performance (Marrucci and Daddi, 2021d). More recently, studies on EMSs have been extended to other topics such as the circular economy (Scarpellini et al., 2020a), green supply chain management (Testa and Iraldo, 2010; Daddi et al., 2021) and eco-innovation (Daddi et al., 2016; Scarpellini et al., 2020b). Nevertheless, despite this proliferation of studies, the debate on EMSs and environmental performance scholars are still debatable.

Certified organisations have generally been associated with better environmental and economic performance. However, some scholars have claimed that in some cases EMS adoption may be a symbolic strategy aimed at increasing the organisation's reputation and stakeholder trust. EMS internalisation has also been a key focus, i.e., the substantial and formal integration of the EMS requirements within organisation activities (Testa et al., 2018b). Testa et al. (2018a) stated that "the level of internalisation of its requirements both in terms of the strategies and daily operational procedures is a key determinant in achieving a real improvement in performance".

Despite the focus on EMS adoption, empirical findings have been contradictory and often lead to controversial results on whether or not certifiable EMSs improve environmental performance. This confusion also hinders a common understanding on the contribution of EMSs to the transition to a circular economy (Marrucci et al., 2019; Daddi et al., 2019).

Although most of the contributions on the link between EMS and environmental performance originally predicted a generally positive association, this has been undermined by the current new branch of studies. There are several reasons that explain the mixed results in the literature.

The first issue is the constructs and indicators used to measure environmental performance. Testa et al. (2014) used the reduction of carbonic anhydride emissions, and highlighted different effects of ISO 14001 and EMAS on environmental performance. The authors suggested that both standards have a clear influence on environmental performance, however while ISO 14001 mainly contributes in terms of short-term environmental performance, EMAS is more effective in the long term. Iraldo et al. (2009) did not select any specific variables, but focused on environmental performance as a general concept. Other studies also considered eco-efficiency, waste production and even legal compliance and the adoption of green practices (Daddi et al., 2011b).

Another aspect is whether or not a study includes other variables such as mediation or the moderation of environmental outcomes. In fact, in addition to internalisation, which has been also studied in relation to ISO 14001, other factors have been used to analyse EMS effects on environmental performance. Daddi et al. (2017a) analysed the role played by the environmental manager's satisfaction in enhancing the environmental performance of EMAS-registered organisations.

The size sample, coverage and reliability can also affect the findings of a study. In the very extensive academic literature on EMS performance, it is not difficult to find quantitative studies with limited sample sizes, i.e., less than 100.

Lastly, the main controversial aspects of the link between EMSs and environmental performance are associated with the methods used to gather information. Most studies used perceptual measures collected through questionnaires to assess EMS effects on environmental performance. Through Likert scales, scholars asked managers to express their perception of organisational performance. However, the self-reporting approach can be easily subject to social desirability bias and other distortions. In fact, most of the previous studies on EMSs have measured the environmental performance in terms of perceptions as opposed to quantitative data (Marrucci et al., 2021c).

Despite these caveats, "intangible benefits" can be obtained by the adoption of an EMS. The adoption of EMAS or ISO 14001 can lead to a better management of environmental compliance, a reduction of environmental risks, a higher environmental involvement and awareness of managers and employees (Marrucci et al., 2021b) and a closer cooperation with institutional stakeholders and local communities (Daddi et al., 2011a).

Even though EMAS adoption is facing a slight decrease (Daddi et al., 2017b), policymakers are constantly working to remove and simply administrative costs and burdens for EMAS and ISO 14001 certified organisations (Daddi et al., 2014).

However, one of the last biggest surveys on EMAS-registered organisations (Marrucci et al., 2021e) confirmed that the internalisation of an environmental management system improves the overall performance of organisations. Without concretely integrating the EMS within the organisation's working life and designing a sustainable monitoring tool, managers may only achieve an adoption which may lead to better social legitimacy, but will not improve organisations' environmental performance.

4.1.1 Environmental certifications of organisations and of their activities/processes

As previously mentioned, the topic of the certification of organisations focuses on the correct management of the activities that fall under organisations' direct control or that they can influence (indirect control). There is a wide range of environmental certifications for organisations, but our work will focus on those most relevant for the diffusion of environmental sustainability in the football world. In particular:

- The EC Regulation for a Community eco-management and audit scheme: EMAS (no. 1221/2009) (paragraph 4.2);
- The UNI EN ISO 14001 standard, Environmental Management Systems (paragraph 4.2);
- The UNI EN ISO 14064 standard, Greenhouse gas emissions – Part 1: Specification with guidance at the organization level for quantification and reporting of greenhouse gas emissions and removals (paragraph 5.2);

However, as explained, other certifications such as the UNI EN ISO 50001 standard on Energy Management Systems, the UNI EN ISO 45001 standard on Occupational Health and Safety Management Systems and so on, could also contribute to football sustainability development.

Among all the certifications, EMAS and especially ISO 14001 are the most widespread. To understand the interest these certification schemes have registered, it is enough to mention that the EMAS regulation, as of June 2021, counts a total of 3,851 organisations and 12,856 sites registered in Europe, while the ISO 14001 standard certified as of December 2020, 348,218 organisations and 568,518 sites worldwide.

There are two fundamental aspects that link together all these standards:

- the field of application is the "organisation";
- "Plan-Do-Check-Act (PDCA)" approach also known as Deming cycle is the basic methodology.

The term organisation is the subject of a specific and fundamental definition reported both by the EMAS Regulation and by the ISO 14001 standard (which we can consider as historical norms and which at the definition level have inspired and fed the information processes in this area): "group, company, firm, firm, body or institution, or parts or combinations thereof, whether associated or not, public or private, which has its own closed administrative functional structure".

This definition is broad and includes not only industrial companies but also service companies, public bodies and institutions. Everything that falls within this definition constitutes a certifiable entity and therefore the field of application can be determined in relation to it. When we talk about the field of application of an ISO standard or of a European regulation, we mean the delimitation of the boundaries of the activities and processes of the organisation to which all the requirements must be applied. A critical aspect in defining these boundaries concerns the so-called "cherry-picking" risk that can compromise the seriousness and credibility of the certification. This practice, explicitly forbidden by the main accreditation and standardisation roles of the various schemes, can be translated into practice by defining the boundaries that include only the best part of the organisation, i.e., the part that is able to comply with the requirements of the scheme of interest, excluding instead from the field of application the challenging activities or processes.

An element of the definition of organisation that places some limits on its wide application is the reference to a "functional and administrative structure" which must be interpreted as possession by the organisation of responsibility, authority, decision-making power, managerial autonomy, availability of human and financial resources, and ability to manage the activities falling within the scope in order to comply with all the requirements of the standard or regulation. Thus, beyond the intuitive perimeter at the organisation's gates of the company, the definition of the borders and therefore of the field of application is definitely more complex in cases where there are multisite organisations or there is the possibility to subdivide the organisation certification into parts (e.g., sectors of a public body).

The Deming cycle or PDCA cycle or, alternatively, the Shewhart cycle is a business management approach that specifically concerns the improvement of production through the optimisation of work processes, the resolution of any critical issues (problem-solving) and the reduction of any type of waste. The Deming cycle is divided into four distinct phases which are repeated, in a cyclical manner, until the achievement of the improvement in productivity, the ultimate goal of the cycle. The four phases are:

1. PLAN or planning phase: without careful planning the organisation cannot proceed with the action. Therefore, the first phase of the Deming cycle involves the execution of a plan: system monitoring, identification of problems and drafting of an intervention plan for the resolution of critical issues;
2. DO or execution phase: from the theoretical plan to its practical application. In this phase the organisation moves on to the execution of the plan for continuous improvement developed during the first phase. At the same time, the data processed during the execution of the plan necessary for the next phase is collected;
3. CHECK or control phase: after execution, the collected data is checked. In this third phase the staff responsible for the continuous improvement of the production systems are called upon to carefully analyse the statistical data obtained during the implementation of the improvement plan. Also in this phase, all possible corrections to be made to the plan to integrate it are evaluated;
4. ACT or action phase: this last phase involves the application of the plan, integrated with any changes, in order to ensure an ever-increasing quality of the organisation's production process. At the end of the Deming cycle, if the production reaches the prescribed improvements, it does not mean that the cycle cannot be reapplied to the production in order to maintain constant quality and improvement over time.

Management systems do not limit the concept of production to the classic realisation of products and goods, but include also the provision of services. Also, by "process" they mean a set of correlated or interacting activities that transform input elements into output elements, adding value and guaranteeing the achievement of results regardless whether the focus is on services or products. Each organisation can therefore divide its management into various business processes which cyclically undertake the path of the Plan-Do-Check-Act approach.

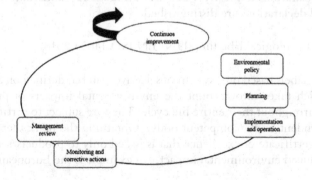

Figure 4.1 The path of the Plan-Do-Check-Act approach

4.1.2 Environmental certification of products and services

Product certification focuses on the environmental aspects and impacts of the life cycle of a manufactured product or service. The product certifications discussed in this book are:

- the European Regulation for the European Union Ecolabel (No. 66/2010, EU Ecolabel);
- the EU Energy Label issued as a result of various EU directives;
- the EU Organic Label issued as a result of various EU regulations;
- the product environmental footprint (PEF) and the organisational environmental footprint (OEF)

Product certification is a formal and voluntary act by which an accredited third party states, with reasonable reliability, that the product conforms to what is declared in a reference technical document. The choice to certify the product is based on the company's desire to differentiate itself within the market, enhancing a set of particular and significant characteristics, rigorously guaranteed by a third party. Voluntary certification therefore allows you to stand out from competitors, enhancing your investments in terms of sustainability in the eyes of various stakeholders (customers, suppliers, etc.).

As regards environmental certifications for products and services, it is possible to distinguish product certifications on the basis of the principles to which they refer. In particular, the following are recognised:

- certifications of excellence, based on compliance with certain requirements;
- transparency certifications, closer to the world of product life cycle assessment.

According to the classification and description of the labels and environmental declarations of the UNI EN ISO 14020:2002 standard, three types of ecological declarations are distinguished.

- Type I ecological labelling (UNI EN ISO 14024:2018)

Voluntary labels based on a system of selective criteria, defined on a scientific basis, which takes into account the environmental impacts of products or services throughout their entire life cycle. They are subject to certification by an independent body (competent body). Obtaining the mark therefore constitutes a certificate of excellence that is issued only to products/services that have a reduced environmental impact. An example is the European Ecolabel.

- Type II ecological labelling (UNI EN ISO 14021:2018)

Self-declarations of an environmental nature by producers, importers or distributors of products, without the obligation of certification by an independent external body. An example is the self-declaration of the amount of recycled material contained in a product (e.g., packaging).

• Type III ecological labelling (UNI EN ISO 14025:2010)

Voluntary declarations based on established parameters that contain a quantification of the environmental impacts associated with the entire life cycle of the product calculated through an life cycle assessment (LCA) system. They are independently audited and presented in a clear and comparable form. An example is the Environmental Product Declaration (EPD), which is internationally valid for three to five years.

Some types of product environmental certification can be used directly on the product or even on the immediate packaging, others are accompanied by claims (including advertising) or declarations intended to attract the attention of potential buyers and influence their choice. Product certification cannot, however, be used to identify a specific manufacturing facility. To be more precise, it is commonly held that due to their characteristics, type I and II labels are mainly aimed at the end consumer (business to consumer, B2C), whilst the type III labels are better used for relations with commercial partners in the production chain (business to business, B2B).

We will mainly focus on type I labels since they offer better assurances of data transparency, credibility of the scheme and the possibility to develop useful solutions for the football world. Attempts to start certification schemes for type II claims are, however, on the increase and judging by some of the single-theme labels (e.g., "carbon footprints" or "water footprints") could already fall into this category.

With the sole exclusion of the Energy Label, all the other environmental product certifications explained below have in common the life cycle thinking concept. This approach, which can be framed as the path of the product or service from "cradle to grave", finds its maximum level of application, both from a structural and technical-regulatory details, within the ISO standards of the 14040 series. The maturation and diffusion of the life cycle approach within the voluntary standardisation processes has marked a fundamental and profoundly innovative step from the perspective with which the environmental certification schemes have been applied.

Firstly, this approach is characterised by the long-term logic which introduces into environmental management the considerations of the impacts that occur after the useful life of a product and before the production process in the upstream phase. Secondly, the life cycle approach aims to promote the logic of circularity, pushing the producer to consider and therefore to deal with all the impacts that are generated even when the product or part of it (packaging, waste, etc.) is under the direct management responsibility of other subjects. Thirdly, this approach helps organisations to broaden the focus of environmental issues from the local company dimension to the "system-product", or rather to the broader scope of operations of the various actors involved in the management of the product or the service.

To meet these needs, which constitute its backbone and the methodological basis, the life cycle approach necessarily requires the collection and consideration of data information that the organisation that wants to obtain the certification does not possess (e.g., environmental data of the extraction of raw materials or of the end-of-life treatment of waste).

The life cycle approach enters the dynamics of certification schemes in different ways. In some cases, the organisation is required to perform an LCA to rigorously derive the environmental indicators to be used in the market communication (e.g., EPD). In other cases, the life cycle analysis is not delegated to the organisation that wants to obtain the label, but is carried out on a one-off basis by a competent body in charge of the label. This competent body characterises the impacts by product category and defines a series of thresholds relating to quantitative environmental indicators. Organisations will have to demonstrate full compliance to these parameters in order to obtain certification (e.g., EU Ecolabel).

Almost all of the products and services covered by the above-mentioned labels are necessary for a football organisation. In order to reduce the environmental impact of their activities, football organisations may start using certified environmental products. The stadium management and the organisation of football events require procurements of high volumes of products and services. Some of the services (e.g., cleaning, catering, grass cultivation, etc.) and the products (e.g., paints, cleaning products, etc.) also have an important environmental impact. The adoption of specific criteria could contribute to the transition towards green behaviours among suppliers, as well as enhance the club's environmental performance.

The EU Ecolabel, EU Energy Label and EU Organic Label guarantee a high level of transparency, reliability and scientific credibility, which meets customers' green demands. And, unlike other environmental information or labelling, no technical understanding is required to read and understand the label. By choosing ecolabelled products, consumers automatically make an environmentally friendly choice.

Supporting these ecolabels could a winning choice for football organisations. Not only do they boost their corporate image, but they can also fulfil supporters' increasing demand for truly environmentally sustainable products. Indirectly, football organisations' actions will also support manufacturers that make credible green choices, and may also increase the diffusion of green products in the daily life of supporters.

4.1.2.1 The EU Ecolabel

The EU Ecolabel is the ecological quality mark of the European Union that distinguishes products and services which, while guaranteeing high performance standards, are characterised by a reduced environmental impact during their entire life cycle. As of September 2021, 2,057 licences have been awarded for 83,590 products (goods and services) in the EU market. Most licences and products are awarded in Spain, Germany, France and Italy.

The EU Ecolabel was established in 1992 by Regulation no. 880/92 and is now governed by Regulation (EC) no. 66/2010 in force in the 27 countries of the European Union and in the countries belonging to the European Economic Area – EEA (Norway, Iceland, Liechtenstein).

The EU Ecolabel is a voluntary ecological label based on a system of selective criteria, defined on a scientific basis, which takes into account the environmental impacts of products or services throughout their entire life cycle and is subject to certification by an independent body (competent body).

Environmental performance is assessed on a scientific basis by analysing the most significant environmental impacts during the entire life cycle of the product or service, also taking into account the average life span of the products and their reusability, recyclability and the reduction of packaging and their content of recycled material.

The Ecolabel criteria, established at European level with a wide participation of interested parties including European consumer and environmental associations, also cover important aspects relating to the health and safety of consumers. They also concern, where relevant, the main social and ethical aspects of the production processes. The EU Ecolabel criteria concern five main environmental hotspots: deforestation and degradation, inefficient waste disposal and non-recycling, inefficient use of resources (water, energy, raw materials, etc.) and products (food waste, excessive use of detergents, etc.), and reduction of carbon emissions.

The EU Ecolabel covers a wide range of product groups such as personal care products, cleaning products, clothing and textile products, paints and varnishes, electronic displays, coverings, furniture and bed mattresses, growing media, soil improvers and mulch, lubricants, paper products and tourist accommodation. However, citizens look for the EU Ecolabel especially for the purchase of "Cleaning" and "Paper" products (Marrucci et al., 2021a). Football organisations consume important quantities of these materials and adopting green criteria for their selection would significantly contribute to boosting sustainability in their strategies. Moreover, supporters might be influenced by these choices and change their household consumption. Product certifications are especially helpful in detailing the technical specifications which contractors must comply with in the provision of the service or product. The EU Ecolabel can be utilised as a means of proof of compliance with technical requirements. Besides the requirements concerning the environmental characteristics of the product, EU Ecolabel also includes requirements concerning the quality, performance and safety of the product (when applicable). Consequently, this label specifically suits the purpose of procurement tenders.

Box 4.1 The role of the EU Ecolabel in football organisations

Football organisations should use the EU Ecolabel for different purposes.

For example, the EU Ecolabel is applicable to cleaning products and detergents. A football club could use numerous kilograms of these products in a year, e.g., they are used to clean the dressing rooms, to clean the offices and meeting rooms located in the stadium and for any other cleaning activity. A football club could decide to buy only ecolabelled detergents to reduce (indirectly) its environmental impact.

Another field where the ecolabel is applicable is accommodation services. There are a lot of hotels certified with the EU Ecolabel and afootball match could create a strong need of hotel rooms for example for away supporters or for home supporters that attend an evening match and don't live in the city of its favourite football team. In this case a football match should try to reduce the impact derived from this "football tourism". The club should identify the hotels certified ecolabel in its city and favour the choosing of those hotels by the supporters. The approaches could be several like for example: establish an agreement with these hotels with special room price for the supporters, create brochures or informative sections of the website where can be found the list of hotels with Ecolabel in the city, communicate this info through the periodical communications that a club has with the main supporters' groups.

Many other products and services can be certified according to the EU Ecolabel and these could be easily consulted on the EU Commission website. Similarly for the case of cleaning products and hotels, the clubs should identify a specific strategy to privilege their consumption.

4.1.2.2 The EU Energy Label

The awareness of having to make a better use of energy resources has led to the need to establish a classification and labelling framework to stimulate the market to be populated by more energy-efficient products. These products should perform the same tasks with less energy use and therefore have advantages for the environment (reduction of energy requirements and CO_2 emissions), for users (lower operating costs due to reduced consumption), for manufacturers (visibility and saleability of advanced models, on which investments have been made in technological development).

The first unitary labelling framework occurs with the Directive 75/1992/EC promoted by the European Union. This directive defined the range of appliances to be subjected to labelling to nine initial types of products: refrigerators, freezers, washing machines, dryers, dishwashers, ovens, water heaters and storage boilers, light bulbs, air conditioners. It also defined two different information elements that characterise the appliances: energy labels (*stricto sensu*) and information sheets. Initially, this contained summary data on consumption, but did not indicate an energy class representing the product. It emphasises the energy consumption of appliances rather than their energy efficiency.

The Directive 75/1992/EC has been replaced by the Directive 30/2010/EC. This directive extended the energy label to other products with a significant impact on energy consumption (not necessarily electricity) and gave more importance the energy efficiency of appliances before their simple absolute energy consumption. For the first time, it introduced energy efficiency classes defining a basic scale from A to G, and expandable with classes A+, A++ and A+++. In other words, the energy class must synthetically reflect the efficiency of an appliance and not its consumption.

In turn, the Directive 30/2010/EC was replaced by Regulation 1369/2017 which changed the labels in March 2021. Despite this, there are no significant changes. The regulation mainly updated the technical criteria of product categories and proposed new energy efficiency classes for all product families, with scales always and only from A to G (classes A+, A++ and A+++ will no longer be used).

In summary, the primary objective of the EU Energy Label is to provide consumers with recognisable, accurate and comparable information on the energy consumption of household appliances, their performance and essential characteristics. Its main feature is the uniformity for all appliances in the same category. This allows consumers to easily compare the distinguishing characteristics of an appliance, such as energy consumption, water consumption or its capacity. In fact, all the information contained on the label is based on standard tests required by European legislation. Currently, the range of products covered is more widespread compared to lists included in the first EU directive of the 1992. EU Energy Label includes air conditioners, cooking appliances (domestic), dishwashers (household), heaters (space and water heaters), light bulbs and lamps, local space heaters, fridges and freezers (household), refrigeration (professional), refrigeration with a direct sales function, solid fuel boilers, electronic displays including televisions, tumble driers, ventilation units (residential), washing machines (household) and tyres. Other products (e.g., electric heaters, hair dryers, electric hobs, steam mops, microwave ovens, electric grills and barbecues, dehumidifiers, kettles, toasters, etc.) are not subject to energy labelling, either because the incidence of their consumption on the overall figures is negligible, i.e., too small to justify the creation of a specific category, or because the differences in consumption between the different models on the market are modest and it would not make sense to categorise them.

The success of energy labelling has favoured the development of increasingly energy-efficient products with better technical characteristics and functional performance. The EU Energy Label had achieved annual energy savings of approximately 150 Mtoe (million tons of oil equivalent) by 2020, approximately equivalent to the annual consumption of primary energy in Italy. However, in addition to environmental benefits, it allows consumers to evaluate the operating costs of each appliance, helping them to choose the appliance with the lowest energy consumption with the same technical characteristics. For consumers, this means an average saving of up to €285 per year on household energy bills. According to the EC (2019), the EU Energy Label is recognised by 93% of consumers and 79% consider it when purchasing energy-efficient products.

As for the EU Ecolabel, football organisations frequently purchase products covered by the EU Energy Label. Considering buying exclusively class A products would allow them to not only strongly decrease their environmental impacts by increasing energy efficiency, but also to achieve important economic savings. Moreover, since the EU Energy Label is so widespread and common among consumers, supporters would easily recognise the effort made by the organisation. This would lead to a twofold effect: from one side, the organisation would improve its environmental reputation, while on the other side, the supporter might be more incline to buy energy efficiency products.

Box 4.2 The role of the EU Energy label in football organisations

As with the EU Ecolabel, the EU Energy Label should be used in detailing the technical specifications to which contractors must comply with in the provision of the service or product. It also should be utilised as a means of proof of compliance with technical requirements.

In particular, the EU Energy Label can be used by football organisations for the selection of air conditioners, ventilation units, cooking appliances, fridges, freezers and refrigeration, dishwashers, washing machines, tumble driers, heaters, boilers, electronic displays (TVs, monitors, signage), light bulbs and lamps, tyres.

4.1.2.3 The EU Organic Label

In 2007, the Council of the EU approved Regulation (EC) No. 834/2007 which defines the principles, objectives and general rules of organic production as well as the methods of labelling organic products. The regulation, which is still in force, is also complemented by various Commission implementing acts relating to the production, distribution and marketing of organic products.

All these pieces of legislation are the legal basis that establishes whether products, including those imported from third countries, can be marketed as organic within the EU. The regulations also define how and when the EU Organic Label can be used. The EU Organic Label provides a coherent visual identity to EU organic products. This makes it easier for consumers to identify organic products and helps farmers market them across the EU.

The EU Organic Label can only be used on products that have been certified as organic by an authorised inspection body or agency. This means that they have met strict conditions for production, handling, transportation and storage. The label can only be used on products that contain at least 95% organic ingredients and which also comply with strict conditions for the remaining 5%. The same ingredient cannot be present in organic and non-organic form.

The European Union rules on organic farming cover agricultural products, including aquaculture and yeast. They include all stages of the production process, from seeds to processed final products. This means that there are specific provisions concerning a wide variety of products, such as: seeds and propagating material such as cuttings, rhizomes, etc. from which plants or crops are grown, live products or products that do not need further processing, feed and products with multiple ingredients or processed agricultural products intended for use as food. EU regulation on organic production excludes products from fishing and hunting wild animals, but includes harvesting of wild plants when certain natural habitat conditions are respected. There are specific rules for wine and aquaculture.

Producing with organic methods means respecting the rules on organic farming, which aim to promote environmental protection, maintain Europe's biodiversity and strengthen consumer confidence in organic products. This regulation governs all sectors of organic production and is based on a series of fundamental principles, such as: ban the use of GMOs, prohibit the use of ionising radiation, limit the use of artificial fertilisers, herbicides and pesticides, prohibit the use of hormones and limit the use of antibiotics, to be used only if necessary for animal health.

This means that organic producers need to take different approaches to maintaining soil fertility and animal and plant health, including: crop rotation, favour the cultivation of nitrogen fixing plants and other green manure crops to restore soil fertility, prohibit the use of mineral nitrogen fertilisers, to reduce the impact of weeds and pests, organic farmers choose resistant varieties and breeds that encourage natural pest control, encourage the natural immune defences of animals and prevent overcrowding to protect animal health.

Farmers must also comply with specific conditions if they wish to market their products as organic. These rules are intended to respect the welfare of animals, to promote their feeding according to their nutritional needs and to protect the health and the environment of the animals. They also help build public confidence, as they ensure that organically raised animals are kept separate from non-organic ones.

According to data from Nomisma's Consumer Survey report, from 2005 to date the value of sales of organic branded products has grown by 220% (Nomisma, 2021). Moreover, the 2021 Organic Market Report published by the Soil Association (Soil Association, 2021) reveals the highest year-on-year growth in 15 years for the organic market, at +12.6%. This report also indicates the desire to eat healthy, the anxiety of avoiding pesticides and chemical residues, and the attention to the environment as the reasons why consumers decide to purchase organic products. In particular, it is the European countries that are major consumers and producers of organic food. According to research by the Soil Association, even though the United States stands out among the countries that sell the most, Germany and France are immediately after the USA. In fact, organic crops represent 2.2% of European crops and 5.4% of cultivated land within the European Union.

Organic fruits and vegetables avoid the load of pesticides and those substances that are normally used to facilitate their long conservation. Organic proteins (e.g., meat, fish, etc.) contain much better fats and fat qualities, think for example of the polyunsaturated fatty acids that are ingested by cows that burn grass living outdoors, and are also not burdened by the pesticides and antibiotics that are widely used in battery farms to avoid contamination. The body of a sportsman is very stressed, if he then receives all these foreign substances (e.g., pesticides, antibiotics, etc.), it is clear that the body must take action to expel them. However, these toxins can accumulate and this can decrease the efficiency of sports performance. Thus, by increasing the health and the performance of their players, football organisations can significantly contribute to reduce the impact on nature.

Box 4.3 The role of the EU Organic label in football organisations

When choosing to use organic products, football and sports organisations are faced with a double opportunity. Football organisations should start adopting only organic food for their players' diets. In fact, several studies proved that for athletes, choosing organic food not only makes sense, but it is definitely fundamental. Carbohydrates (e.g., pasta, bread, cereals, etc.) from organic farming, and especially wholemeal ones, better modulate the absorption of sugars.

Moreover, organic food can be used by football organisations in their VIP area during football matches or, at least, in their facilities' bars, kiosks, other services connected to food. Fostering the adoption of organic products in these contexts would allow them to pursue a twofold approach. It will reduce the direct environmental footprint of the organisations by consuming less impactful products and will raise the awareness of supporters about organic and sustainable consumption.

4.2 Sustainable events with ISO 20121

Events are sometimes, by their nature, high profile and transient, with both positive and negative social, economic and environmental impacts. The ISO 20121:2012 "Event Sustainability Management System" has been drafted to help organisations and individuals improve the sustainability of their event-related activities.

The ISO 20121 specifies the requirements of an event sustainability management system to improve the sustainability of events. It is applicable to all types and sizes of organisations involved in the design and delivery of events and accommodates diverse geographical, cultural and social conditions. At the same time, it requires organisations to recognise their relationship with and impact on society and society's expectations of events.

Figure 4.2 provides an overview of the event sustainability management system model for the ISO 20121.

For operators in the event management sector who want to undertake the path towards sustainable event management, ISO 20121 is the reference point. In fact, one of the main risks of organising a sustainable event is disappointing the expectations of the stakeholders, and obtaining a counterproductive communicative effect that is far removed from the promoter's intentions.

The ISO 20121 standard is a guideline that defines the requirements for the development and implementation of a management system for the sustainability of events, indicating a scheme within which organisers and their suppliers can create a sustainable event and interact with stakeholders in a concept of sustainability understood as the way in which an organisation conducts its activities to obtain an economic return in compliance with ethical, social and environmental protection principles.

Through the integration of the management systems model with the life cycle of events, ISO 20121 aims to define the planning and implementation phases of an event (from the definition of a policy for sustainable development, to the identification of stakeholders and the context in which the event is inserted, from the definition of the resources necessary for the identification of key performance indicators (KPIs), to the operational control) up to the definition of the monitoring of the event to identify and evaluate the performance and consequent actions for improvement.

The ISO 20121 allows an organisation to demonstrate that all financial, economic, social and environmental aspects have been taken into consideration during the organisation of a particular event. In organising an event, organisations will be able to concretely demonstrate their commitment to the environment through the reduction of energy consumption or the use of eco-friendly materials, and towards social principles through fair trade purchases or attention to needs of those with disabilities or food allergies and intolerances.

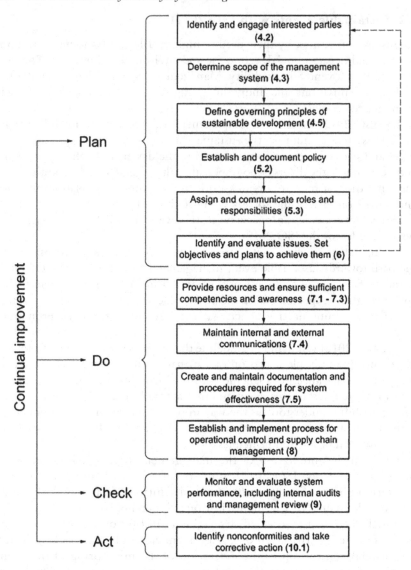

Figure 4.2 Event sustainability management system model for the ISO 20121.

A certified sustainable event is a best practice of corporate social respon-sibility, transmits principles of sustainability to the relevant public, helps to strengthen the competitive positioning of the organisation that promotes it. The ISO 20121:

• Identifies the universal principles for a sustainable event;
• Provides a responsible management model for events and services;

- Can be used for certification purposes, to guarantee consistency and credibility.

The universal principles for a sustainable event are:

- Principle 0: Regulatory Compliance. The fundamental prerequisite of ISO 20121 is compliance with the regulatory framework applicable to the event;
- Principle 1: Inclusiveness – fair treatment and involvement of all stakeholders;
- Principle 2: Integrity – adherence to ethical principles;
- Principle 3: Transparency – sharing of information about the event;
- Principle 4: Management – ability of the organisation to adopt a system for the sustainability of the event.

The path includes the commitment and involvement of all levels and functions of the organisation and the evaluation of all areas of management. It is necessary to identify all stakeholders, and to assess their degree of involvement and accountability. Both internal (e.g., members of the organisation, top management, employees, collaborators, staff, volunteers, etc.) and external stakeholders (e.g., testimonials, institutions, local authorities, associations, sponsors, suppliers, participants, audience, local community, media and press, etc.).

Like the other ISO standards, ISO 20121 is also based on the "Plan-Do-Check-Act" methodology. It provides a systematic framework for the integration of sustainable management practices so as to reduce the impact related to economic, environmental and social. Organisations that implement this system can reduce costs and improve their brand reputation. In addition, the sustainable management of events has beneficial effects on the social, environmental and economic impacts of the event itself at different levels, such as the production of waste, the consumption of energy and water, the control of workers in the event organisation chain, etc.

According to UNEP (2009), an event is sustainable when it is "conceived, planned and implemented in such a way as to minimize the negative impact on the environment and leave a positive legacy to the host community". Developed on the basis of the British standard BS 8901, ISO 20121 constitutes a flexible reference model for organisations that want to demonstrate their commitment to sustainability in the planning and implementation of events.

The standard can in fact be applied to a single event, to a series of events, to organisations specialised in the realisation of events or, again, to service providers such as catering companies and also to locations (e.g., exhibition districts, conference centres, hotels, etc.).

The distinctive elements of the standard can be summarised as follows:

- Definition of the principles of sustainable development and policy. For the definition of these principles, the standard suggests referring to the following: ethical management of resources (stewardship), inclusiveness, integrity, transparency. In addition to these, of course, the organisation can implement others, perhaps referring to the ISO 26001 standard "Guide to social responsibility".

- Evaluation of the significant impacts of the event in the three areas of sustainability: social, environmental and economic. This assessment must take into account the feedback from interested parties.
- Definition of targeted objectives and targets for each of the significant and priority aspects identified with clear release of the actions, timing, resources necessary for their achievement and the method of evaluating the results.
- Definition of the methods of dialogue with the various stakeholders through an exhaustive communication plan for the entire life cycle of the event.
- Organisation of the supply chain from a sustainable perspective with the inclusion of parameters consistent with the principles and policy adopted.
- Performance monitoring, always with reference to the principles and policy adopted by the organisation and taking care to correctly identify and manage the lessons of previous events in order to usefully exploit them for the design of subsequent ones.

The standard focuses on the analysis of the aforementioned three key dimensions of sustainability, clarifying how the organisation, in planning and developing a sustainable event, must pay attention to the adoption of processes and actions aimed at the efficient use of resources, taking care to minimise waste.

Some actions consistent with the main principles of the standard can be:

- Favour service providers or local producers or, again, opt for local or zero-kilometre PGI products;
- Reduce the waste of food offered during the event, by donating what is not used to voluntary associations;
- Foster partnerships with local associations to provide various types of support to the event (e.g., forms of volunteering and assistance during the event);
- Ensure the reuse of assets created for the event to give a second life to everything created specifically for the event;
- Assess the carbon footprint of the event by planning carbon-neutral events, carefully evaluating the reduction of emissions along the entire life cycle of the event itself and planning offsetting initiatives for the benefit of the local community;
- Evaluate the water footprint of the event to measure the extent of the impacts on water resources during the event, promote water efficiency and optimise water resources;
- Design and build buildings and other structures in line with the most qualified protocols such as LEED certifications;

- Promote travel by electric vehicles to the place of the event, through the rental of special shuttles or in any case the use of public transport or, again, by encouraging and rewarding forms of car sharing;
- Promote the choice and use of recyclable materials for the stands;
- Promote the use of biodegradable tableware;
- Where necessary, place ecological chemical toilets;
- Encourage the separate collection of waste with easily identifiable bins and containers;
- Use LED technology lighting in the event venues;
- Manage only online invitations and e-tickets, without the need for paper printouts;
- Avoid the use of plastic or disposable packaging, for example by providing participants with gadgets such as reusable bottles or by placing dispensers for water supply.

The adoption of ISO 20121 entails a number of benefits for organisations, both direct and indirect:

- Cost savings resulting from the reduction of energy consumption, waste reduction or the purchase of local products;
- Reputational advantages deriving from the visibility that an ethical event produces, demonstrating the company's commitment to environmental sustainability and social responsibility;
- Promotion of innovative techniques and technologies that help to use resources more efficiently;
- Dissemination of greater awareness among participants, employees, suppliers and in the local community about the benefits of eco-friendly products and services;
- Social benefits for the area through the creation of employment and business opportunities for local suppliers;
- Development of an efficient and effective systematic approach to the principles of sustainable development;
- Implementation of a system for monitoring and recording sustainability performance;
- Characterisation of the supply chain in a more sustainable sense;
- Increase in the motivation and loyalty of the human resources employed and attraction of the best talents.

ISO 20121 can be merged with other management systems such as ISO 14001, but also with other methodology such as life cycle assessment (LCA), i.e., the systematic analysis of the potential environmental impacts of products or services during their entire life cycle.

In fact, several tools have been used to define and quantify the environmental impacts associated with an event; however, a lack of uniform approaches for conducting environmental evaluations has been revealed. Toniolo et al. (2017) evaluated whether the LCA methodology, which is rarely applied to an event, can be an appropriate tool for calculating the environmental impacts associated with the assembly, disassembly and use phases of an event, analysing in particular the components and the displays used to establish the exhibits. The authors also included in their analysis the issues reported by ISO 20121 involving the interested parties that can be monitored but also affected by the event owner, namely the event organiser, the workforce and the supply chain. The results obtained by Toniolo et al. (2017) show that the main contributors are energy consumption for lighting and heating and the use of aluminium materials, such as bars for supporting the spotlights, carpet and the electronic equipment. This study highlighted the importance of the environmental implications of the energy consumed by heating and lighting, and indicated that the preparation and assembly of an event should always be considered when quantifying the environmental profile of an event.

Musgrave and Pelham (2011) discussed the current demand for sustainability within the event industry by seeking the opinions of seven experts working in various roles within the event industry who all contributed to the development of ISO 20121. The entire group agreed that within a short time period demand for sustainability will grow, making this an attractive business model. The authors recognised the value of an international standard for sustainability like ISO 20121 for the event industry. The authors claimed it was important to raise the profile of sustainability in the event sector.

Practical wisdom in the conference-planning field suggests that green, or environmentally responsible, events result from adherence to various best practices, such as eliminating paper, reducing packaging and recycling. Sustainability standards such as ISO 20121, however, propose a more systematic way of identifying the sustainability issues that stakeholders care about (e.g., accessibility, climate change, waste avoidance and health) and setting continuous improvement objectives to address these priorities through planning decisions. Whereas the former approach is largely tactical, the latter is more strategic and presents opportunities for associations to drive mission-based principles through their event supply chain and demonstrate performance against values that matter to members (McKinley, 2018).

4.3 The ISO 14001 standard and the EMAS Regulation

The ISO 14001 standard and the EMAS Regulation (EC n.1221/2009) represent the key references for environmental certification for organisations and their activities and/or processes. Given their 30-year application, they have already induced and stimulated the development of consolidated methodologies aimed at operationally interpreting and translating the environmental management requirements of the standards into practice. Resuming the

PDCA cycle, the prescriptive contents and the supporting indications for the application of a certification path that meets the requirements of both of them will be presented in the following paragraphs, divided into the following fundamental elements:

- Environmental review: the review is the snapshot of the organisation and its significant environmental aspects by defining suitable criteria in order to assess its environmental impacts. It identifies legal provisions applicable to its activities, examine all the existing environmental management practices and procedures and evaluates the results from the analysis of previous environmental accidents and emergencies;
- Policy and programmes: the environmental policy outlines the organization's approach to its effect on the environment. This statement must come from top management. This is because the policy will affect how every individual performs their job in relation to environmental impact. An environmental management programme is the roadmap the organisation will follow to achieve its environmental objectives and targets. It is a document that provides the details of what must be done, by whom, how and when, for each of the defined objectives and targets;
- Management system: it is the real engine of environmental management, represented by an organisational, managerial, relational and documentary structure that allows the company to constantly feed and move the mechanisms of environmental management;
- Audit and review: these are the internal review of the system and the top management review, in which the results achieved are verified and any corrective actions to be taken are defined. The audit is a systematic, independent, objective and documented process for gathering facts in order to identify areas for improvement and ensure you have best practice processes in place;
- Third-party verification: it is the control phase by an appropriately accredited external subject necessary to obtain the certification. A third-party audit is when an external organisation (a third party) who undertakes an audit of an organisation, where the external organisation does not have a direct relationship to the auditee organisation (the organisation being audited);
- the Environmental Declaration: this is the most important and demanding additional requirement of EMAS with respect to the ISO 14001 standard and concerns the organisation's communication with stakeholders on environmental issues.

Currently not very many football clubs have obtained the ISO 14001. Moreover, most of them are big European clubs such as Manchester United, Juventus FC, Porto FC, etc.

4.3.1 Environmental review

ISO 14001 and EMAS environmental management systems require the organisation to identify its environmental aspects and manage them. The standards establish that the organisation must identify the environmental aspects of its activities, products and services that, within the scope defined for the environmental management system, it can directly monitor and control and those over which it can exercise an influence. The organisation must also determine those aspects that have or can have significant impacts on the environment. Particular emphasis is therefore placed on the definition of an environmental aspect, that is an element of the activities, products or services of an organisation that has, or can have, an impact on the environment. By environmental impact, on the other hand, the standards mean any modification of the environment, negative or beneficial, totally or partially caused by the environmental aspects of an organisation. An environmental aspect is defined as significant when it has, or can have, a significant environmental impact. To decide whether it is a significant environmental aspect, the organisation must have a credible and objective assessment system for environmental aspects. This system is aimed at identifying and assessing the environmental aspects of the organisation and determining which are the most important.

In summary, the environmental analysis is the tool through which an organisation establishes its current position on environmental issues relating to the activities it carries out. The analysis can therefore be assimilated to a photograph that portrays the environmental conditions of the organisation at the time it is carried out, thus constituting the starting point against which the organisation itself will be able to evaluate the progress of its performance over time. The assessment of the environmental aspects must be periodically updated or in any case must be updated whenever substantial changes occur in the organisation, both from the technical and management point of view. The environmental aspects of organisation are identified within the field of application of the environmental management system, taking into account the inflows and outflows associated with the activity, products and services. It is therefore advisable, in order to proceed with the identification of environmental aspects, to construct a detailed picture of the activities that can generate environmental aspects or be connected to them. A good practice is represented by the analysis of the processes that characterise the organisation, through a flow chart that highlights the inputs and outputs relating to the various activities.

Below, we list the main environmental aspects:

* Emissions in the atmosphere, e.g., logistics;
* Water discharges, e.g., pitch irrigation;
* Soil contamination, e.g., pitch management;
* Consumption of resources, e.g., merchandising, food and beverages;
* Energy consumption, e.g., stadium lighting system;

- Waste production, e.g., supporters' waste;
- Land use and consumption, e.g., soil occupation;
- Biodiversity, e.g., green areas outside the stadium;
- Noise, odours, visual impact, etc., e.g., matches, stadiums.

These references are useful, even if not exclusive, for identifying the so-called direct environmental aspects, i.e., environmental aspects associated with the activities, products and services of the organisation over which the organisation has direct management control. Direct aspects are all those aspects directly generated by organisations, on which it can exercise a total management capacity.

It is also advisable, however, that the organisation that aims to obtain an environmental certification also keeps under control the indirect environmental aspects, i.e., environmental aspects that can derive from the interaction of an organisation with third parties and that can be influenced by the organisation itself. These are environmental aspects for which the organisation is able to exert a certain influence, but not the capacity for total management. Some examples of indirect environmental aspects are the following:

- Aspects related to the life cycle of the product/service (design, development, etc.);
- Capital investments and financial assets;
- New markets;
- Choice and composition of the products/services offered;
- Administrative and planning decisions;
- Environmental performance and practices of contractors and suppliers;
- Etc.

Indirect aspects are therefore the environmental aspects that are not generated by activities carried out by the organisation, through its own personnel and structures, but over which the organisation exercises the ability to partially manage or simply influence. Examples of indirect aspects are the hazardous substances used by cleaning companies operating at the organisation's site or the emissions deriving from the means of transport of suppliers. Exercising control, albeit partial, and influence on the environmental aspects generated by contractors and suppliers represents an unavoidable operating mode. Indeed, the standards state that organisations should be able to demonstrate that significant environmental aspects related to procurement procedures have been identified and that such significant environmental impacts associated with these aspects are addressed within the management system. The organisation should also undertake to ensure that suppliers and those acting on its behalf comply with the organisation's environmental policy when carrying out contracted activities.

For a football club, logistic, catering, cleaning, maintenance services can be all considered indirect aspects.

In summary, the analysis of the environmental aspects is divided into two phases: identification and evaluation. In the first it is necessary to break down the processes of the organisation's activity, products and services, in order to identify their interactions with environmental systems (e.g., GHG emissions, wastewater, waste, etc.). In the second, on the other hand, the significance of the environmental aspects identified is evaluated according to a method that the organisation establishes. This methodology must be reproducible and verifiable by independent control. Although there is no single method for evaluating environmental aspects, some criteria that can be used as a reference are:

- Potential to cause environmental damage;
- Fragility of the local, regional and national environment;
- Extent, number, frequency and reversibility of environmental aspects or impacts;
- Existence of environmental legislation and related obligations;
- Importance for stakeholders.

In the case of indirect environmental aspects, it is appropriate to add to these a criterion that takes into account the ability of the organisation to influence them.

A fundamental element of the environmental analysis is the assessment of the environmental legislative compliance of organisations, which involves an assessment of compliance with all applicable legal requirements and other requirements that the organisation subscribes to. By applicable environmental requirements we mean both those related to the compliance of the sites (e.g., fire prevention certificate, compliance of electrical systems, suitability of the refrigerant used in air conditioning systems, etc.), and those related to production activities (e.g., authorisation to discharge wastewater, safety data sheets of hazardous substances, waste management, etc.). Since compliance with environmental legislation is a prerequisite for obtaining environmental certification, during the environmental analysis it is necessary to verify compliance with all the requirements applicable to the organisation.

The 14001 standard expects organisations to understand their context. The context includes defining influences of various factors on the organisation and how they impact the EMS. The general context of the organisation can be classified as:

- Internal context: any actions or products and services that may affect the environmental performance of the football club
- External context: may include legal, economic, social or political issues
- Environmental context: all other environmental aspects that may be susceptible to damage by your organisation's environmental performance

Starting from the context analysis, the organisation must also determine, monitor and review relevant interested parties and detect risks and opportunities and how they affect the EMS.

The organisation should take the time to understand the relevant interested parties' needs and expectations and determine those relevant to the environmental management system, which should be addressed. Moreover, organisations must identify potential risks and opportunities. Risks and opportunities are defined as potential adverse effects (threats) and potential beneficial effects (opportunities). The rationale behind this definition is to have organisations primarily focus their attention on the results related to risk determinations, including both positive and negative effects, rather than simply the uncertainty related to the occurrence of events.

The final result of the analysis should be a complete and updated informative, analytical and evaluation framework of the organisation, capable of summarising the set of interactions of its activity with the environment, providing references for the functionality and effectiveness of environmental management procedures and ensure full legislative compliance. It is therefore appropriate that the initial environmental analysis activities end with the preparation of a summary report, i.e., a concise summary document, to be used as an agile and effective tool in subsequent planning activities for improving environmental performance and management system set-up. A possible index of this document could be the following:

* Description of the environmental characteristics of the territorial context;
* Description of the organisation's activity;
* Description of the management and organisational structure;

THE CLUB'S STAKEHOLDERS

First Team Players	Participants in the Juventus Soccers Schools and in the Juventus Academies	Sponsors and Commercial Partners
Fans		Staff (technical, medical, etc.)
Players' Agents and Representatives	Educational Institutions and Universities	Local and International Organisations and Associations
Youth Sector Players		
	Sports Institutions	Juventus fans, Season ticket holders, Members and spectators at the stadium
Shareholders and Capital Providers	Media	
Competitors (other clubs, their fans and associates)	Public Administration and Law Enforcement	Top Management, employees and associates (stewards)
Families of Juventus athletes	General Public	
Suppliers and their employees		

Figure 4.3 Juventus FC's list of stakeholders according to its sustainability report

- Presentation of the environmental analysis and significance assessment methodology;
- Identification of direct and indirect environmental aspects;
- Analysis of direct environmental aspects and interpretation of results;
- Analysis of indirect aspects and illustration of relations with relevant external parties;
- Summary scheme of the significant direct and indirect environmental aspects.

Box 4.4 Evaluation of direct environmental aspects under normal conditions

Three criteria are applied for the assessment of direct environmental aspects:

- Relevance
- Efficiency
- Sensitivity

Relevance is that parameter that describes the intrinsic potential severity of the environmental impact factor to cause a negative consequence on environmental components.

Efficiency aims to evaluate the organisation's ability to manage the various environmental issues also according to their relevance.

Sensitivity is an evaluation parameter that refers to the environmental and social situation of the area in which the site is located.

Relevance can be evaluated considering the presence of regulatory limit:

1. There is no legal limit;
2. Presence of management constraints deriving from the applicable legislation;
3. There is a legal limit.

The following sub-criteria will be used for the calculation of the efficiency criterion.

Sub-criterion: Intertemporal trend

1. If the indicator shows a significant improvement in performance in the period under consideration;
2. If the indicator shows a fluctuating trend in the period under consideration (and, in any case, worsening / improvements are < 5%);
3. If the indicator shows a significant deterioration (> 5%) of performance in the period under consideration.

Sub-criterion: Presence in the organisation of procedures or practices on the management of the environmental aspect in question.

1. Presence of written procedures on the correct management of the environmental aspect;
2. Existence of (oral) practices on the correct management of the environmental aspect;
3. Absence of procedures or practices on the correct management of the environmental aspect.

The following sub-criteria will be used for the calculation of the sensitivity criterion.

Sub-criterion: Comparison with local municipal plan for the environment

1. If the local environmental plan does not recognise the environmental aspect under analysis as one of the main environmental criticalities of the area;

2. If the local environmental plan recognises the environmental aspect under analysis as one of the main environmental criticalities of the area.

Sub-criterion: Comparison with the sustainability strategy promoted by UEFA

1. The environmental aspect has been assessed as not significant in the UEFA strategy;
2. The environmental aspect has been assessed as averagely significant in the UEFA strategy;
3. The environmental aspect has been assessed as significant in the UEFA strategy.

The value assumed by the three parameters (relevance, efficiency, sensitivity) is given by the average of the scores attributed to each response. The significance value of each environmental aspect is given by the average of the values assumed by the three evaluation parameters. Significance under normal conditions = (Relevance + Efficiency + Sensitivity) / 3

The environmental aspects will be judged significant based on the score attributed to them and in particular:

$V < 1.65$	Not significant environmental aspect
$1.65 < V < 2.00$	Medium significant environmental aspect
$V > 2.00$	Significant environmental aspect

4.3.2 Environmental policy and improvement programme

The results of the initial environmental analysis, i.e., the process of identifying and evaluating the environmental aspects related to the activities carried out by the organisation, constitute a preparatory element for the start of the actual planning phase (PLAN) envisaged by the Deming cycle.

The planning phase makes use of two tools that must be built in sequence:

- The environmental policy of the organisation;
- The environmental improvement programme.

4.3.2.1 Environmental policy

The environmental policy is the tool that has the function of general direction of the environmental management of the organisation. It defines the basic principles and criteria that must be taken into consideration for the subsequent definition of specific objectives linked to the management and control of the significant environmental aspects and the improvement of related performances. It is a short communicative document that responds to two needs of the environmental management system:

- A declaration of intent that must be signed by the top management and made public, representing the commitment that the organisation expresses with respect to the principles of good environmental management and to the improvement of its environmental performance;
- A basic reference that the organisation assumes for the planning of environmental improvement and the definition of systemic and operational methods for managing environmental aspects and for periodic checks on the adequacy of the effectiveness of the management system.

It therefore assumes an internal value as an essential tool in the mechanism for defining objectives and achieving results. It also assumes an external value as a tool through which the organisation expresses its commitments relating to the management methods of its environmental aspects and communicates them to all stakeholders. From the first point of view, environmental policy must be an effective tool in setting criteria for establishing objectives and goals. From the second point of view, it must be sufficiently clear, understandable and faithfully represent the commitments that the organisation assumes. The policy must be signed by the top management, meaning the group of people capable of assuming strategic and political commitments. In fact, a commitment at the highest levels is required, since the fulfilment of the expressed commitments will involve both in the short and long term the entire organisation and its organisational, human and financial resources. It must include a series of elements that are explicitly required by ISO 14001 and reinforced in their relevance by the EMAS Regulation:

• Commitment to continuous improvement of environmental performance, to be understood as constant commitment over time to reduce negative impacts and to effectively manage the aspects connected to the organisation's activities;
• The adoption of the principle of prevention of the original environmental impacts produced by the activities carried out;
• The commitment to and compliance with the legal requirements applicable to the activities of the organisation and other requirements that the organisation has voluntarily signed.

For the drafting of the policy, the results of the environmental analysis must be taken into account. The general objectives for improving the environmental performance of organisations must in fact be based on the evidence of the most important and critical environmental aspects. The environmental policy is drawn up during the construction phase of the environmental management system and then periodically reviewed in order to be always updated with respect to the evolution of the organisation. Both the ISO 14001 standard and the EMAS Regulation explicitly require that the environmental policy must be communicated and must be available to all interested parties, both internal and external to the organisation. In particular, it is requested that it is disseminated to all people who work directly or indirectly for the organisation. It must also be made available to the public.

Box 4.4 Manchester United's environmental policy

ENVIRONMENTAL POLICY STATEMENT

Manchester United recognises its responsibility to ensure a safe and healthy environment and will endeavour to maintain sound environmental performance through our ISO14001 environmental management system. This policy will be implemented by maintaining legislative compliance and having clearly outlined objectives, targets, management responsibilities and employee involvement to continually improve our performance.

Our management systems reflect the unique nature of our business as a major sporting venue, team and brand. We will regularly audit our performance to highlight areas for improvement and measure our progress. We expect the same of our major suppliers and contractors, and will continue to run and develop our best practice supplier environmental management programme. We are also moving towards a more sustainable procurement programme. Contractors working on refurbishment schemes and new construction are expected to meet appropriate environmental standards.

As a world class sporting business, we have a strong relationship with both our commercial partners and our supporters. We will look for ways in which we can leverage our position to influence their environmental activities and encourage them to help us to improve our environmental performance.

Our customers are also becoming more environmentally aware, so we will promote our environmental management programme to them and ensure that we maintain our Green Tourism Business Scheme.

We take our stewardship over the land we occupy, associated water resources and air quality seriously.

WE TAKE OUR STEWARDSHIP OVER THE LAND WE OCCUPY, ASSOCIATED WATER RESOURCES AND AIR QUALITY SERIOUSLY.

(Continued)

- We actively manage the biodiversity of the Carrington Nature Reserve and use it as an educational tool when practical. All other landscaping and grounds maintenance is planned with the most positive practical environmental impacts in mind.

- We will prevent pollution to the land, air or water as a result of our activities. We will avoid hazardous processes or materials where suitable alternatives are available.

- We have achieved the Carbon Trust Standard and will continue to build on our developed carbon and renewable energy strategy, to improve our performance further.

- We have already installed rainwater harvesting and taken steps to manage our water use. We will continue to strive to reduce our water consumption across all sites, whilst maintaining pitches and other facilities to a standard expected of a world class sporting venue.

We recognise the need to move towards an economy that keeps valuable resources in circulation. We have taken steps to reduce the amount of waste we produce and divert all operational waste from landfill. We also aim to minimise the use of non-renewable materials, improve our recycling rates and use more recycled materials.

This policy will be reviewed at least annually, and will be brought to the attention of all employees and made available to all stakeholders including the general public via our web-site manutd.com or on request.

Authorised by R Arnold,
Group Managing Director
Manchester United Limited

4.3.2.2 Environmental improvement programme

The long-term general principles and criteria established and disseminated through the environmental policy serve to guide the planning of organisations and aim to continuously pursue the improvement of environmental performance over time. The environmental planning of organisations is based on a document called the "environmental programme". The programme can be considered an element of primary importance because it is through its implementation that the improvement of environmental performance pursued through the use of the environmental management system is substantiated. The implementation of the programme, the examination of its correct application and its periodic updating must ensure the achievement of the environmental improvement objectives and the environmental target defined by the organisation. In fact, the ISO 14001 standard and the EMAS Regulation require the organisation to establish, implement and maintain objectives and targets. By objective, the standards mean a general purpose of overall improvement usually referred to by the organisation in a specific category of significant environmental aspects. A target is a detailed performance requirement (i.e., quantified with the use of specific environmental indicators) linked to an objective and to one or more significant environmental aspects. The achievement of the target set for one or more environmental aspects allows the achievement of the objective. The objectives and targets must be set in coherence with the environmental policy and therefore in coherence with the aspects that emerged as the most significant from the environmental analysis. They must be able to carry out continuous improvement in line with the management and technological options that are considered applicable in light of the operational, financial and commercial needs of the organisation. The environmental programme is the tool with which the organisation intends to achieve objectives and targets. All the interventions planned for this purpose with a predefined time horizon will therefore be placed in the environmental programme. Interventions may be both simple and short term, or more articulated and necessarily to be carried out over a longer term. In the latter case, the intervention can be divided into single implementation steps (e.g., feasibility study, design, construction, testing, etc.).

Being the true fulcrum of the environmental management system, it is essential for the organisation to identify a clear path of resources and timescales that allows the achievement of the objectives set out in the environmental policy. The process by which the environmental programme is drawn up, monitored and kept updated details as follows:

- Drafting of the environmental programme;
- Implementation of the environmental programme;
- Examination of the progress of the environmental programme;
- Updating or new drafting of the environmental programme.

This process, with the related organisational roles and responsibilities, must be documented. The programme is drawn up, in its first draft, on the basis of the significant environmental aspects resulting from the environmental analysis and within the framework of the general principles and criteria established with the environmental policy. It therefore includes all the interventions that organisations plan to implement in the programming period to improve environmental performance, with particular reference to significant environmental aspects. Each planned intervention must be defined by describing in detail:

- The methods of intervention;
- The significant environmental aspect to which the improvement is intended;
- The quantification of the improvement objective pursued, indicated using specific performance indicators;
- The organisational figures responsible for carrying out the intervention;
- The amount of resources needed for carrying out the intervention;
- The expected implementation times.

It is therefore clear that the environmental programme as a whole will have to be set up bearing in mind the feasibility with respect to the resources that organisations will be able to make available, in terms of time, human and financial resources and also in the light of the organisation itself.

Box 4.5 Example of a football organisation's environmental programme

N.	Environmental aspect	Action	Target	Deadline	Monitoring	Resources	Responsible	State
1	Water consumption	Installation of water flow optimiser	-5%	Dec 22	N. of water flow optimisers installed	€1,000	Maintenance department	DONE
2	Energy efficiency	Installation of LED lamps in the office area	-10%	Dec 22	N. of LED lamps installed	€2,500	Maintenance department	DONE
3	Energy efficiency	Changing of the air conditioners	-5%	Sept 23	N. of air conditioners changed	€30,000	Maintenance department	ONGOING
4	Single use plastics avoidance	Reusable cups	-10%	Dec 22	N. of single use cups purchased	€1,500	Catering services	ONGOING
5	Material efficiency	Purchase of recycled paper	100%	Sept 22	N. of paper purchased	€1,000	Purchasing department	DONE
6	Waste production	Recycling of the organic matter produced during turf maintenance	100%	Dec 22	% of organic waste sent to recycling	€500	Turf maintenance department	ONGOING
7	Air emissions	Purchase of electric cars	100%	Dec 23	N. of electric cars	€100,000	Purchasing department	ONGOING

4.3.3 Environmental management system

The next step after planning is to create an organisational and management structure consistent with the identification and evaluation of the environmental aspects, the commitments identified in the environmental policy, the objectives and targets set in the improvement programme, as well as with the regulatory requirements applicable to the organisation.

As part of its general management system, the organisation must define the management, organisational and technical structure: the environmental management system (EMS). It represents the heart and engine of the organisation's activities and processes aimed at managing environmental aspects and implementing the environmental improvement strategy. Once the organisational structure has been defined, it is also necessary to understand the training needs for each of the figures involved in the environmental management system and to define the operating procedures for the correct management of the significant environmental aspects, as well as for the correct functioning of the system itself. The design and implementation of an EMS does not require an organisational revolution, but rather a rationalisation and systematisation of some processes that are already active before the moment of its introduction within the organisation (e.g., waste management). Without prejudicing the full autonomy of the organisation to adapt its structure and requirements of the EMAS and ISO 14001 in accordance with its technical and managerial needs, some elements must be considered in the system definition process. In particular, an organisation must:

- Adapt its organisational structure by defining the structure of the management system and the organisational departments involved, indicating the related duties;
- Involve the staff by providing suitable methods for raising awareness, training and increasing skills in the management of environmental aspects;
- Define and implement effective working methods for the correct management of environmental aspects and a suitable response to emergencies;
- Monitor its environmental performance, the functioning of the system and provide effective methods for resolving any non-compliance;
- Define the communication processes, both top-down and bottom-up, between the various organisational departments and towards external stakeholders.

DEFINITION OF ROLES AND RESPONSIBILITIES IN ENVIRONMENTAL MANAGEMENT

Establishing a clearly defined organisational structure, consistent with the environmental problems that the organisation must manage, adequate for the objectives it intends to pursue, is an essential element to ensure the effectiveness of the environmental management system. Each organisation will define the organisational structure of its environmental management system in line with its own characteristics and management approach. There are, however, some general principles that organisations can take into account when implementing their management structure. First of all, it is necessary to assign responsibilities and define the roles for all the functions that are involved in the management of environmental aspects or that, through their activities, can generate a direct or indirect environmental aspect. To provide the departments and human resources operating in the organisation all the references and coordinates useful for correctly carrying out the activities that are required in the context of environmental management, a precise and detailed definition of the following must be implemented:

- The roles that each figure in the organisation must cover in environmental management;
- The responsibilities assigned to these figures with regard to environmental aspects;
- The duties and tasks assigned within the environmental management system;
- The working methods with which everyone must carry out these tasks and duties.

Particular attention must be paid by the organisation to the balance between the responsibilities attributed and the powers delegated to each function involved in the EMS, in order to ensure that this is able to fulfil its role in the decision-making and management processes concerning the environment. The organisation can make use of various tools that specify the responsibilities, duties and tasks in environmental management for each function: organisation charts, matrix of responsibilities, job descriptions, function charts, etc. These tools represent a valid documentary support that can prove to be very useful in the operation of the organisation. An instrument certainly capable of providing a synthetic and functional representation of the corporate organisational structure is the organisation chart. This can be drafted at different levels of detail: representing the entire organisational structure in a single diagram, or representing different organisational areas separately. However, it is advisable to create a specific organisation chart that provides a clear picture of the roles and responsibilities within the organisation in the field of environmental management, to which job descriptions can be associated that define in detail the tasks assigned to the various figures present in the organisation chart itself.

Secondly, the fundamental role that top management assumes in the correct functioning of the management system should be emphasised. The top management must, first of all, be able to express and transmit their commitment to the implementation of the principles defined in the environmental policy to all staff, in order to strengthen awareness on the importance of environmental issues and the opportunity to adopt pro-environmentally friendly behaviours.

It is also advisable to identify a figure within the organisation to be entrusted with the role of operational coordination of environmental management activities. This figure, usually identified as the "environmental manager" or the "manager of the environmental management system", must not, however, be conceived as a specialist function that solely guarantees all activities related to environmental management and assumes all the responsibilities and connected charges. Instead, it must be seen as a support and stimulus to the Top Management and to all the remaining personnel of the organisation in environmental management.

In order to keep EMS active, it is essential that the organisation ensures the availability of adequate resources. This means that the organisation must guarantee the availability of technical, financial and human resources capable of achieving a correct and effective management of environmental problems. The organisation must have the knowledge and the technical and technological equipment suitable for guaranteeing the improvement in environmental performance that it has set itself as its main objective. Secondly, the economic and financial planning, fundamental for the normal activities of organisations, should be extended in order to include the budgetary aspects and needs deriving from environmental management. Finally, it is essential that the human resources on which the organisation relies for the implementation of the EMS, as well as all the personnel involved in the activities that affect the environmental performance of the organisation, are able to contribute to the achievement of the objectives it has defined. Defining roles and responsibilities, working methods, training, information and communication are essential aspects to ensure effective and sound environmental management.

Box 4.6 Football organisations' Environmental Manager job description

1. Leadership & commitment – the Environmental Manager shall facilitate the involvement of the top management of the Club in environmental issues. This objective can be reached through the following activities:

- Promote the inclusion of the protection of the environment as a value of the Club i.e., promoting its inclusion in the vision or the policy of the Club;
- Involve all managers of the different departments in periodical meetings in order to update them about the ongoing initiatives in the field of environmental management identifying their possible roles and responsibilities;

(*Continued*)

- Discuss with the top management in order to ensure that adequate resources (organisational, human and financial) are allocated to the enactment of the environmental issues in the activities of the Club.

2. Operational management – the Environmental Manager must ensure that the Club's operations and processes are carried out in a manner to eliminate or mitigate (as far as possible) negative environmental impacts, and eliminate or mitigate the risk of unexpected harmful events and environmental emergencies. This objective can be reached through the following activities:

- Ensure legal compliance to environmental regulations (at EU and national level) and an effective management of environmental aspects of operations (at all levels and functions), and thus attend to the allocation of roles and responsibilities to the Club's personnel within the boundaries of the extant organisational arrangements of the Club;
- Arrange, manage and monitor the collection, deposit, conferment, disposal of waste from all Club structures;
- Establish processes for the implementation and control of planned (temporary and permanent) changes to operations and processes that may have an impact on environmental performance (changes in location or work conditions, new technologies, changes in work organisation, etc.);
- Identify environmental actions to be implemented in the activities present in the training centre that could have an impact on the environment (e.g., restaurant, hotel, management of chemical products for the management of the pitch, etc.);
- Establish, implement and periodically review (in coordination with safety manager) processes necessary to prepare for, and respond to, potential emergency situations;
- Adopt actions to reduce the environmental impacts connected with the arrangement of team matches (e.g., incentives for public mobility, requests about waste management, etc.);
- Coordinate its activities with the Purchasing Department in order to assure the inclusion of green criteria in purchasing procedures;
- Establish periodical meetings with the Sponsorship Department in order to identify possible collaborations with sponsor in the field of environmental sustainability.

3. Internal and external communication & involvement – the Environmental Manager shall attend to external communication, environmental reporting and disclosure initiatives, in close collaboration with the Club's Communication and Social Responsibility departments and other operational units of the Club. To these aims, the following responsibilities are envisioned:

- Establish and maintain internal channels (e.g., dedicated email account, newsletter, intranet webpage, website, etc.) for the dissemination of information and news regarding the environmental initiatives of the Club;
- Ensure that any reports or suggestions from organisational members regarding the environmental aspects of operations and processes are provided with timely feedback;
- Establish and maintain channels for the external communication (e.g., dedicated webpage on the institutional website, newsletter, etc.) of the Club's environmental improvement initiatives, reaching the Club's most salient stakeholders (e.g. football clubs, football supporters, other football national and international institutions, stadium owners, local communities, etc.);
- Cooperate to possible environmental reporting initiatives (such as a Sustainability or Social Responsibility Report) to ensure a transparent disclosure of the Club's environmental performance and a widespread dissemination of the Club's efforts towards environmental improvement in close collaboration with Communication and Social Responsibility departments;
- Provide environmental info and data to any external media partner that will require these kinds of info;
- Arrange periodical dissemination events about environmental initiatives of the Club in order to contribute to the awareness raising of all football stakeholders;
- Represent the contact person of the FSR Department of national and international football institutions (National Football Federation, UEFA, FIFA);
- Promote an organisational culture and work environment that values environmental sustainability, by:

  - Communicating the importance of effective environmental management and environmental compliance for the Club's activities and the sport sector;
  - Leading and supporting the Club's personnel so that they will actively contribute to the integration of the Environmental Policy in daily activities and to the achievement of environmental objectives;
  - Providing support to other relevant management roles to demonstrate their leadership for environmental improvement and how it applies to their respective areas of responsibility.

(Continued)

4. Training & awareness – the Environmental Manager shall ensure that appropriate training is periodically provided to the Club's personnel, according to their training needs, skills and competences. To this aim, the following responsibilities are envisioned:

- Identify, map and periodically reassess the necessary skills and competences for personnel who perform work activities under the Club's control and which affect its environmental performance and its ability to comply with legal obligations;
- Periodically define and implement a periodic training and awareness plan (e.g., on an annual base) aimed at meeting the training needs of the Club's personnel (or external people who work for the Club) in the reference period, by detailing (i) the supplying body, (ii) training modalities, (iii) personnel addressed and (iv) verification of learning;
- Support, facilitate and monitor the participation of the Club's personnel in the training initiatives, by eliminating potential barriers to attendance.

5. Planning & monitoring – the Environmental Manager shall lead, supervise and coordinate the monitoring of the Club's environmental performance and the planning of possible improvement actions. To this aim, the following responsibilities are envisioned:

- To establish the key relevant data to monitor, the periodicity of data collection and the performance indicators to elaborate;
- Periodically collect the environmental data, elaborate the performance indicators, discuss them with specific identified departments (including the top management);
- Identify possible improvement actions to be planned and coordinate periodical meetings with the Club's managers in order to collect suggestions to plan environmental objectives and to share possible actions that will involve their department.

AWARENESS RAISING, TRAINING AND PARTICIPATION

An effective EMS is achievable provided that all personnel, regardless of their duties and function, are adequately informed and trained. The primary objective of the information and training activities is to raise awareness among staff in order to actively involve them in the management of environmental aspects and in the pursuit of the organisation's improvement objectives. It is also necessary to ensure that any person who performs, for the organisation itself or on its behalf, tasks that may cause one or more significant environmental impacts identified by the organisation has acquired the necessary competence. The principles contained in the environmental policy must be transferred to employees at all levels and put into practice in their respective operational areas. It is a process of maturation of the organisational culture which, affecting individual behaviour, requires time and a gradual development. It is therefore reasonable that the training and awareness-raising activities are designed and conducted in parallel with the implementation of the environmental management system. The ISO 14001 standard and the EMAS Regulation in fact emphasise the need to spread environmental awareness to all workers, and in particular on:

- The importance of compliance with environmental policy, procedures and management system requirements;
- Significant, real or potential, environmental impacts resulting from the organisation's activities and benefits for the environment due to the improvement of their individual performance;
- Roles and responsibilities to achieve compliance with environmental policy, system procedures and requirements, including emergency readiness and the ability to react;
- The potential consequences of deviations from the specified operating instructions procedures.

Worker training activities must be primarily aimed at encouraging behavioural change processes through learning dynamics that allow highlighting problems as well as helping to solve them. For this reason, the training must give answers to the learning needs of workers in the cognitive, operational and behavioural areas. For each of these areas, different tools for training activities must be prepared. Depending on the learning needs, different ways of training and information can be created.

Training is essential to create the organisational conditions for the assimilation of the culture of prevention and is aimed to transfer skills that are not limited to a specific area of activity. Information is a simplified form of training: it transfers content that can be assimilated even if advanced forms of interactivity are not developed. To promote real participation and propensity to change behaviours, a worker training programme should never be limited to the communication of knowledge, but also act on the acquisition of values and attitudinal mental disposition.

DEFINE AND IMPLEMENT CORRECT WORKING METHODS FOR THE MANAGEMENT OF ENVIRONMENTAL ASPECTS AND EMERGENCY SITUATIONS

One of the most important requirements of the environmental management system certainly concerns the ability of the organisation to define and apply working methods that guarantee the implementation in the field of principles of environmental policy and the achievement of improvement objectives.

The organisation must therefore identify which operations and activities are associated with the significant environmental aspects in line with its policy, objectives and targets. It is therefore necessary to start from the results of the environmental analysis to identify the operational activities to which the most relevant direct and indirect aspects are associated and to define the most suitable actions and behaviours in order to ensure that these are carried out while minimising the impact on the environment. Once the mapping of the activities concerned has been completed, it is necessary to plan the correct working methods and ensure that these are carried out in the best conditions.

There is a widespread belief that writing down the working methods in procedures and operative instructions where detailing the criteria to carry out the activities can constitute a useful support for the organisation. In fact, the formalisation of working methods makes it possible to rationalise and standardise the actions and operations that are carried out to finalise a specific activity of the organisation.

The objective to be pursued in the formalisation of the EMS must be to achieve a degree of documentation proportionate to the actual needs of the organisation, especially in relation to its complexity and the problematic nature of managing its environmental aspects. An organisation can choose the level of formalisation that best suits it as neither procedures nor operating instructions are subject to any type of constraint or requirement. They should therefore be proportionate to the management needs of the organisation. When deciding on the correctness of the procedures it is necessary to keep in mind the size and complexity of the organisation, the nature of the environmental impacts and the competence of the operators in charge of carrying it out. Simple diagrams, schemes and matrixes can sometimes represent a simple and effective solution to provide the necessary information.

An important aspect, underlined by the ISO 14001 standard and the EMAS Regulation, concerns the management and surveillance of suppliers and contractors. The actions that the organisation can take to manage relations with these figures may concern:

- The introduction of environmental performance requirements rules in the tender specifications and contractual clauses relating to their non-compliance;
- Performing audits on contractors and suppliers to verify compliance with the environmental requirements of the service specifications;
- The preparation of internal structures on the site and/or temporary structures to facilitate correct behaviour by contractors and suppliers;
- The definition of internal procedures for the selection, qualification and control of the activity of contractors and suppliers;
- Sanctions against suppliers and contractors resulting from the outcome of the audit, control and surveillance activities;
- The definition and sharing with contractors and suppliers of plans and procedures for the management of emergencies in the plants.

PERFORMANCE MEASUREMENT, MONITORING AND IMPROVEMENT

The ISO 14001 standard and the EMAS Regulation require the organisation to establish and maintain documented procedures to regularly monitor and measure the main characteristics of its activities and operations that can have a significant impact on the environment. This includes recording information that makes it possible to follow the progress of environmental requirements, operational controls and compliance with the organisation's objectives and targets. The measurement and surveillance activity therefore allows the collection of quantitative data which, elaborated in the form of synthetic indicators, provide important information for evaluating the organisation's performance, the effectiveness of the EMS and its ability to achieve environmental objectives.

We can therefore distinguish two elements of the monitoring system, in addition to the audit activities that the organisation must implement:

• Management monitoring;
• Performance monitoring.

The first category includes periodic monitoring of the state of implementation of the objectives and monitoring of the effectiveness of controls. An organisation must therefore establish operating procedures to effectively monitor the level of achievement of the improvement objectives over time. It is advisable for this verification to take place at least every six months in order to be able to intervene promptly if problems arise with compliance to the deadlines set by the organisation. With regard to the surveillance of the relevant environmental parameters, it is necessary for the organisation to define in a timely manner the monitoring and control activities necessary to guarantee a high level of its environmental performance and to verify their implementation and effectiveness.

The second category concerns the measurements of the environmental performance of the organisation to verify both the achievement of the targets set in the programme, through the use of the identified performance indicators, and the compliance with operational criteria, as well as for the monitoring of environmental accidents.

The monitoring of environmental performance also has the objective of monitoring the significance of the environmental aspects previously deemed relevant for the organisation and of identifying new ones.

According to the requirements of the ISO 14001 standard and the EMAS Regulation, the organisation must finally define responsibilities and authorities to deal with and analyse any non-compliance (NC), to decide the actions to mitigate any impact caused and to correct the activities that have generated the NC and prevent them from happening again in the future.

"Non-compliance" means a failure to satisfy one or more requirements defined by the organisation through its management system, by the reference standards, by the applicable legislation and regulations, that negatively affect environmental performance.

The organisation should introduce a procedure that describes the methods for identifying, documenting, evaluating and treating NCs and managing corrective and preventive actions. The latter are undertaken to avoid the repetition of NC due to systematic factors, eliminating the causes by activating preventive measures. Any corrective and preventive action taken to eliminate the causes of NC must be adequate to the importance of the problems and commensurate with the environmental impact faced.

THE COMMUNICATION PROCESSES WITHIN THE ENVIRONMENTAL
MANAGEMENT SYSTEM

The commitment to an EMS also requires the development of an adequate and systematic communication activity regarding environmental aspects. The environmental communication flows of an organisation must be directed both internally and externally. In fact, the ISO 14001 standard and the EMAS Regulation require that the organisation, in relation to its environmental aspects and EMS:

•   Ensures internal communications between different levels and functions of the organisation;
•   Receives, documents and responds to requests from external stakeholders.

To foster internal communication, it is useful for the organisation to activate adequate channels, tools and methods. The information tools must be effective and efficient. The information and communication flows must be bidirectional, in order to allow workers not only to be informed, but also to express requests and suggestions and to receive adequate and timely feedback. In other words, to be involved and to participate in the environmental management.

The creation and maintenance of relationships and opportunities for the interaction with external stakeholders on environmental issues can activate a fruitful mechanism for exchanging information with the organisation. External communication can take place through different channels and tools depending on the target audience:

•   Institutional communication (e.g., public administrations, institutions, control bodies, etc.) ;
•   Marketing communication (e.g., participation in fairs and conferences, publications in specialised magazines, sustainability reports, etc.);
•   Communication to suppliers;
•   Communication to other stakeholders (e.g., associations, population, public meetings, etc.).

The organisation, however, must not only pay attention to the flow of outgoing information, but also be concerned with tools and activating suitable channels for the reception and management of all incoming information. It is only by keeping in mind the bidirectional value of communication and external relations that the organisation can enjoy all the advantages deriving from a strategic setting of relations with the outside world. To achieve this, the organisation could implement a complaints collection system in order to prevent any unwanted effects.

Box 4.7 An example of environmental communication and stakeholder involvement in a Football Federation

The Italian Football Association (FIGC) in collaboration with Seria A League, Serie B League, Lega Pro (third division league), National Grassroots League (LND), Italian Footballers' Association (AIC), Italian Football Coaches Association (AIAC), CoRiPet, ENI and Lete (FIGC sponsor) has developed the "Charter on the environmental sustainability of football", a tool that aims to redefine the organisational and operational perimeter in the context of football events. The Charter was drawn up for the benefit of the Italian football family and aims to define the functional guidelines for a practical application of the principles of environmental sustainability in terms of governance, infrastructure management, event management, partnerships and involvement of stakeholders and fans.

Membership of the "Charter on the environmental sustainability of Italian football" is free and open to all Italian clubs, both professional and amateur, and is granted by filling in a form provided by their respective leagues, through which the club provides an expression of interest in the proposed issues. The participating clubs will be included in a special list and subsequently involved by the FIGC in the management of the initiatives that will be undertaken.

4.3.4 Audit and review

4.3.4.1 Audit

One of the fundamental activities that make up the "Check" phase of the Deming cycle is the internal audit activity. Once the EMS has been implemented, in the organisation arises the need to evaluate its efficiency, effectiveness in guaranteeing the expected performance and the ability to achieve the objectives set in the environmental programme.

Every organisation that intends to implement an EMS is therefore called upon to programme adequate methods of verification and internal control, both to reach a sufficient initial level in terms of environmental performance and to effectively monitor the results produced by the virtuous circle of continuous improvement.

The operational scheme designed by the ISO 14001 standard and the EMAS Regulation reserves particular importance to the role of auditing activities. The standards define the environmental audit as "a systematic, independent and documented process, aimed at obtaining the audit evidence and evaluating it objectively, to determine to what extent the EMS audit criteria established by the organization are respected". Through the auditing activity, the organisation therefore sets itself the goal of carrying out a verification:

- Of merit, on environmental performance, on EMS compliance with the criteria and principles that guide it, on the adequacy of the system regarding the productive, technological, organisational and managerial characteristics of the organisation, as well as on its ability to achieve the improvement objectives;
- Of the method, on the correct application of the EMS and on the compliance of the adopted behaviours compared to the established rules.

The evaluation must be systematic, i.e., based on certain and recognised methodologies; objective, i.e., deriving from objective, verifiable and reproducible evidence in a systematic audit process; documented, i.e., based on existing documents to guarantee the traceability of such evidence; periodic, i.e., carried out with scheduled regularity in order to start ensuring the continuous improvement cycle over time.

There are three types of audits:

- First-party audits, carried out by someone from the organisation itself to ensure the organisation meets the procedure that has specified itself;
- Second-party audits, carried out by those who have an interest in the organisation (e.g., audits carried out by customers at their suppliers);
- Third-party audits, carried out by independent external audit bodies.

In addition to the indications contained in ISO 14001 and the EMAS Regulation, the main reference standard for conducting audits is ISO 19011:2018 "Guidelines for auditing management systems". This standard consists of three main chapters, including the modalities with which audits are planned, with which the audit activities are carried out and the auditor's competence requirements are addressed.

If it is true that the fundamental objective of implementing an EMS is the management planning of the environmental aspects related to an activity, a correctly set and developed audit programme is an indispensable element to achieve this objective. From a management point of view, the ISO 14001 and EMAS standards require the organisation to establish and maintain procedures for the periodic conduct of audits, taking into account the results of previous audits and the environmental importance of the activities to be audited.

The training of internal auditors or the selection of external auditors is an important moment to ensure the success of the audit activities. The reliability of the process and the results are in fact linked, on the one hand, to the independence and impartiality of judgment of the auditors and, on the other, to their competence. The audit activity must also be adequately prepared and properly planned, identifying the objectives and scope of each audit or audit cycle. The audit cycle is the period in which all areas or activities of an organisation are audited. Planning therefore assumes a high importance in responding to the need to establish the phases of the audit cycle in order to ensure the verification of all areas covered by the EMS in the reference period.

4.3.4.2 Review

The definition of responsibilities is a fundamental step in the structuring of an environmental management system. In particular, the figures belonging to top management have significant strategic and decision-making responsibilities.

Top management must first define the principles of the policy, set the objectives and decide the programmes, guaranteeing adequate resources. In addition to this, the top management must also supervise the management and ensure the functioning of the environmental management system by promoting, supervising, verifying and reviewing the objectives, the programmes and the system itself. From this perspective, the top management of the organisation must periodically review the management system in order to assess its adequacy and effectiveness in implementing the policy and programmes.

In the logic of continuous improvement, the review activity essentially aims to identify the areas of the management system that present any room for improvement. Once the critical points have been identified, the top management of the organisation can redefine the objectives and/or components of the EMS in order to pursue the identified improvement opportunities.

The review carried out by top management must cover all the organisation's activities and all environmental management activities. Particular attention must be paid to the review of the policy, objectives and programmes.

First, through this activity, top management aims to ensure that the commitments expressed in the policy are up to date with respect to the evolution of the assessment of environmental aspects. Second, it aims to assess the degree of achievement of performance improvement goals. Finally, to evaluate the consistency of the objectives with respect to the commitments undertaken and the congruence of the means of the time allocated with respect to those necessary. The review activity will therefore identify any needs and opportunities for updating and improving the policy, objectives, programmes and system.

4.3.5 Third-party verifications

As we have seen, environmental audits represent one of the fundamental tools for maintaining and improving the environmental management system.

Audits can be internal or external. The distinction essentially depends on the purpose of the audit. In the first case they are carried out by the same organisation for internal purposes. The verification can result in a judgment of compliance or non-compliance with the ISO 14001 standard. Audit results are aimed at the needs of control, surveillance and continuous improvement within the organisation.

Third-party or external audits are those that end with the issue of a certificate of compliance by independent third-party bodies. In these cases, the organisation's decision to adopt an environmental management system goes hand in hand with the objective of ensuring adequate visibility of this attestation of compliance, in a widespread and recognisable way by the market, economic operators and other relevant stakeholders. The organisation therefore appoints an independent third party to assess and certify the compliance of the environmental management system with the requirements established by ISO 14001.

Given the relevance of the third-party verification, the problem of "certifying the certifier" then arises, i.e., ensuring that the certification bodies that issue these certificates meet the ethical, organisational, technical and professional requirements established by standards of international application. This compliance is, in turn, ensured through an evaluation and accreditation system recognised internationally and nationally.

The particular value of accreditation consists in providing a certification with authority of the technical competence of the bodies responsible for ensuring compliance with the applicable standards. Accreditation is defined by legislation as an attestation by a national accreditation body that certifies that a given assessment body meets the criteria established by the harmonised standards and, where appropriate, any other additional requirements, including those defined in the relevant sectoral programmes, to carry out a specific conformity assessment activity (art. 2, Reg. EC/765/2008).

4.3.6 EMAS Regulation and the environmental declaration

The Eco Management and Audit Scheme (EMAS) was established in 1993 by the European Community with a regulation. Initially conceived for industrial sites only, in 2001, with EC Regulation No. 761, it was extended to all economic and non-economic realities. It is one of the voluntary instruments activated under the 6th Environment Action Programme (2001–2010). EMAS has the objective of favouring a rationalisation of the management capacities of organisations from an environmental point of view. It is based not only on compliance with the limits imposed by law but also on the continuous improvement of environmental performance, on the creation of a new and trusting relationship with institutions and with the public and on the active participation of employees. It allows the organisations that voluntarily adopt it, following verification by an accredited and independent subject, to be registered in an "EMAS Register" which is made public.

The environmental management system required by the EMAS standard is based on the ISO 14001 standard. In fact, all the ISO 14001 requirements are included in EMAS, while the open dialogue with the public is pursued by requiring organisations to publish (and keep updated) an Environmental Declaration. Within this document, organisations must report information and salient data regarding their environmental aspects and impacts.

ISO 14001 and EMAS share the goal of guiding organisations towards continuous improvement of environmental performance through the introduction of an EMS. The inclusion of the ISO 14001 standard within the EMAS standard means that it can represent a preliminary stage for the pursuit of the more rigorous EMAS registration. The differences between the two standards have significantly narrowed following the changes made to ISO 14001 in 2015, in particular, legislative compliance is a mandatory requirement in both cases, the involvement of suppliers and attention to indirect environmental aspects is present thanks to the "introduction of the Life Cycle Prospective", a strong focus is placed on both standards to involve all personnel and to increase the responsibility of top management. However, some differences still persist.

Table 4.1 Main differences between EMAS and ISO 14001

EMAS	ISO 14001
Voluntary public instrument, created through an EU regulation, with an institutional supervision system	Voluntary and private system; it is not created by laws, but by voluntary agreements within the ISO between the representatives of the national standardisation bodies
Registration is done by an independent third party accredited by a public institution	The environmental certification is issued by private third parties, accredited by the various national accreditation bodies
Valid in Europe (European instrument)	Valid worldwide (international instrument)
The main interlocutors are the public and the institutions	The main interlocutor is the market
Obligation to draw up the environmental declaration for the public disclosure of environmental performance	Less oriented towards external communication
Possibility of district/territorial registrations	Single organisations only
Less widespread	More widespread

With the Regulation 1221/2009 (EMAS III) the legislator reiterates that openness, transparency and periodic communication of environmental information are crucial elements in order to differentiate EMAS from other similar systems.

Among the needs of the interested parties in recent years the demand for environmental quality has gradually assumed increasing importance, i.e., requests for organisations to demonstrate responsible behaviour towards the use of environmental resources. Demonstrating organisations' environmental quality is therefore connected to the theme of the perception of stakeholders and therefore to environmental communication. Environmental connection can be defined as any process of exchange of significant information with stakeholders which has as its object the relationship between the organisation and environmental protection.

The EMAS Regulation defines the environmental declaration as a "clear information to the public and other stakeholders on the following elements concerning an organization: structure and activities, environmental policy and environmental management system, environmental aspects and impacts, program, environmental objectives and targets, performance environmental compliance with applicable regulatory obligations relating to the environment".

In a nutshell, with the environmental declaration an organisation draws up and validates by independent and impartial subjects a public document with which it explains and disseminates to the outside world the steps taken to adopt and maintain over time an environmental management system aimed at improving its environmental performance.

References

Daddi, T., Frey, M., Iraldo, F., Nabil, B. (2011a). The implementation of an Environmental Management System in a North-African local public administration: the case of the City Council of Marrakech (Morocco). *J. Environ. Plan. Manag.*, 54(6), 813–832, doi:10.1080/09640568.2010.537543

Daddi, T., Magistrelli, M., Frey, M., Iraldo, F., (2011b). Do environmental management systems improve environmental performance? Empirical evidence from Italian companies. *Environ. Dev. Sustain.*, 13(5), 845–862. doi:10.1007/s10668-011-9294-8

Daddi, T., Testa, F., Iraldo, F., Frey, M., (2014). Removing and simplifying administrative costs and burdens for EMAS and ISO 14001 certified organizations: evidences from Italy. *Environ. Eng. Manag. J.*, 13(3), 689–698. doi:10.30638/eemj.2014.073

Daddi, T., Iraldo, F., Testa, F., (2015). Environmental Certification for Organisations and Products: Management approaches and operational tools. Routledge Research in Sustainability and Business, Routledge. ISBN: 9781138784734.

Daddi, T., Testa, F., Frey, M., Iraldo, F., (2016). Exploring the link between institutional pressures and environmental management systems effectiveness: an empirical study. *J. Environ. Manage.*, 183, 647–656. doi:10.1016/j.jenvman.2016.09.025

Daddi, T., Iraldo, F., Testa, F., De Giacomo, M. R., (2017a). The influence of managerial satisfaction on corporate environmental performance and reputation. *Bus. Strategy Environ.*, 28(1), 15–24. doi:10.1002/bse.2177

Daddi, T., De Giacomo, M. R., Frey, M., Iraldo, F., (2017b). Analysing the causes of environmental management and audit scheme (EMAS) decrease in Europe. *J. Environ. Plan. Manag.*, 1–20. doi:10.1080/09640568.2017.1395316

Daddi, T., Ceglia, D., Bianchi, G., de Barcellos, M.D., (2019). Paradoxical tensions and corporate sustainability: A focus on circular economy business cases. *Corp. Soc. Responsib. Environ. Manag.*, 26(4), 770–780. Doi:10.1002/csr.1719

Daddi, T., Heras-Saizarbitoria, I., Marrucci, L., Rizzi, F., Testa, F., (2021). The effects of green supply chain management capability on the internalisation of environmental management systems and organisation performance. *Corp. Soc. Responsib. Environ. Manag.*, 28(4), 1241–1253. doi:10.1002/csr.2144

EC, European Commission, (2009). Regulation (EC) No 1221/2009 of the European Parliament, the council. On the voluntary participation by organisations in a community eco-management and audit scheme (EMAS), repealing regulation (EC) No 761/2001 and commission decisions 2001/681/EC and 2006/193/EC. *Off. J. Eur. Union.*

European Commission (EC), (2019). Special Eurobarometer 492: Europeans' attitudes on EU energy policy, Directorate-General for Communication. Brussels.

EU EMAS Register, (2021). http://ec.europa.eu/environment/emas/register/reports/reports.do accessed December 2021.

International Organization for Standardization (ISO), (2017). The ISO survey of management system standard certifications - 2017 - explanatory note. https://isotc.iso.org/livelink/livelink/fetch/8853493/8853511/8853520/18808772/00._Overall_results_and_explanatory_note_on_2017_Survey_results.pdf?nodeid¼19208898&vernum¼-2. Accessed on December 2021.

Iraldo, F. Testa, F. Frey, M., (2009). Is an environmental management system able to influence environmental and competitive performance? The case of the eco-management and audit scheme (EMAS) in the European union. *J. Clean. Prod.*, 17(16), 1444–1452. doi:10.1016/j.jclepro.2009.05.013

Marrucci, L., Daddi, T., Iraldo, F., (2019). The integration of circular economy with sustainable consumption and production tools: Systematic review and future research agenda. *J. Clean. Prod.*, 240, 118268. doi:10.1016/j.jclepro.2019.118268

Marrucci, L., Iraldo, F., Daddi, T., (2021a). Investigating the management challenges of the EU Ecolabel through multi-stakeholder surveys. *Int. J. Life Cycle Assess.*, 26, 575–590. doi:10.1007/s11367-021-01866-5

Marrucci, L., Daddi, T., Iraldo, F., (2021b). The contribution of green human resource management to the circular economy and performance of environmental certified organisations. *J. Clean. Prod.*, 319, 128859. doi:10.1016/j.jclepro.2021.128859

Marrucci, L., Iannone, F., Daddi, T., Iraldo, F., (2021c). Antecedents of absorptive capacity in the development of circular economy business models of small and medium enterprises. *Bus. Strategy Environ.*, article in press. doi:10.1002/bse.2908

Marrucci, L., Daddi, T., (2021d). The contribution of the Eco-Management and Audit Scheme to the environmental performance of manufacturing organisations. *Bus. Strategy Environ.*, article in press. doi:10.1002/bse.2958

Marrucci, L., Daddi, T., Iraldo, F., (2021e). The circular economy, environmental performance and environmental management systems: the role of absorptive capacity. *J. Know. Manage.*, article in press. soi:10.1108/JKM-06-2021-0437

McKinley, S., (2018). Meetings with a mission: The Unitarian Universalist Association's systematic approach to advance sustainability. *Glob. Bus. Organ. Excell.*, 37(2), 12–23. doi:10.1002/joe.21838

Musgrave, J., Pelham, F., (2011). Will sustainability change the business model of the event industry? *Worldw. Hosp. Tour. Themes*, 3(3), 187–192. doi:10.1108/17554211111142149

Nomisma (2021). Coop Report 2020 - Economy, consumption and lifestyles of Italians today and tomorrow. Italy.

Scarpellini, S., Marín-Vinuesa, L.M., Aranda-Usón, A., Portillo-Tarragona, P., (2020a). Dynamic capabilities and environmental accounting for the circular economy in businesses. *Sustain. Account. Manag. Policy J.*, 11(7), 1129–1158. doi:10.1108/SAMPJ-04-2019-0150

Scarpellini, S., Valero-Gil, J., Moneva, J.M., Andreaus, M., (2020b). Environmental management capabilities for a "circular eco-innovation". *Bus. Strategy Environ.*, 29(5), 1850–1864. doi:10.1002/bse.2472

Soil Association, (2021). Organic Market Report. Scotland.

Testa, F., Iraldo, F., (2010). Shadows and lights of GSCM (green supply chain management): Determinants and effects of these practices based on a multi-national study. *J. Clean. Prod.*, 18, 953–962. doi:10.1016/j.jclepro.2010.03.005

Testa, F., Rizzi, F., Daddi, T., Gusmerotti, N.M., Frey, M., Iraldo, F., (2014). EMAS and ISO 14001: the differences in effectively improving environmental performance. *J. Clean. Prod.*, 68, 165–173. doi:10.1016/j.jclepro.2013.12.061

Testa, F., Iraldo, F., Daddi, T., (2018a). The Effectiveness of EMAS as a Management Tool: A Key Role for the Internalization of Environmental Practices. *Organ. Environ.*, 13(1), 48–69. doi:10.1177/1086026616687609

Testa, F., Boiral, O., Iraldo, F., (2018b). Internalization of environmental practices and institutional complexity: Can stakeholders pressures encourage greenwashing? *J. Bus. Ethics*, 147(2), 287–307. doi:10.1007/s10551-015-2960-2

Toniolo, S., Mazzi, A., Fedele, A., Aguiari, F., Scipioni, A., (2017). Life Cycle Assessment to support the quantification of the environmental impacts of an event. *Environ. Impact Assess. Rev.*, 63, 12–22. doi:10.1016/j.eiar.2016.07.007

United Nations Environment Programme - UNEP (2009). Annual report. Seizing the green opportunity. UNEP Division of Communication and Public Information, Publishing Service Sector, Nairobi. ISBN:978–92-807-3071-5.

5 Life cycle assessment as a support for sustainable football

The environmental footprint approach dates back to the 1960s with the first applications of the method of analysing the life cycle of products and subsequently affirmed with the now consolidated acronym LCA (life cycle assessment).

However, this method has undergone a process of profound transformation and considerable diffusion since the beginning of the 2000s. Considered for many years the prerogative of large multinationals, with the internal skills and know-how, as well as the resources to invest in the application of the method. In recent years, however, the LCA has spread to many sectors other than the classic industrial realities (Bartolozzi et al., 2018).

In particular, producers (as well as stakeholders and consumers) have understood that the organisation's environmental responsibility cannot be confined within the organization's gates. On the contrary, an approach based on the need to transmit the environmental commitment to the entire value chain relating to the product or service that is offered on the market is consolidated: from suppliers and customers, to logistics, to the final consumer.

In its most rigorous and orthodox version, the LCA studies the environmental aspects and potential impacts throughout the life of the product or service, "from cradle to grave", i.e., from the acquisition of raw materials, through manufacture and use, up to the end-of-life phase. The main categories of environmental impact taken into consideration concern the use of resources, human health and potential environmental impacts such as climate change, depletion of the ozone layer, acidification, etc.

Particularly interesting is the performance of comparative LCA studies, capable of identifying the best solutions from an environmental point of view in a given context. Important for comparison is the identification of a standardised methodology, which allows carrying out comparable studies thanks to the identification of the same unit of measurement and the same assumptions.

The environmental footprints of products and services and the voluntary schemes that certify their reliability, represent a competitive opportunity that many organisations are deciding to seize to communicate their commitment and the excellence of their performance to the market, avoiding the risks of the so-called greenwashing. The footprint is not considered by organisations

DOI: 10.4324/9781003228271-5

only as a number to be associated with their product or service, but also as a competitive opportunity to use a powerful, clear and direct vehicle for communication between all the players in the commercial chain.

5.1 Life cycle assessment and the ISO 14040 standards

In recent years, various methodologies have been implemented in order to identify, study and evaluate the environmental impacts associated with a product, service or organisation. The need to develop this type of instrument has matured as a result of increasing pressures coming mainly from external actors to the organisation asking for more and more consistently information and guarantees regarding the environmental compatibility of products or services (Iraldo et al., 2014). This new need has pushed organisations, research structures and both national and international standardisation bodies to develop methodologies able to respond to the new needs developed by stakeholders.

Since the early evolutionary stages of these systems, one of the main problems was how to correctly measure the impacts related to a product or a service. In fact, it is known that during the life cycle of a product/service, which starts from the extraction of raw materials and reaches the end of its useful life and eventual recovery and disposal, a series of impacts on the environment are generated. The impacts assume a very different significance and importance depending on of the phase of the life cycle considered. Therefore, it became extremely important to extend the study through an overall vision of the product/service, avoiding a partitioning of the individual phases for which the results could be misleading.

To date, the main tool capable of assessing the impacts during the entire life cycle of a given product/service is represented by the methodology called "life cycle assessment" (LCA). This tool is able to measure environmental impacts through an analysis that starts from the extraction of raw materials (or when are "subtracted" from the environment), passing through all the processes of transformation that they undergo until their "return to the earth", i.e., after the final waste disposal processes. This path is also defined as "from cradle to grave".

Actually, as early as the1960s, several studies were carried out in order to quantify the emissions, the waste generated, the use of resources and energy consumption associated with the development of products. The important results obtained aroused particular interest and served as model and booster for the progressive diffusion of these models of assessment.

At the same time, some limitations emerged from the very first application phases due, in particular, to the non-comparability of the results as obtained through the application of different methodologies. To cope with this gap, in the 1990s, both national and international standardisation bodies tried to harmonise and rationalise the methodological references, arriving at the emanation of the family of ISO 14040 standards (Environmental Management - Life Cycle Assessment), published since 1997.

The SETAC (Society of Environmental Toxicology and Chemistry) in a 1993 study provided a definition of the LCA methodology which is still today valid and widely used:

> a process to evaluate the environmental burdens associated with a product, process, or activity by identifying and quantifying energy and materials used and wastes released to the environment; to assess the impact of those energy and material uses and releases to the environment; and to identify and evaluate opportunities to affect environmental improvements. The assessment includes the entire life cycle of the product, process, or activity, encompassing extracting and processing raw materials; manufacturing; transportation and distribution; use, re-use, maintenance; recycling, and final disposal (SETAC, 1993).

Today the ISO 14040:2021 and ISO 14044:2021 standards constitute the main reference for the dissemination of the LCA.[1] The ISO 14040:2021 standard provides the principles and the reference framework to conduct a life cycle analysis study while the ISO standard 14044:2021 provides methodological information. In particular, this series of ISO standards has the following articulation:

* UNI EN ISO 14040:2021 – Principles and Framework
* UNI EN ISO 14044:2021 – Requirements and guidelines
  a. The goal and scope definition of the LCA;
  b. The life cycle inventory analysis (LCI) phase;
  c. The life cycle impact assessment (LCIA) phase;
  d. The life cycle interpretation phase;
  e. Reporting and critical review of the LCA;
  f. Limitations of the LCA;
  g. Relationship between the LCA phases;
  h. Conditions for use of value choices and optional elements.

Life cycle assessment according to the general standard must understand the following steps:

1. The definition of the objective and scope of the study;
2. Inventory analysis;
3. Impact assessment;
4. Interpretation of results and suggestions for improvement.

The standard recognises the usefulness of the LCA tool in identifying opportunities for improving the environmental aspects of the product/service in different stages of the life cycle, in identifying the most appropriate indicators to measure environmental performance, in guiding the design of new products/services/processes in order to minimise their environmental impact and in supporting the strategic planning of organisations and policymakers. According to this logic, LCA is often also used as informative and scientific

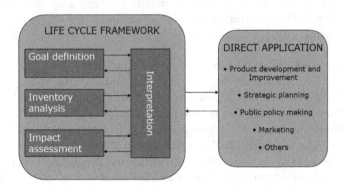

Figure 5.1 ISO 14040 Life cycle assessment diagram: methodology phases and application

substrate to implement strategies for organisations' communication, or in the definition of tools that can be used for these purposes, such as the aforementioned type II claims (environmental product declarations) or type I (ecological labelling programmes).

The four phases of the LCA do not have to be interpreted individually as each single phase is strictly interdependent with the others.

The first phase regards the defining of the purpose and objectives of the LCA study. In particular, it is important to be clear over the reasons why the analysis was conducted, the intended use of its results and the type of audience they are intended for. The scope of the study must be defined and within it the following topics must be clearly described and considered:

- The functions of the product/service system (or of the product/service systems in case of comparative studies[2]);
- The functional unit;
- The boundaries of the product/service system (defined by the standard as "the elementary set of process units connected between each other as regards resource and energy, which pursue one or more defined functions");
- The types of impact, the impact assessment methodologies and the subsequent interpretation;
- The quality requirements of the initial data;
- The limits and assumptions of the analogical model of reality that characterises the product/service system object of the LCA, which is created to study their environmental impacts.

One of the main aspects is the definition of the functional unit which aims to provide a reference to link the incoming and outgoing flows with respect to which that will be included in the measurements and assessments and that will be provided, interpreted and discussed in the study results. The standard defines incoming flow as the resources or energy that enter into a process unit (resources can consist of raw materials or products). While outflow means the resources or energy that come out of a process unit (resource can be made up of raw materials, intermediate products, products, emissions and from waste).

The functional unit is therefore the unit of measurement of the performance of the system and must define the analysed product/service not in its physical characteristics, but in its function and in the service that it provides. Table 5.1 shows some examples of possible units functional related to different product/service systems.

Another very important aspect in the implementation of an LCA study is the definition of the system boundaries, or the identification of single operations (units) that make up the process, with the related inputs and output, and which must be included in the study. Borders must be geographical, technological and temporal. All "process units" within system boundaries must be interconnected, i.e., receive their own inputs from the "upstream" units and provide their outputs as inputs to the units "downstream", following the scheme of the process studied.

Generally, in order to consider a complete LCA study, the boundaries of the system must start from the raw materials extracted from the earth and end with the disposal of waste that returns to the earth. In this case we speak of a study "from cradle to grave". It can happen, especially in the case of intermediate products/services, that the study limits the analysis to the gates of the organisations, and therefore the phases of distribution, use and end of life are excluded from the confines of the system. In this case it is called a "from cradle to gate" study.

The second phase in the study of an LCA is the inventory analysis of the life cycle (life cycle inventory – LCI). This phase includes the data collection and calculation procedures that allow the types of interaction that the system has with the environment to be quantified. Such interactions may concern, for example, the use of resources and emissions into the air, the releases into water and soil associated with the product/service system, etc. (Daddi et al., 2017). Essentially, the analysis of the life cycle inventory involves the collection of production data, the supply and consumption of raw materials, semi-finished products and auxiliary products, energy and water

Table 5.1 Examples of functional units

System	Examples of functional units
Provision of hotel services	• 1 guest • 1 room
Electricity production and distribution	• 1 kWh fed into the network • 1 kWh provided to the user
Football organisations	• 1 player • 1 football match

consumption, air emissions, wastewater and waste generated in the production process, the logistics of distribution, the use phase of the product/service and its disposal once it reaches the end of its useful life.

The inventory phase through data collection often involves one modification of the analysis itself. In fact, the acquisition of data allows you to obtain a greater knowledge of the system studied which, therefore, could bring out the need to identify new types of data or request a reinterpretation of those already collected. It is also important to keep in mind that the activities necessary for compiling a life cycle inventory often require commitment and the involvement of a number of subjects external to the organisation, even if not directly included in the production process, but that are "responsible" for the upstream and downstream phases of the production cycle (Testa et al., 2017).

In particular, this is true for the retrieval of data and information on life cycle stages such as the production and transport of raw materials, "outbound" logistics and sale of products, the stage of use by the consumer or of the end user and disposal or any methods of recovery of the product at the end of its life or of the waste that is generated in all the phases indicated above. Sometimes, however, the unavailability of the information and data necessary for making the inventory may cause the review of the objective or scope of the LCA study.

In relation to this issue, in recent years both private and public sector entities – which are increasingly aware of the growing relevance that the LCA tool is gaining in the context of organisations' environmental strategies – have developed several databases. These entities have undertaken a process of elaboration and development of databases now publicly available for organisations interested in applying the methodology to their products/services.

Particular attention should be paid to the quality of the data collected for the creation of the inventory, which strongly determines the significance of the study results. In LCA studies it is therefore appropriate to use the highest possible percentage of so-called specific data, i.e., data that refer exactly to the system considered or to a "technologically equivalent" system (i.e., a system with similar energy sources, raw materials, process phases and plant structure). These can be primary data, i.e., directly collected in the field and referred to the specific analysed plants and processes; or secondary, i.e., taken from the existing technical literature or from databases specifically prepared but referring to an "equivalent" system. The equivalence respect to the system actually studied must be evaluated on the basis of the similarity and appropriateness of the data used according to temporal, geographical and technological criteria. On the other hand, all secondary data referring to generic systems (e.g., average data relating to different technologies) are called generic. The use of generic data in an LCA study can significantly affect the quality of the results, so it is always important to contain as much as possible the percentage of generic data of the total (in the case of certification schemes, there are often defined maximum thresholds for the use of generic data).

For data collection, flow diagrams of the production process are often used as a starting point. On their basis, specific checklists are developed and allocation procedures are defined. The flow diagrams allow to easily schematise all the process units that make up the considered system, highlighting the relationships between them. Since a production process can generate, together with the main product/service, several co-products or by-products, the need often arises to define rules able to assign to the outputs a quota of consumption and impacts related to the analysed operations. Such criteria of distribution, defined as allocation methods, are generally divided into two types:

- Allocation based on physical quantities: the environmental impacts are distributed proportionally to product and co-products on the basis of certain physical parameters such as volume, mass, energy, etc.;
- Economic allocation: in this case the distribution of the environmental impacts is proportional to the economic value of the product and of the co-products. This method is used when the physical allocation is not easily applicable.

A particularly interesting strength of the inventories made in the LCA field is represented by the methodology for measuring energy consumption that allows calculating not only the share of energy directly consumed in each phase of the production system, but also the share of indirect energy necessary to be able to produce fuels and electricity that normally power the industrial processes and whose values vary from country to country depending on the level of efficiency associated with the different methods of production and processing of energy.

Figure 5.2 shows some Eurostat data that demonstrate how wide can be the gap between the energy mixes of different nations.

Any differences that have consequences on the calculation of energy consumption of a product/service system can be measured through LCA techniques. The importance of the energy mix can be easily understood taking into consideration a single operation which can be carried out in two different establishments. The first one is located in a country where electricity generation is mainly dependent on fossil fuels (as in Italy or Poland) and the other one instead is performed in a country like Austria or Croatia where there is a consistent use of hydroelectricity. Such an operation, which will have an identical direct energy consumption, will however be characterised by different values with regard to indirect energy, i.e., the "primary" energy shares necessary to produce and make available the energy that directly feeds the operation. In this specific case, given the greater efficiency of hydroelectric power, the overall energy consumption index will be in favour of the operation carried out in Austria/Croatia compared to the one carried out in Italy/Poland.

Following the inventory phase, we find the phase of the life cycle impact evaluation where the environmental consequences generated by the analysed

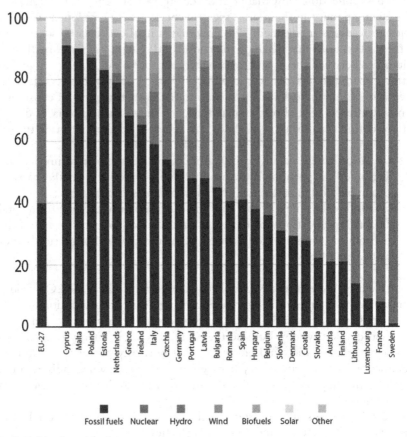

Fossil fuels   Nuclear   Hydro   Wind   Biofuels   Solar   Other

Fossil fuels include coal, gas and oil products.
Biofuels include solid (e.g. wood), liquid (e.g. biodiesel) and gaseous (e.g. biogas) biofuels.
Other includes electricity from geothermal, non-renewable waste, heat from chemical sources and other sources.   **Source: Eurostat**

Figure 5.2 EU production of electricity by source, 2018 (%)

system are assessed. This phase aims to evaluate the potential environmental impacts caused by the analysed processes, products/services or activities, using the information collected during the inventory phase.

One or more impacts can be associated with each environmental aspect. The LCA technician is responsible for choosing the level of detail and the impacts to be assessed, in line with the objectives and field of application defined during the first phase of the study. In this context, by aspect we mean the immediate physical result deriving from a specific operation (e.g., CO_2 production resulting from combustion processes). While by impact we mean the more general environmental "problem" associated with the aspect (e.g., example the greenhouse effect resulting from CO_2 emissions).

Table 5.2 lists the various impact categories and related units of measure used in this phase of the LCA.

The ISO 14044 standard provides for two phases of impact analysis. The first one is mandatory and made up of three sequential activities:

- Selection of the impact categories to be considered and the related indicators (climate change $\Rightarrow CO_2$, ozone layer depletion $\Rightarrow$ CFC11, etc.);
- Assignment of inventory results to the selected impact categories (classification);
- Calculation of the indicators of each impact category (characterisation).

The second, which is optional, is divided into:

- Comparison between the calculated indicators and the reference values (normalisation);
- Determining the importance of each single environmental impacts (weighing).

The classification consists of organising the inventory values of all gaseous, liquid and solid emissions, caused directly and indirectly from the considered operations, associating them with the different impact categories. The characterisation, on the other hand, determines in a homogeneous and quantitative way the contribution of the single emissions, expressed through the category indicators, calculated thanks the use of the characterisation coefficients of each pollutant available in the scientific literature (e.g., "IPCC – Intergovernmental Panel on Climate Change", "WMO – World Meteorological Organization", etc.).

Table 5.2 List of the impact categories included in an LCA study

Impact category	Unit
Climate change	kg CO_2 eq.
Ozone depletion	kg CFC11 eq.
Ionising radiation, HH	kBq U–235 eq.
Photochemical ozone formation, HH	kg NMVOC eq.
Respiratory inorganics	disease inc.
Non-cancer human health effects	CTUh
Cancer human health effects	CTUh
Acidification terrestrial and freshwater	mol H+ eq.
Eutrophication freshwater	kg P eq.
Eutrophication marine	kg N eq.
Eutrophication terrestrial	mol N eq.
Ecotoxicity freshwater	CTUe
Land use	Pt
Water scarcity	m^3 depriv.
Resource use, energy carriers	MJ
Resource use, mineral and metals	kg Sb eq.

Given the complexity of the methodological approach, of the elaborations and of the calculations, normally LCAs are conducted, from the setting up of the study up to the evaluation phase, with the support of specific software and also equipped with databases (more or less complete) of secondary data that can be used to surrogate the impossibility of collecting environmental data in the field, especially for the phases of the life cycle that escape the management control of the organisations and/or are located in places geographically far away. SimaPro and Gabi, available in constantly updated versions, are probably the most used software for LCA calculation.

Then, there are two optional phases called normalisation and weighing through which it is possible to aggregate the results of the different categories of impact thus obtaining a single score that allows the environmental impact of the analysed system to be evaluated as a whole. Both methods require a strong subjective factor and therefore are often not fully embraced by the international scientific community.

The interpretation of the results takes place in the last phase of the LCA study. They are analysed in order to obtain specific information that should be used to improve the environmental performance of the analysed product/ service system. This phase, therefore, has the aim to present, as clearly and completely as possible, the results of the previous phases. It also supports the decision-making process in the elaboration and planning of improvement interventions. The aims set in the initial phase of the study come to fruition in the actions that are defined following the phase of data interpretation. It may also be necessary at this stage to make a review of some fundamental steps of the study (e.g., the field of application, the type and quality of the data collected, etc.) in order to achieve the defined goal.

As also suggested by the standard, it is essential to collect in a detailed report the results obtained in the study in order to eventually share them with the interested public. This aspect, obviously, is closely linked with the purposes of the study and the significance that the organisations would give to the results (Testa et al., 2016).

As we have seen, an LCA study can be implemented for different purposes which can range from process improvements to product/service innovation, up to support for marketing communication on the product/service. If the LCA study aims to be part of an organisation's company communication strategy in order to show its commitment and effort in the environmental field, it is advisable, though not essential, to provide the results of the study in a document that should be as clear and detailed as possible (Vizzotto et al., 2021).

The final document must therefore be calibrated according to the type of audience it is intended for, with differentiations in the language and in the degree of detail assumed. The report must necessarily contain the key elements of the study that must be reported as clearly as possible. The report must provide in-depth information regarding the assumptions, data, information and methodologies with which the LCA study was performed and, very importantly, the sources from which they have been extrapolated. A document prepared in this way can guarantee the reader of the accuracy and reliability of the information contained therein. Finally, it is highly recommended that the LCA study is evaluated and certified by an independent third party for example as part of a validation scheme of environmental product declaration (so-called ISO type III environmental labels).

The brief overview of the LCA methodology presented in this section highlights the complexity of the tool and the different limitations due to the availability of certain data and the subjectivity of certain stages. On the other hand, the strong potential of the instrument is also highlighted. In particular, the outputs of an LCA study can certainly come to fruition in improvement actions on the environmental performance of a product, service or organisation and therefore of greater competitiveness of the organisations that adopt it.

LCA can also play a crucial role in managing relationships with the supply chain. In fact, the involvement of suppliers can effectively contribute to the management and reduction of the environmental impacts generated along the supply chain. In this way, organisations would be able to significantly contribute to the development of an environmentally oriented competitive strategy (Testa and Iraldo, 2010).

In particular, cooperative strategies offer effective solutions that aim to manage the complexity associated with some products/services by contributing to the identification of more sustainable solutions. Developing actions that aim to involve all the players in the supply chain who contribute to the environmental impact of a product/service along its entire length life cycle therefore represents a formidable opportunity to concretely improve environmental performance.

This road, however, might be full of obstacles to overcome. The environmental impact of a product/service often involves actors and stages of life cycle with which the organisation has sporadic contact or a low ability to influence their choices. These aspects make complex structuring forms of collaboration. In addition, the presence of commercial intermediaries such as distributors of raw materials, suppliers of secondary materials, etc., contribute to the "loss of direct contact" between the organisation and other actors who play a key role in the life cycle of a product/service by reducing its ability to influence (or simply to collaborate with) the supply chain actors.

While the development of green products/services within an organisation can generally be implemented in a short time, the same initiatives which require collaboration between organisations along the supply chain often rely on the need for specific information, necessary for the definition of a profitable collaboration, but that can sometimes be so difficult to get that it ends up hindering the development.

The diffusion of these difficulties has contributed to the development of methodologies and managerial solutions aimed not only at accounting for impacts associated with the life cycle of a product/service, but also with the actual involvement of suppliers in the analysis and quantification of these impacts. In particular, the LCA entailed a more intense management of the supply chain and the *supply chain management* required more in-depth knowledge of the environmental impacts and of the phases where they are generated.

The growing use of LCA has promoted the adoption of the "inter-organisational" approach in environmental management. Thanks to the LCA organisations are now aware of the fact that a significant amount of the environmental impacts related to the life cycle of their own products/services not only takes place outside the "organisation's boundaries", but, in many cases, they are due to activities that are not even under their direct management control.

The use of the LCA is conducive to an intensification of the organisation's commitment towards the other actors of the "product/service system" thanks to a more in-depth understanding of the environmental aspects related to the life cycle. However, the supplier selection policy may be heavily conditioned by the characteristics of the product/service and by the market. The information obtained through an LCA on the downstream impact of a product/service should be included in the selection procedures and in the tender specifications, in order to guide the evaluation and choice of suppliers in line with the attention that the organisation dedicates to the life cycle.

To sum up, there are numerous factors that lead to the identification of LCA as an effective tool for the improvement of the environmental performance along the supply chain.

First of all, the LCA must be considered a tool strongly linked to the context of the organisation, i.e., LCA results are strongly connected with the purpose and scope of the study. In this logic the supply chain represents one of the privileged contexts to which the LCA must refer and in which it must develop.

Second, strict requirements must be defined not only to preserve trust between the actors involved but also transparency in sharing some data. In this sense, the collaboration between the actors of the supply chain is at the same time a factor that favours the application of the LCA and an element that is strongly strengthened when this tool is applied correctly and effectively.

Third, LCA requires drivers that derive from long-term environmental targets and that derive from both external factors (competition intra and inter-sectoral; pressure from various stakeholders, etc.) and internal (interest in developing new knowledge, need to have reliable information, etc.). The sharing of environmental targets with the actors of the supply chain therefore represents a necessary condition for both the strategies of Green Supply Chain Management and for an effective LCA.

5.2 The methodology of the European Commission for the environmental footprint: similarities and differences with the LCA approach

The first and most relevant news regarding the recent development and the diffusion of the LCA approach is undoubtedly represented by its transposition and enhancement in the context of European legislation. In particular, a central element of the European strategy is related to the usability and the credibility of information on the environmental performance of products and services.

In fact, it is necessary that such information is used consistently and appropriately, whether it is the result of scientific evaluation methods, based on the life cycle approach (Life Cycle Thinking). They should also be able to dialogue with consumers positively influencing their purchasing behaviours.

In this context are particularly relevant the two methodologies that allow measuring the environmental performance of the entire life cycle of products/services (product environmental footprint – PEF) and organisations (organisation environmental footprint – OEF).

The two methodologies are based on the international organisations standards that regulate the implementation of LCA studies, introducing many important improvements compared to these standards, such as:

- Introducing a clear definition of the categories which express the type of potential environmental impacts to carry out a comprehensive life cycle assessment on;
- The obligation to assess the quality of the data;
- The introduction of minimum requirements regarding data quality;
- More precise technical instructions to address some critical issues of LCA studies (such as allocation, etc.).

The development of the PEF and OEF methodologies allows to consolidate the development of the two reference standards and allow the development of the rules that will regulate the methods of calculating the environmental footprint of product categories (Product Environmental Footprint Category Rules, PEFCR) and organisation sectors (Organisation Environmental Footprint Sector Rules, OEFSR), including the development of environmental reference parameters (so-called "characterisation factors") for each category of impact.

Particular attention was also paid to the following initiatives:

- Definition of methods and mechanisms for control and verification of the reliability of the studies carried out in accordance with the aforementioned methodologies;
- Development and "formalisation" of innovative and shared approaches for the communication of such information to consumers;
- Identification of benchmarks for each product category and for each sector, in order to encourage and nurture a communication that can also leverage comparative dynamics, at least with the average performance of the reference sector or with a scale of performance levels set in relation to the identified benchmark.

In the intentions of the European Commission, consolidation and dissemination of the PEF and OEF methodologies and the development of reference rules for the different categories of products/services and sectors will allow to define with greater clarity "what is a green product/service/organization", eliminating those uncertainties that characterise the current situation.

The development of these methodologies also allows providing further indications on the use of clear, precise and relevant environmental self-declarations in marketing and advertising to avoid unfair commercial practices. In particular, the Commission recommends a number of principles to be applied when communicating information on the environmental performance of products and organisations such as transparency, accessibility, reliability, clearness, comprehensiveness and comparability.

All these "qualities" of the information on environmental impacts of products/services and organisations are effectively prosecutable through the application of the LCA method in terms of interpretation of the PEF and the OEF.

As previously reported, the PEF has a twofold objective: to harmonise the calculation of the environmental footprint of products, and facilitate comparison as a stimulus to competitiveness. This methodology is based on the LCA, and on the ISO reference standards, but with respect to the LCA as defined in the standard and in the various guidelines available, introduces further methodological specifications.

The potential areas of application for the PEF methodology are reported within the Recommendation 2013/179/EU:

- Optimisation of processes along the life cycle of a product;
- Support of product design minimising environmental impacts along the life cycle;
- Communication of life cycle environmental performance information on products (e.g., through documentation accompanying the product, websites and apps) by individual companies or through voluntary schemes;
- Schemes related to environmental claims, in particular ensuring sufficient robustness and completeness of claims;
- Reputational schemes giving visibility to products that calculate their life cycle environmental performance;
- Identification of significant environmental impacts in view of setting criteria for ecolabels;
- Providing incentives based on life cycle environmental performance, as appropriate.

The PEF was developed as part of a pilot action that began in 2013 and ended in April 2018, which involved more than 2,000 stakeholders and over 300 companies (representing on average 70% of the European market of the selected products) with the aim to develop specific rules for the products involved. These rules, called Product Environmental Footprint Category Rules (PEFCR), are specific rules of product/service that define in detail how to conduct a PEF study for the specific application. They are analogous to the Product Category Rules (PCR) defined in the Environmental Product Declaration (EPD) system, but they differ in two main elements:

- Greater level of detail and prescription;
- Greater participation of interested parties in the definition of the rules. In fact, they have been drawn up with the involvement of at least 51% of the market.

Since the PEFCR are based precisely on the general provisions of the calculation methods of the environmental footprint, they allow heavily simplifying the work of the analyst as they define: the modelling choices, the data to be used, the significant environmental aspects, the types of data to be collected. In this way the results of different evaluations will be more comparable within a given product category, regardless of who carried out the study.

The execution of a PEF study, and the main methodological requirements, are defined in the following main documents:

- Recommendation 2013/179/EU
- PEFCR Guidance

The structure of the PEF study is similar to the structure of a LCA study as defined in ISO 14040 and 14044 standards, and therefore includes the following steps:

1. Definition of the objectives and the field of application;
2. Analysis of the resources and emissions (inventory of incoming and outgoing data relating to the different phases of the product life cycle);
3. Evaluation and interpretation of the environmental footprint;
4. Communication of the environmental footprint.

The PEF methodology, although it has many similarities with the LCA (e.g., it is based on the analysis of the life cycle of, the structure of the process is similar, etc.), is characterised by some technical aspects that act as additional guiding elements compared to ISO 14040 and 14044. Providing these technical prescriptions makes it possible to decrease the arbitrariness present in the choices characterising an LCA study, where it is not always clear how to deal with some aspects of the modelling. To compare products/services belonging to the same category, the PEF methodology requires strict guidance that minimises subjective interpretations and the choices made by the analyst during the modelling phase. In fact, the PEF aims to be a reproducible and harmonised methodology, and provides specific technical requirements on a number of elements, including:

- Definition of the functional unit;
- Impact assessment method;

- Interpretation;
- Multifunctionality management of recycling and energy recovery;
- Data quality requirements.

DEFINITION OF THE FUNCTIONAL UNIT

A product/service system can have numerous possible functions. Moreover, the function chosen for the study depends on the goal of the study. Once the function has been chosen, the functional unit that satisfies the chosen function should be identified. The ISO 14040 standard defines the unit functional as "the quantified performance of a product/service system to be used as a unit of reference in a life cycle assessment study". In order to define the functional unit comprehensively and unambiguously, the PEF identifies the following aspects that should be considered:

- "What": the product or service provided;
- "How much": the quantity necessary to perform its function;
- "How long": the duration of the product or service;
- "How well": the expected quality level.

It is also necessary to determine an adequate reference flow which represents the quantity of product necessary to satisfy the defined function, which also takes into account the duration of the product/service.

IMPACT ASSESSMENT METHOD

The assessment of the impacts according to the PEF methodology foresees the same four steps of the ISO standard: classification, characterisation, normalisation and weighting. Normalisation and weighting are only used to support the interpretation of the results. The method recommended by the PEF for the impact assessment is the ILCD method, as defined in the document "Recommendations for Life Cycle Impact Assessment in the European context ILCD Handbook" (2011). The ILCD method consists of 16 categories for which the recommended midpoint characterisation method is indicated by the European Commission. The recommended methods and characterisation factors are classified according to their quality in three levels:

- Level 1: recommended and satisfactory;
- Level 2: recommended, but some improvements are needed;
- Level 3: recommended, but to be applied with caution.

INTERPRETATION OF THE RESULTS

One of the most important phases of the PEF study is represented by the interpretation of the results. In this phase, the impact categories, the phases of the cycle of life, the most relevant processes and direct flows of the analysed system are identified. This identification allows the organisation to identify the activities of the product/service system that can be improve in terms of environmental performance. In addition to the possibility of improvement, another important aspect is the communication of information on the product/service and its environmental footprint to the consumer.

The identification of the most relevant impact categories is based on the normalised and weighted results, sorted from highest to lowest (in terms of contribution percentage). Specifically, only the categories that cumulatively contribute to at least 80% of the total environmental impact (excluding categories related to toxicity since the methods are not yet robust enough) are selected. With the same procedure, contribution cumulatively higher than 80% of the total environmental impact, the impact categories for each significant environmental category are selected for the analysis of the phases of the most relevant life cycle. The life cycle phases that obligatorily must be considered in this analysis are: acquisition of raw materials, product/service production, distribution and storage, use phase and end of life. The same procedure is also applied for the identification of multiple processes and relevant flows. As regards flows, the concept of materiality is applied taking into consideration those on which there is the direct possibility to intervene, i.e., the flows related to the foreground processes.

END-OF-LIFE MULTIFUNCTIONALITY MANAGEMENT

Multifunctionality at the end of life results every time a product can be recovered from the material point of view, with recycling, or energetic, with incineration. If a material is recycled and becomes part of another system, it is necessary to understand how to consider its end life in the previous and next systems. The PEF manages this aspect through the CFF – Circular Footprint Formula, described in the PEFCR Guidance (v. 6.3). Through this formula, the entire life cycle is evaluated, starting from the production of the material. This formula is composed of three main values: materials, energy and disposal.

DATA QUALITY REQUIREMENTS

As regards the data quality requirements, the PEF methodology applies the principle of materiality, i.e., focus on what is important. The data quality criteria used are four:

• Technological representativeness (TeR): identifies the degree to which the inventory data represent the process with respect to its technological characteristics which are documented in the descriptive information of the dataset;
• Temporal representativeness (TiR): describes the representativeness of the process with respect to time. Technology changes rapidly over time and, thus, TiR is closely linked to TeR;

- Geographic representativeness (GR): identifies the degree to which the inventory data represent the process with respect to the geographical context;
- Accuracy/uncertainty.

Representativeness (technological, temporal and geographical) defines the measure with which processes describe the system, while precision indicates the way data have been obtained and their relative degree of uncertainty. The data quality index (Date Quality Rating – DQR) is calculated by adding the quality index for each quality criterion, divided by the total number of criteria.

To understand the type of data to be collected in a PEF study, the PEFCR shows the DNM –Data Need Matrix – through which it is possible to understand the type of data to be collected and the necessary quality. All the processes required for modelling must be evaluated using this matrix. In particular, for the processes identified as most relevant for the analysed system, the PEF requires that data must be characterised by a level of higher quality than less relevant processes.

Within the PEFCR is reported the list of specific data that an organisation must necessarily provide. The PEFCR also provides the default data for all those processes for which organisations have no type of control or no possibility of accessing information from suppliers. Even for secondary data, however, compliance with a certain level of quality is required.

Within the PEF context, the quality assessment is done on two levels: both on the single dataset and on the entire study. Even data quality is analysed at two levels: the dataset and the activity data. In fact, as part of the PEF methodology, the amount of a given product/material/energy is called activity data. When the wording "secondary dataset" is shown in the table, it refers to the data present in the database. While when it is reported as a "specific data company" the collection of the data is mandatory (activity data).

The DNM is based on the level of influence of the organisation on each analysed process:

- The process is managed by the organisation that applies the PEFCR;
- The process is not managed by the organisation, but it has access to specific information regarding the process;
- The organisation does not manage the process and does not have access to specific data.

Therefore, for the data over which the organisation has direct control, collection is mandatory. However, if data are not under the organisation's control, a certain quality is required in relation to the ability to find them. The quality thresholds reported within the matrix are an obligation that must be fulfilled in order to ensure that the study complies with the PEF requirements. Quality rating represents a big difference between PEF and LCA studies. In fact, in an LCA study the data is evaluated in a qualitative way, expressing an opinion on a wide range of criteria (greater than those considered in the PEF), but without translating quality into scores.

5.3 Life cycle assessment of grassroots football matches

According to a study conducted by the energy company Selectra, sport contributes between 0.3% and 0.4% of the planet's global emissions. Although such a figure may seem small, that's a bigger carbon footprint than Barbados and is roughly the same as Denmark's.

During the football EURO 2016 matches the environmental footprint reached almost 3 million tonnes of CO_{2-eq}, almost equivalent to the annual environmental footprint of 3,000 European inhabitants (UEFA, 2016).

It is extremely important that football organisations start assessing their environmental impact through scientifically grounded methods. By conducting an environmental footprint of their main activities, football clubs would identify environmental improvement opportunities. This analysis also aims to identify the most impactful processes, so-called "hotspots", associated with the activities of football clubs.

In the frame of the ERASMUS+ GREEN COACH and GOALS, we calculated the environmental footprint of a football match of an average EU grassroots club. Since the environmental impacts of a football club may differ according to geographical conditions, technical features and so on, we decided to collect that from different grassroots clubs located all over the Europe in order to create a "hypothetical" average club obtained by calculating the average environmental footprint of all the collected footprints.

The environmental footprint is based on a life cycle approach. An LCA assesses and quantifies the environmental impact of a product or service over its entire life cycle. The main phases of an LCA are goal and scope setting, inventory analysis, life cycle impact assessment (LCIA), and interpretation. An inventory analysis provides information on all relevant energy and material inputs, and on the emission of toxic and non-toxic pollutants, but that alone does not provide enough information to guide decision-making. To be able to understand the consequences of these inputs and emissions, we need to translate them into environmental impacts. The impact assessment phase provides this translation.

This analysis was made on the data obtained through a data collection campaign that was conducted in 2021 in eight European countries (Belgium, France, Kosovo, Lithuania, Norway, Portugal, Romania and Sweden).

The environmental footprint assessment was conducted in order to assess the impact of a football match. The analysis focused on calculating the environmental footprint of a single amateur football match (e.g., lighting of the stadium, use of equipment, mobility of athletes and supporters, etc.).

This document attempts to comply with the requirements of:

* Guide to the Product Environmental Footprint (PEF), Annex II of Recommendation 2013/179 / EU; PEFCR "Guidance version 6.3", with the exception of all the parts that are already attributable to existing PEFCR. Deviations from the requirements of PEFCR Guidance 6.3 have been made based on old versions of the Guidance or on expert judgment;

- ISO 14040:2006 – Environmental management – Life cycle assessment – Principles and framework;
- ISO 14044:2006 – Environmental management – Life cycle assessment – Requirements and guidelines /14043.

This PEF report is not meant to be periodically reviewed. This study follows the requirements for the data collection and quality control procedures described in chapter 7.19 of PEF Guidance 6.3.

A total of 31 data collection questionnaires were collected throughout the data collection campaign (see Table 5.3). It is worth noting that the sample is exclusively composed of grassroot football clubs.

The scope of the study is to assess the product environmental footprint of a football match, considering the following system boundaries:

- Energy and water consumption associated with the football match processes (i.e., irrigation of the pitch, lighting, showers of the players, heating of the locker rooms);
- Production and end of life of the sport apparel and equipment (sport leather shoes, T-shirts, shorts, sport suits, balls, sport bags, goalkeeper pants, socks, winter jackets, rain jackers, goalkeeper gloves);
- Production and end of life of waste materials associated to the football match, and related production of the corresponding materials (paper, plastic, glass, metal, household waste, plus wastewater treatment);
- Transport of the players to the football pitch (home team and away team);
- Transport of the public attending the football match (home team and away team).

The functional unit of the study is one match played on a football pitch. The life cycle model has been designed in accordance with the system boundaries. All the data have been collected directly by the teams involved in the study, as previously described.

Table 5.3 Sample description

Country	Number of respondents
Belgium	5
France	5
Kosovo	3
Lithuania	5
Norway	4
Portugal	3
Romania	3
Sweden	3
Total	31

The specific model assumptions, for each process included in the assessment, are reported in the following subsections. All the life cycle secondary datasets used in the model belong to the Ecoinvent 3.6 database.

Energy and water consumption associated to the football match processes
For the production of electricity consumed (low voltage), the national mix of sources has been applied, unless it was differently specified in the questionnaires.

Water consumed has been considered as tap water from the municipal aqueduct, unless specified otherwise in the questionnaires.

Production and end of life of the sport apparel and equipment
For the production of the sport apparel and equipment, generic assumptions about the type and weight of materials have been made according to secondary data.

For the whole life cycle of sport leather shoes, data from a previous life cycle assessment carried out by our research group in the frame of the LIFE PREFER have been used.

For the end-of-life scenario of each material, national statistics reported in the Annex C for the PEF methodology have been applied.

The PEF CFF (Circular Footprint Formula) has been applied to the model in order to properly balance the burdens and the credit of recycling operations. This formula is composed of three parts:

- The material part;
- The energy part;
- The disposal part.

The first section of the "material" part of the Circular Footprint Formula (CFF) needs to be applied to input materials as follows:

$$\text{Material}\left(1 - R_1\right)E_V + R_1 \times \left(AE_{recycled} + (1 - A)E_V \times \frac{Q_{sin}}{Q_P} \right)$$

where,

- R_1 (recycled content) varies between 0 and 1;
- A (allocation parameter) can be set at 0.2, 0.5 or 0.8 according to the market demand for secondary raw materials (0.2 for high demand, 0.8 for low demand, 0.5 for the other cases);
- Qsin/Qp (quality degradation ratio of the recycled material) is 1 or lower depending to the loss of quality after recycling operations;
- E_v are the specific emissions and resources consumed (per functional unit) arising from the acquisition and preprocessing of virgin material;

- $E_{recycled}$ are the specific emissions and resources consumed (per functional unit) arising from the recycling process of the recycled (reused) material, including collection, sorting and transportation process.

The second section of the "material" part of the Circular Footprint Formula (CFF) needs to be applied at the end of life, in case of recycling takes place as follows:

$$+(1 - A)R_2 \times \left(E_{recyclingEoL} - E_V^\star \times \frac{Q_{sout}}{Q_P} \right)$$

where,

- R_2 is the recycling rate (% of the material which is bound to be recycled)
- A is the allocation parameter (it allocates the burden and benefit of recycling according to market demand for recycled materials);
- Q_{Sout}/Q_p is the quality degradation ratio of the recyclable material;
- $E_v^\star$ are the specific emissions and resources consumed (per functional unit) arising from the acquisition and preprocessing of virgin material assumed to be substituted by recyclable materials (i.e., the "credits" for avoiding the use of virgin material);
- $E_{recyclingEol}$ are the specific emissions and resources consumed (per functional unit) arising from the recycling process at EoL, including collection, sorting and transportation process (i.e the "burdens" related to the recycling operations).

The energy section of the CFF refers to the incineration process taking place at the end of life of the disposed materials, according to the following formula:

$$\text{Energy}(1 - B)R_3 \times \left(E_{ER} - LHV \times X_{ER,heat} \times E_{SE,heat} - LHV \times X_{ER,elec} \times E_{SE,elec} \right.$$

where,

- R_3 is the incineration rate (% of the packaging material which is bound to be incinerated);
- B is the allocation parameter (it allocates the burden and benefit of incineration). In PEF studies the B value shall be equal to 0 as default;
- E_{ER} are the specific emissions and resources consumed (per functional unit) arising from the energy recovery process (e.g., incineration with energy recovery, landfill with energy recovery, etc.);
- LHV is the Lower Heating Value of the material in the product that is used for energy recovery;
- $X_{ER,\,heat}$ and $X_{ER,\,elec}$ are the efficiency of the energy recovery process for both heat and electricity;
- $E_{SE,\,heat}$ and $E_{SE,\,elec}$ are the specific emissions and resources consumed (per functional unit) that would have arisen from the specific substituted energy source, heat and electricity respectively.

Finally, the last section of the CFF refers to the landfill process, according to the following formula:

$$\text{Disposal}(1 - R_2 - R_3) \times E_D$$

where,

- R_2 is the recycling rate (% of the packaging material which is bound to be recycled);
- R_3 is the incineration rate (% of the packaging material which is bound to be incinerated);
- E_D are the specific emissions and resources consumed (per functional unit) arising from disposal of waste material at the EoL of the analysed product, without energy recovery.

For the current study the average vales included in the PEF Annex C have been applied for the aforementioned parameters.

Production and end of life of waste materials associated with the football match
Starting from the list of waste materials associated with a football match, as reported in the single questionnaires provided by teams involved in the study, the corresponding average production processes of the raw materials have been designed in the model by using secondary datasets taken from Ecoinvent database.

For the end-of-life scenario of each material, national statistics have been applied, according to the before mentioned PEF Annex C, for R_2 (% of recycling), R_3 (% of incineration with energy recovery) and the remaining fraction sent to landfill.

The PEF CFF (Circular Footprint Formula) has been applied to the model in order to properly balance the burdens and the credit of recycling operations.

Transport of the players to the football pitch
In accordance with the information reported in the single questionnaires provided by teams involved in the study (average distance, average transportation means used), the transport processes of the players to the football pitch have been modelled with secondary datasets taken from Ecoinvent database.

Transport of the public attending the football match
In accordance with the information reported in the single questionnaires provided by teams involved in the study (average attendance, average distance, average transportation means used), the transport processes of the public attending the football match have been modelled with secondary datasets taken from Ecoinvent database.

Table 5.4 summarises the data quality attached to each type of data used.

Table 5.4 Data quality: level of completeness

Process	% of football teams providing specific data	Notes
Energy consumption	80.65%	25 teams out of 31 reported specific data, while for the remaining 6, national average has been used
Water consumption	77.42%	24 teams out of 31 reported specific data, while for the remaining 7, national average has been used
Waste generation	80.65%	25 teams out of 31 reported specific data, while for the remaining 6, national average has been used
Sport apparel	87.10%	27 teams out of 9 31 reported specific data, while for the remaining 4 national average has been used
Transport operations (average distances for home and away games and means of transportation)	93.55%	29 teams out of 31 reported specific data, while for the remaining 2, national average has been used

To calculate the results of the impact assessment in the characterisation phase, all substances are multiplied by a factor that reflects their relative contribution to the environmental impact, quantifying how much impact a product or service has in each impact category.

The PEF methodology proposes a default list (Table 5.5) of impact categories which relate to:

- Emissions into air,
- Emissions into water,
- Use of natural resources,
- Toxicity,
- Use of land.

According to the European Commission's Joint Research Centre – Institute for Environment and Sustainability[3], the recommended characterisation models and associated characterisation factors are classified according to their quality and reliability into three levels (or a mix of them):

- "I" (recommended and satisfactory);
- "II" (recommended but in need of some improvements);
- "III" (recommended, but to be applied with caution).

Impact category	Impact category Indicator	Unit	Characterisation model	Robustness
Climate change, total	Radiative forcing as global warming potential (GWP100)	kg CO_2 eq.	Baseline model of 100 years of the IPPC (IPCC, 2013)	I
Ozone depletion	Ozone depletion potential (ODP)	kg CFC11 eq.	Steady-state ODPs as in WMO (2014) + integration	I
Ionising radiation, HH	Human exposure efficiency to U^{235}	kBq U-235 eq.	Human health effect as developed by Dreicer et al. (1995) and Frischknecht et al. (2000)	II
Photochemical ozone formation, HH	Tropospheric ozone concentration increase	kg NMVOC eq.	LOTOS-EUROS model (Van Zelm et al., 2018) as implemented in ReCiPe 2008	II
Particulate matter	Impact on human health	disease inc.	PM method recommended by UNEP (2016)	I
Non-cancer human health effects	Comparative Toxic Unit for humans (CTU_h)	CTU_h	USEtox model 2.1 (Fankte et al., 2017)	III
Cancer human health effects	Comparative Toxic Unit for humans (CTU_h)	CTU_h	USEtox model 2.1 (Fankte et al., 2017)	III
Acidification terrestrial and freshwater	Accumulated Exceedance (AE)	mol H+ eq.	Accumulated Exceedance (Seppälä et al., 2006; Posch et al., 2008)	II
Eutrophication freshwater	Fraction of nutrients reaching freshwater end compartment (P)	kg P eq.	EUTREND model (Struijs et al., 2009 as implemented in ReCiPe 2008)	II
Eutrophication marine	Fraction of nutrients reaching marine water end compartment (N)	kg N eq.	EUTREND model (Struijs et al., 2009 as implemented in ReCiPe 2008)	II
Eutrophication terrestrial	Accumulated Exceedance (AE)	mol N eq.	Accumulated Exceedance (Seppälä et al., 2006; Posch et al., 2008)	II
Ecotoxicity freshwater	Comparative Toxic Unit for ecosystems CTU_e	CTUe	USEtox model 2.1 (Fankte et al., 2017)	III
Land use	Soil quality index Biotic production Erosion resistance Mechanical filtration Groundwater replenishment	Pt	Soil quality index based on LANCA (Beck et al., 2010; Bos et al., 2016)	III
Water scarcity	User deprivation potential (deprivation-weighted water consumption)	m³ depriv.	Available WAter REmaining (AWARE) as recommended by UNEP (2016)	III
Resource use, energy carriers	Abiotic resource depletion (ADP ultimate reserves)	MJ	CML 2002 (Guinéé et al., 2002; Van Oers et al., 2002)	III
Resource use, mineral and metals	Abiotic resource depletion – fossil fuel (ADP fossil)	kg Sb eq.	CML 2002 (Guinéé et al., 2002; Van Oers et al., 2002)	III

The characterised results for the average team emerged before normalization and weighting, distributed for the relative environmental aspects included in the study, are shown in Tables 5.6 and 5.7 and Figure 5.3. All data reported refer to the functional unit of one match played, according to what was stated in previous paragraphs of the current report. The characterised results indicate the absolute impact of one football match.

Our environmental impact assessment was modelled using LCA Simapro 9 and the ILCD-midpoint+ method v. 1.11 (October 2019 version), released by the European Commission's Joint Research Centre in 2012. Moreover, the ILCD method assesses the environmental impacts in different impact categories of interest, such as global warming, abiotic depletion, acidification, eutrophication, human toxicity, among others. The ILCD method provides characterisation factors, as recommended in the ILCD guidance document (EC-JRC, 2011), to quantify the contribution of the different flows to and from a process to each impact category and normalisation factors to allow a comparison across indicators. Characterisation quantifies the extent of the contribution of flows to each impact category (for example, expressing the contribution of CH_4, N_2O and CO_2 to the climate change category, by means of CO_2 equivalence factors). Normalisation is an optional step used to express the characterised impact indicators in a way that allows comparison to each other. Normalisation standardises the indicators by dividing their characterised values by a selected reference value, translating into an assessment of how much the investigated process contributes to a given category with reference to a value considered acceptable or unavoidable in a given point in space and time. The weighting has an essential role to support the identification of the most relevant impact categories, life cycle stages, processes and elementary flows (describing a resource consumption or emission) to ensure that the focus is put on those aspects that matter the most. With weighting, results may be summed across impact categories to arrive at a single score indicator for an LCA.

All our impact assessment results were normalised and weighted in order to select the most relevant impact categories and to obtain single scores results expressed as Eco-Points (Pt). According to the ILCD 2011 method, the normalisation factors (NFs) are based on Benini et al. (2014), while the weighting factors are based on EC (2014) (all impact categories receive the same weight in the baseline approach). Moreover, in the present study the weighting excluded three toxicity-related impact categories (human toxicity cancer, human toxicity non-cancer and freshwater ecotoxicity) since according to the EF method they are not seen as sufficiently robust to be included in external communications or in a weighted result.

Table 5.6 Characterised results of PEF (non-normalised and non-weighted, absolute value)

Impact category	Unit	Total	Electricity	Water	Packaging production	Sportswear and equipment	Transport	Waste
Climate change	kg CO_2 eq	2,228.10	637.37	67.02	8.31	79.37	1,419.14	16.90
Ozone depletion	kg CFC11 eq	4.5E-04	4.8E-05	4.5E-06	9.3E-06	1.3E-04	2.6E-04	1.2E-06
Ionising radiation, HH	kBq U-235 eq	254.37	123.79	23.19	1.00	6.75	98.26	1.40
Photochemical ozone formation, HH	kg NMVOC eq	7.27	1.15	0.22	0.03	0.16	5.66	0.05
Respiratory inorganics	disease inc.	9.6E-05	6.3E-06	3.1E-06	5.7E-07	2.0E-05	6.4E-05	1.7E-06
Non-cancer human health effects	CTUh	3.4E-04	9.5E-05	2.9E-05	2.1E-06	2.1E-05	1.3E-04	6.3E-05
Cancer human health effects	CTUh	1.2E-04	8.3E-06	1.8E-05	5.2E-07	1.8E-05	7.3E-05	3.4E-06
Acidification terrestrial and freshwater	mol H+ eq	9.53	2.37	0.37	0.05	0.53	6.11	0.11
Eutrophication freshwater	kg P eq	0.66	0.37	0.05	0.00	0.02	0.20	0.02
Eutrophication marine	kg N eq	2.72	0.40	0.07	0.01	0.18	1.60	0.46
Eutrophication terrestrial	mol N eq	23.53	3.61	0.68	0.09	1.48	17.33	0.34
Ecotoxicity freshwater	CTUe	5,007.98	259.29	202.90	9.48	581.94	3,827.95	126.43
Land use	Pt	14,831.51	1,385.41	464.08	469.64	335.51	12,013.75	163.12
Water scarcity	m^3 depriv.	7,784.18	75.82	8,392.78	3.73	27.40	123.02	838.57
Resource use, energy carriers	MJ	31,822.22	9,623.60	1,138.58	126.45	1,293.16	19,542.02	98.41
Resource use, mineral and metals	kg Sb eq	3.0E-02	2.7E-03	3.1E-04	2.4E-04	7.8E-03	1.9E-02	1.4E-04

Table 5.7 Characterised results of PEF (non-normalised and non-weighted, percentage)

Impact category	Electricity	Water	Packaging production	Sportswear and equipment	Transport	W.
Climate change	29%	3%	0%	4%	64%	1*
Ozone depletion	11%	1%	2%	28%	58%	0*
Ionising radiation, HH	49%	9%	0%	3%	39%	1*
Photochemical ozone formation, HH	16%	3%	0%	2%	78%	1*
Respiratory inorganics	7%	3%	1%	21%	67%	2*
Non-cancer human health effects	28%	9%	1%	6%	38%	18*
Cancer human health effects	7%	15%	0%	15%	60%	3*
Acidification terrestrial and freshwater	25%	4%	1%	6%	64%	1*
Eutrophication freshwater	55%	7%	0%	3%	31%	4*
Eutrophication marine	15%	3%	0%	7%	59%	17*
Eutrophication terrestrial	15%	3%	0%	6%	74%	1*
Ecotoxicity freshwater	5%	4%	0%	12%	76%	3*
Land use	9%	3%	3%	2%	81%	1*
Water scarcity	1%	108%	0%	0%	2%	-11
Resource use, energy carriers	30%	4%	0%	4%	61%	0*
Resource use, mineral and metals	9%	1%	1%	26%	63%	0*

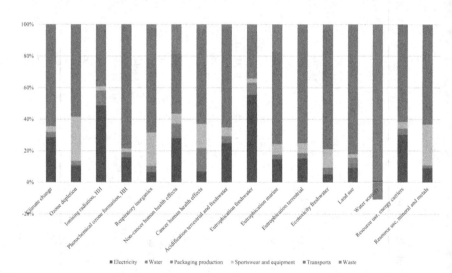

Figure 5.3 Characterised results of PEF (non-normalised and non-weighted)

Although normalised results and weighting scores are perceived as relevant for decision-making, further development is needed to improve uncertainty and robustness, especially in the case of weighting (Pizzol et al, 2017).

The normalised and weighted results for the average team are shown in Table 5.8 and Figure 5.4. All data reported refer to the functional unit of one

Table 5.8 Weighted and normalised results of PEF (single score)

Impact category	Unit	Total	Electricity	Water	Packaging production	Sportswear and equipment	Transport	Waste
Climate change	mPt	63.73	18.23	1.92	0.24	2.27	40.59	0.48
Ozone depletion	mPt	1.31	0.14	0.01	0.03	0.37	0.76	0.00
Ionising radiation, HH	mPt	3.24	1.58	0.30	0.01	0.09	1.25	0.02
Photochemical ozone formation, HH	mPt	9.13	1.44	0.27	0.03	0.21	7.11	0.06
Respiratory inorganics	mPt	14.36	0.94	0.47	0.09	3.03	9.58	0.26
Non-cancer human health effects	mPt	-	-	-	-	-	-	-
Cancer human health effects	mPt	-	-	-	-	-	-	-
Acidification terrestrial and freshwater	mPt	11.40	2.84	0.44	0.06	0.63	7.30	0.13
Eutrophication freshwater	mPt	7.62	4.23	0.56	0.04	0.19	2.33	0.28
Eutrophication marine	mPt	3.01	0.44	0.08	0.01	0.20	1.77	0.51
Eutrophication terrestrial	mPt	5.20	0.80	0.15	0.02	0.33	3.83	0.08
Ecotoxicity freshwater	mPt	-	-	-	-	-	-	-
Land use	mPt	0.94	0.09	0.03	0.03	0.02	0.76	0.01
Water scarcity	mPt	61.29	0.60	66.08	0.03	0.22	0.97	-6.60
Resource use, energy carriers	mPt	43.49	13.15	1.56	0.17	1.77	26.71	0.13
Resource use, mineral and metals	mPt	42.15	3.80	0.44	0.34	10.87	26.51	0.19
Total	mPt	266.85	48.27	72.29	1.10	20.17	129.46	-4.45

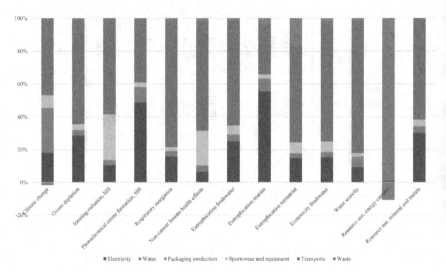

Figure 5.4 Weighted and normalised results of PEF (single score)

match played, according to what was stated in the previous paragraphs of the current chapter.

According to the PEF methodology the most relevant impact categories are those contributing to reach the 80% threshold of the cumulated weighted results. Thus, as shown in the previous tables and figures, the most relevant impact categories are:

- Climate change;
- Water scarcity;
- Resource use, energy carriers;
- Resource use, minerals and metals;
- respiratory inorganics.

Moving to the most relevant life cycle phases, transport operations is the largest contributor (though it is not under direct control of the football team) followed by water consumption, electricity and "sportswear and equipment", as shown in Table 5.9.

It is interesting to see that, if we consider the total results without the transport impacts, which are not under the direct control of the football team, the major areas of possible intervention aimed at improving the overall footprint seem to be:

- Water consumption;
- Electricity;
- Sportswear and equipment.

Table 5.9 Weighted results of PEF (life cycle phases contribution) – Single score

	Single score (weighted results – percentage)
Electricity	18%
Water	27%
Packaging production	0%
Sportswear and equipment	8%
Transports	49%
Waste	-2%

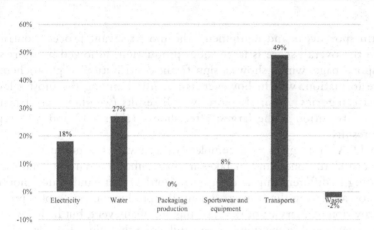

Figure 5.5 Weighted results of PEF (life cycle phases contribution) – Single score

Table 5.10 Weighted results of PEF (life cycle phases contribution) – 16 impact categories

act category	Electricity	Water	Packaging production	Sportswear and equipment	Transports	Waste
nate change	29%	3%	0%	4%	64%	1%
ne depletion	11%	1%	2%	28%	58%	0%
sing radiation, HH	49%	9%	0%	3%	39%	1%
tochemical ozone formation, H	16%	3%	0%	2%	78%	1%
piratory inorganics	7%	3%	1%	21%	67%	2%
a-cancer human health effects	–	–	–	–	–	–
cer human health effects	–	–	–	–	–	–
lification terrestrial and eshwater	25%	4%	1%	6%	64%	1%
ophication freshwater	55%	7%	0%	3%	31%	4%
ophication marine	15%	3%	0%	7%	59%	17%
ophication terrestrial	15%	3%	0%	6%	74%	1%
oxicity freshwater	–	–	–	–	–	–
d use	9%	3%	3%	2%	81%	1%
er scarcity	1%	108%	0%	0%	2%	-11%
ource use, energy carriers	30%	4%	0%	4%	61%	0%
ource use, mineral and metals	9%	1%	1%	26%	63%	0%

Table 5.11 Weighted results of PEF (life cycle phases contribution – transportation excluded) – Single score

	Single score (weighted results – percentage)
Electricity	35%
Water	53%
Packaging production	1%
Sportswear and equipment	15%
Waste	-3%

Within sportswear and equipment, the most relevant process contributing to the overall score is large shoes production, followed by sport suits and sports bags, which shows a significant contribution to photochemical ozone formation, which, however, is not listed among the most relevant impact categories. At single score overall results (weighted results), sport suits' contribution is the largest after shoes. Tables 5.12 and 5.13 report these results.

An LCA study gives us a complete overview of the product or service studied. On the one hand, it takes into account all environmental aspects including 16 different impact categories. On the other hand, it does not limit itself to calculating the impacts during the production phase of a product, the provision of a service or the carrying out of an event, but includes all the impacts generated in the supply chain and along the value chain.

Nevertheless, understanding and communicating LCA results it is not always easy. LCAs generate very technical results that most of the time

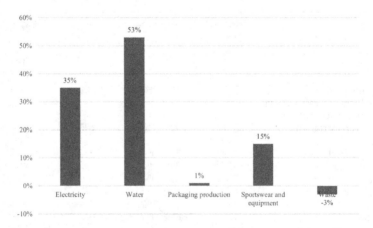

Figure 5.6 Weighted results of PEF (life cycle phases contribution – transportation excluded) – Single score

le 5.12 Characterised results of PEF (sportswear and equipment contribution)

act category – Total tswear and equipment	Shoes	Balls	Gloves	Sports suits	Sports bags	Winter jackets	Rain jackets	T-shirts	Shorts	Socks
gle score	80.7%	0.9%	0.0%	6.6%	5.0%	0.0%	0.0%	4.6%	2.3%	0.0%
one depletion	0%	0%	0%	1%	0%	0%	0%	0%	0%	0%
ising radiation, HH	0%	0%	0%	0%	0%	0%	0%	0%	0%	0%
tochemical ozone ormation, HH	0%	0%	0%	0%	0%	0%	0%	0%	0%	0%
spiratory inorganics	14%	0%	0%	0%	0%	0%	0%	0%	0%	0%
n-cancer human ealth effects	0%	0%	0%	0%	0%	0%	0%	0%	0%	0%
ncer human health ffects	0%	0%	0%	0%	0%	0%	0%	0%	0%	0%
dification terrestrial nd freshwater	2%	0%	0%	0%	0%	0%	0%	0%	0%	0%
rophication reshwater	0%	0%	0%	0%	0%	0%	0%	0%	0%	0%
rophication marine	1%	0%	0%	0%	0%	0%	0%	0%	0%	0%
rophication errestrial	1%	0%	0%	0%	0%	0%	0%	0%	0%	0%
toxicity freshwater	0%	0%	0%	0%	0%	0%	0%	0%	0%	0%
d use	0%	0%	0%	0%	0%	0%	0%	0%	0%	0%
ter scarcity	0%	0%	0%	0%	0%	0%	0%	0%	0%	0%
source use, energy arriers	4%	0%	0%	2%	1%	0%	0%	1%	1%	0%

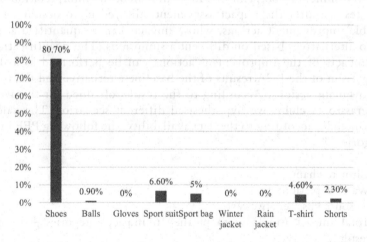

Figure 5.7 Weighted results of PEF (Sportswear and equipment contribution)

are difficult to interpret even for experts, let alone for consumers or for football fans.

To overcome this barrier, using similar LCA methodologies, it is possible to convert and translate data expressed in technical units of measurement

Table 5.13 Weighted results of PEF (Sportswear and equipment contribution)

	Single score (weighted results – percentage)
Shoes	80.7%
Balls	0.9%
Gloves	0%
Sports suits	6.6%
Sports bags	5%
Winter jackets	0%
Rain jackets	0%
T-shirts	4.6%
Shorts	2.3%

such kg of CO_2 eq., m^3 depriv., MJ, etc., into more comprehensible definite quantities.

Table 5.14, using the characterised results of the PEF of an average EU grassroot football match, shows the equivalence to facilitate LCA communication for the main impact categories, i.e., carbon footprint (kg of CO_2 eq.), water footprint (m^3 depriv.) and resource consumption (MJ).

LCA can be used by football organisations to compare different scenarios and identify the most sustainable one. In fact, for the aim of reducing the environmental footprint of a football match, the interpretation of the LCA results, after the impact assessment, allowed us to design a list of possible improvement actions, whose impacts can be quantified according to alternatives based on different assumptions. The quantification of the impacts of the improvement actions can be performed as a direct comparison of the LCA results of the baseline alternative and the related improvement actions. According to the results obtained for the average EU grassroots clubs, we hypothesised different scenarios. The calculations include, according to the data availability, the following PEF impact categories:

- Climate change;
- Water depletion;
- Resource use, energy carriers;
- Total impact (single score pf the 16 impact categories – weighted results).

Table 5.15 reports all the proposed improvement actions, as well as the different alternatives and assumptions.

Tables 5.16–5.29 show the results of the analysis of each improvement action. The improvement actions were calculated in relation to the baseline, i.e., how much will the environmental footprint change if the club would adopt this improvement action?

Table 5.14 Possible equivalence by impact category for the average EU grassroots football match

Impact category			
"Climate Change" 2228.1 kg of CO_2 eq. are equal to...	the kg of CO_2 eq. issued by travelling	49,734.38 km by high-speed train	Around 33 times the distance Rome–Berlin
	the kg of CO_2 eq. issued by travelling	18,567.50 km with a medium-sized car	Around 12 times the distance Rome–Berlin
	the kg of CO_2 eq. absorbed by	297.08 trees	
	the kg of CO_2 eq. in a year to produce the energy needed to run	25.23 electric ovens	
	the kg of CO_2 eq. in a year to produce the energy needed to run	278,512.50 smartphones	
"Water scarcity" 7784.18 m^3 depriv. are equal to...	m^3 of water consumed in one day by	31,826.72 Italian inhabitants	
	m^3 of water consumed in one season to irrigate	31,136.72 square metres of land planted with tomatoes	
	m^3 of water consumed for washing	44,481.03 cars	
	m^3 of water consumed to fill	3.11 Olympic swimming pools	
	litres of water consumed on average to make	93,785.30 5-minute showers	
"Eutrophication freshwater" 0.66 kg P eq. are equal to...	kg of phosphorus eq. issued by	1,100 washing cycles in the washing machine	
"Photochemical ozone formation" 7.27 kg NMVOC eq. are equal to...	kg of NMVOC eq. issued by traveling	6,923.81 km with a medium-sized car	4.5 times the distance Rome–Berlin
"Resource use" 31822.22 MJ are equal to...	MJ consumed to light for	106.07 minutes a football stadium for the World Cup	
	MJ consumed in a year to heat	103.32 sqm of an apartment	

Table 5.15 List of the possible improvement actions

Action N°	Description	Alternatives and related assumptions
1	Led lights vs. halogen lights	Baseline: halogen lights on during the match Improvement: led lights on during the match (led lig consumption -90% of halogen light)
2	Life extension (2 and 3 years) for football kit	Baseline: 1 football kit (sport suit in polyester+shirt+socks+shorts) each year per player Improvement 1: the football kit lasts 2 years Improvement 2: the football kit lasts 3 years Improvement 3: the football kit lasts 5 years
2 bis	End-of-life scenario for football kit	Baseline: football kit to landfill Improvement 1: football kit sent to recycling (1 reuse e.g., donation) Improvement 2: football kit sent to recycling (2 reuse e.g., donation)
3	Water well vs. public water (per m³ of consumed water)	Baseline: all water consumption comes from public water Improvement 1: all water comes from wells
4	Car sharing: 3 people 1 car vs. 4 people 1 car (100 km)	Baseline: 2 people in 1 car Improvement 1: 3 people in 1 car Improvement 2: 4 people in 1 car
5	Team bus vs. players' cars (100 km – 16 people per team)	Baseline: no bus, all players in cars, 2 persons per car Improvement 1: team bus, no players with cars
6	Adoption of photovoltaic panel kwh	Baseline: no solar energy production Improvement 1: panel of 15 kw
7	Reusable water bottle vs. single-use bottle	Baseline: single-use bottle (1 litre, plastic weight 35 g Improvement 1: refillable bottles made of aluminium (used 1,000 times with 200 g of water consumed p single washing)
8	Adoption of water flow optimiser	Baseline: no water flow optimiser (16 litres per minu per shower) Improvement: water flow optimisers in all showers a toilets (-30% consumption)
9	Duration of the shower	Baseline: 1 shower, 8 minutes per player (16 litres per minute per shower) Improvement 1: shower lasts 4 minutes instead of 8
10	Duration of the lights after the end of the match (2,000 w halogen – 13 lamps per pitch)	Baseline: keep the lights on 1 hour before the match 30 minutes after the match (tot 3 h) Improvement 1: keep the lights on only for 1 hour instead of 1.5 hours before and after the match (tot 2.5 h) Improvement 2: keep the lights on only for the durat of the match (tot 1.5 h)
11	Separate collection vs. no separate collection	Baseline: all waste to landfill Improvement: all waste to recovery
12	Diesel/petrol car vs. electric car (use phase: 100 km)	Baseline: diesel/petrol car used Improvement: electric car used (EU electricity mix applied)
13	Jumpsuit in cotton vs jumpsuit in polyester	Baseline: jumpsuit in 100% polyester Improvement 1: jumpsuit 50% polyester 50% cotton Improvement 2: jumpsuit 100% cotton
14	Virgin plastic seats vs. recycled plastic seat	Baseline: 1 seat 100% virgin PET Improvement 1: 60% virgin PET, 40% recycled PET

5.16 ACTION 1 – Led lights vs. halogen lights (results per h of lighting) – EU average electricity mix

ACT CATEGORIES	Climate change	Water scarcity	Resource use, energy carriers	Total environmental footprint
IONS	kg $CO_{2\text{-eq}}$	m³ depriv.	MJ	mPt
line: halogen lights on during e match	11.25901	2.5725217	229.67355	1.1589949
ovement: led lights on during e match	1.125901	0.25725217	22.967355	0.11589949
erence improvement/baseline	– 90%	– 90%	– 90%	– 90%

5.17 ACTION 2 – Life extension (2 and 3 years) for football kit (per person)

ACT CATEGORIES	Climate change	Water scarcity	Resource use, energy carriers	Total environmental footprint
IONS	kg $CO_{2\text{-eq}}$	m³ depriv.	MJ	mPt
line: 1 football kit (sport suit polyester+shirt+socks+shorts) ch year per player	30.435302	10.441406	446.55219	9.8622058
ovement 1: the football kit lasts years	15.217651	5.220703	223.27609	4.9311029
ovement 2: football kit lasts years	10.145101	3.4804686	148.85073	3.2874019
ovement 3: football kit lasts years	6.0870605	2.0882812	89.310438	1.9724412
erence improvement 1/baseline	– 40%	– 40%	– 40%	– 40%
erence improvement 2/baseline	– 67%	– 67%	– 67%	– 67%
erence improvement 3/baseline	– 80%	– 80%	– 80%	– 80%

5.18 ACTION 3 – Water well vs. public water (per m³ of water)

ACT CATEGORIES	Climate change	Water scarcity	Resource use, energy carriers	Total environmental footprint
IONS	kg $CO_{2\text{-eq}}$	m³ depriv.	MJ	mPt
line: all water consumption mes from public water	0.34568043	43.088611	5.8702258	382.9643
ovement 1: all water comes om wells	0	42.95	0	338.15639
erence improvement/baseline	– 100%	0%	– 100%	– 12%

5.19 ACTION 4 – Car sharing: 3 people 1 car vs. 4 people 1 car (per 100 km)

ACT CATEGORIES	Climate change	Water scarcity	Resource use, energy carriers	Total environmental footprint
IONS	kg $CO_{2\text{-eq}}$	m³ depriv.	MJ	mPt
line: 2 people in 1 car	16.068112	1.4631609	219.96904	2.871165
ovement 1: 3 people in 1 car	10.712075	0.97544062	146.64603	1.91411
ovement 2: 4 people in 1 car	8.0340559	0.73158046	109.98452	1.4355825
erence improvement 1/baseline	– 33%	– 33%	– 33%	– 33%
erence improvement 2/baseline	– 50%	– 50%	– 50%	– 50%

Table 5.20 ACTION 5 – Team bus vs. players' cars (per person-km)

IMPACT CATEGORIES	Climate change	Water scarcity	Resource use, energy carriers	Total environmen footprint
ACTIONS	kg CO_{2-eq}	m³ depriv.	MJ	mPt
Baseline: no bus, all players in car, 2 people per car	257.08979	23.410575	3519.5046	45.938641
Improvement: team bus, no players with car	160.71297	2.5744491	2369.9066	19.106606
Difference improvement/baseline	– 37%	– 89%	– 33%	– 58%

Table 5.21 ACTION 6 – Adoption of photovoltaic panel (per kwh)

IMPACT CATEGORIES	Climate change	Water scarcity	Resource use, energy carriers	Total environme footprint
ACTIONS	kg CO_{2-eq}	m³ depriv.	MJ	mPt
Baseline: no solar energy production	0.43303935	0.098935002	8.8335987	44.576686
Improvement: panel of 15 kw	0.080118348	0.075601724	0.99067483	22.773482
Difference improvement/ baseline	– 81%	– 24%	– 89%	– 49%

Table 5.22 ACTION 7 – Reusable water bottle vs. single-use bottle (per l)

IMPACT CATEGORIES	Climate change	Water scarcity	Resource use, energy carriers	Total environmen footprint
ACTIONS	kg CO_{2-eq}	m³ depriv.	MJ	mPt
Baseline: no single-use bottle 1L, plastic waste produced	0.13436689	0.061517012	2.9528352	31.348018
Improvement: refillable bottles	0.001107614	0.008838144	0.013396519	0.18962814
Difference improvement/ baseline	– 99%	– 86%	– 100%	– 99%

Table 5.23 ACTION 8 – Adoption of water flow optimiser (per minute of shower)

IMPACT CATEGORIES	Climate change	Water scarcity	Resource use, energy carriers	Total environmen footprint
ACTIONS	kg CO_{2-eq}	m³ depriv.	MJ	mPt
Baseline: no water flow	0.005530887	0.68941778	0.093923613	6.1274288
Improvement: water flow optimiser on showers	0.003871621	0.48259244	0.065746529	4.2892002
Difference improvement/ baseline	– 30%	– 30%	– 30%	– 30%

5.24 ACTION 9 – Duration of the shower (per shower per person)

IMPACT CATEGORIES	Climate change	Water scarcity	Resource use, energy carriers	Total environmental footprint
ACTIONS	kg $CO_{2\text{-eq}}$	m^3 depriv.	MJ	mPt
Baseline: 1 shower, 8 minutes per player	0.044247096	5.5153422	0.7513889	49.01943
Improvement: shower lasts 4 minutes instead of 8	0.022123548	2.7576711	0.37569445	24.509715
Difference improvement/baseline	- 50%	- 50%	- 50%	- 50%

5.25 ACTION 10 – Duration of the lights after the end of the match (per hour)

IMPACT CATEGORIES	Climate change	Water scarcity	Resource use, energy carriers	Total environmental footprint
ACTIONS	kg $CO_{2\text{-eq}}$	m^3 depriv.	MJ	mPt
Baseline: keep the lights on 1 hour before the match and 30 minutes after the match	33.77703	7.717565	689.02066	3.4769847
Improvement 1: keep the lights on only for 1 hour instead of 1.5 hours before and after the match	22.51802	5.1450433	459.3471	2.3179898
Improvement 2: keep the lights on only for the duration of the match	16.888515	3.8587825	344.51033	1.7384923
Difference improvement 1/baseline	- 33%	- 33%	- 33%	- 33%
Difference improvement 2/baseline	- 50%	- 50%	- 50%	- 50%

5.26 ACTION 11 – Separate collection vs. no separate collection (per kg of waste treated)

IMPACT CATEGORIES	Climate change	Water scarcity	Resource use, energy carriers	Total environmental footprint
ACTIONS	kg $CO_{2\text{-eq}}$	m^3 depriv.	MJ	mPt
Baseline: all waste to landfill	32.815208	16.943585	461.04702	4.6585854
Improvement: all waste to recycling	21.728622	9.5493397	356.55725	3.4289228
Difference improvement/baseline	- 34%	- 44%	- 23%	- 26%

5.27 ACTION 12 – Use of diesel/petrol car vs. electric car (per 100 km)

IMPACT CATEGORIES	Climate change	Water scarcity	Resource use, energy carriers	Total environmental footprint
ACTIONS	kg $CO_{2\text{-eq}}$	m^3 depriv.	MJ	mPt
Baseline: use of diesel/petrol car	32.136224	2.9263219	439.93808	5.7423301
Improvement: use of electric car	16.731583	4.5580566	285.7725	3.4740813
Difference improvement/baseline	48%	56%	- 35%	- 40%

Table 5.28 ACTION 13 – Jumpsuit in cotton vs. jumpsuit in polyester (per jumpsuit)

IMPACT CATEGORIES	Climate change	Water scarcity	Resource use, energy carriers	Total environment footprint
ACTIONS	kg CO_{2-eq}	m³ depriv.	MJ	mPt
Baseline: jumpsuit made of 100% polyester	4.5961417	2.0296678	78.147054	0.44493392
Improvement 1: jumpsuit made of 50% polyester/50% cotton	9.6804004	86.249844	111.15944	1.7778377
Improvement 2: jumpsuit made of 100% cotton	14.764659	170.47002	144.17184	3.1107416
Difference improvement 1/baseline	111%	4,149%	42%	300%
Difference improvement 2/baseline	221%	8,299%	84%	599%

Table 5.29 ACTION 14 – Virgin plastic seats vs. recycled plastic seats (per seat)

IMPACT CATEGORIES	Climate change	Water scarcity
ACTIONS	kg CO_{2-eq}	m³ depriv.
Baseline: 1 seat 100% virgin PET	5.34	1.65
Improvement: 1 seat 60% virgin PET 40% recycled PET	3.47	0.98
Difference improvement/baseline	- 35%	- 41%

Notes

1 The 2021 versions, however, present only small changes compared to the 2006 versions which are the milestones of the LCA technical literature.
2 The LCA can also be used to compare the environmental impacts connected to alternative products, services or processes.
3 ILCD (International Reference Life Cycle Data System) Handbook "Framework and requirements for LCIA models and indicators", "Analysis of existing Environmental Assessment methodologies for use in LCA" and "Recommendation for life cycle impact assessment in the European context" (http://lct.jrc. ec.europa.eu/).

References

Bartolozzi, I., Baldereschi, E., Daddi, T., Iraldo, F., (2018). The application of life cycle assessment (LCA) in municipal solid waste management: A comparative study on street sweeping services. *J. Clean. Prod.*, 182, 455–465. doi:10.1016/j. jclepro.2018.01.230

Benini L., Mancini L., Sala S., Manfredi S., Schau E. M., Pant R., (2014). Normalisation method and data for Environmental Footprints. European Commission, Joint Research Center, Institute for Environment and Sustainability, Publications Office of the European Union, Luxemburg. ISBN: 978–92–79–40847-2. doi:10.2788/16415

Daddi, T., Nucci, B., Iraldo, F., (2017). Using Life Cycle Assessment (LCA) to measure the environmental benefits of industrial symbiosis in an industrial cluster of SMEs. *J. Clean. Prod.*, 147, 157–164. doi:10.1016/j.jclepro.2017.01.090

EC, (2014). Environmental Footprint Pilot Guidance document, - Guidance for the implementation of the EU Product Environmental Footprint (PEF) during the Environmental Footprint (EF) pilot phase, v. 5.2. https://ec.europa.eu/environment/eussd/smgp/pdf/Guidance_products.pdf

EC-JRC, (2011). ILCD Handbook. Recommendations based on existing environmental impact assessment models and factors for Life Cycle Assessment in European context.

Iraldo, F., Testa, F., Bartolozzi, I., (2014). An application of Life Cycle Assessment (LCA) as a green marketing tool for agricultural products: the case of extra-virgin olive oil in Val di Cornia, Italy. *J. Environ. Plan. Manag.*, 57(1), 78–103. doi:10.1080/09640568.2012.735991

Pizzol, M., Laurent, A., Sala, S., Weidema, B.P., Verones, F., Koffler, C., (2017). Normalisation and weighting in life cycle assessment: quo vadis? *Int. J. Life Cycle Assess.*, 22(6), 853–866. doi:10.1007/s11367-016-1199-1

Society of Environmental Toxicology and Chemistry (SETAC), (1993). Guidelines for Life-Cycle Assessment: A "Code of Practice". From the SETAC Workshop held at Sesimbra, Portugal 31 March – 3 April 1993.

Testa, F., Iraldo, F., (2010). Shadows and lights of GSCM (Green Supply Chain Management): determinants and effects of these practices based on a multi-national study. *J. Clean. Prod.*, 18(10–11), 953–962. doi:10.1016/j.jclepro.2010.03.005

Testa, F., Nucci, B., Tessitore, S., Iraldo, F., Daddi, T., (2016). Perceptions on LCA implementation: evidence from a survey on adopters and nonadopters in Italy. *Int. J. Life Cycle Assess.*, 21, 1501–1513. doi:10.1007/s11367-016-1106-9

Testa, F., Nucci, B., Iraldo, F., Appolloni, A., Daddi, T., (2017). Removing obstacles to the implementation of LCA among SMEs: A collective strategy for exploiting recycled wool. *J. Clean. Prod.*, 156, 923–931. doi:10.1016/j.jclepro.2017.04.101

UEFA, (2016). Social responsibility & sustainability – Post event report, 2016. Quantis International, Lausanne, Switzerland. https://www.uefa.com/MultimediaFiles/Download/OfficialDocument/uefaorg/General/02/42/47/58/2424758_DOWNLOAD.pdf

Vizzotto, F., Testa, F., Iraldo, F., (2021). Towards a sustainability facts panel? Life Cycle Assessment data outperforms simplified communication styles in terms of consumer comprehension. *J. Clean. Prod.*, 323, 129124. doi:10.1016/j.jclepro.2021.129124

6 Climate change and circular economy in football organisations

6.1 Circular economy: a new paradigm

The circular economy is a particularly effective strategy of change in the name of sustainability as it aims to radically review the traditional model of production and consumption. In recent years, the attention of companies and other socio-economic actors on the challenges of sustainability has steadily increased. The main interpretation of the circular economy concept is that, given the effort that is made to extract resources from nature and to transform them into products or services with economic value, it makes no sense to use them only once or, in any case make a limited use of them, but use them as many times as possible in closed cycles. The natural consequence of this approach is that, if the value contained in the resources is used several times, the pressure on virgin raw materials is reduced and the overall environmental impact is reduced. For this reason, the circular economy model is inspired by natural models and natural flows of matter and energy, highlighting the importance of creating cycles of high value and quality materials. This has significant implications for the design of products and services on many of its essential dimensions: on the nature, type and quantity of raw materials needed and on how they are used (efficiency), on business models, on how goods and services are used in the consumption phases, on how they are managed at the end of their life cycles, on logistics, on technological innovation to support the extension of the useful life of products, on their recycling and recovery, etc.

Given the growing interest in the circular economy as a sustainable development strategy to improve the efficient use of resources and the competitiveness of businesses and markets, the circular economy model does not present a stable theoretical construct or a set of homogeneous operational indications (Marrucci et al., 2019). Consequentially, it is interpreted and applied in different ways at different levels (micro, meso, macro) and in different geographical contexts.

This also depends on the fact that the circular economy draws impetus and inspiration from different economic theories and approaches. From environmental and ecological economics to industrial ecology, passing through cradle-to-cradle, performance economy and blue economy, to biomimicry.

DOI: 10.4324/9781003228271-6

Offering a framework composed of principles, objectives, solutions, and rising to a general notion gravitating on the different approaches, it also becomes necessary to read circular economy through the lens of management (Marrucci et al., 2021). In this way, it is possible to provide a more operational approach which is also more usable to various organisations.

Moving from a linear economic model to a circular one also represents a response from some worrying trends which are recorded at the global level. In particular, the volatility of the prices of some resources, the estimates on the availability of some materials and finally the expected three billion new consumers by 2030 that will push the demand for goods and services to unprecedented levels. Dependence on scarce resources exposes organisations to some significant risks such as increased procurement costs, reduced revenues, business continuity, etc. It is clear that the use of resources is closely linked to economic stability. Natural resources, such as biomass, fossil fuels, metals, water, etc., provide the basis for the goods, services and infrastructures that make up our current socio-economic systems. In general, global growth has become increasingly dependent on commodity trading, while price volatility has become a determining factor for trade and production all over the world. The impact of resources then plays an important role in many conflicts and migrations.

The use of these natural resources is one of the main causes of the most urgent impacts on human and planetary well-being. The extraction and processing of natural resources causes more than 90% of the global loss of biodiversity, water stress and more than half of the global greenhouse gas emissions. Additionally, resource use causes waste pollution and emissions, including particulate matter and toxic chemicals.

The connection between the use of materials and climate change is clear and evident. It has been calculated that 62% of global greenhouse gas emissions are released in the extraction, processing and production of products and services. While only 38% are issued in the distribution of products and services. For all these reasons, recycling, resource efficiency and circularity business models have great potential for reducing emissions (Gusmerotti et al., 2020).

A systemic approach for the application of circular strategies could actually be fundamental in the fight against climate change. Decoupling the use of natural resources and the environmental impacts of economic activities from human well-being is an essential element in the transition to a more sustainable future. Decoupling can bring substantial social and environmental benefits, including redressing past environmental damage, while supporting economic growth and human well-being. We speak of relative decoupling, when the use of resources or the pressure on the environment grow at a slower rate than the economic activity that causes it. On the other hand, we speak of absolute decoupling when the use of resources or the pressure on the environment decrease while economic activity continues to grow. In general terms, however, the decoupling of well-being from the use of resources occurs when the service provided or the human satisfaction per unit of use of resources increases. In other words, it allows well-being to increase regardless of the use of resources.

Although the concept of the circular economy is widely used by academics and practitioners, its meaning is still debated. In fact, Yuan et al. (2006) said that there is no commonly accepted definition of circular economy. Initially, the most common explanation was provided by the Ellen MacArthur Foundation (2012) which defined it as

> an industrial system that is restorative or regenerative by intention and design. It replaces the end-of-life concept with restoration, shifts towards the use of renewable energy, eliminates the use of toxic chemicals, which impair reuse, and aims for the elimination of waste through the superior design of materials, products, systems, and, within this, business models.

Kirchherr et al. (2017) analysed more than one hundred definitions in order to obtain a "final" definition, suggesting that circular economy

> is an economic system that replaces the "end-of-life" concept with reducing, alternatively reusing, recycling, and recovering materials in production/distribution and consumption processes. It operates at the micro level (products, companies, consumers), meso level (eco-industrial parks), and macro level (city, region, nation, and beyond), with the aim of accomplishing sustainable development, thus simultaneously creating environmental quality, economic prosperity and social equity, to the benefit of current and future generations. It is enabled by novel business models and responsible consumers.

However, as explained in Korhonen et al. (2018a; 2018b) the notion of circular economy is based on a fragmented collection of ideas derived from a variety of scientific disciplines and research areas. For instance, the concept of circular economy can also be traced to industrial ecology, industrial ecosystem and symbiosis, zero waste and emission, design and resource efficiency and many, many others.

Given the lack of a univocal and recognised definition of circular economy, in order to have a decision-making framework that can have, at the same time, a theoretical and operational nature, the system of principles on which organisations can base circular choices and strategies becomes fundamental. Three principles that have been linked to the circular economy since the beginning of the diffusion of this concept and that have played a prominent role are the so-called 3Rs:

• Reduction: of the consumption of resources, of waste production and of the generation of emissions in the life cycle processes of a product or service;

- Reuse: of waste and products, possibly after repairs (refurbishment or remanufacturing) or directly, wholly or in part, as components of other products;
- Recycling: waste in order to use it as a secondary raw material.

Through the 3Rs approach it is clearly possible to achieve the transition from a linear model (take-make-dispose) to a circular model.

More recently, a specific standard on circular economy has been published by the British Standard, i.e., BS 8001:2017. BS 8001:2017 tries to reconcile the far-reaching ambitions of the circular economy with established business routines. The standard contains a comprehensive list of circular economy terms and definitions, a set of general circular economy principles, a flexible management framework for implementing circular economy strategies in organisations, and a detailed description of economic, environmental, design, marketing and legal issues related to the circular economy (Pauliuk, 2018).

By focusing on principles, the BS 8001:2017 standard has the explicit purpose of facilitating the implementation of the principles of the circular economy in organisations, identifying and defining six of them. Figure 6.1 reports all the principles with a brief explanation.

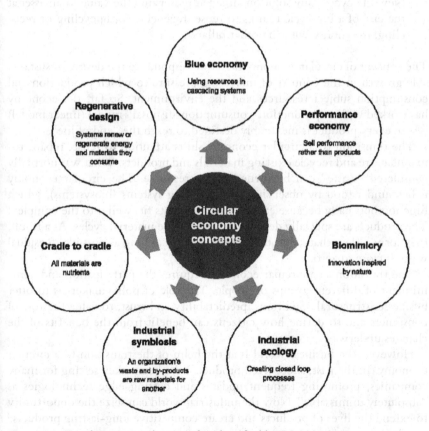

Figure 6.1 Circular economy's principles identified by BS 8001:2017

The circular economy is a strategic ally for sustainable development. Its broader vision is essential to review the approach to addressing the issues of scarcity of resources, global warming and waste management. The circular paradigm is based on five pillars, which can stand individually or in combination with each other:

- Sustainable resources: use renewable energy sources and biodegradable, recyclable or renewable materials;
- Product as a service: a new concept of ownership, with organisations able to offer a single service that can be used by many, rather than the same product replicated for multiple individuals, maximising the utilisation factor and the useful life;
- Sharing platforms: tools for sharing and collaboration between users and owners, to optimise the costs of goods and services and the resources used to produce them;
- Extension of useful life: produce from the beginning to obtain a longer life cycle, providing greater possibilities for updating, repairing and re-manufacturing products;
- New life cycles: any solution aimed at preserving the value of an asset at the end of a life cycle thanks to reuse, regeneration, upcycling or recycling, in synergy with the other pillars.

The concept of circular economy therefore responds to the desire for sustainable growth in the context of increasing pressure to which production and consumption subject resources and the environment. So far, the economy has worked with a "production-consumption-disposal" model (linear model) where every product is inexorably destined to reach the "end of life".

The transition to a circular economy shifts attention to reuse, repair, re-manufacture and recycle existing materials and products. What was normally considered "waste" can be turned into a resource. The circular economy is best understood by observing natural living systems (biosystems), which function optimally because each of their elements fits well into the complex. The products are specially designed to fit into the material cycles. As a result, they form a flow that keeps the added value for as long as possible. Residual waste is close to zero.

The transition to a circular economy requires the participation and commitment of different groups of people. The role of policymakers is to offer businesses structural conditions, predictability and trust, to value the role of consumers and to define how citizens can benefit from the benefits of the changes underway.

However, the business world is at the helm of the transition to a circular economy. In the past, short-lived products have been a key setting for many companies, promoting frequent updates and cutting-edge technologies as "absolutely unmissable". Now the industrial world can seize the opportunity to extend the lives of products and create competitive long-lasting products.

A circular project is the starting point for the development of any new product or service of the circular economy. Greater cooperation within and between supply chains can decrease costs, waste and damage to the environment. Advances in eco-innovation offer new products, processes, technologies and organisational structures. Organisations might discover new markets by moving from selling products to selling services and developing business models based on renting, sharing, repairing, upgrading or recycling individual components. Many business opportunities for SMEs might also arise from this new approach (Marrucci et al., 2022).

Quickly understanding the opportunities of the circular economy and addressing its challenges depends on the widespread support of society (Khan et al., 2020). It is essential to involve NGOs, business and consumer organisations, trade unions, schools and universities, research institutes and other stakeholders at all levels of government. In the transition to a circular economy, these subjects can operate as facilitators, leaders and multipliers. Action is also needed to communicate the ideas and benefits of the circular economy to people in everyday life (in the workplace, in schools, among local communities). Social networks and digital communication media can attract many consumers to new circular products and services.

Making sustainable choices should become easier (more accessible, attractive and affordable) for all consumers. A number of factors affect their decisions, including the behaviour of other people, the way they receive information or advice, or the immediate costs and benefits of their choices.

Now the transition to the circular economy is supported by an increasing number of policies and initiatives. However, specific political, social, economic and technological barriers to wider practical implementation and acceptance still persist:

- Organisations often lack the awareness, knowledge or ability to put circular economy solutions into practice;
- Today's systems, infrastructures, economic models and technology can block the economy in a linear model;
- Investments in efficiency improvement measures or innovative business models remain insufficient, as they are perceived as risky and complex;
- Demand for sustainable products and services may continue to be low, particularly if these involve changes in behaviour;
- Prices often do not reflect the true cost of the use of resources and energy for society;
- The political signals for the transition to a circular economy are not strong and consistent enough.

The circular economy represents a paradigm for decoupling economic growth and the consumption of natural resources. This objective requires the definition of new production models based on a set of actions and strategies aimed at reducing the consumption of resources, improving efficiency and reducing the production of waste. However, although the concept of circular economy is deeply connected to environmental sustainability, as the circular economy represents a strategy for sustainability, they should not be considered as synonyms. Rather, it is necessary to be able to distinguish the specificities of the circular strategy in the framework of sustainable development in order to connote and focus it on specific aspects of the processes, products, services and actions that can be implemented. Although the strategies aimed at sustainable development have areas in common and boundaries that are not always clear, to optimise the synergies and avoid distortions it is good to know how to distinguish circular aspects from purely environmental ones. The aspects of circularity must also be wisely mixed in the management of sustainability in order to avoid trade-offs or unwanted effects, making it even more difficult to achieve and maintain that balance between the various dimensions of sustainable development. From this point of view, according to a holistic, systemic and divided cycle-based approach, the overall effect of a circular choice or a purely environmental and climatic choice must be wisely evaluated and considered.

There can be numerous factors that push an organisation to undertake a circular economy strategy (Khan et al., 2021). Personal and competitive factors are elements capable of pushing companies towards green strategies. An organisation may decide to internalise environmental issues and its daily practices in order to increase internal productivity and thus improve its competitive position. Additionally, a proactive environmental strategy is associated with cost reduction benefits through the adoption of operational actions that increase resource efficiency, productivity and reduce waste. Other initiatives are linked to reducing the environmental impact of products, processes and services in order to differentiate products and services and target environmentally sensitive consumers. These internal motivations, based specifically on economic and competitive aspects, can undoubtedly be traced back to the circular choices.

First of all, it must be considered that the circular economy is based on the concept of resource efficiency which is intrinsically linked to the optimisation in the use of materials and therefore in cost savings. Furthermore, in connection with the issue of economic competitiveness, it is necessary to consider the need and the will of organisations to reduce the risk associated with their supply chain.

It is clear that circular choices based on closed cycles, reuse of resources, extension of the value of resources, renewable resources, regenerative and restorative intentions can contribute to reducing the risks of supplying raw materials. This may happen thanks to the fact that the circular model intends to change the typical assumptions of the procurement and post-consumption phases. In this sense, it is possible to associate the reduction of procurement risks with circular economy choices.

Sometimes organisations pursue environmental protection in order to respond to internal pressures of a more ethical nature even if this limits their profits. The environmental values and attitudes of top managers are an important factor in explaining the environmental proactivity of an organisation. When managers have a high environmental commitment and are aware of the advantages and disadvantages of environmental management tools, they tend to give more importance to environmental issues within organisations.

The external context is generally considered one of the main reasons behind the adoption of a circular environmental strategy. From an environmental point of view, public authorities are the most obvious example of external pressure, as they essentially act on environmental topics by enacting mandatory laws or by providing a clear signal of their support for a specific practice. Another example of external pressures was the decision by organisations to require suppliers to demonstrate that they have an efficient environmental management system or that they can offer products or services with specific environmental attributes. Pressures for the adoption of environmental practices can also be generated by various stakeholders such as shareholders, investors, employees, suppliers, customers, etc. who directly or indirectly intervene in the life of the organisation under various aspects.

To summarise the main drivers of the circular economy, Gusmerotti et al. (2019) pointed out, as a recurring theme, the efficiency of processes which generate cost reduction or in any case maximisation of the use of inputs and their reduced environmental impact (of processes, products and services). Many organisations believe that increasing their efficiency (cost reduction) and customer satisfaction are the main reasons that led them to undertake circular economy actions. A good number of organisations are in any case firmly convinced that the improvement of environmental performance represents the relevant motivation, in part and driven by the need to comply with the laws and in part by acquiring a competitive advantage over competitors. A small number of organisations believe that the adoption of circular economy initiatives has been stimulated by the need to implement corporate values, reduce the risks associated with the supply of raw materials, increase business attractiveness and anticipate future regulatory obligations. On the other hand, very few organisations have adopted circular practices to imitate practices adopted by competitors or to reduce their dependence on raw materials. Another primary theme is the improvement of the corporate image aimed at capturing new customers sensitive to environmental sustainability issues and new market opportunities. Of particular interest is the issue of the circular economy also as an opportunity for organisational growth at the level of available knowledge and organisational models. The issue of collaboration is also central through the opportunity to create new partnerships. The circular economy is also seen as a chance to strengthen and improve its distinctiveness and competitiveness. On the other hand, there is very little input deriving from the regulatory and incentive aspects, which usually represent recurring drivers for the sustainability of organisations. The internal drivers also clearly emerge, of an economic and competitive nature, but also of values and ethics. The drivers related to regulation are considered important in general but there is no specific pressure deriving from a current regulatory framework in the field of circular economy. It should be noted the lack of awareness about the supply risks and about the dependence on virgin raw materials, which, evidently, are not yet considered real drivers.

6.2 Rethinking football business models in a circular way

The *take-make-dispose* economic model, based on the use of inputs deriving from natural and traditional resources and materials available in unlimited quantities, has been the predominant model for centuries. However, in recent decades there has been an unprecedented growth in the demand for these resources, the supply of which has proved to be subject to significant limits. This has called into question for the first time the current economic system, based on a linear approach. The concept of circular economy began to develop in response to the crisis of the traditional model, due to the need to deal with the limited resources used by the economic system. The circular economy is an economy designed to be restorative and regenerative by design and intention. The materials of biological origin are designed to re-enter the biosphere, while the materials of technical origin are designed to circulate within a flow that foresees the minimum loss of quality. The circular economy is based on renewable energy sources, aimed at minimising the use of inputs, tracking and eliminating the use of toxic chemicals that make it difficult to recover and recycle products at the end of their life and drastically reduce waste production through careful planning and design.

Until the early 2000s, however, the economic system spontaneously followed another pattern of development: the abundance of resources determined the affirmation of the model based on linearity. Today, however, there are many critical elements, supported by various global trends, which are calling into question the inescapability of the current linear system. The prices of goods traditionally considered commodities (including natural resources) have undergone and continue to undergo a significant increase in their cost. Experts have estimated that vital elements for industry such as critical raw materials could run out in a very short time, unless the industry rethinks how they are used and exploited. Three billion new consumers are also expected by 2030, which will push the demand for goods and services to unprecedented levels. The dependence on scarce resources exposes organisations to some significant risks, such as increased costs, reduced revenues connected with greater uncertainty of the same, and also the risk of brand reputation.

Maintaining the linear model of resources exploitation, according to a "business as usual" logic, would mean confronting a constantly bigger price volatility and a probable inflation of fundamental commodity goods, in particular of raw materials and natural resources. It is estimated that the increase in the cost of resource extraction will have an even greater impact on business than the future reduction in resource availability. In light of these trends, on the one hand, many organisations are starting insuring against these risks and, at the same time, changing the industrial model in order to make growth and profits less dependent on those resources that are becoming increasingly scarce. On the other hand, policymakers are also setting themselves a paradigm shift, aiming to transform the linearity of production systems into circularity. However, the ideal model of the circular economy does not reflect today's reality in the production, consumption and, above all, waste recovery and valorisation system. First of all, in every phase of the circular model, significant quantities of waste and scraps are still produced today, in relation to the number of materials used during the same phase. Although there are therefore initiatives aimed at pursuing circularity, the current situation is still far from the "closure of the cycle", or rather the possibility of using, recovering or really recycling everything that would be discarded. Thus, on the one hand, the quantities of raw materials used are still very consistent and growing. While, on the other hand, the recovery capacity is still undeniably limited.

By focusing on the different phases of the ideal circular economy model, it is possible to identify the main causes behind what are defined as losses, i.e., all those points in the cycle in which there is no closure, but rather a loss of efficiency through the spill from the production or consumption system of materials or energy that is still potentially useful and exploitable. The causes that generate the efficiency losses in terms of non-valorisation of waste are many and can concern all the actors involved in various management phases of the material flows that pass through the various steps of the life cycle of the products and services that are on the market:

- *Information asymmetries.* In many cases, consumers and producers have little or no knowledge of the environmental impacts caused by a product or service, as well as of the related external costs inflicted on the community.
- *Business priorities.* Traditionally the emphasis from corporate strategies is placed on very short-term targets and not on broader objectives such as improving environmental performance.
- *Market barriers.* Production sectors and markets suffer from a strong distortion in the price of products, which is unable to reflect the costs associated with the environmental impact of the production chains from which they originate. It thus happens that the organisations that pollute the most sustain lower fixed and variable costs (loading the environmental ones on the community) since they do not invest in innovation, thus being able to set lower prices for their products/services. In the absence of corrective measures, this guarantees them better competitive performance, especially in a recessive economic phase like the current one, in which price competition is extremely important for a consumer who is more attentive to the convenience of the products he buys.
- *Habit and culture.* Shopping habits and consumer culture undoubtedly have a great weight in determining the possibilities of recovering the

material to produce recycled products that will be successful in the market. Today the recovery of secondary raw materials is held back by the difficulty of getting the final consumer to accept products with a lower performance than more conventional competing products.

- *Geography and infrastructural development.* The great distances and the extension of the geographical boundaries due to the ever-increasing globalisation impede and hinder the application of the so-called reverse logistic, which presupposes the management of the movement of products backwards in the supply chain, from the final destination to the initial producer or a new subject in the chain in order to recover the returns or dispose of the product correctly.
- *Technology.* There can be issues with the rate of innovation and replacement of technologies, often capable of inhibiting the development of solutions that can allow a high recovery rate of secondary raw materials.
- *Regulation.* It is not uncommon that regulatory nature limitations are also imposed, making it difficult to close cycles and therefore the circularity of industry processes.

The described barriers generate forces that distract potential resources from the system and, in particular, business strategies from the circular model. These forces derive from a series of cultural, technological, institutional, market, etc. inactions. It is these inactions that have continued to push the economic system on to the tracks of the linear system. If there are barriers that make it too expensive, demanding or even impossible to introduce innovations inspired by circularity from a technical, regulatory and/or financial point of view, it is clear that the system will not spontaneously change its evolutionary direction. Only by overcoming these barriers will it be possible to achieve the circularity of the economy. If the barriers are too high, the inactions continue, inhibiting the spontaneous development of circular economy practices. The reality of recent years has shown that in many cases it is possible to overcome the barriers by adopting business models inspired by circular economy principles, which, moreover, have been also found to be successful under a competitive profile. Many experiences have shown that this is possible thanks to the activation of internal organisational factors that allow the overcoming of barriers, acting as a driver, able to push the organisation itself, and, often, to encourage other actors of the supply chain towards the closure of the cycle.

It is possible for organisations to spontaneously develop effective solutions in terms of circular business models, thanks, above all, to the motivational drivers and strategic choices that arise from the action of internal circular factors within the company. Moreover, these factors often require collaboration with other actors in the supply chain who are interested in obtaining a target in terms of valorising resources and materials and therefore closing cycles. Among the factors that stimulate the birth of these circular business models, some are particularly effective. In particular, entrepreneurial spirit deriving from a management sensitive to environmental issues; creation of synergies and savings thanks to a greater cooperation between the various actors operating along the supply chain; exploration of new market opportunities; identification of competitive challenges deriving from the scarcity of a resource/raw material, or the risks associated with its rising prices or supply difficulties.

A business model represents a set of strategic decisions that establish how organisations create, transfer and acquire value based on their internal activities and their relationships with stakeholders. The business model represents for organisations a driving force of competitiveness that contributes to the definition of their position in the market with respect to the competitors.

The design of the business model is therefore a strategic priority for organisations. The new circular economy paradigm requires organisations to adapt their business model or create a new one. The business models of the circular economy are united by some traits that characterise them in the form of management styles, innovative approaches, cooperative actions or operational solutions. In the process of developing these models, the adoption of typical actions of the circular economy such as reverse logistics, the assessment of the durability of products, redistribution, reuse, remanufacturing and recycling are added or replaced to the more typical entrepreneurial activities, requiring new technologies and skills.

The value proposition of organisations in a circular economic model can also be based on product service systems, thus offering products with less physical content, which do not foresee ownership by customers, with respect to which customers can take advantage of multiple services. It is a functional business model, that involves switching to pay-per-use approach, in which customers pay for a use they can derive from the products or services or to obtain certain results. Another element of interest is the need to cooperate not only with the players in the supply chain, but also with customers, i.e., a system based on the acquisition of a set of services rather than ownership of the asset.

Different approaches to the circularity of organisations can be identified according to the different approach adopted by the organisations in terms of integration of circular principles and the consequent benefits that the organisations can achieve (Gusmerotti et al., 2020).

Market-driven. Organisations that adopt a pricing scheme or marketing campaigns based on the use and reuse of products, but in which internal practices and product design procedures do not seem to reflect an authenticity in the circular approach. It is a model where organisations focus on market acceptance of the pay-per-use model, without modifying aspects related to product design, internal activities or suppliers. In this case, the focus is on revenue and the benefit of market penetration.

Efficiency-driven. Organisations that put circular principles as a starting point for the planning and development of activities which are effectively based on the relationships with suppliers, but which do not focus on the creation of a circular economic model visible to their final customers, either on price or in marketing campaigns. In this case, the attention of the organisations is upstream, or rather on the cost structure, and their advantage is linked to efficiency.

Circular embeddedness. Circular organisations both internally and externally. In particular, this type of organisation not only manages the production system according to the principles of the circular economy, but also the involvement of suppliers in its circular production system. Moreover, the communication to customers is focused on the implementation of circular practices.

This classification allows us to understand how the approaches to the circular economy and its drivers can be different. There may be market-driven approaches, that is guided by enhancing the adoption of circular practices towards the consumer. Efficiency-driven approaches, which aim at improving efficiency and containing costs. Lastly, more holistic approaches that include the integration of circular economy principles in all phases of the organisation.

Several studies have focused on the link between the strategies and constitutive actions of circular business models and the fundamental principles of the new paradigm. In particular, organisations and scholars focused on controlling the balance between limited stocks and flows of renewable resources; encourage the use of recycled materials, components and products; minimise the negative externalities of consumption production systems by applying new business models. According to Gusmerotti et al. (2020) the main examples of circular business models are:

- *Regenerate.* This model focuses on the transition to renewable energies and materials, e.g., the valorisation of organic waste into energy sources or raw materials for other chains.
- *Share.* This model is based on a sharing economy perspective in which people share goods and assets. Therefore, the property loses its importance. Products are designed to last longer, and maintenance focuses on facilitating the reuse of the products and extending their useful life. Co-ordination between people is clearly necessary for the feasibility of the model.
- *Optimisation.* This model is heavily based on technological development. Organisations use digital manufacturing technologies, big data and remote control to reduce waste in production systems along supply chains.
- *Loop.* This model uses biological and technical cycles. Collaboration and coordination along supply chains are essential to close loops and convert waste and useful resources.

- *Virtualisation.* This model is very focused on services. Organisations that follow this approach tend to replace physical products with virtual and dematerialised products, while increasing customer satisfaction.
- *Exchange.* This model includes the transformation of obsolete and non-renewable goods into more advanced and renewable goods.

In addition to these main business models, scholars and technicians have identified many alternative forms of circular development. It is therefore a question of analysing your own scenario in order to identify the best solution and the best business model for your organisation.

Lastly, according to the BS 8001:2017, these are the main circular economy business models that can be adopted by an organisation as shown in Table 6.1.

More recently, UEFA teamed up with partners to champion circular economy practices at the UEFA Champions League final 2022 hosted in Paris. UEFA and PepsiCo tested several food and beverage circular economy practices with the aim of transitioning to zero waste by 2026. In particular, they tested:

- Menu boards with environmental labels;
- Reusable EcoCups to provide 100% of the cups for spectators;
- PepsiCo PET bottles made with 25–100% recycled PET (rPET);
- Draft dispensers to provide most of the beer;
- PepsiCo hospitality areas to reuse glasses for future events;
- Aluminium cans and glass bottles separation and recycling procedures;
- PepsiCo LED boards to embed "Please Recycle" messaging;
- Uneaten sandwiches and desserts to be donated to local charity;
- Unused food that cannot be donated to be collected and used for methanisation;
- Water fountains installed in the UEFA offices removing need for bottled water.

The circular economy practices centred around the "4Rs framework" (reduce, reuse, recycle, recover) – outlined in UEFA's sustainability strategy – to collect data which can then define a baseline for improvement action. This will then ultimately contribute to the future publication of UEFA's Guidelines for Circular Economy in food and beverages at football matches. The number of practices implemented will increase at every subsequent UEFA Champions League final until reaching the objective of zero waste to landfill. The implementation is part of the F&B Circularity Project, a collaboration between UEFA and PepsiCo, which aims to support the UEFA Champions League's transition to circular food and beverage practices and has involved ten clubs participating in this season's competition. Utilising data gathering and stakeholder consultation to help update guidelines, the project has been rolled out on a pan-European basis, with the likes of Benfica, Inter,

Table 6.1 Overview of circular economy business models

Circular economy business models	Brief description	Examples
ON DEMAND		
Produce on demand (Made to order)	Producing a product or providing a service only when consumer demand has been quantified and confirmed. Minimises raw material demand and avoids over-stocking.	Airplanes are only manufactured once ordered. Other items are produced based on user/customer votes (e.g., most popular T-shirt designs are made available for sale).
DEMATERIALISATION		
Digitisation	Replacing physical infrastructure and assets with digital/virtual services. This offers advantages over tangible products, but without reducing the perceived value to the customer.	Move from physical video/DVD stores to online film and music services etc., digital as opposed to camera film or vinyl records.
PRODUCT LIFE CYCLE EXTENSION/REUSE		
Product life cycle extension	New products are designed to be durable for a long lifetime.	Leading high-grade German washing machines.
Facilitated reuse	Reuse with or without any repair/upgrade and supplied either free of charge (FOC) or resold.	FOC: furniture reuse networks. Resold: online auction and for sale websites.
Product modular design	Design product to be modular so that components are updated, but not the whole item.	Modular construction or mobile phones.
REMANUFACTURE AND MANUFACTURE WITH SECONDARY MATERIALS		
Refurbish, remanufacture and recondition	Product gets a next life after remanufacturing – the process of restoring the product or part functionality to "as-new" quality; facilitated by design for disassembly. Enables the producer to put the products back into the market to earn a second or subsequent income from a second or subsequent user.	Remanufactured products, parts and components provided with "as-new" performance and reliability at a reduced cost compared with new. Major Japanese car manufacturer offering genuine exchange parts remanufactured from returned used parts which are inspected and rebuilt to meet the same quality standards and performance as new and carry the same warranty.

Manufacture by secondary material (value optimisation) including recycling	Creating products through secondary materials from recovered waste.	Plastic bottles recycled into fleece jackets, fishing nets used in carpet manufacture, or reclaimed timber used to make furniture.
Incentivised return	Incentivises customers to return used/unwanted items back to the producer via a convenient system. Producer then either recycles materials or remanufactures the product. Incentive usually in the form of a discount offered on a new product for surrendering the old one.	Financial or alternative incentive offered for the return of used or unwanted electrical items.
PRODUCT AS A SERVICE/PRODUCT SERVICE SYSTEMS (PSS)		
Lease agreement	Leasing access to and not selling ownership of a product/service. This can be on a B2B or B2C basis. In general, an "operating lease" model is likely to be best suited for PSS models in the context of a circular economy as ownership of the asset is retained by the lessor and can be combined with service or performance-based business models. The lessee's capital outlay is typically lower when compared to outright purchase when taking depreciation, maintenance and disposal/replacement costs into account. The lessor typically benefits from higher overall profitability during the lease period and retains ownership.	Lease agreements on power tools, TVs and DVD players etc. over say a 6–12 month contract.
Performance based (Pay for Success)	Company delivers product performance or defined results rather than the product/service itself. The customer purchases a defined level of performance, where the company's primary revenue stream comes from payments for performance delivered or demand-fulfilment. Ownership remains with the operating company.	Leasing a washing machine for 1000 washing cycles or providing a pick-up and delivery laundry service.

(Continued)

Circular economy business models	Brief description	Examples
SHARING ECONOMY AND COLLABORATIVE CONSUMPTION		
Peer to Peer (P2P) lending	P2P lending of products/services, mainly between members of the public or between businesses, but where no direct financial transaction occurs, or income is secured. More socially driven, rather than commercial, where access might strengthen community relationships. For B2B lending, business benefits might include reduced costs over directly sourcing the products/services concerned.	More traditionally dependent on the participation and generosity of community members to share their goods/services. Increasing interest in community-based lending of skills/know-how. Facilitates the sharing of overcapacity or underutilisation (e.g., electric drills or lawnmowers, cars or apartments, etc.)
Sharing platforms/ resources	Shared access or "collaborative consumption" amongst users, either individuals or organisations, but where some form of transactional arrangement (which could be financial) is provided. Enable increased utilisation rate of products and services by making possible shared use/ownership among consumers. Enabling customers to access a product, rather than owning it outright, and use it only as needed.	Renting out private parking spaces; shared ownership of products (e.g., pressure washer purchased between several neighbours). Bike-sharing systems in cities (e.g, self-service cycle hires schemes in London and Paris, etc.). This system can also be viewed as a lease agreement given that the user has to take out a subscription. The main difference is that the per cycle hire retention period is typically very short (e.g., same day) and payment is not reoccurring.

Dortmund, Porto, Milan, Man City, Juventus and Leipzig all taking part. It has already led to the creation of a best practices database with international institutions, the formation of a clubs' consultation group to share knowledge and discuss common challenges, and a feasibility analysis of practical implementation of practices at two pilot stadiums. This project aligns with UEFA's Circular Economy Policy which, by 2030, aims to embed the 4Rs approach in all operations to minimise the impact of football on the environment and drive resource efficiency and cost savings. UEFA also aims at achieving zero plastic waste and food waste – within UEFA, across UEFA events and collaboratively across European football – by 2030.

UEFA catalyses circular economy solutions together with partners and stadiums/event venues, with a particular focus on product packaging, plastics, single-use items, food loss and waste. Furthermore, it integrates circularity criteria in the UEFA Stadium Infrastructure Regulations as well as in UEFA campus facility management. The organisation also creates and continuously updates a repository of best practices targeting football, capturing innovations and lessons learned across member associations, leagues and clubs.

UEFA launched its Circular Economy Guidelines as part of UEFA's Football Sustainability Strategy 2030. The guidelines include three sections: an introduction to the circular economy concept and the 4R framework; best practice and factsheets in the food and beverage domain from various football stakeholders (created with the support of UEFA's commercial partner PepsiCo); and an outlook into forthcoming circular economy focus areas – energy and water, apparel and football equipment, and event materials (signage, brand production and furniture, and IT equipment). The guidelines provide simple, practical and essential information on key aspects of the circular economy. It is a tool that will help national associations, event organisers, clubs and other football stakeholders navigate this complex subject and start the journey towards zero plastic and food waste (to landfill) football matches by 2030.

All these efforts can be connected to the European Strategy for Plastics in a Circular Economy. Our society, economy and environment are all negatively affected by the way plastics are currently designed, produced, used and discarded. The amount of plastic litter is growing, hurting marine ecosystems, biodiversity and potentially human health. The strategy pursues an ambitious approach for plastic packaging recyclability and contains a strong response on microplastics which are a significant source of marine pollution. Football is not exempt from single-use plastic products, especially, but not only, in the food and beverages area, e.g., cotton bud sticks, cutlery, plates, straws and stirrers, balloons and sticks for balloons, food containers, cups for beverages, beverage containers, cigarette butts, plastic bags, packets and wrappers, wet wipes and sanitary items. Where sustainable alternatives are easily available and affordable, football organisations should start moving away from single-use plastic. Other activities that may be carried out are: reducing consumption through awareness-raising measures, introducing design requirements in the procurement phase, introducing labelling requirements – to inform consumers about the plastic content of products, disposal options that are to be avoided, and harm done to nature if the products are littered in the environment – and introducing waste management and clean-up obligations for catering services and other users of single-use plastic products.

Below you can find some examples of circular best practices related to the football world divided according to the circular economy phases.

PROCUREMENT

Water. Day after day there is a high consumption of water in flushing, baths, clothes washing and diverse washes. Since these operations do not require the use of potable water, the recovery of rainwater for these operations is increasingly seen as a key point in the strategy to combat water lack. Compact stormwater systems allow the treatment and storage of rainwater and grey water in order to allow their reuse in conditions of total efficiency and hydraulic-sanitary safety. Rainwater and grey water after treatment can be reused in the following ways:

- Washing of floors and/or stadium benches after each game or at cleaning times;
- Discharge of flushing;
- Irrigation of turf area.

To complement, it will be of interest to use:

- Flow reducers on all faucets and showers in the stadium;
- Install shuffling with double discharges;
- Flow reducers in compressors used for cleaning the stadium.

Materials. From this point of view, since stadiums' managers always have to substitute a significant number of damaged seats after each match, it would be the case to look for seats made from recycled materials instead of virgin plastic ones. It would be great if they were made with the PET bottle collected thanks to the stadium's waste management system.

Energy. Environmentally proactive stadia can decide to move ahead of energy efficiency and directly generate green energy, such as solar energy. Sports facilities frequently offer sufficient space for installing photovoltaic panels – whether on roofs or in the immediate vicinity of the stadium. It is important to note that photovoltaic plants are not only of interest for new buildings, but they can also be retrofitted to existing sports facilities. The energy generated is usually not directly supplied to the sports facility, but is fed into the power supply network. Installing solar or wind power plants allows reducing energy costs, while reducing climate-altering emissions.

DESIGN

Speaking of the circularity concept of durability, the example of temporary structures and installations could easily fall under this reuse principle. Large sport events usually use a large number of temporary structures and installations, such as tents, containers, barriers, stands, that are built within and aside venues for operational needs. Smart design choices also allow efficient use of existing materials, including modular structures, to reduce the amount of customised manufacture. These temporary facilities include tents for catering and medical aid, restaurant and sanitary facilities, media centres and offices, terraces and stands. Temporary facilities are always very important, since most activities – such as catering, shows, games and exhibitions – take place in the area surrounding the actual sporting event. Even a complete sports facility can be erected as a temporary construction. Low-waste and resource-saving construction methods are therefore of particular importance in this area.

PRODUCTION

Lighting constitutes a relevant energy-intensive activity in stadium management. However, it offers several smart and economically efficient opportunities for improvement based on the adoption of energy-saving and cost-efficient technologies. First, the adoption of energy-saving light bulbs, such as LED or fluorescent lights, as a replacement for more energy-intensive incandescent or halogen light bulbs, produces relevant energy savings. Besides adopting LED lights, which are considered particularly efficient in the case of field lighting, efficiency could be improved by adopting a modular regulation system for floodlights, which allows regulating the intensity of floodlighting according to a specific timing or demand, in order to avoid lighting the pitch at full capacity when not necessary.

DISTRIBUTION

The transportation between venues of the sporting event can be transformed into a more environmentally sustainable service by operating environmentally friendly vehicle fleets. This best practice aims to transform all vehicles employed during the staging of a sporting event, especially VIP and staff vehicles, into environmentally friendly transportation. For example, organisers may plan to use fuel-cell vehicles and hybrid vehicles to reduce the impact that VIP and staff transportation as well as fans' mobility from the venues may have on the event's carbon footprint. The organisation of environmentally friendly vehicles requires planning during the preparatory phase of the event as well as during the actual staging of the event. Overall, it requires strong cooperation between the event organisers and the sponsors, which are usually the main providers of VIP transportation.

CONSUMPTION

Football events require reusable cups to be provided to the visitors. The advantages of a reusable cup system are plain for all to see. Provided there is an adequate collection and cleaning system, one cup can be used several times at one event. The concept is adding an extra step of logistics to the event management since reusable cups must be returned washed after use. However, it adds several benefits including lower CO_2 emissions, higher user satisfaction, less cleaning and a potential economic benefit.

RECYCLING

The waste generated in the stadium can easily be aggregated to that generated in households and commerce. In football events, food waste represents an important kind of waste, thus, a system of separate waste collection has to be set up both in the common areas open to the public and in the technical areas reserved for staff and service providers.

The choice of the different waste fraction to collect separately should be taken considering:

- The local waste management's regular practices (which are the fractions that are normally collected separately in that municipality) and the local waste facilities;
- The type of waste that is normally produced in every specific venue's areas (e.g., food waste in restaurant and kiosks in the immediate vicinity of the stadium before the matches, special waste in the infirmary etc.).

In order to set up an efficient waste management collection system during football events, it is necessary to engage different actors like the event organiser, venue and stadium authorities, site owners and host cities, hospitality services and licensed souvenir providers, commercial partners, concessions stand operators, cleaning service providers, waste management operators, hotels, sponsors, other partners and organisations, etc. The bottom line is that the stadium needs to develop a separate collection scheme as similar (if not same) to the one deployed by the local authority in order to facilitate the collection and treatment afterwards. There are cases where a certain local or regional authority had good separate collection performances, but these good results are missing in football games. Football games, given the number of people attending them and the amount of waste can easily improve the overall local waste management performance.

All teams committed to pack up all such concession food on game nights for redistribution to local shelters and other places that serve people in need (distributed to charities working with people living in conditions of poverty). Several tons of food are diverted from landfills and incinerators and it can reduce greenhouse gas emissions through this initiative.

6.3 Measuring the circularity of football organisations and events

The measurement of circularity represents an essential requirement for the implementation of the transition path from a take-make-dispose economic model to a model having the circular economy as a reference paradigm. It is based on the monitoring of physical and economic aspects of the examined systems (e.g., organisations, supply chains, sectors, etc.) in order to acquire useful information to identify areas for improvement and establish new priorities. In this context, it therefore becomes necessary to define precise references to measure the level of circular economy. These references should be standardisable, verifiable and, above all, replicable despite the specificity of the activities to be monitored. To date, there is no single and universal measurement approach that allows organisations to adequately grasp the complexity and multiple aspects involved in the path towards the circular economy. The monitoring of indicators relevant for circularity helps to stimulate performance at the level of organisation, sector and socio-economic system.

Indicators are defined as "values derived from parameters capable of providing synthetic information relating to a specific phenomenon" (Marrucci and Daddi, 2022). Indicators are recognised as having a series of advantages and benefits, such as the ability to condense dynamic and complex phenomena into manageable and meaningful forms, the ability to be communicative on topics of interest, the ability to indicate whether a given target can be reached or not. They can also be used as managerial and support tools, as well as helping to support the decision-making process.

With regard to the measurement of the circular economy, it should be added that the indicators can constitute, thanks to their different potential uses, a real springboard towards the adoption of more circular practices. They can in fact be used as performance indicators (Key Performance Indicators – KPIs), helping organisations to define their own internal and external benchmarks. Indicators can be also used to provide information for product or service labels in order to guide the consumer in their choices. Furthermore, they can become the foundations on which developing changes in the organisational structure or favour the exchange of information between the actors belonging to the same supply chain.

The development of specific tools for measuring the circular economy starts from understanding what are the requirements and aspects that make a circular process. Moreover, it is also crucial to have the knowledge of which actions can be undertaken or not by a specific organisation so that its own processes and peculiar activities can become in all respects circular. The starting point is represented by the identification of which are the phases of a given process affected by the paradigm of the circular economy.

Many authors agree in identifying the following six phases as part of the circular economy: procurement, design, production, distribution, use and of end-of-life management. These phases represent the processes whose performances, once measured, can give a vision of how much of a given system is circular. Circularity, in turn, can be implemented by working on each of the aforementioned phrases by adopting actions to maximise circularity.

In order for a process to be classified as circular it must meet at least one of the following requirements:

*   Reduction of natural resources consumption: the main objective is the reduction of the exploitation of limited stocks of natural resources through the efficient use of resources, water and energy;
*   Reduction of the emission level;
*   Reuse, recovery and recycling of materials and products: the objectives are to prevent the production of waste, minimise incineration and disposal in landfills and reduce the loss of materials and energy;
*   Implementation of the use of renewable and recyclable resources: reduction of the use of non-renewable natural resources in favour of renewable and more sustainable ones;
*   Implementation of product durability: extension of the average life of products, moving to new models of the *use-oriented* type, such as leasing or pooling, encouraging and favouring the reuse of products and their components, using more and more recyclable material.

Similar aspects, therefore, represent dimensions that must be measured and which the development of specific indicators for the circular economy must take into account.

As part of research activities and experimental projects in the field of the circular economy conducted in recent years with organisations in various sectoral and territorial contexts, the authors, together with other researchers[1] of the Institute of Management of the Sant'Anna School of Advanced Studies, have developed a tool aimed at measuring the levels of circularity of processes, products and services, with the aim of supporting both activities of engagement and that of real circular economy management.

The tool for measuring circularity builds a list of questions broken down for each stage of the production of goods and services: procurement, design, production, distribution, use and end-of-life management. Each of these questions provides for a type of qualitative-quantitative response, to be expressed through the use of specific values, percentages or on a scale.

The indicators that are part of the tool are focused on actions that are, at the same time, circular flagships, emerging from best practices of various types and circularity hotspots, emerging from previous studies; belonging to different phases of the cycle of production and consumption of goods and services, with particular reference to the organisational dimension.

Below, for each phase, some examples of indicators belonging to the circular economy measurement tool are reported.

For the procurement phase, the indicators were defined to map the role of secondary raw materials in the set of incoming inputs in the process/product and the adoption of sustainable energy supply systems. We also considered possible actions to minimise packaging, an essential aspect in terms of reducing the use of resources. From a managerial point of view, the ordering/purchasing systems and the optimisation of routes by suppliers have been included in the measurement process, as they are capable of measuring the ability of an organisation to reduce waste, on the one hand and to reduce overall its environmental impact on the other.

A set of questions was defined for the design phase, aimed at understanding whether the organisation has adopted any standards for sustainable design taking into account compliance with the circular economy criteria.

For the production phase the questions include the efficient management of resources, both in the technological dimension and the organisations' ability to better manage energy and water resources, for example by creating closed cycles for these critical resources.

Table 6.2 Some examples of measures for the procurement phase.

PROCUREMENT
Use of recycled raw materials (or semi-finished products) Adoption of systems to optimise the ordering/purchasing process to avoid waste Request for optimisation of routes for the procurement of raw materials Minimisation of raw material packaging required Supply from renewable sources

Source: Gusmerotti et al. (2020)

Table 6.3 Some examples of measures for the design phase.

DESIGN
Adoption of guidelines and references for the eco-compatible design of products / services / events that include indications concerning "circularity" Realisation of LCA studies for the assessment of environmental impacts Design choices that aim to prefer secondary raw materials Design choices that aim to facilitate reuse

Source: Gusmerotti et al. (2020)

Table 6.4 Some examples of measures for the production phase.

PRODUCTION
Adoption of management methods / technologies / tools for the most efficient use of raw materials (excluding energy and water) Reuse of waste in the process Water reuse Implementation of interventions for the energy efficiency of the process Chemicals reduction

Source: Gusmerotti et al. (2020)

For the distribution phase, particular attention is given to the average distance travelled for the supply in order to assess whether the organisation has adopted a distribution design aimed at reducing the impact of the transport phases and being able to support local supply chains. For the transport phase, the tool also takes into account the adoption of forms of sustainable mobility, considered as a crucial practice of the circular economy, and the optimisation of transport.

For the use phase, the measurement tool of circularity includes questions about the information kit provided to the consumer in order to adopt suitable practices for sustainable use.

As regards the end-of-life phase and, specifically, the management of waste, it aims to investigate the capacity of the organisation to manage its waste with the aim of recovering material (recycling); the ability to prevent their production, in particular with respect to the flow of packaging; and the adoption of peculiar schemes of the circular economy, such as, in this case, the take back of products/components with the purpose to ensure the maintenance of the value of the same over time, in the same or in other production cycles.

Table 6.5 Some examples of measures for the distribution phase.

DISTRIBUTION
For its vehicle fleet, preference for rented/purchased vehicles meeting circularity criteria (e.g., vehicles powered by second/third generation biofuels, vehicles with a lower environmental impact (e.g., Euro 5 or 6 Vs. Euro 3; vehicles powered by LNG) and/or means for which there are specifications on the presence of secondary raw materials Optimisation of routes and loads Predilection for sustainable mobility (e.g., train versus plane)

Source: Gusmerotti et al. (2020)

Table 6.6 Some examples of measures for the use phase.

USE
Implementation of awareness / information campaigns aimed at promoting circular economy objectives Information to the user of the best ways to use products / services

Source: Gusmerotti et al. (2020)

Table 6.7 Some examples of measures for the end-of-life phase.

END-OF-LIFE
Recovery of material from waste Separate waste collection Adoption of product withdrawal schemes at the end of life, in order to reuse parts or components that still have value Adoption of solutions to minimise the presence of pollutants

Source: Gusmerotti et al. (2020)

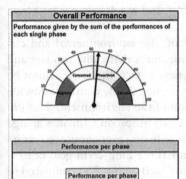

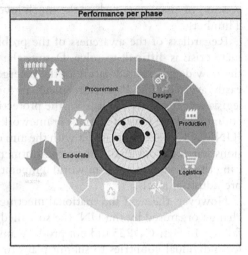

Figure 6.2 Graphical representation of the results obtained thanks to the Circularity tool. Source: Gusmerotti et al. (2020)

Figure 6.2 shows how collected information is returned thanks to the application of the tool.

The first information that is returned is related to the type of approach to the circular economy that the organisation has, considering four main profiles on a scale from 0 to 100: beginner, concerned, proactivist and circular.

The first category includes organisations that have a relatively low circularity performance. The category "concerned" considers the organisations that have evidently embarked on a path of maximisation of circularity, not yet fully mature. The last two categories represent the more mature organisations in which circularity is an integral part of strategies and business value, both in the proactivist and in the circular species, so obviously the results achieved by the organisation are unquestionably high.

A measure of the circularity performance for each phase is also provided, considering the results of the different phases related to the above categories. This makes clearer to organizations which steps require additional reflection and action.

6.4 Climate change: the challenge of this era

In recent times, there has been nothing but talk about the environmental emergency and global warming whose imminence, in terms of climatic cataclysms that are now visibly taking place, has caught us a little off guard. After decades of warnings from scientists all over the world, now we try to run for cover, messing up laws and directives, before reaching the terribly imminent point of no return. However, the constant ineffectiveness of every attempt to remedy has awakened public opinion, also thanks to the intervention of characters such as the much loved – and much criticised – Greta Thunberg.

Regardless of the awareness of the problem, the environmental and climate crisis is difficult to solve. Despite the measures that came too late and the now deeply rooted nature of the emergency, in fact, the crisis cannot be easily averted. The Paris Agreement, in force since 2015, is the worldwide legislation currently in place for the protection of the environment. The 196 countries of the United Nations Framework Convention on Climate Change (UNFCCC) have stipulated it with the aim of reducing greenhouse gas emissions starting from 2020. Their commitment has the long-term goal of limiting the average increase in world temperature well below 2°C compared to preindustrial levels.

However, the next international meeting, the 25th conference on climate change organised by the UN, the so-called COP25, was considered to be a failure. In fact, COP25 did not produce anything binding on the obligation for individual countries to submit plans to further reduce their greenhouse gas emissions, necessary to achieve the goals set by the Paris Agreement in 2015.

The surprise that the imminent alarm caused was indicative of the lack of knowledge of the origin of the problem. The first international measures to stem it date back to the 1990s, when people began to think that the extreme industrialisation faced during the century had led to relevant consequences. In reality, however, pollution as we understand it today has more distant origins in time and dates back to the Industrial Revolution.

The advent of modern industries, transport that uses fossil fuels and the need for a more efficient and faster life have generated the phenomenon we are still dealing with now. Not surprisingly, the origin of the term smog dates back to the nineteenth century, when large cities began to be submerged by new mists of smoke. A multitude of innovations radically changed peoples' way of living and with it their relationship with the environment.

Only from the second half of the 1960s onwards we can see the first change in the attitude of industrial organisations to the way they interacted with the environment. We can pinpoint the birth of the first green practices by companies to this period.

In the early 1970s the economic and social effects of environmental degradation, caused by the unsustainable use of natural resources and as a consequence of industrial activity, began to exert a pressure on industry to improve its performance. The combined influence of public and community opinion, environmental pressure groups, "green" political parties, and the media, (at local, national and global level) targeted policymakers and brought forth a regulatory regime which demanded high levels of compliance of the large industrial organisations.

The major environmental catastrophes which occurred during the 1980s served to strengthen the public belief that most environmental problems were connected with the activities of large organisations While during the 1990s, the public concern about SMEs' contribution to the deterioration of the environment also rapidly increased.

From the year 2000 onwards, the possibility of combining competitive advantages and eco-efficiency became more evident in businesses. Environmental aspects became an integral part of corporate strategy and a factor to be taken into consideration in all corporate functions. Integration occurred both on a strategic and operative level and the environment became an almost moral obligation for business owners and was demanded by external stakeholders as well.

However, companies are not always able to develop a corporate vision in which environmental and economic aspects are integrated. This condition causes a decoupling between the actual environmental performance and the external image of the company. In these circumstances, the economic benefits are only short term, linked to a temporary improvement in the corporate reputation, while the environmental actions are only superficial and mainly linked to communication activities.

Yet, although global warming is a phenomenon linked to industrialisation, environmental changes have deeper roots than a few centuries. Over the course of our planet's history, the environment has changed several times. Just think of the countless ice ages and climatic changes faced over the millennia. All changes, however, occurred naturally and autonomously. The appearance of man, on the other hand, has totally changed things. When the primates began to make their way on Earth, in fact, they put in place the so-called "homination" process, according to which they adapted to the environment and laid the foundations to move from the animal state to the one closest to what we are today. But before we left the wild stage and became fully human, our ancestors had to go through a further process, i.e., civilisation. Through this passage, from the adaptation of bodies and consciences to the environment, we have come to the adaptation of the environment. Unlike other living beings, who live according to their habitat, in fact, man builds his own according to his needs, melds it and modifies it.

Moreover, in recent decades, household consumption habits have changed as a result of the widespread, albeit unequal, increase in income, globalisation, technological innovations – such as the Internet and cell phones – and the aging of the population. Nevertheless, all these improvements of the life have a cost on the environment. Climate change, loss of natural resources, extinction of species and environmental damage caused by emissions and waste can result from unsustainable patterns of consumption and production.

Understanding consumption habits means understanding human behaviour. In fact, through this data we can understand how the global use of resources has changed and what their environmental impact is. The consumption of goods and services such as food, drink, accommodation, mobility, tourism, etc., in fact, determines a growing pressure on the territory, which must now be managed with awareness.

The first data to report is related to basic necessities, food and drink, which have a high environmental impact due to the costs (economic, human and environmental) related to the production, transformation, transport and composting of food. In addition, the number of electrical and electronic goods we buy and replace – such as TVs, computers, cell phones and appliances – has increased over the past 20 years and this has increased both the demand and consumption of electricity of households. Travel, especially by car and plane, has grown, increasing energy consumption and greenhouse gas emissions. In addition, cities are expanding, incorporating the suburbs, with a consequent increase in the consumption of energy, resources, transport and land. Finally, what characterises the most developed countries is the growing number of trips for recreational purposes: tourism marks record numbers every year and travel usually takes place by car or plane, the environmental costs of which we already know. To these must be added the energy and water consumption, the use of land and the production of waste, wastewater, etc. of the holidaymakers on site.

Consumerism is an increasingly widespread phenomenon in more developed countries and consists of the need or the desire to always grab new consumer goods and products. This unbridled rush to buy is largely caused by continuous and pressing advertising campaigns that tend to make us appear to have indispensable needs that are perhaps not so urgent, indeed these needs are often fictitious: all this only to increase production. All of this, however, has negative effects, first of all, pollution and the indiscriminate exploitation of the natural resources present on the planet. Consumerism is the main enemy of environmental protection: if new goods are always produced, as well as the costs of production and pollution resulting from production processes, we must consider that what we owned becomes a surplus, a waste. It becomes waste not because it is old or broken but only because it is outdated or no longer stylish.

However, consumer spending is changing toward a higher share of overall spending on services. This development may contribute to relative decoupling of environmental pressures from economic growth, since service sectors generally have lower environmental intensities than average. Further improvement should be addressed mainly on product categories showing a higher environmental intensity (i.e., transport, food and drink and housing goods). In particular, in each product category demand should be oriented towards more environmentally friendly products.

Overall, the challenge is to create a virtuous circle: improving the environmental performance of products and services throughout their life cycle, promoting and stimulating the demand of better products and production technologies, and helping consumers to make better informed choices. Nevertheless, this call for actions should be answered not only by public institutions or manufacturing companies. All the sectors of our society should start working to foster the transition towards a more sustainable world.

Our planet is facing unprecedented challenges in terms of climate and environment which, taken together, pose a threat to our well-being. However, we still have time to take decisive measures. The task may seem daunting, but we can still reverse some negative trends, adapt to minimise damage, restore crucial ecosystems and better protect what we have. To achieve long-term sustainability, we must consider the environment, climate, economy and society as inseparable parts of the same entity.

Green transition, environmental protection, ecological science: these issues, until recently relegated to the fields of activism or academic research, are finally at the centre of public debate. The effects of the climate crisis are now evident even in the eyes of those who are most reluctant to accept its reality, and a rethinking of our ways of life and of the development models of society is required – individually, socially and politically.

6.5 Football fighting climate change

Climate change has also some direct effects on football, especially in terms of increasingly hot fields and injuries and heatstroke becoming more and more frequent. While playing in the heat has always been an aspect of the game, things are different now. Some examples of the problems raised by the increasingly hot days emerged with the matches of the Women's World Cup and the African Cup conditioned by the great heat. In Egypt, a player from Nigeria was hospitalised for severe dehydration during a training session. There is an increased risk of heat-related injuries during matches. In fact, as with head injuries, players try to stay on the pitch as long as possible for the good of their team, to the detriment of health.

The problem has already arisen at the 2014 World Cup in Brazil and will most likely present itself in an even more accentuated way also during the events scheduled for the next few years, starting with the 2022 World Cup in Qatar. On this issue, in European football, for example, La Liga, the Spanish championship, has committed itself with matches between May and September never scheduled before 7.30pm to avoid athletes' problems with high temperatures, due to global warming. And even greener is the Bundesliga, the German tournament, with some clubs that have adopted anti-pollution policies: from the photovoltaic section in the Werder Bremen stadium with 200,000 solar cells, enough energy for 300 apartments to the Augsburg stadium, the first carbon-neutral arena, to the Borussia Moenchengladbach's on-site well that supports the water supply. There is also Hoffenheim, who will plant trees in a Ugandan forest to offset the carbon emissions in his stadium. While in England, Forest Green Rovers became famous, a small club that offers vegan menus at the stadium for fans, a wooden structure, zero emissions with solar panels on the roof and strictly natural lawn.

English football struggles to stay afloat. Literally. Every year in Great Britain over 62,000 football matches, at all levels, are cancelled due to flooding, heavy snow and extreme weather events that are becoming more and more frequent.

According to BBC Sport, which has calculated the number of damages to English football linked to the crazy climate, there are minor clubs that are even in danger of disappearing, because they are unable to manage the costs of floods caused by rising seas or rivers along which fields are often built.

Carlisle United, a small club from the fourth division (League Two), had to contend with two massive floods in 2005 and 2015. The last time, when storm Desmond engulfed the country, the Carlisle players, returning from an away game, found the pitch completely flooded. The season ended with two opposing teams lending their playing fields. But when the owner of Carlisle United, after paying the costs for the refurbishment of the field, tried to take out insurance that would cover the damages in case a similar event was to happen again in the future, the bitter surprise arrived. No company wanted to take out the insurance. The reason? Predictive models of atmospheric conditions in the area predicted that new climatic events of that magnitude will be increasingly frequent. In the event of a third flood there will hardly be a future for Carlisle United. The history of Carlisle United is emblematic of how climate change could completely disrupt the world of sport in the UK and around the world.

In 2018, the United Nations created the Sports for Climate Action Framework which seeks to make the sports industry more responsible and involved in the fight against climate change by uniting sports organisations and the communities that support them with a series of principles to safeguard the future of the planet.

UEFA and the European Commission (EC) have teamed up for the latest round of UEFA club competitions to kick off #EveryTrickCounts – a new awareness campaign in which football stars and freestylers mobilise against change climatic. #EveryTrickCounts is part of the UEFA "Respect" programme on football and social responsibility and was launched during matches of the men's Champions League, Europa League and Europa Conference League through an advertising spot that saw the participation of Luis Figo, Delphine and Estelle Cascarino and Gianluigi Buffon.

The video was broadcast on television, on social networks and on stadium screens. In the video, the four players show how simple changes in our daily lives can make a big difference in the fight against climate change. The spot is in line with a key objective of UEFA's commitment to the European climate pact, whereby communities and organisations are invited to help the European Union respect the Green Deal and Europe's transition towards an economy with net zero greenhouse gas emissions by 2050. More recently, Juventus FC published its first Climate Report where the club reports its GHG inventory and the actions taken to reduce their emissions.

Juventus FC, in addition to the measurement of Scope 1 and Scope 2, offsets the emissions through UN certified emission reductions (CERs), carbon credits generated by climate-friendly projects vetted by the UN following rules approved at intergovernmental level and with international oversight, providing a high level of credibility to the offsetting regime.

The global football movement can and must play a leading role in the race towards a more sustainable world. With its global reception, its influence,

This inventory includes the following Scope

Scope 1: includes direct emissions from sources owned or controlled by your organization.

Scope 2: includes indirect emissions from the purchase of electricity, steam, heating and cooling consumed by your organization.

ENERGY PURCHASED AND METHANE CONSUMPTION	2019-2020	2020-2021
Energy GJ		
Electricity purchased	40,537.20	40,953.73
Headquarters	1,206.1644	1,433.74
Store¹	1,311,629.6	1088.59
JTC Continassa	3,145.87	4,384.61
JTC Vinovo	4,698.35	5,120.86
Stadium Complex²	30,345.18	29,006.53
District Heating	45,874.52	49,833.26
Headquarters	1,496.98	1,764.08
JTC Continassa	24,836.79	25,303.86
Stadium Complex	19,490.75	22,765.32
District Cooling	3,477.82	4,364.02
Headquarters	1,177.70	1,692.09
JTC Continassa	2,300.11	2,671.93
Methane Consumption	19,251.34	17,896.87
JTC Vinovo³	19,251.34	17,896.87

1 Starting from the 2018/2019 season, the data refers to all the stores: Turin (Garibaldi and Nizza) and Rome
2 Starting from the 2017/2018 season, "Stadium Complex" refers to all the areas adjacent to it (i.e. outdoor parking lots), JMedical and the Juventus Museum
3 To convert consumption values from m3 to GJ, we have used the UNFCCC standardised baselines applicable to Italy for the years in concern (for 2019 we have adopted the most recent baseline available at the time of drafting the Sustainability Report).

CO2EQ EMISSIONS (t)	2019-2020	2020-2021
Total CO2EQ Emissions (Scope 1 e Scope 2-location based)	9,005.96	8,793.70
Total CO2EQ Emissions (Scope 1 e Scope 2-market based)	4,636.95	4,884.42
Scope 1	1,629.09	1,588.87
Methane⁴	1,081.82	1,006.36
Company Car Fleet²	557.28	582.51
Scope 2 - market based	2,997.86	3,295.55
Scope 2 - location based	7,366.86	7,660.75
Electricity: location based³	4,369.0	4,305.2
Electricity: market based⁴	0,0	0,0
District Heating⁵	2,786.39	3,030.14
District Cooling	211.47	265.41

1 CO2 equivalent emissions from the consumption of gas for heating include the following greenhouse gases: CO2 (carbon dioxide); CH4 (methane); N2O (nitrous oxide). Sources: Emission factors - ISPRA (2020); Global Warming Potential - IPCC (2013).
2 CO2 equivalent emissions of the car fleet have been calculated on the basis of average road transport emissions in Italy (ISPRA). The following greenhouse gases were taken into account for the calculation of CO2 equivalent emissions: CO2 (carbon dioxide); CH4 (methane); N2O (nitrous oxide). For the fleet travel distance, with a view to precise future reporting, values of 15,000 kilometres per year were assumed, with the exception of the Alfa Romeo Stelvio, Maserati Levante and Jeep Cherokee vehicles, for which a travel distance of 20,000 kilometres per year was assumed.
3 CO2 emissions deriving from the use of electricity - calculated using the location-based method - were obtained from "European Residual Mixes 2018", (AIB). In particular, the Italian "Total supplier mix", which represents the emission factor associated with the mix of technologies used in Italy for the production of electricity, was chosen
4 CO2 emissions deriving from the use of electricity - calculated using the market-based method - were obtained from "European Residual Mixes 2018", (AIB), in particular, the Italian "Residual Mix", which represents the emission factor of electricity generation quotas remaining after the use of specific tracking systems for the energy sources used, such as certificates of Guarantee of Origin, was chosen. Starting from the 2018/2019 season, an emission factor of 0 has been considered, as the Company now purchases electricity produced entirely from renewable energy sources.
5 CO2 emissions deriving from the consumption of district heating and cooling, in line with the production technology used for their generation, were obtained assuming the emission factor associated with the productivity of an average cogeneration plant in Italy (ISPRA 2019) as reference.

Figure 6.3 GHG inventory of the Juventus FC. Source: Juventus FC (2022)

its resources and its ability to inspire hope, sport must be a guide to change. Football fans are ready to follow the discipline and their favourite athletes in the fight against the climate. If the sports industry can collectively prioritise sustainability and change the way it operates in the fight against climate change on a scale necessary to have a major impact, it will not only safeguard its own future, but surely others will follow the path taken to living in a world where humans and nature thrive together.

If we want to sum up the efforts that football should adopt against climate change, we can identify three main objectives:

- Make the sports sector zero impact on carbon emissions by 2050;
- Leverage the influence of sport to mobilise billions of fans to take concrete action;
- Use partnerships, which are fundamental for sport, to facilitate innovation and the sharing of new technologies and infrastructures to facilitate the transition to a carbon-free world.

6.6 Measuring football organisations' climate change impact: ISO 14064

Adherence to international, national and local initiatives in terms of reducing the impact generated on climate change requires the ability to calculate, monitor and report climate-altering emissions (i.e., greenhouse gas emissions) and/or emission reductions over time or the removal of greenhouse gases from the atmosphere generated by the activities carried out by organisations or by the implementation of specific projects.

This ability can allow organisations to properly manage their strategic positioning with respect to the issue of climate change, with a view to:

- Reduce the risks associated with non–compliance with the requirements of good environmental practice on the subject of "climate change" that the market or the reference stakeholders consider increasingly important and, indeed, communicate effectively with respect to the opportunities offered by a "virtuous" positioning;
- Be able to adhere in a reasoned and effective way to initiatives and voluntary emission reduction schemes that are consistent with and support the strategies and policies undertaken;
- Have the tools to respond effectively to any mandatory obligations that the community and national legislation has decided to place on the organisation;
- To produce the organisation in the logic of the new tools (regulated or voluntary) based on market mechanisms, through which it is possible to directly enhance the results obtained in terms of reductions or removals from the interventions or projects carried out in economic and financial terms.

These elements of innovation have contributed in recent years to the development of companies, institutions, public administrations and other types of subjects of the need to:

• Quantify the emissions or removals related to organisations' activities or specific projects undertaken correctly and effectively;
• Identify the most appropriate tools to be used to support the development and implementation of organisations' strategy for climate change, and to monitor its concrete results;
• Be able to report with credibility organisations' emissions or contribution to the mitigation of climate change, and to be able to demonstrate the validity of the monitoring and reporting mechanisms adopted;
• Set up and plan the reduction or removal projects in a functional way to report in a credible and effective way the results and possibly to obtain the forms of valorisation envisaged by the programme or the reference scheme;
• Be able to immediately provide, also from a communicative point of view, a measure of the performance obtained or a demonstration of the organisation's contribution to the mitigation of climate change.

To provide certainty about the possible ways to meet these needs, the world of standardisation has recently started to develop some standard rules on the subject.

Today the reference standards are summarised in the ISO 14064 standard published in 2006 and relating to the requirements for the quantification, monitoring, reporting and reductions of emissions obtained by an organisation, within the scope of its activities or with reference to specially prepared and developed projects.

The ISO 14064 standard is made up of three separate and relatively autonomous parts. The first two (ISO 14064-1 and 14064-2), in particular, establish the requirements for reporting emissions and overall emissions reductions linked to the activity of an organisation (the ISO 14064-1 standard) or linked to the implementation of a specific project aimed at reducing emissions or increasing the removal of greenhouse gases (the ISO 14064-2 standard). Two different reporting objects, therefore (on the one hand the activities carried out by the organisation, on the other the focus on a single specific project), to meet different standardisation needs, born in connection with the opportunity or need to guarantee accuracy, effectiveness and credibility in greenhouse gas emissions claims.

A third standard of the same group (ISO 14064-3) is functional to the use of the previous two and identifies the principles and requirements for the verification of greenhouse gas inventories (14064-1) and for the validation or verification of reduction projects of greenhouse emissions (14064-2). This third standard can be used by the same organisations to internally verify (first- or second-party verifications) the inventory or the project carried out and must be taken as a reference by the independent subjects (typically the verification and certification bodies) who are in charge of the external verification (third-party verification).

In fact, the application of the ISO 14064 standards is more robust if it is subjected to external verification and then validated by an autonomous and authoritative subject. The ISO 14064 standards are verifiable standards (not certifiable) or can be subjected to a third-party verification, which gives rise to a report containing evidence of compliance with the established requirements.

At the same time, the application of the rules makes it possible to standardise the approaches and rules established for the reporting of emissions. In this way, different experiences and the results associated with them can be comparable, both when they refer to the same voluntary or mandatory scheme, both when they refer to different schemes or are independently developed with respect to possible schemes and initiatives. The aim is of proposing requirements of general application, but characterised by the necessary rigour.

For example, the results obtained at the organisation or project level are not evaluated in absolute terms but in comparison with a reference scenario (constituted at the organisation level by the framework of emissions and/or removals in the absence of ad hoc policies already structured, and at the project level from the foreseeable future scenario in the absence of the project itself).

The ISO 14064-part 1 standard defines the requirements for quantifying and reporting the greenhouse gas emissions generated by an organisation and the reductions or removals of emissions obtained. It refers to a specific tool, namely the inventory of greenhouse gases. The inventory describes the picture of the emissions generated by each of the emission sources related to the organisation's activity, as well as the removal of greenhouse gases carried out by so-called "absorbers". The standard therefore establishes the ways in which the inventory must be designed and developed, managed, used in communication for the purposes of reporting the results achieved and, finally, verified.

The application of the provisions of the standard (as well as for the purposes of verification for its own sake, or third-party validation) can be part of a programme or initiative for the achievement of objectives for reducing the organisation's emissions which the organisation has joined, and in this case allows it to demonstrate that adherence to the programme is pursued in an effective manner. The inventory must take into account all the different greenhouse gases, considering their specific potential for impact on global warming and reporting all the values by the ton of CO_2. The inventory must also comply with a series of basic principles, indicated by the standard to ensure "fair and correct" accounting (including, by way of example, those of consistency, accuracy, transparency) and must be a coherent tool with respect to the needs of the so-called "intended user" or the subject (internal or external to the organisation) identified as the one who will use the information contained therein to conduct assessments and make decisions.

The "guarantee level", or the degree of assurance of the information contained, must be linked to these needs. The third-party verification will verify the consistency of the methods of preparing the inventory with the requirements of the reference standard given the level of guarantee required by the organisation.

The first step for the inventory of greenhouse gases is the definition of the organisational boundaries of the inventory and the identification of the emission and removal sources that must be taken into account. In fact, the standard indicates the need to structure the inventory by aggregating the sources of emission and removal into groups, defined as "installations", on the basis of a spatial, organisational or technical criterion. The set of all installations that are considered relevant to the inventory defines the organisational boundaries.

The relevance of the installations is assessed on the basis of a control criterion (the emissions are accounted for if the source is subject to the operational or financial control of the organisation), on a proportional basis (the emissions are accounted for on the basis of the proportion of the total attributable to the organisation), or other possible criteria in the event that the application of ISO 14064 constitutes part of the adhesion to a specific emission reduction programme.

The second step consists of defining the operational boundaries of the inventory, which are identified by recognising the operations carried out within the organisation and associating the respective issues or removals with them, organised into three different categories:

*   Direct emissions (and their possible removal), or the emissions directly originating from the installations located within the organisational boundaries;
*   Indirect emissions from energy consumption, connected with the generation of energy, in its various forms, acquired externally and used by the organisation;
*   Other indirect emissions, i.e., emissions that the organisation can only partially control as they originate from outsourced activities, from external services connected with the organisation's activities, from the life cycle perspective of the organisation's products/services outside its organisational boundaries, etc.

The third step consists of quantifying the emissions and any corresponding removal of greenhouse gases. Overall, several steps must be implemented and documented. In fact, it is necessary to:

*   Identify all sources of emissions and all absorbers that originate the removals;
*   Select appropriate methodologies for quantifying emissions and removals (or adopt the methods indicated by any reference programme or initiative);
*   Select and retrieve any organisation activity data required by the calculation methodologies;

- Identify or develop the emission factors that make it possible to calculate the emissions generated, starting from the activity data;
- Calculate greenhouse gas emissions and removals on the basis of the chosen calculation methodologies, using activity data and emission factors.

However, the inventory does not consist solely of the framework of emissions and removals related to the organisation. The ISO 14064-1 standard requires a series of complementary elements, namely:

- The planning and implementation of actions or projects aimed at reducing or preventing emissions or at achieving or increasing the removal of greenhouse gases (for example, actions to reduce consumption or increase efficiency energy, for the management of company mobility or even CO_2 storage interventions). The effect of the actions carried out will result in lower overall emissions generated by the organisation which will be described in the inventory of greenhouse gases. The organisation is required to document the actions carried out and quantified and, if it intends to report and communicate the actions, to describe the details (spatial and temporal boundaries, the calculation approach of the results obtained and the calculation made);
- The creation of a greenhouse gas inventory to be used as a baseline to use it as a comparison with periodic inventories. The organisation must therefore identify a reference year and compose, similarly to what has been done for the inventory of greenhouse gases, the framework of "historical" emissions and removals. The choice of the reference year takes place both on the basis of the availability of historical data and on the basis of any emission reduction targets, assumed by the organisation independently or as part of a specific programme or initiative, expressed in terms of reduction with respect to the amount issued in a base year.

The organisation must also meet a series of management requirements in order to ensure the necessary level of quality of the information entered in the inventory. In practice, it involves drawing up and applying various procedures (a tool similar to that envisaged, for example, in environmental management systems) to ensure:

- Compliance with the basic principles and operational requirements established by the standard, as well as consistency with the needs of the intended user;
- The correctness of the process of creation and periodic review of the inventory;
- The definition of responsibilities and organisational roles related to the creation of the inventory;

- The planning, implementation and verification of the necessary training activity for the figures involved;
- The creation and maintenance of a data collection system;
- Carrying out periodic checks on the accuracy of data collection (including calibration of any measuring instruments);
- The management of errors and omissions;
- The management of documentation and archiving of relevant records;
- The planning and implementation of internal audits and periodic reviews, both of a technical nature (relating to the functioning of the detection and accounting system) and of a management nature (relating to problems or opportunities for organisational improvement).

As can be seen, the management requirements are very similar, if not equal, to those required for an environmental management system. All elements of such a management system (procedures, records, etc.) must be documented for internal or third-party verification purposes. In particular, internal audits must be conducted on the basis of a specific plan and by competent and independent (albeit internal) personnel from an administrative, technical and organisational point of view, defined in advance in the technical details, communicated internally and documented. The audits (internal and external) must be carried out with a level of detail corresponding to the level of guarantee previously defined.

A final element envisaged by the ISO 14064-1 standard is the "Report on greenhouse gases" that the organisation must prepare, to be used as an internal and external information tool, to support audits and as a complement for compliance with certain programmes or reduction of emissions initiatives which the organisation has adhered to. The report, to be prepared on the basis of a specific procedure that defines its planning, timing, format, method of dissemination, etc., contains a description of the inventory of greenhouse gases, a series of mandatory elements (relating to organisational responsibilities, technical details of the inventory – period covered, methodologies used – at the reference baseline, verifications conducted and level of assurance), and possibly a series of optional elements (e.g., strategies and objectives of the organisation relating to greenhouse gas emissions, reduction actions or absorption envisaged or the results of those implemented, any programmes or initiatives in which the inventory is framed, additional environmental performance indicators or benchmark elements).

The ISO 14064-2 standard, on the other hand, defines the requirements for quantifying, monitoring and reporting activities aimed at obtaining reductions in greenhouse gas emissions (or increases in the removal of greenhouse gases) organised in the form of a project.

What is meant by "project"? A reduction project of greenhouse gas emissions (or removal of greenhouse gases) is intended as a set of activities aimed at modifying a trend scenario (i.e., the situation that would occur in the absence of the activities to be carried out), generating a reduction in greenhouse gas emissions (or an increase in removals). The results obtained from a project defined in this way can be quantified, monitored and communicated with a view to reporting in order to be recognised and validated. The validation of the results obtained through the project can give rise to instruments susceptible to economic valorisation, such as emission credits.

Unlike part 1, part 2 of ISO 14064 was in fact expressly developed to provide methodological support for the implementation of projects that typically fall within voluntary or compulsory schemes (or programmes), of an international, national or local character, aimed at accounting and recording the results obtained from individual projects carried out by a proponent. To the proponent is thus provided the possibility of enhancing the reductions in emissions or removals of greenhouse gases obtained through the recognition and validation of certified reduction quotas. These reduction quotas can be used to satisfy the commitments undertaken by the proposer or assigned in a compulsory manner, or to intervene on a market that attributes them an economic exchange value.

The ISO 14064-2 standard therefore intends to define the requirements for quantifying, monitoring and effectively communicating the results obtained from an emissions reduction project, with the aim of guaranteeing the effectiveness of the process that leads to the realisation of a project. These requirements may therefore coincide with or be adopted by programmes or market instruments which, on the basis of the reporting carried out, foresee the release of emission credits or other assets to be sold and purchased on a market.

The implementation of a greenhouse gas project is typically divided into two main phases: the planning phase and the implementation phase. The ISO 14064-2 standard recognises these two phases and establishes the requirements that must be taken into consideration for their development.

The planning phase is described through a typical process: the project is conceptually set up; is evaluated in terms of feasibility; is approved; is subjected to a phase of consultation with the stakeholders; the realisation of the project is planned; the project plan is again submitted to the stakeholders; finally, the project is definitively approved.

If the project is part of a greenhouse gas programme, final approval takes place through a validation of the project by the competent bodies provided by the programme and its subsequent registration. The requirements envisaged by ISO 14064-2 relating to the planning phase are intended to ensure the development of effective tools for managing the various phases of the process described above.

The proposer must first of all make a description of the project and its reference context in a project plan. This plan must include:

• The explanation of the aims and objectives pursued, the location and conditions existing before the start of the project;
• The ways in which the reductions in greenhouse gas emissions or the removals of greenhouse gases envisaged by the project will be obtained;

- The quantification of the reductions or removals (expressed in tons of CO_2 equivalent);
- The risks that may affect the achievement of the expected results in terms of reductions or removals;
- The roles and responsibilities assigned for the implementation of the project and the possible framing of the project in an initiative or programme relating to greenhouse gases;
- The eligibility of the project with respect to any reference programme, the environmental impact assessment, when required by the legislation applicable to the project, the results of the consultation phases with the stakeholders and the methods undertaken for ongoing communication with them;
- Scheduling the start and end of the project, the path of the different phases of the project and their timings.

Based on the project description, the proposer must define a method and criteria for identifying and evaluating the sources of emissions, absorbers and reservoirs of greenhouse gases linked or affected by the project. Based on the procedure, the elements related to the project are then identified and assessed. Subsequently, the proposer is asked to identify and evaluate, establishing appropriate methods and criteria, the potential reference scenarios or scenarios that could occur in the absence of the envisaged project. The elements to consider for the construction of the scenarios are:

- The types of projects already existing or alternative to the one considered, the activities and technologies alternative to those envisaged by the project in question, capable of providing the same level of products and/ or services;
- The availability and reliability of available data;
- Other elements such as the anticipated legislative, technical, economic, socio-cultural, environmental, geographical innovations or changes, pertinent to the location and the project period envisaged.

The construction of the reference scenario (such as to guarantee the same level of activity, products or services of the project in question) must take place through a procedure defined in advance and aim at identifying the differences between the project scenario (i.e., the scenario will occur with the implementation of the project) and the reference one, to calculate the additional reductions determined by the project itself. The latter must be determined according to a prudential criterion, or by adopting hypotheses that guarantee not to incur an overestimation of the differential effects of the project. To this end, after having constructed the reference scenarios, the proposer must identify sources, absorbers and reservoirs of greenhouse gases that would be consequent to them.

The next step requires the proposer to identify the elements to be monitored in order to obtain an estimate of the reductions and removals that can be correlated with the project, or the differential results attributable to it. For this operation, it is necessary to identify the elements that are relevant to the project as they are a) controlled by the proponent, b) related to the flows of matter and energy resulting from the project, or c) influenced by changes in the reference context (e.g., market) resulting from the project.

The elements relevant to the project, if directly comparable, will be verified with respect to the correspondents of the reference scenario. If different (and therefore relevant for the purposes of monitoring the differential results of the project) and monitored in an economically feasible way, they will be included in a monitoring plan which will aim to quantify the reductions and removals of related greenhouse gases. To this end, the methodologies for calculating reductions and removals and any necessary emission or removal factors must be properly defined.

The implementation phase of a reduction or removal project is also described through a typical process: the project activities begin; the performance of the activities (for example the production of energy, products or services) defines the project period; during the project period, periodic checks are carried out on the results obtained and the units of greenhouse gases reduced or removed are recognised; at the end of the project period a final report is presented on the overall results (reductions or removals of greenhouse gases) obtained with the project; the project ends definitively. Even for this second phase, the requirements foreseen by ISO 14064-2 aim to guarantee the development of effective tools for the management of the different phases of the typical process. In order to periodically monitor and verify the results resulting from the implementation of the project activities, the proposer must define procedures and methodologies to calculate the emission reductions or removals variations as the difference between the detected emissions or removals and those foreseen by the reference. The difference is calculated for each greenhouse gas and for each emission source, absorber or reservoir of greenhouse gases. The values of each difference must be expressed in tons of CO_2 equivalent using the values of the Global Warming Potential for each of the greenhouse gases.

Other specific procedures must be set up to ensure:

- The management of the quality of data and information, which must also include an assessment of the uncertainty related to the calculation methodologies and the quality of the data available. The objective of data quality management is to reduce, as far as possible, the level of uncertainty relating to the quantification of emissions reductions or increases in removals;
- The registration, compilation and analysis of the data necessary for the calculation of reductions and removals. Registration must take place having made a series of elements relating to the monitoring to be conducted

traceable and traceable: the purpose; the data and information to be communicated in the units of measurement indicated; the monitoring methods (possible estimation approaches, modelling, measurement and calculation methods); timing and frequency of monitoring based on the knowledge and information needs of the recipients; roles and responsibilities defined to ensure the conduct of monitoring; the methods of documentation, localisation and storage of data and records;

* The calibration and maintenance of any measurement equipment used;
* Documentation management.

The design and compliance with ISO 14064-2 requirements must undergo third-party verification and validation. Verification takes place starting from an assertion, or an affirmation made by the proposer, relating to the results obtained by the project. Moreover, in connection with this need, a specific project reporting tool must be prepared, or a "Report on greenhouse gases", which has a function corresponding to the relationship envisaged, at organisational level, by ISO 14064-1 and must therefore be functional to the needs of the supposed recipient (or "intended user") of the information contained. The report will therefore contain a summary of the project and its salient elements (location, duration, timing), of the reference scenario and of the reductions or removals obtained, with a demonstration of their additional character.

In the event that the project in question is part of a programme linked to greenhouse gases, aimed at making it possible to exploit the results achieved, this may provide specific methods and procedures for: the certification and recognition of reduced or removed greenhouse gas units (in connection with the monitoring carried out periodically); the final verification of emissions reductions or the increase in removals determined by the project as a whole (in connection with the final report on greenhouse gases); the final certification of achieved results.

In many cases, the need or opportunity perceived by an organisation today is not being able to report effectively and credibly the picture of its greenhouse gas emissions and the reduction actions implemented, but of being able to declare immediately the achievement of an environmental objective or performance expressed in terms of climate-altering emissions produced, and therefore linked to one's contribution to the fight against climate change. A need similar, in practice, to the one that can be satisfied through declarations, labels and environmental labels that can immediately communicate the virtues of a product, service or organisation or confirm its characteristics of environmental excellence. In the specific case linked to the fight against climate change, an excellent performance that can be interesting to communicate concerns the ability to cancel the negative contribution that the organisation's activity or a product or service would cause under normal conditions, or to be carbon neutral.

The issue of carbon neutrality was born in the early 2000s as a proposal addressed to organisations (but also individuals) to qualify their business, their product or service, or even individual events or trips. The commonly envisaged procedure foresees:

*   An analysis and quantification of the emissions attributable to the object in question;
*   A study on possible interventions for the direct reduction of the emissions generated and the implementation of the interventions themselves;
*   Adherence to specific initiatives to "offset" the emissions generated that cannot be directly reduced, which guarantee the creation and/or conservation of forest areas in such a way that the financed action leads to an absorption of greenhouse gases corresponding to the residual emissions generated.

The completion of this path allows organisations to affirm neutrality with respect to climate-altering effects, which can be communicated through a special logo or trademark, a certificate, registration in a special register or other methods. The appreciation of the result is therefore a function of the widespread recognition of the brand or logo, the credibility of the organisation that issues them and, connected to it, the rigorousness with which emissions, reductions and compensations are quantified.

With the expansion of the application of carbon neutrality as a form of environmental qualification, validated by private organisations, over the years the need has arisen to give certainty to the terminology used, the processes conducted, the verifications performed and the validation methods relating to the obtaining a "certification" of neutrality with respect to climate-altering effects.

More recently, the Science Based Targets initiative (SBTi) mobilises the private sector to take urgent climate action. By guiding companies in science-based target setting, they enable them to tackle global warming while seizing the benefits and boosting their competitiveness in the transition to a zero-carbon economy. The logic adopted by the SBTi is very simple:

1. Defining and promoting best practice in science-based target setting;
2. Providing technical assistance and expert resources to companies and financial institutions who set science-based targets in line with the latest climate science;
3. Bringing together a team of experts to provide organisations with independent assessment and validation of targets;
4. Leading the Business Ambition for 1.5°C campaign, mobilising companies to set science-based targets in line with a 1.5°C future.

Science-based targets provide a clearly defined pathway for companies and financial institutions to reduce greenhouse gas (GHG) emissions, helping prevent the worst impacts of climate change and future-proof business growth.

Targets are considered "science-based" if they are in line with what the latest climate science deems necessary to meet the goals of the Paris Agreement – limiting global warming to 1.5°C above preindustrial levels.

For instance, quoting again the Juventus FC's climate report, the club assess its direct and indirect greenhouse gas emissions. In fact, by analysing and publishing its Scope 1^2 and Scope 2^3 emissions, the club has been able to gain an understanding of its carbon footprint and aims to deepen its reporting efforts, collecting, where possible, data and information that can provide an increasingly accurate picture of its direct and indirect impacts in relation to CO_2 emissions.

Several clubs have started working on their carbon footprint, but, as explained in Chapter 5, this might provide only a partial overview of the real environmental impacts of football. Aware of the efforts that calculating an environmental footprint requires, this approach can provide a more holistic and complete perspective of the pressures exerted by a club on the environment.

The subjects interested in reporting neutrality perceive the need to adhere to rigorous and truly effective schemes and initiatives but also, and above all, concern the need on the part of potential recipients of a declaration neutrality (customers, users, etc.) to be able to recognise performance actually achieved compared to mere greenwashing operations.

Notes

1 In particular, it is worth mentioning Dr. Natalia Maria Gusmerrotti and Dr. Filippo Corsini.
2 Scope 1: includes direct emissions from sources owned or controlled by your organisation.
3 Scope 2: includes indirect emissions from the purchase of electricity, steam, heating and cooling consumed by your organisation.

References

Ellen MacArthur Foundation, (2012). Towards the Circular Economy Vol. 1: an economic and business rationale for an accelerated transition. https://www.ellenmacarthurfoundation.org/publications/towards-the-circular-economyvol-1-an-economic-and-business-rationale-for-an-accelerated-transition

Gusmerotti, N.M., Testa, F., Corsini, F., Pretner, G., Iraldo, F., (2019). Drivers and approaches to the circular economy in manufacturing firms. *J. Clean. Prod.*, 230, 314–327. doi:10.1016/j.jclepro.2019.05.044

Gusmerotti, N.M., Frey, M., Iraldo, F., (2020). Management dell'economia circolare. Principi, drivers, modelli di business e misurazione. FrancoAngeli. ISBN:9788891791627

Juventus FC (2022). Juventus Climate Report 2020/2021.

Khan, O., Daddi, T., Iraldo, F. (2020). The role of dynamic capabilities in circular economy implementation and performance of companies. *Corp. Soc. Responsib. Environ. Manag.*, 27(6), 3018–3033. doi:10.1002/csr.2020

Khan, O., Daddi, T., Iraldo, F. (2021). Sensing, seizing, and reconfiguring: Key capabilities and organizational routines for circular economy implementation. *J. Clean. Prod.*, 287, 125565. doi:10.1016/j.jclepro.2020.125565

Kirchherr, J., Reike, D., Hekkert, M., (2017). Conceptualizing the circular economy: an analysis of 114 definitions. *Resour. Conserv. Recycl.*, 127, 221–232. doi:10.1016/j.resconrec.2017.09.005.

Korhonen, J., Nuur, C., Feldmann, A., Birkie, S.E., (2018a). Circular economy as an essentially contested concept. *J. Clean. Prod.*, 175, 544–552. doi:10.1016/j.jclepro.2017.12.111.

Korhonen, J., Honkasalo, A., Seppälä, J., (2018b). Circular economy: the concept and its limitations. *Ecol. Econ.*, 143, 37–46. doi:10.1016/j.ecolecon.2017.06.041.

Marrucci, L., Daddi, T., Iraldo, F., (2019). The integration of circular economy with sustainable consumption and production tools: Systematic review and future research agenda. *J. Clean. Prod.*, 240, 118268. doi:10.1016/j.jclepro.2019.118268

Marrucci, L., Daddi, T., Iraldo, F. (2021). The circular economy, environmental performance and environmental management systems: the role of absorptive capacity. *J. Knowl. Manag.*, article in press. doi:10.1108/JKM-06–2021-0437

Marrucci, L., Iannone, F., Daddi, T., Iraldo, F. (2022). Antecedents of absorptive capacity in the development of circular economy business models of small and medium enterprises. *Bus. Strategy Environ.*, 31(1), 532–544. doi:10.1002/bse.2908

Marrucci, L. and Daddi, T., (2022). The contribution of the Eco-Management and Audit Scheme to the environmental performance of manufacturing organisations. *Bus. Strategy Environ.*, 31(4), 1347–1357. doi:10.1002/bse.2958

Pauliuk, S., (2018). Critical appraisal of the circular economy standard BS 8001:2017 and a dashboard of quantitative system indicators for its implementation in organizations. *Resour. Conserv. Recycl.*, 129, 81–92. doi:10.1016/j.resconrec.2017.10.019

Yuan, Z., Bi, J., Moriguichi, Y., (2006). The circular economy; a new development strategy in China. *J. Ind. Ecol.*, 10, 4–8. doi:10.1162/108819806775545321.

7 Green marketing, environmental communication and greenwashing in football

7.1 Environmental sustainability as a green marketing strategy

Green marketing and environmental communication are assuming a central role in organisational strategies, stimulating organisations to strengthen their environmental commitments and to transmit to the market, in an increasingly consistent way, the performance of their products and services and the results achieved in this field.

In a context characterised by the proliferation of generic and indistinct environmental messages and by the multiplication of channels and the ways in which these are conveyed, organisations are now called upon to make a qualitative leap, which frees green marketing strategies from the logic of a market niche and aims at promotion on a much larger competitive scale.

On the one hand, consumers ask to be sure of actually contributing, through their purchase act, to the improvement of the environment. On the other hand, they require that the qualities, in terms of functional and aesthetic performance of the "green" product/service, are similar to those of conventional products/services, and that the price is not (excessively) higher.

However, being competitive in terms of quality and price is not enough: the real challenge for marketing is to make the environmental improvement associated with the consumption of products or the use of services concrete, "perceptible" and "distinctive", and to this message add an equally solid and recognisable communication of the commitments undertaken and the results achieved on which the "green" identity of an organisation and its brands rests.

This objective can be achieved above all through an adequate communication of environmental issues. When the information that reaches the public concerns pollutants, resource consumption and effects on the ecosystem, the most relevant problem for an organisation is how to communicate its commitment in an effective and understandable way, combining the completeness and credibility of environmental information with simplicity and attractiveness of the message.

This need is particularly pressing in current market scenarios, in the face of the growing reputational risks that an organisation can face if the various

DOI: 10.4324/9781003228271-7

stakeholders perceive its communication as "greenwashing", i.e., an attempt to claim false merits without a real and demonstrable commitment to improve the environmental performance of its activities, products and services.

In this logic, it has become increasingly evident that an effective strategy requires tools and methods that are not the simple adaptation of those already available for traditional marketing and communication. In fact, the consumer has evolved. They have become increasingly attentive to the environmental consequences of purchasing choices and much more willing, than in the past, to change consumption habits in relation to variables that escape only the conventional parameters of quality and price. The reference context in which purchasing decisions take place has changed profoundly, not only in terms of market growth and globalisation, but also from the point of view of the possibilities offered by the new information and communication technologies, which now allow the individual consumer an availability and speed of access to information and a possibility of interaction with organisations and with other individual consumers unthinkable in the more recent past.

Environmental marketing was instituted with the aim of developing, promoting and enhancing products and services capable of generating a reduced environmental impact compared to the alternatives offered on the market (Iraldo, 2018). Historically, environmental marketing strategies have developed on the thrust of the increasingly significant trend of consumers to express conscious purchasing choices, aimed at rewarding organisations committed to ecology and preferring "more sustainable" products and services from an environmental, ethical and social point of view.

However, there is no "typical" consumer oriented in any case to ecological consumption choices, or willing to buy the product/service sold as "preferable from an environmental point of view" regardless of the quality performance and effectiveness of use of the same (Pretner et al., 2021). Today, a detailed analysis of market trends indicates that there is no "prototype" of green consumer, but there are different (and numerous) types of consumers and customers who, in certain circumstances, prove to be more inclined to purchase environmentally friendly products.

Today, the consumption of the most sustainable products and services is ready for a qualitative leap, which frees marketing strategies from the logic of a niche market and instead aims at promotion on a much wider competitive scale (Iraldo and Melis, 2020). On the one hand, consumers, regardless of their socio–economic connotations, ask to be sure that they can actually contribute to improving the environment by purchasing green products. On the other hand, they demand that the qualities, in terms of functional and aesthetic performance of the ecological product, are similar to those of conventional products and that the price is not higher or at least not "excessively higher" than the price of the conventional one.

For an "ecological" product or service, however, being competitive in terms of quality and price is not enough. The real challenge for green marketing is to make the environmental improvement associated with the consumption of products or the use of services concrete and perceptible, to "convince" the customer/consumer of the real usefulness of his role in protecting the environment (Testa et al., 2015). The ability, on the part of the organisation, to make visible or tangible for the customer the environmental advantages linked to the choice of its product or service is therefore essential. In this respect, not all products and services are the same.

For some types of products, the highest environmental performance can be highlighted right from the visual contact at the point of sale. For most products, but especially services, however, the environmental improvement cannot be perceived at the time of purchase. Consumers must "experience it" through the use of the product or the provision of the service. In other cases, the consumer must "trust" the organization, as in the case where the consequences on the environment will never be visible or tangible to the average consumer (Testa et al., 2018a).

Today, the main challenge for organizations is finding an effective mix between completeness and credibility of environmental information, on the one hand, and simplicity and attractiveness of messages on the other.

Despite the importance that green marketing has reached in industrial sectors, in the football world the implementation of environmental management practices is not so linked with marketing and communication reasons. In fact, a survey carried out by LIFE TACKLE and administered to more than 100 European football managers reported the varying motives and drivers of the adoption of environmental practices. As shown in Figure 7.1, all the drivers connected with marketing and communication are relegated to the lowest positions.

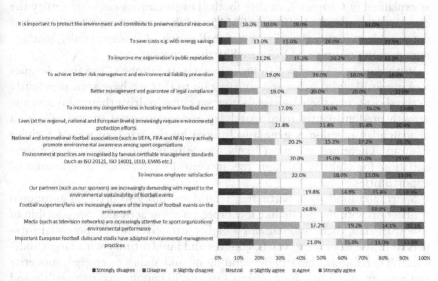

Figure 7.1 Motivations for adopting environmental management practices. Source: LIFE TACKLE (2021)

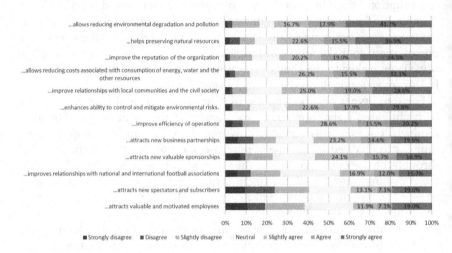

Figure 7.2 Expected benefits of environmental practices adoption. Source: LIFE TACKLE (2021)

Neither sponsors nor fans nor the media seems to be interested in environmental activities carried out by a football organisation. Moreover, football managers do not see relevant benefits in terms of increased sponsorship, spectators or subscribers (Figure 7.2).

However, the football world may be penalised by the fact that currently no certification exists that is directly connected with a football match. In fact, as explained in Chapter 4, to date football organisations can only certify the organisation using ISO 14001 or EMAS and the event using ISO 20121. It is not possible to certify the service "football match". Consequentially, marketing opportunities may be hampered by this situation.

With domestic broadcast rights values across Europe's "big five" leagues looking unlikely to grow at a similar rate to that we have seen previously in the short term, the emphasis is now on clubs to drive their own revenue growth predominantly from matchday and commercial sources. Growth in matchday revenue is generally limited by the size and use of a club's stadium. Therefore, the most likely source of revenue growth and differentiation for clubs is through the successful exploitation of commercial opportunities.

Sport, and football in particular, retains an ability to drive an emotional connection with the public like few other genres or activities. Sponsorship of a football club, therefore, remains a highly attractive tool for potential partners to utilise in order to reach, connect and build affinity with target audiences. Therefore, a club's understanding of, and ability to engage, monetise and activate, its fanbase is critical to a successful commercial partnership and is a key factor in driving sponsorship rights value.

It is worth noting that in the football world marketing activities can be split into two main areas: B2B marketing, i.e., searching for sponsors and other revenues; and B2C marketing, i.e., season ticket campaigns, ticketing, sports sales. Most of the time in the marketing department there are also three other areas: communication, i.e., multichannel fan engagement; external relations, i.e., third-party management (municipality, NGOs, etc.); and events, i.e., internal and external event manager.

7.2 Developing accurate communication on environmental sustainability

Over time, communication of a social nature, i.e., the external disclosure of compliance with ethical principles, environmental factors and social equality, has undergone a significant evolution from being a marketing factor, aimed at obtaining a potential competitive advantage, to being an essential element for the creation of long-term value for companies.

For some decades, non-financial reporting has become an essential element for traditional businesses. They are increasingly oriented towards the creation of profit in the long term, which needs a tool capable of transmitting to the outside, and in particular to the main stakeholders, the idea that the activity is carried out in a sustainable manner, i.e., in compliance with ethical principles, social values and the environment. In the football field, interest in non-financial reports has grown much more recently, above all thanks to a series of external impulses.

The UEFA regulations on financial fair play certainly represent the most general of these impulses as, despite ultimately posing financial constraints, they repeatedly stress the need for football clubs to operate in a sustainable manner and demonstrate the ability to have an economic–financial equilibrium in the long term. These new constraints have led football clubs to suddenly change their approach to budgetary issues.

There is also no doubt that it is clear to football organisations that showing themselves to the outside as an entity capable of innovating, respecting people and the environment and, more generally, operating in compliance with ethical and social principles represents a source of value. In this sense, it is sufficient to think of the economic damage that a football club can suffer if shadows of racism fall on them or, in terms of relations with lenders, if there is any doubt about compliance with financial fair play.

For these reasons, the sustainability report represents a particularly useful tool that should not be given up. It is also worth underlining how, ultimately, the purpose is always and in any case of a financial nature, it follows that an approach towards integrated reporting would be even more capable of improving strategic efficiency and showing the ability to create value.

The major football clubs are increasingly oriented towards the integration of financial reporting with information relating to sustainability issues. The need to converge towards this new approach, oriented to the medium-long term, derives from the need to strategically plan social activity in order to ensure compliance with a series of parameters imposed at the level of the European federation.

The adoption of Directive 2014/95/EU on the disclosure of non-financial and diversity information (referred to as the "Non-financial Reporting Directive" –NFRD) set the EU on a clear course towards greater business transparency and accountability on social and environmental issues. The directive serves as a vital instrument in terms of advancing the EU's agenda for CSR. The European Union (EU) Non-Financial Reporting Directive requires all large companies[1] (whether listed or not) and, starting from 1 January 2026, all listed SMEs (excluding micro-enterprises) to disclose certain types of non-financial and diversity information in their yearly management reports. Non-Financial Statement Disclosure Categories include:

- Environmental;
- Social and employee matters;
- Anti-bribery and anti-corruption;
- Diversity;
- Human rights;

With respect to those issues, the NFRD requires companies to disclose information about their business model, policies (including implemented due diligence processes), outcomes, risks and risk management, and Key Performance Indicators relevant to the business.

As of today, the NFRD does not introduce or require the use of a non-financial reporting standard or framework, nor does it impose detailed disclosure requirements such as, for instance, a list of indicators per business sector.

Although sustainability reports are spreading, currently less emphasis is given to environmental impacts, on the other hand some social aspects are very popular. Another characteristic of the sustainability reports of football clubs concerns the management of the facilities whether they are owned or not. The issue is very relevant as showing how safety can be managed within the structure, or issues relating to the achievement of the plant, means increasing the potential in terms of turnover. To these specific characteristics is then added the usual part relating to governance, employees, social inclusion and so on.

Although the reasons that lead football clubs to choose to add a sustainability report to their financial statements are similar, these reports still have significant differences between them and little comparability. Furthermore, some of them are very respectful of international standards while others do not yet fully fulfil their function.

The most common international standards related to sustainability reporting are the Global Reporting Initiative (GRI) Standards. They are a series of globally recognised parameters that regulate and help companies, institutions and individuals of all kinds in analysing the environmental impact measures they exert on the planet. The GRI Standards refer to the environmental aspects, yes, but also to the economic and social aspects that every activity should respect in order not to leave a negative footprint on the ecosystem.

The GRI is pioneering in its field, and its standards are today an essential reference point for reporting the sustainability of companies around the world. The various reports are collected in a database that can be consulted by all: the GRI Sustainability Disclosure database.

The GRI Standards have an interconnected and modular structure, so that they can be easily updated without creating interdependencies between them that can be subverted in the event of the addition or removal of new rules. There are three sets of thematic standards covering respectively:

- Economy (GRI 200);
- Environment (GRI 300);
- Social (GRI 400).

Football organisations that adopt the GRI Standards will reap benefits both internally and externally. These parameters make it possible to collect information relating to liability, allowing activities to identify potential risks and address them, possibly transforming them into opportunities or strengths. In practice, the GRI Standards not only provide an opportunity for the organisation to change old polluting habits, but analyse waste to reduce costs and increase the efficiency of all processes.

Within the context of issues related to the environment and sustainability, the possible recipients of the organisation's communication flows are all those categories of subjects who, for various reasons, have an interest in the environmental performance of the same: consumers, customers' intermediates, local communities, suppliers, distributors, employees of the organisation, etc. (i.e., ideally, all stakeholders as a whole).

Each category naturally has specific characteristics in terms not only of values, interests and expectations, but also of the ability to receive, understand and appreciate the messages addressed to it. At the same time, the motivations that push an organisation to communicate with stakeholders vary profoundly in relation to the type of subject considered. For a supplier of raw materials, the goal may be, for example, to involve the supply chain in the development of initiatives aimed at qualifying its product as ecological throughout its life cycle. With respect to the local community of reference, the goal may be to build consensus with respect to an industrial development project in the area. In relation to the market, the organisation may wish to communicate the excellence of its product/service, both in terms of quality and in terms of environmental performance, etc.

The first step that an organisation that intends to develop an environmental communication strategy should take is therefore to identify the recipients it intends to address. The choice of the recipients of the communication requires a careful assessment not only of the current situation and characteristics of the organisation, but also of its prospects for future growth and development, in relation to both its internal potential and the opportunities offered by the market in a dynamic context in continuous evolution.

The identification of the recipients of the communication strategy cannot therefore ignore the knowledge and understanding, by the organisation, of the context in which it wants to communicate. The organisation should consider, first of all, the needs, expectations and perceptions of its possible interlocutors with respect to the variables that can affect their purchasing and consumption choices – with reference to product communication – or with respect to their consent with reference to communication in general.

Following this approach, a useful starting point for the organisation is to relate the set of subjects with which it interacts to the set of variables that can affect their choices and assessments, with the aim of reconstructing an overall picture of the relative importance and weight that each of these stakeholders' attribute to each of the variables considered.

An organisation interested in maintaining and developing its reputation and in making its offer as close as possible to the expectations of demand is therefore confronted with the need to identify the factors that influence the consensus and choice of a green product and to evaluate its weight. For the purchase reasons, to develop a strategy that takes into consideration the most significant ones and to coherently identify the contents of the environmental communication.

In particular, the most significant variables that come into play in the dynamics of green consumption and in consumer purchasing decisions are:

- Price;
- Quality and performance;
- Visibility of the environmental characteristics of the product and the commitment of the organisation;
- The image and reputation of the organisation and its brand;
- Environmental information;
- Guarantees and certifications;
- The proximity (with respect to the consumer) of the environmental effects linked to the product.

In the process of maturing their purchasing decisions, the consumer pays increasing attention to the corporate image. In many cases, in fact, it is difficult for a consumer who is particularly sensitive to environmental issues to consider a product by dissociating it from the perceived image and credibility of the organisation and its brands.

It therefore becomes important for the consumer to also understand the behaviour of the organisation through the consolidation of a "positive" environmental image. This is able to influence the purchase act through trust and brand loyalty mechanisms in cases where the company has taken a position strongly oriented towards the enhancement of its environmental commitment in its sector (Boiral et al., 2017).

Information is the main tool to make the consumer aware of both the environmental value of the product and the environmental commitment of the organisation. The objective of environmental information is twofold. First, to highlight the environmental benefits linked to the consumption of the product. Second, to emphasise the commitment of the organisation on the environmental front, so that this positively affects the environmental image of the product.

In consideration of the particular contents of environmental information, it is necessary that the forms of communication go beyond the traditional promotional channels which, in this case, can sometimes be of little impact on the consumer.

A further element that can compensate for the lack of ecological visibility of the product, or the impossibility of "experimenting" with it through use, is represented by the forms of guarantee relating to the factors previously analysed (environmental commitment of the organisation and information). When the consumer relies on the organisation's environmental image or product information to guide his purchasing choices, he needs, as we have seen, certainty about the truthfulness of the signals he receives.

In these terms, the organisation's commitment to improving the environmental performance of its activities, products and services acquires greater credibility if "validated" by visible, recognised and accredited forms of certification.

Consumers need clarity and transparency towards both information regarding companies and their environmental commitment in general and information regarding the green characteristics of products. In both cases, the presence of forms of certification and guarantees issued by third parties can represent, for consumers, a strong element of credibility and a guarantee of the truthfulness of what the organisation communicates (Macellari et al., 2021).

Organisations that choose to communicate on environmental issues today measure themselves with a growing competence, awareness and maturity of the recipients of their communication flows. It was anticipated that this requires the adoption of more careful and responsible strategies than in the past in relation to the type and characteristics of the information transmitted, whatever the tool and channel used to disclose it. Faced with this need, a series of standards aimed at defining the requirements and characteristics that environmental information should possess in order to be accurate.

The ISO 14063 and ISO 14021 standards, respectively dedicated to the environmental communication of organisations and environmental product communication, have taken on particular importance. The latter in particular was conceived with the aim of promoting and promoting the harmonisation of so-called environmental claims.

Environmental communication can be defined as a process of sharing information with interested parties in order to build trust, credibility and partnership, to raise awareness and to support decision-making processes (Testa et al., 2018b). It is necessary to consider the issue of environmental communication as strategic for organisations. In today's competitive scenario, communication on organisations' environmental performance has become a strategic activity to increase brand reputation and respond to the growing accountability constraints provided for by current environmental legislation.

Therefore, the UNI EN ISO 14063:2020 standard is of considerable help, since it allows organisations to appropriately structure environmental communication with other interested parties such as customers, suppliers, investors, communities, etc. ensuring an approach inspired by transparency, data appropriateness, corporate credibility and clarity of presentation. The key principles of ISO 14063 can be summarised as follows:

- Transparency: making the processes, procedures, methods, data sources and assumptions used in environmental communication available to all interested parties (taking into account confidentiality), informing them of their role.
- Appropriateness: making sure that the information provided is relevant to interested parties, using formats, language and media that meet their interests and needs, allowing full participation.
- Credibility: communicate honestly and fairly and provide information that is true, accurate, material and not misleading, using recognised and reproducible methods and indicators.
- Ability to respond: ensure that communication is commensurate with the needs of interested parties, respond to their requests and concerns comprehensively and promptly, inform them on how requests have been received, processed and satisfied.
- Clarity: make sure the approaches and language used are understandable to stakeholders.

For an organisation it is extremely important to follow these requirements in order to avoid greenwashing, i.e., the process of conveying a false impression or providing misleading information about how a company's products are more environmentally sound.

7.3 Avoiding greenwashing and the risk of greenwashing in football organisations

An attempt to classify the reasons that can make it difficult for an organisation to undertake a green communication and marketing strategy requires, in the first instance, distinguishing between two "typical situations" that are profoundly different from each other:

- The case in which the organisation's hesitations and perplexities towards environmental communication are attributable to the fact that it does not really have a green identity – neither in terms of culture and values of the organization, nor in terms of ability to offer the market products or services with ecological characteristics;

- The case in which the fears of the organisation are instead linked to the difficulty of effectively enhancing its real commitment to environmental protection and/or concrete results in terms of environmental performance of its products or services.

In the first case, the fears of the organisation are certainly well founded. The adoption of a green strategy based on the communication of a generic sensitivity towards the environment, not supported by concrete commitments and results, inexorably exposes the organisation to the risk of damaging its image towards stakeholders and its credibility on the market, up to the actual loss of customers and the erosion of market shares by competitors.

This happens as consumers, customers and, in general, all stakeholders are developing a growing environmental awareness and are proving capable of recognising and correctly evaluating an ecological message, at least of "distrusting" it if this is vague, generic, superficial.

These are all those situations attributable to so-called greenwashing phenomena, a term coined to indicate the situations in which an organisation employs more resources to affirm its environmental sensitivity and/or the environmental benefits of its products (through communication, advertising, marketing, etc.) rather than implementing measures that are truly capable of reducing their environmental impact. In other words, the attempt to "dye green" products, services, activities and commercial brands leads the organisation to commit one or more "mistakes", which the market is able to recognise, consequently suffering damage in terms of image, reputation and credibility.

In summary, greenwashing can be defined as "an action that deceives the public, emphasizing the environmental credentials of a company or its product or service, when these are unfounded or irrelevant" (Testa et al., 2018c).

Beyond the definitions, it should be emphasised that a greenwashing action does not necessarily imply the organisation is acting in "bad faith". In fact, much more frequent is the origin of a greenwashing phenomenon due to the superficiality of the approach to environmental communication and/or a lack of knowledge of environmental issues that the organisations intend to communicate to the market and to stakeholders.

Table 7.1 summarises some of the most frequent types of greenwashing. Not infrequently, a misleading communication from an environmental point of view jointly presents more than one of these cases. At the same time, it should be noted that not all greenwashing "sins" are equally "serious" and expose the organisation to the same risks, in terms of sanctions, image and reputation, etc. Finally, it should be emphasised that the phenomenon of greenwashing affects not only individual products or services, but can affect the organisation as a whole. Regardless of the specific episode that gives rise to the phenomenon (for example, the advertising of a single product), it is the organisation as a whole that risks, in the long term, paying the negative consequences.

Table 7.1 Greenwashing: the most frequent cases

Vagueness and absence of information	Do not provide information (data or specific characteristics) to support what is stated through advertising or product packaging, or provide vague and generic information. If the information exists, there should be no hesitation or fear in communicating it. In this case, the difficulty may rather relate to how to effectively communicate information, through the use of appropriate languages, styles and channels.
Irrelevant feature	Emphasise a single characteristic of the advertised product, deeming it sufficient to classify it as "green", but completely ignoring other more important aspects.
Hidden trade-off	This is certainly the most frequent sin as companies do not violate any rules but simply fail to tell the whole story of the product well, where the raw materials come from, how they are processed and what are the environmental characteristics that distinguish the product, how it is made, transported to large retailers, how it is packaged, how they come and if some materials are recycled, how many greenhouse gases are released into the environment ... these is just some of the information that could really interest consumers, but which is sometimes omitted by leveraging only one aspect that has been tried to improve such as the packaging produced using a smaller quantity of plastic.
"Fake" brands and certifications	Provide data and information presenting them as "certified", but which do not require the intervention of an independent third party, which guarantees procedures and truthfulness (for example: the affixing, on the packaging of products, of "fake" brands and ecolabels, which do not correspond to a real certification process of the declared environmental qualities).
No proof	The sin of lack of evidence consists in boosting the green characteristics of certain products or of the production activity itself without having any (third-party) evidence or certifications to support what is being said.
Lesser of two evils	In this case, the company relies on the description of the lesser evil which, in fact, is always an evil. The information that is given is true in this case but in any case it hides what is behind it which is much worse.
Fibbing	As the word fibbing itself says, telling falsehoods is obviously a case of greenwashing, this is now less practiced but still exists. While it is legally punishable, some organisations still offer fake messages in their advertisements.

Nowadays the communication on green topics in the football world is still relatively new. Thus, there have not yet been any big scandals connected to greenwashing. However, to better explain the different sins of greenwashing, we hypothesised some greenwashing cases in the football world.

A football organisation may be accused of vagueness and absence of information if, after declaring that the match is net zero carbon, it will not provide the study that demonstrates this claim.

By only communicating that the shirt of the football club is made without dangerous substances for the environment and for human health, a football club may be accused of focusing on an irrelevant feature. In fact, this statement is true of all similar products since the CE label, which is mandatory for products in the market, requires that kind of control.

To even compensate the carbon footprint of one single match might be not enough to avoid the risk of greenwashing. In fact, communicating "green" initiatives not included in the context of an overall vision and commitment of the organisation towards the environment can generate the "inconsistency of the commitment" sin. Football organisations should create a consistent and robust strategy on green topics, rather than focusing on single isolated event.

The adoption of uncertified logo on products used by a football organisation or on events managed by football organisations is probably the most common form of greenwashing. However, football organisations may be accused of greenwashing even if they do not use any label, but use images and claims that deliberately suggest and evoke an environmental sensitivity that does not correspond to reality.

7.2 Greenwashing: some possible cases in the football world

n	Possible greenwashing risk	Improved claims
energy consumed ring the football is 0% renewable	*Fibbing* There are solar photovoltaic panels that powered the lighting system of the stadium, but there is also a connection with the national grid which is powered only by renewable sources	The claim is formally correct, but the organisation simply does not purchase or produce energy from renewable sources
ur matches, we not use products ntaining CFCs	*Irrelevant feature* CFCs have been banned for over 30 years	It is not possible to create a claim on this topic since it is an irrelevant topic due to the fact that all products cannot contain CFCs
his stadium, we e green seats"	*Vagueness and absence of information* "Green" is a too broad concept. The claim must contain more detailed information	In this stadium, we use seats produced with 50% of recycled plastic
matches are vironmentally endly"	*Absent of proof* The claim is too generic and the concept "environmentally friendly" cannot be scientifically proved	We measure using LCA analysis the environmental impacts of our matches and are trying to reduce them
g a personal logo at can resemble her green rtification	*"Fake" brands and certifications* Using logo that look likes green certifications that do not exist	Our T-shirts are certified according to the EU Ecolabel
football pitch one of the most stainable since we e only organic oducts	*Hidden trade-off* The use of the organic products is just a part of the activities connected to pitch maintenance. Heating the pitch with lamps to facilitate the growth grass for instance is a more impactful activity	We use only organic products for the maintenance of the pitch
ur air travel, we e only sustainable iation fuel (SAF)	*Lesser of two evils* Even if the organisation really use SAF, they use airplanes for travel when the use of train would be feasible	Whether it is not possible to use the train, we travel by airplanes powered only with sustainable aviation fuel

The examples of greenwashing reported easily lead to the conclusion that an organisation that – not being able to count on the real ecological characteristics of its products – decided to renounce a communication strategy in an environmental sense, would make a correct choice, protecting itself from the risk of running into one of the situations outlined (or other similar ones) and therefore to be, sooner or later, "disheartened" by the market.

In more detail, two possible scenarios would open:

- The first connected to a passive attitude on the part of the organisation which, while acknowledging the existence in the market of a willingness to reward "greener" products and organisations really committed to environmental protection, decided to continue producing "conventional" products. In this case, as we have seen, the organisation would not in any case be protected from a possible loss of competitiveness. Working for the environmental improvement of products is not (anymore) only the response to a market request, but also connected to the necessity to comply with the increasingly numerous and specific requirements that organisations are (or will soon be) required to comply with.
- The second, more ambitious, scenario would be for the organisation to start from the current inconsistency of environmental credentials and commitment, to undertake a path aimed at seriously investing in the design, research and innovation of its products, in order to develop and/or enhance its environmental performance. Of course, even this path would not be without difficulties and obstacles, for example in terms of:
  - *Costs* – Developing more environmentally conscious processes can improve the performance of the organisation – in terms of reducing waste, optimising the use of raw materials and energy, etc. – but it may also require significant costs (reorganisation, related to different procurement choices, etc.), as well as investment in new technologies. Furthermore, it is often necessary to develop new types of products and therefore the problem of eliminating or modifying existing plants and/or using stocks of products that do not meet the new environmental standards arises;
  - *Organisational complexity* – The development of green products requires, not infrequently, organisational changes within the organisation. These changes are linked, among other things, to the need to operate in an integrated manner and with a strong inter-functional approach, which overcomes the barriers between the different processes which take place within the same organisation. Added to these, there are the difficulties connected with the need to integrate the organisation's work with the work of other players in the production chain;
  - *Organisational culture and internal resistance of the organisation* – Often, organisations show a strong inertia to change, linked to the weight that the roles, routines, processes and consolidated procedures assume

within them. The diffusion of an organisational culture that has the defence of the environment among its values can cause, from this point of view, friction and conflicts, to the extent that the environmental values are "destabilizing" compared to the current values and balances that regulate the activity of the organisation;

-   *Technological limits* – Significant efforts in terms of technological, process and product innovation are often required to improve environmental performance. In particular, there may be objective limits to the organisation's ability to significantly improve its environmental performance by applying the technical and scientific knowledge at its disposal.

The second type of fears, on the other hand, include all those situations in which the protection of the environment and the improvement of environmental performance are actually part of the culture and objectives of the organisation. In these cases, if among the products offered by the organisations there are one or more with ecological characteristics that can be valued as "excellent" in the market, the obstacle to be overcome (to avoid "greenwashing") does not concern the inconsistency of one's own environmental commitment, but the difficulty of being able to transform a real environmental performance advantage into a competitive advantage recognised by the market. Also in this case, it is possible to identify different scenarios, which can be classified in terms of "syndromes".

The first scenario can be defined as a standard syndrome in which the organisation fears that the communication of its commitment from an environmental point of view – referring only to some of its activities, products or services – could highlight the absence of this commitment in other areas and for all the remaining "traditional" products that it continues to offer in the market. In other words, the organisation fears that effective communication of the performance and environmental characteristics of one of its products (or one of its "lines" of ecological products) may lead consumers to believe that the other products – not being able to boast equal performance – are polluting.

A second scenario refers to the existence of a so-called universal judgment syndrome, or the fear that excessive emphasis on the current environmental sensitivity of the organisation highlights the absence of the same sensitivity in the past, resulting in damage to the organisation's image. The perception of "mature" and aware consumers could in fact be that the organisation until then had not been transparent with respect to the environmental impact of its products. Again, the "syndrome" could lead the organisation to undertake to give up green marketing, or to implement it with many cautions and limitations, making it ineffective.

Other scenarios refer to a syndrome that could be defined as partner displacement, to indicate all those situations in which the organisation fears that communicating its environmental commitment could put other organisations with which it has important commercial relations and which do not have difficulties with the same sensitivity and/or the same will or ability to translate it operationally. Think, for example, of partnerships between organisations, but also and above all of supply chain relationships. An organisation motivated to communicate the environmental excellence of its products to the market could be dissuaded from taking this path if its suppliers (or some of these) cannot boast equally excellent environmental performance and, at the same time, there are a number of reasons which induce the organisation not to change these same suppliers (because they are historical partners with whom it has a consolidated relationship, for market reasons, etc.). This type of fear may arise today more than in the past if we consider that the concept of a supply chain associated with the purchased product has now become familiar and that the information needs expressed by consumers are very often not limited to the finished product, but also concern the guarantees relating to its supply chain or its entire life cycle.

The displacement effect could, on the other hand, not be limited to relations with commercial partners, but also manifest itself in those competitive with competitors. This is the case, for example, of advertising campaigns aimed at promoting the environmental excellence of an organisation's products through the communication of quantified environmental performance (such as water and energy consumption, etc.). The organisation could fear the reaction of competitors, where they were able to communicate performances superior to their own and even put them in direct comparison within the so-called "comparative advertising".

A fifth syndrome could be defined by client disorientation, to indicate those situations in which the organisation fears that, given the consolidated image it has with the public, a strongly environment-based communication may be too innovative, giving the impression of a strong discontinuity with respect to the past and thus creating mistrust towards the set of activities of the organisation.

The exposure of some of the most frequent situations that an organisation that is considering the adoption of a green marketing strategy may face, shows how there may be non-trivial or superficial reasons that can act as a barrier to its effectiveness and development. Despite the diversity that characterises these syndromes, it is clear that the organisation must evaluate them against the possible competitive advantages and market benefits that can derive from the offer of innovative products with a strong environmental connotation. The positive feedback that consumers and intermediate customers can offer and the opportunity to expand the targets and market shares thanks to an effective green marketing strategy often lead to overcoming the syndromes described above, or to consider them as inherent risks to innovation, but for this very reason they are often remunerated by being a "first mover", or rather by choosing to undertake this strategy in advance of competitors.

There should therefore be no doubt that a correctly set green marketing strategy, after overcoming the aforementioned syndromes, can lead the company to "collect" significant results on the market. It is clear, in fact, that only through an adequate communication strategy is it possible for organisations that are truly able to offer excellent products and services from an environmental point of view. The strategy should:

- Describe to the market the real environmental benefits linked to the product and service;
- Ensure a balance between environmental performance and traditional performance in terms of quality, effectiveness of use, aesthetics, etc.;
- Base the environmental excellence of the product/service on an approach of collaboration and integration with the supply chain;
- Provide the customer and the consumer with information to fully exploit the potential environmental benefits of the product, without contradicting the image or reputation gained in the past.

According to New Weather Institute (2021) the oil and gas multinationals and various air and automotive companies – considered large carbon emitters and therefore responsible for the current global climate crisis – have invested hundreds of millions of dollars in sports sponsorship projects. This can be considered as a greenwashing strategy aimed at making the world of sport believe that these industrial giants are particularly sensitive to ecological issues and therefore have in no way contributed to the climate catastrophe we are witnessing.

New Weather Institute (2021) focused on around 250 advertising and sponsorship agreements signed between the world's leading sports teams and organisations and large high-carbon industrial conglomerates, from car and airline companies to large oil and gas companies. The authors stated that while sport appears to be at the forefront of the climate emergency, it floats on a sea of sponsorship deals with the world's major polluters.

As already mentioned, the report drawn up by the New Weather Institute, in collaboration with the climate charity Possible and the Rapid Transition Alliance, identified a dense network of advertising and sponsorship deals between the protagonists of 13 sports, including football, cricket and tennis, and the largest polluting industries in the world. Football has concluded the largest number of deals, receiving 57 sponsorships from high-carbon industries, i.e., oil and gas companies and some airlines.

The report explains that the automotive industry is the most present high-carbon sector in the global sports sponsorship market, with 199 agreements covering all sports. Airlines rank second with 63 deals, followed by major oil and gas companies such as Gazprom and Ineos, whose deals have been harshly criticised by many climate campaign activists.

It was no coincidence that when Ineos was about to become a sponsor of Team Sky Cycling in 2019, a spokesperson for the chemical company confirmed the company's commitment to promoting the circular economy. The car manufacturer Toyota is the largest sponsor, totalling 31 agreements, followed by the airline Emirates with 29 partnerships.

Melissa Wilson, a member of Britain's rowing team for the Tokyo Olympics, claimed that allowing polluting industries to sponsor sports organisations and clubs in the face of the climate emergency would be no different from trying to push athletes to dope. Instead, sport and athletes should favour "clean sport" in every way and by every means and become the real protagonists of the global effort to achieve the goal of zero carbon emissions.

The authors define the phenomenon as "sportwashing", which occurs when heavily polluting industries sponsor sport to carve out a fictitious role as supporters of a healthy activity, while in reality they are pumping lethal pollution into the atmosphere. In fact, they would be the ones who pollute the air that athletes breathe, ending up destroying the climatic stability on which every sport undeniably depends.

These big polluters would take the place of the major tobacco companies, becoming the new sports sponsors par excellence. The sponsorship of tobacco in sports is prohibited, but now, for the same reason the agreements with the industrial giants of climate pollution should also be suspended to safeguard the health of people, sport and the planet.

Major events, not only sporting events, leave indelible traces of their passage. Cathedrals in the desert such as the Vela di Calatrava built for the 2009 World Swimming Championships in Rome or the Cesana bobsleigh track for the 2006 Turin Olympics, an immense concrete crater that defaces the mountains that not even Milan Cortina 2026 has deigned to take into account. Not to mention the highway that gets lost in the Amazon rainforest for the 2014 World Cup in Brazil or the inhabitants of the East End neighbourhoods evicted to make way for the 2012 London Olympics. Natural, landscape, social and economic devastation that leaves deep wounds to the ecosystem of the planet.

For this reason, the organisation of the Qatar 2022 World Cup, together with FIFA, published in September sensational and sensationalist reports on the fact that the competition would be "the first carbon neutral in the entire history of the World Cup". After the more than 2 million tons of carbon dioxide produced by the 2018 World Cup in Russia, the 450 thousand produced by Euro 2020, the first hypotheses endorsed by FIFA last summer were that Qatar 2022 would have produced 3.2 million tons. A few months later, however, FIFA itself signed a report according to which emissions would have been zero.

But as a recent Carbon Market Watch analysis writes, all of this is not true[2]. As explained by the authors of the analysis, the carbon neutral result is not achieved with a drastic reduction in emissions but with a complex logical and financial architecture. Firstly, the pollution produced by the construction of infrastructures, and not just stadiums, would be missing from the count. Secondly, the system for the assignment of polluting credits, already in itself not very stringent, would have been further affected by a series of permits, concessions and financial schemes built specifically to get to the announcement of zero emissions. A mechanism that, continues the author, discredits not only the organisers of Qatar 2022 but also those who, like FIFA and the world press, lend themselves to certifying these operations.

7.4 Creating an ESG conscious football world

The acronym ESG (Environmental, Social, Governance) is becoming more and more popular and is characterising the strategies and communication of companies and organisations in many different sectors. ESG intends to represent and above all measure (and in the future certify) the ability of companies to calibrate and manage their impact in environmental, social and governance terms.

ESG indicates a real rating, often known as a sustainability rating, which is expressed on the environmental, social and governance impact of a company or organisation operating in the market. The ESG rating appears increasingly important today because it represents an index that (also) allows investors to have a greater and deeper understanding of the sustainability of a company.

It extends the concept of "traditional" sustainability of a company represented by economic sustainability and the ability to generate new value for investors, to the concept of sustainability towards society and the environment and the ability to generate value for the environment and for society.

Actually, the ESG rating consists of a series of factors that make it possible to express an assessment of the risk and performance profile of an investment in terms of the impact of the company in relation to the type of market in which it operates, the initiatives and to the strategies that distinguish it.

E for *Environmental* concerns the relationship with the environment and includes initiatives and operations aimed at reducing the risks associated with climate change and the impact at the climate change level also in terms of respect for biodiversity, attention to population growth and in general management of resources such as water, land, air, vegetation. CO_2 emissions are the other major issue (and parameter) that falls within the environmental category.

S for *Social* concerns all corporate and organisational decisions and activities that have a social impact such as respect for civil and labour rights, attention to working conditions, gender equality and the rejection of all forms of discrimination, the ability to contribute to the social fabric and to the territory in which the company lends its work through initiatives that increase well-being and that improve the quality of life of the inhabitants. This also includes issues such as combating the use of child labour and for organisations with complex supply chains having real control over all those supply chains.

G for *Governance* concerns the strategies and decision-making choices of companies and organisations in terms of remuneration ethics, respect for the rules of meritocracy, respect for shareholders' rights and fighting against any form of corruption, rules in the composition of the Board of Directors. Governance is also representative of the identity of the company, the organisation, the strategy, the attitude and determination with which it aims to implement the ESG principles, i.e., the ability to define and implement organisational forms and concrete actions that are for everyone the effects in the condition of implementing these principles in everyday life. The governance that feeds the ESG parameters relates to organisational models in which these principles are an integral and substantial part of the company "mechanisms". They are a strategic choice equipped with means, resources, objectives and control tools so that it is effectively implemented.

Like any industry careful to present itself as modern and developed, football across Europe is also incorporating the doctrines of sustainable finance and ESG issues. The desire of the clubs to be in step with the times in terms of sustainability and environmental development certainly has something to do with it.

The increasing popularity of ESG as a lens through which to view sustainability risks and opportunities has increased familiarity with many of the environmental, social and governance factors that affect an organisation. Football has become a regular business like any other and increasingly clubs are professionalising their management, and thus face more scrutiny from a range of stakeholders, including investors and sponsors. While clubs are always under pressure to deliver financial results, we don't see the same expectations towards environmental, social and governance (ESG) impacts. Not only does football contribute to the country's economic and socio-cultural prosperity, but it also has great potential to lead by example through driving sustainability performance, transforming the nation's passion into a vehicle for positive change. However, there is work to be done. Clubs are exposed to a series of ESG risks that if not managed have an increasing ability to damage reputations and their licenses to operate, and ultimately dent their profitability. They engage daily with job sectors identified as at the highest risk for modern slavery, including temporary hospitality and security staff, and have lengthy supply chains that must be managed responsibly and ethically. However, very little attention is paid – or at least is not publicly disclosed – to these risks.

Moving forwards, clubs should be considering:

1. Multidimensional thinking
    Clubs are doing great things – particularly around community engagement and energy efficiency. However, a more holistic approach is required: one that encompasses responsible sourcing, promotes healthy choices, respects human rights and is open and transparent about how the stadiums are being run and what teams and fans are being supplied with, in terms of goods (kit, food and beverage) and services (cleaning, construction and maintenance).
2. Collaborating with peers, suppliers and broad civil society
    Platforms for collaboration are increasingly evident and accessible. Clubs have an opportunity to engage with peers, suppliers and broader

civil society to share both successes and difficulties, learn from others and benefit from collective action.

3. Communicating with fans, investors and sponsors

Clubs must be accountable for their impacts and answer not only to investors and regulators' disclosure demands, but wider society as well. Clubs should communicate to their stakeholders what they are doing – or how they are investing their resources. Key benefits include maintaining their license to operate as well as contributing to promoting a club's image. They have great potential to lead by example, educating their fans about sustainability issues and promoting best practice in the wider sports sector. So, why not go beyond simple financial disclosures, build a sustainability strategy and tell their stories to society?

On 28 March 2022, the SE European Football Index was published by Standard Ethics whose objective is to monitor the situation of European clubs in terms of sustainability. At a European level, considering the 15 major clubs currently listed, it emerges that the level of disclosure is, in general, still low on issues related to sustainability and that, apart from two companies that have good ESG reporting, all the others are struggling to align to the international indications of the UN, OECD, EU.

From the analysis of Standard Ethics, which was essentially based on the economic dimensions of the companies examined, as well as on some other characteristics such as the quality of disclosure and the availability of ESG data, it therefore emerges that:

- 13% of the companies adopt sustainability-oriented policies and an adequate reporting system;
- 67% of the companies still have a low level of disclosure, even if 20% of them have embarked on a path to improve ESG reporting;
- 20% of companies still have unsatisfactory sustainability management.

Rating	Outlook	Company	ISIN	Rating	Outlook	Company	ISIN
EE-		Borussia Dortmund	DE0005493092	E		Celtic Football Club	GB0004339189
E+		Juventus Football Club	IT0000336518	E		S.S. Lazio	IT0003621783
E	pos.	AFC Ajax	NL0000018034	E		Benfica	PTSLB0AM0010
E		Manchester United	KYG5784H1065	E		Brondby	DK0010247956
E		Galatasaray Sportif	TRAGSRAY91X9	E-		Fenerbahce Futbol	TREFBAH00019
E		Besiktas	TRABJKAS91X6	E-		Trabzonspor	TRETRBZ00016
E		Olympique Lyonnais	FR0010428771	E-		Sporting CP	PTSCP0AM0001

Figure 7.3 Index Constituents from 28th March 2022. Source: SE European Football Index

Only in two cases were structured policies clearly oriented towards sustainability and standard extra-financial reporting present, i.e., Borussia Dortmund and Juventus Football Club. In the case of Roma, and to a lesser extent Ajax, analysts have found evidence that a path has been started in that direction.

In general, the sector of listed football teams does not offer high-quality public reporting (especially on non-financial issues) and rarely also offers an adequate and full English translation of its website and relevant documentation. Finally, the main sustainability governance tools, such as Codes of Ethics and ESG policies, do not appear widespread (or are not well structured).

The perception is that – with some exceptions – listed football clubs, although involved in businesses that go beyond mere sports – merchandising, advertising, television rights, stadium management and more – do not follow the example of other economic sectors. In other words, they find it difficult to professionally analyse their social, environmental and economic impact, to offer standard ESG reporting and above all to articulate a convincing system of governance of sustainability.

Notes

1 Number of employees greater than 500 and, alternatively, a balance sheet greater than 20 million or net revenues greater than 40 million.
2 https://carbonmarketwatch.org/2022/05/31/fifa-world-cup-in-qatar-scores-own-goal-with-misleading-carbon-neutrality-claim-new-report/

References

Boiral, O., Heras-Saizarbitoria, I., Testa, F., (2017). SA8000 as CSR-Washing? The Role of Stakeholder Pressures. *Corp. Soc. Responsib. Environ. Manag.*, 24(1), 57–70. doi:10.1002/csr.1391

Iraldo, F., (2018). Green Marketing: how can a Product's Environmental Footprint be effectively communicated to consumers?: a case study with Carlsberg beer. *Econ. Energy Environ. Policy*, 2, 167–186. doi:10.3280/EFE2018-002009

Iraldo, F., Melis, M., (2020). Oltre il greenwashing: linee guida sulla comunicazione ambientale per aziende sostenibili, credibili e competitive. Edizioni Ambiente. ISBN 978-8866273141

LIFE Tackle, (2021). The environmental management of professional football events: a survey of football managers. https://lifetackle.eu/assets/files/Report_survey_manager_LIFE_TACKLE.pdf

Macellari, M., Yuriev, A., Testa, F., Boiral, O., (2021). Exploring bluewashing practices of alleged sustainability leaders through a counter-accounting analysis. *Environ. Impact Assess. Rev.*, 86, 106489. doi:10.1016/j.eiar.2020.106489

New Weather Institute, (2021). Sweat not oil. Why sports should drop advertising and sponsorship from high-carbon polluters.

Pretner, G., Darnall, N., Testa, F., Iraldo, F., (2021). Are consumers willing to pay for circular products? The role of recycled and second-hand attributes, messaging, and third-party certification. *Resour. Conserv. Recycl.*, 175, 105888. https://doi.org/10.1016/j.resconrec.2021.105888

Testa, F., Iraldo, F., Vaccari, A., Ferrari, E., (2015). Why Eco-labels can be Effective Marketing Tools: Evidence from a Study on Italian Consumers. *Bus. Strategy Environ.*, 24(4), 252–265. doi:10.1002/bse.1821

Testa, F., Boiral, O., Iraldo, F., (2018a). Internalization of Environmental Practices and Institutional Complexity: Can Stakeholders Pressures Encourage Greenwashing? *J. Bus. Ethics,* 147, 287–307. doi:10.1007/s10551-015-2960-2

Testa, F., Boiral, O., Heras-Saizarbitoria, I., (2018b). Improving CSR performance by hard and soft means: The role of organizational citizenship behaviours and the internalization of CSR standards. *Corp. Soc. Responsib. Environ. Manag.*, 25(5), 853–865. doi:10.1002/csr.1502

Testa, F., Miroshnychenko, I., Barontini, R., Frey, M., (2018c). Does it pay to be a greenwasher or a brownwasher? *Bus. Strategy Environ.*, 27(7), 1104–1116. doi:10.1002/bse.2058

8 Fostering behavioural changes in football fans

8.1 Theoretical framework of behavioural change

The Theory of Planned Behaviour (TPB) is a model that explains human behaviour as a consequence of an intention which in turn is the result of the interaction between different beliefs, namely the attitude, the subjective norms of the acting individual and the perception of control. It is an extension of the previous Theory of Reasoned Action (TRA).

The TRA provides that the behaviour is preceded by the intention to put it into practice; this, in turn, is determined in a contemporary way by the attitude towards behaviour and subjective norms.

The TRA, developed by Fishbein and Ajzen (1975) and Ajzen and Fishbein (1980) assumes that behaviour is determined by the intention, defined in terms of subjective probability, that an individual performs a particular action, such as purchasing a product. The intention, in turn, would be determined by the attitude – favourable or not - towards the specific behaviour

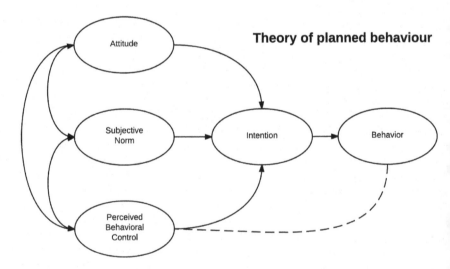

Figure 8.1 Graphical representation of the TPB

DOI: 10.4324/9781003228271-8

and by the subjective norm, understood as the perception of the individual of how much the adoption of the behaviour is approved or disapproved by specific people or target groups.

The model also assumes that attitudes towards behaviour depend on beliefs relating to the consequences, in terms of cost-benefits, of adopting the behaviour itself (behavioural beliefs), as well as on the assessment of each of these consequences. Similarly, subjective norms are seen as a function of the perception of normative pressure (normative beliefs), as well as the motivation to act in accordance with the expectations of target groups.

Ajzen (1991), to overcome the limits of the TRA by Fishbein and Ajzen (1975), introduces a new element, thus formulating the TPB. The new variable introduced consists of perceived behavioural control, that is the perception that a subject has of being able to carry out the desired behaviour. This control affects the intention to implement a given behaviour and the actual behaviour itself (for example from a market perspective this behaviour could be the purchase of a product).

Perceived behavioural control must be differentiated from actual effective control, that is, the actual control exercised by the person over the behaviour. The perceived behavioural control is, with respect to the real control, its proxy, that is an indirect measure of it and concerns only the subjective perception, not the effective control of the individual over the behaviour. It also differs from the locus of control (Rotter, 1966). You may have an internal locus of control but feel you have no control over behaviour. While the locus of control is the individual's perception of internal or external control kept constant in daily life, the perceived behavioural control is uniquely situational, therefore linked to the context of the individual behaviour considered. Finally, perceived behavioural control differs from self-efficacy (Bandura, 1977), which is actually considered a part of it. Some believe that they cannot consider perceived behavioural control and self-efficacy as interchangeable due to differences in the conceptualisation of the two concepts. However, self-efficacy is one of the two components of perceived behavioural control (the other is perceived control). Perceived behavioural control also has a direct influence on behaviour, but the intention to perform the behaviour is equally to have a greater influence on the performance of the behaviour.

Similarly to attitudes and subjective norms, perceived behavioural control is a function of control beliefs, which represent the subjective estimate of the possibility of accessing the resources and opportunities necessary for the execution of the behaviour. They are based, to a small extent, on past behaviour, while, to a greater extent, on indirect information and on the experiences of friends and acquaintances (Ajzen and Madden, 1986).

Ajzen and Madden (1986) have proposed two versions of their model: the first is based on the assumption that perceived behavioural control has an independent effect on intentions, in the sense that intention about a behaviour is only expected to form when the person believes he has the means to perform the behaviour itself; the second also considers the possibility of a direct influence of perceived control on behaviour, which can only be foreseen when it is assumed that perceived behavioural control functions as a partial substitute for effective control over internal and external factors that could interfere with the execution of the behaviour. Therefore, the direct path from perceived behavioural control to behaviour represents a non-volitional determination of action.

In this context Ajzen introduces the perceived behavioural control to the relationship and influence scheme that the attitude has on the behaviour. The limits of the TRA are thus overcome, which provided for a systematic evaluation of the "subjective norms" (the expectations that other people significant to us have with respect to our behaviour, that is, approval or disapproval, and our motivation to please them), the systematic evaluation of the consequences of the behaviour and the evaluation of expectations for the value of the object of the behaviour (this is always better understood if you think about buying a product).

The TPB has been frequently used to investigated consumers behaviours according to green aspects and several drivers have been identified (Testa et al., 2021). For this reason, it is necessary to better frame the consumer's attitude towards eco-sustainable products/services.

Starting from a survey called "Attitudes of Europeans towards building the single market for green products" conducted by the European Commission in the 2013, which investigated the attitudes and behaviours of Europeans towards "green" products/services, we will be able to better frame this topic. The term "green" refers to products/services that have a lower negative impact on the environment during their production, in terms of use or disposal, compared to other products/services that perform the same functions and satisfy the same type of need.

During the purchase decision, consumers take into consideration different aspects of the product. From Figure 8.2 it can be seen that 84% of respondents declare that they pay attention to the environmental impact of products. The environmental impact of products is preceded in importance by the quality of the product, which occupies the first position with 97%, and by the price of the product which is considered important by 87% of consumers. The name of the brand is not very relevant (46%).

The attention declared for the environment is consistent with the data concerning the declarations about the types of "green" behaviour already implemented; 84% of consumers claim to have practiced separate collection and a similar percentage said they have reduced energy consumption.

And 70% of Europeans say they have reduced their water consumption to the minimum necessary and have reduced their consumption of disposable products (64%). The percentage of those who declare they have purchased local or "eco-friendly" products amounts to 64%, while 52% said they did so only if this product is guaranteed by a label that ascertains its sustainability.

Just over half of respondents (56%) said they had chosen a way to travel that was as sustainable as possible. Almost 40% of respondents claimed that they used the car less frequently for environmental reasons and replaced it with other, more environmentally friendly, alternative ways.

	Quality	Price	Environmental impact	Brand
Very important	65%	40%	38%	14%
Rather important	32%	47%	46%	32%
Not very important	2%	10%	12%	36%
Not important	1%	2%	3%	17%
I don't know	0%	1%	1%	1%

Figure 8.2 Features of products/services considered during the purchasing phase by respondents

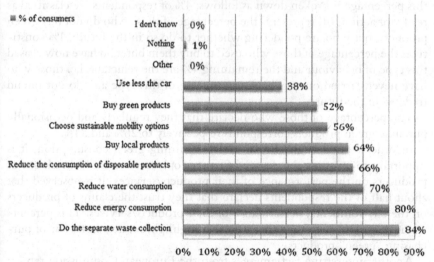

Figure 8.3 Green actions adopted by respondents

At the basis of these actions declared by European consumers, there is above all the perception that buying eco-sustainable products can really make a difference for the environment (89%), followed by another motivation concerning the perception of qualitative parity between eco-friendly versions of products and conventional counterparts (74%).

With regard to the frequency of "green" purchasing behaviours practiced and the purchase intentions declared by the interviewees, a wide range of statements emerges from the survey that fall within these possibilities:

- Regular: this is the category of consumers who often buy low environmental impact products;
- Occasional: this is the category of consumers who sometimes buy products with a low environmental impact;
- Ready to buy: this is the category that includes consumers who have never bought products with a low environmental impact, but are sure to buy them in the future;
- Thoughtful: this is the category that includes consumers who have never bought products with a low environmental impact, but they might start doing it in the future;
- Recidivist: this is the category of consumers who habitually bought products with a low environmental impact, but have now stopped;
- Reluctant: this is the category of consumers who have never bought and do not intend to buy products with a low environmental impact.

Respondents were asked to choose from a series of statements, the one that best described their buying behaviour in general.

In total, 15% of European citizens do not buy eco-friendly products and this percentage is broken down as follows: 4% of respondents are classified as ready for action, 6% represents the percentage of those who do not buy green products, but who are pondering whether to do so in the future, 1% constitutes the percentage of those who used to buy them but who have now ceased this type of behaviour and the remaining 4% are the reluctant, i.e. those who have never carried out a behaviour purchase of this type and do not intend to do so in the future.

The percentage of those who declare that they regularly and occasionally purchase green products corresponds respectively to 26% and 54%.

In order to understand the attitudes regarding green consumption, it is important to examine the degree of trust people have towards the claims of producers on the performance of their products/services. It is observed that about half of the respondents declare that they trust the claims of producers on the environmental performance of their products/services. This percentage is consistent with the other data that highlight reasons in favour of purchasing "green" products.

Another interesting fact emerges from the European Commission report: 77% of respondents say they would be willing to pay more for environmentally

Which of the following statements best describes your behavior?

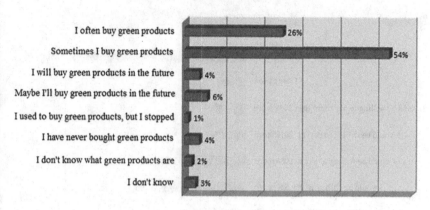

Figure 8.4 Green purchasing decisions made by respondents

How much do you trust the claims of producers on the environmental performance of their products/services?

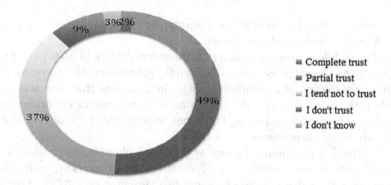

Figure 8.5 Respondents' trust of green claims

friendly products, if they were sure that they really are. The amount of the additional price that consumers would be willing to pay for green products varies considerably: 37% would be willing to pay 5% more, 28% would pay 6–10% more, 7% would be willing to pay 11–20% more and only 5% would be willing to pay 20% more for this type of product. This is a fact that undoubtedly reveals a positive attitude of consumers towards "green" products, as long as organisations offer guarantees regarding the environmental benefits.

Although green consumption is a growing phenomenon in various sectors and the survey seems to highlight positive trends and attitudes towards

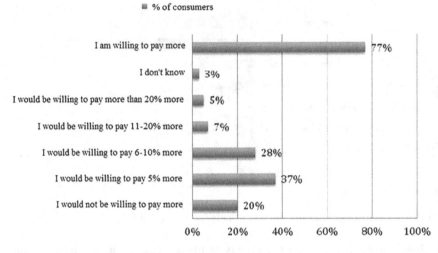

Figure 8.6 Respondents' willingness to pay for green products/services

sustainability, there is nevertheless a significant gap between eco-compatible purchasing attitudes and behaviours.

In fact, while a growing number of consumers declare in surveys that they are ready to adopt environmentally friendly behaviours, also showing their willingness to support a premium price in the awareness that their action can really make a difference for the environment, these positive intentions rarely translate into consistent buying behaviour, making this type of behaviour a typically niche phenomenon.

This trend is commonly known as the "30:3 phenomenon", since while around 30% of consumers say they want to buy responsibly, only 3% of purchases reflect these declared intentions (Mezger et al., 2020). This circumstance has profound implications for organisations that produce and/or market green products/services, since launching products/services on the basis of purchase intentions declared in market research will, most likely, result in costly market failures, as it is now commonly accepted that intentions are not significantly related to behaviour.

In an attempt to address this gap problem, two different lines of research have emerged in the literature on ethical and sustainable consumption. The first is focused on the methodological limitations of the market research commonly used to assess the purchasing intentions of green consumers and the subsequent behaviour. These authors suggest that people may respond in an idealistic way, producing what is commonly known as social desirability bias, i.e., the disturbing effect that comes into play when the subject, who responds to an interview or a questionnaire, has the opportunity to give answers that can be considered socially more acceptable than others (Chung and Monroe, 2003; Krumpal, 2013; Larson, 2019).

The second line, to which most of the existing literature on the subject is attributable, adopts a different approach to the problem of the gap between green purchasing attitudes and behaviours. It recognises the distortion of social desirability as a factor only partially responsible for this gap. It also identifies other factors that directly or indirectly hamper the translation of green attitudes into coherent purchasing behaviours (Padel and Foster, 2005; Bray et al., 2011; Chaihanchanchai and Anantachart, 2022).

In order to intercept the variables responsible for the gap between attitude and behaviour, Carringtion et al. (2010) have developed a model which, in addition to developing a cognitive approach, recognises the complexity of the decision-making process of the conscious consumer by also including the surrounding environment. In fact, the model integrates environmental variables into the cognitive perspective in order to reflect the complexity of the purchase decisions that occur in real life.

The internal and environmental factors that are integrated into the model constitute elements that refer, respectively, to the cognitive and behavioural traditions. The cognitive perspective of human behaviour is based on internal mental processes that play a decisive role in behaviour: these lines of study seek to understand the interaction and correlation between cognitive constructs, such as beliefs, attitudes and intentions. The behavioural perspective, on the other hand, is based on measures of observable behaviour, where the environment plays a decisive role in determining actual behaviour.

The holistic model of Carrington et al. (2010) is based on the assumption that there are contextual elements that help explain the gap between purchase intentions and actual behaviour. This model therefore addresses the problem of the gap between attitudes and behaviours in the context of green consumption, focusing on the gap between green purchasing intentions and real purchasing behaviour. It seeks to overcome the defects of the merely cognitive perspective, exploring the mediating effect of "implementation intentions" and integrating the moderating effects of the variable "actual behavioural control" and situational factors. While intentions specify a desired final point and signal a commitment to achieve this result, implementation intentions specify the plan to implement these intentions, i.e., "when situation X occurs, I will reply with the Y behaviour".

The empirical evidence from this study suggests that when people form implementation intentions, the likelihood that they translate their intentions into consistent purchasing decisions increases significantly. Implementation intentions positively mediate the relationship between intentions and behaviours, because these simple plans help individuals become aware of their intentions, protect them from unwanted influences and avoid conflict, as well as provide an important aid for individuals to change their current purchasing habits and create new ones.

Both situational factors (e.g., visual temptation) and those internal to the individual (e.g., habits or moods) have the potential to block, deflect and conflict with a certain intention. The implementation intention protects and maintains the intention by allowing the subject to control his behaviour in the situational context.

The deviation of intentions and behaviour, however, is not determined only by the cognitive processes of consumer evaluation. They, in fact, find themselves in an environment that is built outside their mind and that environment has a demonstrable effect on actual behaviour.

There are two types of environmental stimuli that influence consumer behaviour: the situation and the object (Belk, 1975). The situation refers to a single definite moment in time and space and such situational characteristics are momentary. On the contrary, the object factor refers to the characteristics of the product/service that are lasting and to the characteristics of the brand that are general.

As regards the situational context, it is possible to identify five main factors: surrounding physical environment (i.e., visibility, positioning, information, etc.), surrounding social environment (i.e., presence of other people, roles and interactions, etc.), time perspective (i.e., period of the day, time since the last purchase, etc.), task definition (i.e., scope of the purchase), previous states (i.e., momentary moods, such as anxiety, hostility and excitement and momentary constraints, such as illness, fatigue and money).

Many situational factors are unconscious to the individual, but still have an effect on purchasing behaviours. In order to also observe the situational factors that are not perceived at the level of awareness, the objective measures refer to the characteristics of the situational environment that exist a priori to the interpretation of the subject. Examples of possible subconscious factors include the presence of other people in the immediate vicinity, the effect of lighting, perfume and music in the place, etc. The intention-behaviour deviation can be positively or negatively moderated by situational factors.

Marketing strategies applied to sustainable products/services, which increase effective control over behaviour or help the consumer to accurately construct the imaginary scenario, can be effective in reducing the gap between attitude and behaviour. Effective strategies can consist of equipping the sales area with more staff so that they interact with the consumer, ensuring the visibility of the product/service compared to competing offers, carrying out tactical price promotions and using clear images to communicate effectively and symbolically the quality of the product/service.

8.2 The role of football fans in the environmental sustainability of football

Even though football matches and international football tournaments can generate relevant environmental impacts in terms of waste generation, mobility, energy and water consumption, etc., football plays an increasingly important role in promoting and supporting environmental sustainability. Together with the goal of reducing the environmental footprint of football activities, it is essential to exploit the popularity of football as a means of increasing general environmental awareness through inspiring, unifying and engaging millions of people in adopting behaviours and actions for the protection of the environment.

Within the framework of the LIFE TACKLE (Teaming-up or A Conscious Kick or the Legacy of Environment) project, and aimed at promoting actions for improving the environmental management of football events and the environmental awareness of fans and spectators, a survey on the level of information and awareness of football supporters in relation to environmental management topics was carried out.

The survey was carried out between May 2019 and January 2020 and was physically administered to a sample of spectators/fans during Italian Premier League ("Serie A") or UEFA Nations League official football matches that took place in three European pilot stadiums of the LIFE TACKLE project: the "Luigi Ferraris" stadium in Genova, Italy, the Stadio Olimpico in Rome, Italy, and the Friends Arena in Stockholm, Sweden.

A total of 1,423 questionnaires were collected. However, given the non-mandatory nature of the answers to the questions of the survey, the number of actual respondents varies depending on the question. To allow a correct interpretation of the data, each graph takes into consideration the exact number of actual responses for each question. The minimum number of responses obtained from a question is indicated in brackets below each graph relating to a group of questions.

The sample is mainly composed of young male adults: in particular, about 70% of respondents are male, while the remaining 30% are female (Figure 8.7). Over 50% of respondents are under 34 years old, of which the most populated age group in the sample is between 15 and 24 years old (25.4%), followed by the age group between 25 and 34 years old (20.8%). The third most populated age group is between 45 and 54 years old, which represents

Table 8.1 Questionnaires collected by the LIFE TACKLE's survey on supporters

Date	Country	Stadium	Match	N. of respondents
05/05/2019	Italy	"Luigi Ferraris", Genova	Genoa–Roma	270
20/05/2019	Italy	Stadio Olimpico, Rome	Lazio –Bologna	149
26/05/2019	Italy	Stadio Olimpico, Rome	Roma –Parma	198
25/09/2019	Sweden	Friends Arena, Stockholm	AIK-Göteborg	75
05/10/2019	Sweden	Friends Arena, Stockholm	AIK-Örebro	110
12/10/2019	Italy	Stadio Olimpico, Rome	Italy-Greece	146
15/10/2019	Sweden	Friends Arena, Stockholm	Sweden-Spain	160
02/11/2019	Sweden	Friends Arena, Stockholm	AIK-Sundsvall	80
19/01/2020	Italy	"Luigi Ferraris", Genova	Genoa-Roma	235
Total	1,423			

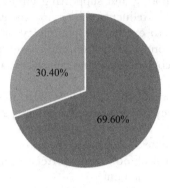

■ Male ■ Female

Figure 8.7 Gender of respondents (n. 1,367)

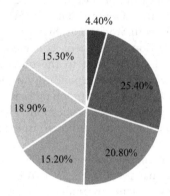

■ < 15   ■ 15-24   ■ 25-34   ■ 35-44   ■ 45-54   ■ > 55

Figure 8.8 Age of respondents (n. 1,404)

about 19% of the sample, while 15.3% of the sample is over 55 years of age and 15.2% of the sample is aged between 35 and 44. Only 4.4% of respondents are under the age of 15 (Figure 8.8).

With regard to the level of education, most of the respondents (over 55%) have completed high school, while almost 20% hold a bachelor's degree and almost 15% hold a master's degree. Few respondents have completed secondary school (8.3%), while very few have a doctorate degree (1.4%) or have completed primary school only (0.9%) (Figure 8.9).

In terms of the distance travelled by fans and spectators to reach the stadium, most of the respondents in the final sample (over 55%) travelled less than 20 km (of which the majority, 35.5%, travelled between 5 and 19 km, while 14.4% travelled between 1 and 4 km, and only 5.3% travelled less

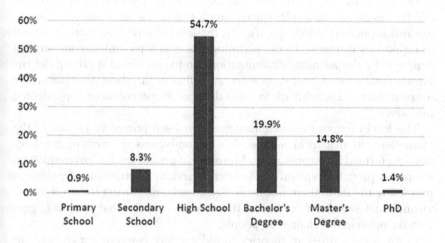

Figure 8.9 Level of education of respondents (n. 1,400)

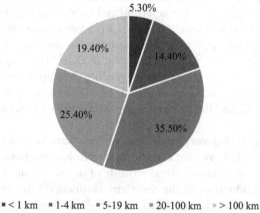

■ < 1 km   ■ 1-4 km   ■ 5-19 km   ■ 20-100 km   ■ > 100 km

Figure 8.10 Travel distance to the stadium (n. 1,398)

than 1 km). About 25% of respondents travelled between 20 and 100 km, while almost 20% travelled more than 100 km to get to the stadium: these percentages are noteworthy in terms of the environmental impact related to the mobility of supporters (Figure 8.10).

8.2.1 Measuring the environmental awareness of supporters

The first part of the survey assessed football supporters' environmental awareness by investigating (1) their environmental values, (2) environmental behaviour in daily life and (3) perceived knowledge of environmental issues.

Understanding the level of environmental awareness of supporters is crucial for designing and implementing environmental actions that are oriented towards supporters. More specifically, the level of environmental awareness of supporters can serve in the planning phase as a preliminary measure to design and tailor adequate dissemination campaigns aimed at raising the environmental awareness of supporters, as well as in the phase of performance measurement as a benchmark to assess the effectiveness of those implemented initiatives.

The level of environmental awareness has been proved to be one of the main elements that influence people's responsiveness to environmental actions performed by organisations. Moreover, a greater level of environmental awareness partially explains the greater behavioural intentions of people in protecting the natural environment. Ultimately, measuring the level of environmental awareness can be the first step in a process that aims to trigger positive behavioural change on people.

In psychology different theories consider values as important antecedents of behaviours, orienting individuals in how to judge the surrounding reality. The rationale is that personal values influence how people make decisions, judging what is right and what is wrong and thus orienting their behaviours. The higher the environmental values of a person among his/her values, the more probable he/she will adopt a pro-environmental behaviour.

The large majority of respondents – more than 90% – agree or strongly agree with each of the four sentences regarding the importance of (1) protecting the environment and natural resources, (2) preventing pollution, (3) respecting the Earth and living in harmony with other species and (4) fighting climate change.

These results show a very high level of environmental values of supporters, who strongly believe that the natural environment should be preserved. However, such pro-environmental attitude of supporters does not necessarily imply an actual adoption of the most environmentally friendly behaviours, as explained above by the so-called attitude-behaviour gap. For instance, if

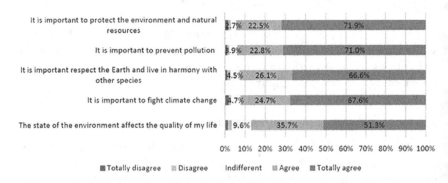

Figure 8.11 Environmental values of respondents (n. 1,393)

a football fan possesses high values towards the environment but he does not perceive that he can effectively contribute to the global cause of protecting the environment with his personal behaviour, he will be discouraged from translating its values into concrete actions. In this report, 13% of respondents are indifferent or disagree with the fifth statement, which is *"The state of the environment affects the quality of my life"*. This result highlights that the impact of the state of the environment on the supporters' quality of life is not perceived as important as their environmental values, which may be one of the factors that contributes to the existence of the attitude–behaviour gap.

One of the aims of raising environmental awareness among football supporters is to promote their environmentally responsible behaviours in daily life, both at home and during sport events. Sport organisations and policymakers can implement various marketing campaigns, such as the use of green advertising or the involvement of sport athletes and celebrities to trigger behavioural change. In order to identify the environmental practices that need to be fostered among supporters, it is necessary to measure their current level of engagement with those environmental practices. Moreover, assessing the supporters' environmental behaviour in daily life allows to empirically validate the relationship between values and actual behaviours, theoretically discussed by many scholars. Behaviours in daily life are measured in this report by assessing supporters' frequency of adoption of seven sentences, each corresponding to a good practice of environmental behaviour.

"Carrying out separate collection", *"preventing food and water waste"* and *"reducing energy consumption"* emerge to be the most implemented environmental behaviours. The three behaviours have in common that they refer to environmental actions rather than environmental products. Among the three,

Figure 8.12 Environmental behaviour in daily life (n. 1,395)

"carrying out separate collection" has the most widespread adoption with the 85% of respondents that have always or often adopted such environmental behaviour. Most likely, the legal obligation to comply with this practice in many municipalities has raised the frequency of its adoption.

"Preventing food and water waste" is often or always adopted by almost 80% of respondents, while "reducing energy consumption" by 75%. High levels of adoption of these environmental behaviours can be explained by the personal benefits associated with those environmental practices. They are win-win solutions since safeguarding the natural environment allows supporters to save money, such as paying cheaper energy and water bills.

The same consideration is not easily replicable with the environmental behaviours that belong to the category of environmental products, i.e., "*using recycled products*", "*using recycled materials*" and "*purchasing sustainable products*". Lower levels of adoption are associated with those behaviours. Management scholars in the field of environmental sustainability demonstrated that green purchasing intentions are strongly influenced by price and quality. If prices of greener products are higher and/or their quality is lower, consumers are not willing to buy those products. This scientific evidence may be empirically confirmed by the data of this report, where three out of the four least adopted environmental behaviours belong to the category of environmental products.

Finally, the level of adoption of the behaviour "*using public transport*" needs to be individually discussed. Around 1,000 questionnaires have been filled in by Italian supporters probably living in Rome or Genoa, which are the cities where the questionnaires have been collected. These are two cities where the urban mobility is strongly affected by local historical development, land morphology and transport management. Taking a bus or other public transport is an environmental behaviour where many factors are taken into account by citizens, such as time of travel, quality, availability of the service and comfort. Therefore, the 23.3% of the respondents who answered that they never or rarely used public transport evaluated the poor performance of the abovementioned factors together with the potential environmental benefits. As a managerial consequence, local authorities and municipalities should try to increase the performance of such services in order to incentivise the use of public transport by supporters, and by more citizens in general.

Assessing supporters' perceived level of knowledge of issues related to environmental sustainability is fundamental in order to measure their environmental awareness. In this report, we investigated separately general aspects related with environmental protection, such as climate change or renewable energies, and specific aspects related with individual environmental behaviours such as how to properly carry out separate collection or recognise recycled products. Measuring knowledge on environmental aspects represents a crucial factor for interpreting people's responsiveness to environmental sustainability, especially in the sport industry where the supporters' proximity to clubs and sport organisations furtherly magnifies their reactions to environmental actions or programmes implemented. For instance, if supporters are not aware of climate change, they will probably be less interested, and even not favourable, towards climate change mitigation actions. Knowledge is the basis for triggering people's interest and willingness to change. Moreover, environmental campaigns of awareness raising should be targeted at increasing the adoption of supporters' pro-environmental behaviours, according to their specific level of knowledge on environmental aspects. In this regard, assessing how supporters perceive to adopt individual environmental actions in a well-informed way is crucial for making accurate interventions.

The results to the first set of sentences depict a similar trend in respondents' framing of general environmental aspects. The highest level of agreement was scored by "*climate change*", where 78.1% of respondents agree or totally agree to be well informed, while the lowest level of agreement belongs to "*renewable energies*", where the percentage of respondents who agree or totally agree with being well-informed on this topic is 70.7%.

Such results homogeneity may indicate that supporters do not individually delve into different environmental topics, receiving the same level of information from newspapers, social media or other communication channels. Consequently, their perceived level of information on general environmental aspects emerges to be similar and rather high among very different topics such as waste management and renewable energies.

Raising environmental awareness among supporters is also important to keep people informed on different environmental aspects, so that individuals can take decisions and act as consciously as possible.

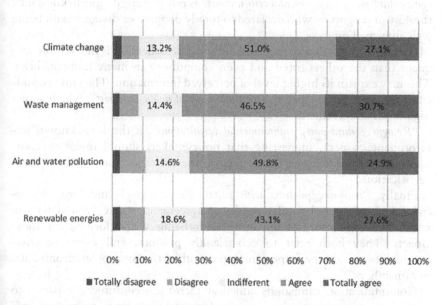

Figure 8.13 Fans' perceived level of information on aspects related to environmental protection (n. 1,361)

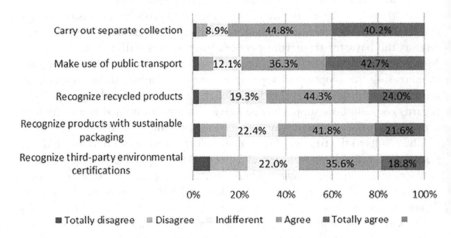

Figure 8.14 How supporters act in a well-informed way on the listed aspects related to environmental sustainability (n. 1,369)

With regard to the perceived knowledge on environmental aspects relating to individual behaviours, the results are much more heterogeneous than the previous ones. More than 85% of respondents agree or totally agree with being well-informed on "*how to properly carry out separate collection*", while "*recognize third-party environmental certifications*" is not perceived as well-known by the 45% of supporters who declared to totally disagree or disagree with being well-informed on it.

Certainly, the action of carrying out separate collection is much more frequent than the others listed and even compulsory in many municipalities. This may explain its higher level of perceived information. The same consideration is valid for the practice of "*make use of public transport*", which shows high levels of agreement.

"*Recognize third-party environmental certifications*" is the least known environmental aspect, suggesting that policymakers should invest in communication by informing consumers on the existence and utility of those certifications.

Finally, "*recognize products with sustainable packaging*" and "*recognize recycled products*" scored similar results of agreement, where around 65% of respondents agree or totally agree with being well-informed on those aspects. They both refer to eco-friendly products and green purchasing intentions, a very important topic within the area of environmental sustainability.

Communication campaigns aimed at increasing consumers' capacity to recognize sustainable products are fundamental in order to reward companies' efforts of using recycled materials or sustainable packaging.

8.2.2 Perceptions and expectations of fans about the environmental management of football

Because of its unique powerful cultural phenomenon football brings together people from all over the world and also generates large amounts of waste among impressive consumption of energy and water. Studies have demonstrated that the ecological footprint of football matches is considerable, yet, in recent years relatively little attention has been dedicated to the environmental impact generated by this sport. Throughout the last decades citizens have generally become increasingly attentive to environmental issues, stirring the need of industries and governments to update the level of attention towards environmental management. The same phenomenon is occurring today in the world of football, where football actors are increasingly becoming accountable for the ecological footprint generated during football matches.

In order to understand and better evaluate the ongoing cultural shift regarding environmental management of football matches it is crucial to understand football fans' perception of the importance of environmental management of football matches.

Respondents have generally shown that amongst fans there is an overall concern towards the environmental impacts of football matches. Well above the majority of respondents, in fact 86.3% of fans that answered the questionnaire, declared that they agree or totally agree that football should take care of environmental protection in the same way it takes care of other issues such as discrimination. Amongst those, the grand majority, 54.2%, said they would totally agree, thus demonstrating the strongest sentiment towards environmental protection. Similarly, 69.6% of respondents answered that they agree or totally agree that they would be much happier to attend a football match if they knew it was environmentally friendly. Among those respondents, 41.4% selected the option "totally agree" to show that they would gain happiness if the matches they attended were environmentally friendly.

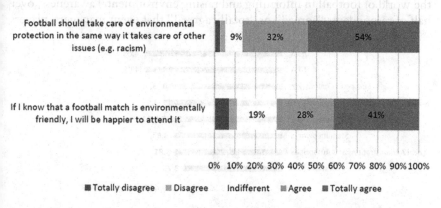

Figure 8.15 Fans' expectations of environmental management in the world of football (n. 1,394)

Another interesting aspect revolving around the cultural shift regarding environmental management is the football fan's opinion regarding who should be responsible for initiatives of environmental protection in the world of football.

The level of importance of the promotion of initiatives of environmental protection ascribed to the different organisations working in the world of football has been measured by giving respondents a list of eight different international/European/national/regional/local organisations working or influencing football management at different levels (UEFA, FIFA, European Commission, National Governments, National Football Associations, Stadium owners, Local Administrations and Authorities and Football Clubs). Fans had to attribute a level of importance ranging from 0 to 5, zero standing for "not important" and five standing for "very important" in order to evaluate whom, according to football fans, should be the most accountable for stirring environmental protection initiatives in this realm. Very interestingly the biggest organisations working at an international and European level, FIFA and UEFA, are seen by football fans as the most accountable entities for the encouragement of environmental protection initiatives in football. Both FIFA and UEFA scored a level of importance of 4.05. Not too far behind, with a level of importance equaling 3.92, the European Commission is viewed by fans as the third most important entity in the advancement of environmental protection in football. Right behind, with a score of 3.91, both National Governments and National Football Associations are the fourth and fifth most accountable entities in the eyes of football fans. Interestingly, according to respondents the least accountable organisations are the ones operating at the local level, such as Stadium owners (3.83), Local Administrations and Authorities (3.81) and Football Clubs (3.75).

Another question submitted to football fans regarded the role of different football actors in raising awareness on environmental protection.

When testing the perception of the role of different subjects operating in the world of football in informing and raising environmental awareness, over half of respondents "agreed" or "totally agreed" that event managers, players

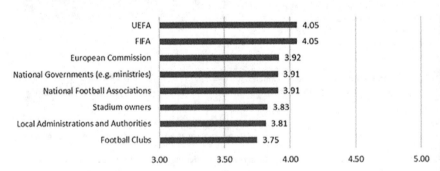

Figure 8.16 Level of importance given to each organisation in promoting initiatives of environment protection in football (n. 1,367)

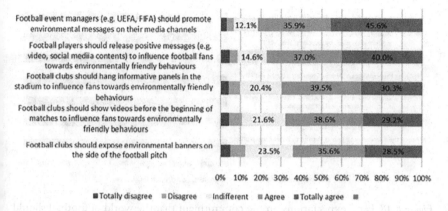

Football event managers (e.g. UEFA, FIFA) should promote environmental messages on their media channels — 12.1% / 35.9% / 45.6%

Football players should release positive messages (e.g. video, social media contents) to influence football fans towards environmentally friendly behaviours — 14.6% / 37.0% / 40.0%

Football clubs should hang informative panels in the stadium to influence fans towards environmentally friendly behaviours — 20.4% / 39.5% / 30.3%

Football clubs should show videos before the beginning of matches to influence fans towards environmentally friendly behaviours — 21.6% / 38.6% / 29.2%

Football clubs should expose environmental banners on the side of the football pitch — 23.5% / 35.6% / 28.5%

0% 10% 20% 30% 40% 50% 60% 70% 80% 90% 100%

■ Totally disagree　■ Disagree　Indifferent　■ Agree　■ Totally agree　■

Figure 8.17 Fans' perception about the different subjects operating in the world of football and their role in informing and raising awareness on environment protection (n. 1,394)

and football clubs all have to play a role. In this section of the questionnaire football fans were asked their opinions on whether football event managers such as UEFA and FIFA should promote environmental messages on their media. Many respondents (45.6%) totally agree that football event managers should promote environmental awareness raising. Another 35.9% checked the option "agree", meaning that the majority of respondents (over 81%) believe that football actors such as UEFA and FIFA should be the driving forces of environmental communication within the realm of football. The majority of football fans engaged in the questionnaire (77%) also answered that they agree or totally agree that football players should release positive messages on environmental protection, such as through videos and social media contents. Of these 77%, the majority said that they totally agree. When respondents were asked about the role that football clubs should play, the majority said that they agree or totally agree that clubs should hang informative panels in the stadium to influence fans (69.8%), that clubs should show videos promoting environmental protection before the matches (67.8%) and that they should expose banners on the sides of the football pitch (64.1%). Interestingly, when asked about the role that football clubs should play, fans tend to become slightly more indifferent than when asked about the role of football managers or football players.

Respondents were also asked about their expectation with regard to the commitment that the world of football should give to seven different environmental topics.

Overall, in all seven cases the majority of respondents "agreed" or "totally agreed" that the world of football should commit to these issues. Most fans (89%) believe that waste reduction is an important environmental issue that the world of football should commit to. Plastic consumption reduction is the second most voted on topic; 87.5% of respondents checked the boxes "agree"

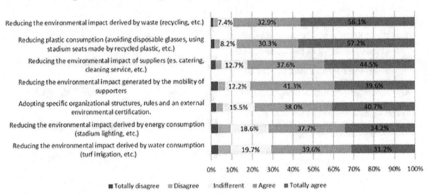

Figure 8.18 Fans' expectations on the commitment that the world of football should devote to environmental issues (n. 1,370)

or "totally agree". Reducing the environmental impact of suppliers such as catering and cleaning services is the third most voted topic; (82.1%) said that they agree or totally agree. In this case the number of fans that state to be indifferent increases over 4 percentage points from when asked about the reduction of plastic waste, and over 5 percentage points compared to when asked about waste reduction. When asked about whether the world of football should commit to the adoption of specific organisational structures, rules and external environmental certification, the majority (78.7%) of respondents agree or totally agree, but the percentage of fans that remains indifferent increases to 15.5%. The percentage of indifferent respondents increases also when asked about whether football should commit to the reduction of environmental impacts deriving from energy consumption (18.6%) and to reducing the environmental impact derived by water consumption (19.7%). Nevertheless, in both cases the majority of fans agree or totally agree that these topics are important and that the world of football should commit to them. And 71.9% of respondents agree or totally agree that the ecological footprint linked to energy consumption is a key subject and 70.8% of respondents agree or totally agree that football should commit to reducing the environmental impact derived from water consumption.

8.2.3 The role and pro-environmental attitude of fans during football events

Even if behavioural intentions do not correspond to actual behaviours, it is important to assess the supporters' level of willingness to adopt environmentally friendly behaviours, especially during football matches. Different environmental actions may correspond to different supporters' intentions. Many factors can influence the willingness of adopting a specific action, such as the level of knowledge concerning the environmental benefits caused by the

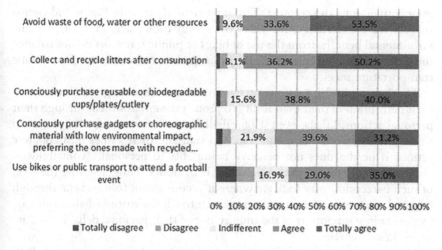

Figure 8.19 Fans' willingness to adopt environmental behaviours during a football match (n. 1,343)

action, or the cost to implement it. Figure 8.19 illustrate the supporters' answers concerning their willingness to adopt five environmental behaviours.

Almost 90% of supporters agree or strongly agree with the willingness to *"avoid waste of food, water or other resources"* and *"collect and recycle litters after consumption"*. The first action is both economically convenient and environmentally friendly: a win-win behaviour that is easily adoptable. The second action does not require any effort in terms of money or time but a minimum effort in looking at the right bin where to put the right trash. The two actions are both well-known and frequently performed at home; this facilitates supporters' willingness to also adopt them during football matches.

Regarding the environmental behaviours of *"consciously purchase reusable or biodegradable cups/plates/cutlery"* and *"consciously purchase gadgets or choreographic material with low environmental impact, preferring the ones made with recycled materials"*, respondents results show lower intentions to adopt them compared to the previous actions (78.8% and 70.8% of respondents respectively totally agree or agree with these two behaviours). For instance, these green purchasing intentions may lead to extra costs for supporters. The price factor may be an explanation of respondents' lower level of agreement. Moreover, the action of purchasing gadgets or choreographic material with low environmental impact may also appear to be difficult to be interpreted and implemented.

Finally, a lower score compared to the others is attributed to the willingness to *"use bikes or public transports to attend a football event"*: here it is interesting to note that 20% of respondents strongly disagree or disagree with this environmental behaviour. Such behavioural unwillingness of respondents may be explained by the negative influence of external factors concerning the use of public transport, which are not related to environmental issues, such as the scarce quality of the public transport service, the poor connections and comfort. This is particularly true for Rome and Genoa that are the two Italian cities where the survey took place. Probably, the environmental benefits from the use of bikes or public transport do not balance the perceived inconvenience in terms of quality and comfort of the public transportation service.

The behavioural intentions of supporters can be strongly influenced by their perception of their own ability to protect the environment through their personal actions. Likely, even if a football fan possesses strong environmental values, he/she would be demotivated to translate their values into concrete actions if he/she does not perceive being able to personally contribute to environmental protection through their behaviours. Thus, assessing the level of such perception may indicate where it is convenient to intervene through targeted environmental campaigns in order to fill the attitude-behaviour gap, by persuading supporters of the importance of their personal behaviours during football matches.

The responses collected do not present similar results. In particular, 80% of supporters agree or strongly agree that they have freedom in deciding whether to take environmentally friendly actions, however only 1/3 of supporters disagree or strongly disagree with the statement *"there is not much I can do individually to protect the environment"*. This means that supporters believe they have the possibility to adopt individual environmentally friendly actions, but they do not perceive that those individual actions can strongly benefit the environment.

The first managerial implication is that sports managers are committed towards environmental sustainability and desire to promote environmentally friendly behaviours among their fans, they should focus on communicating the contribution that each person can individually give to tackle environmental issues, such as climate change, air and water pollution. Thus, increasing

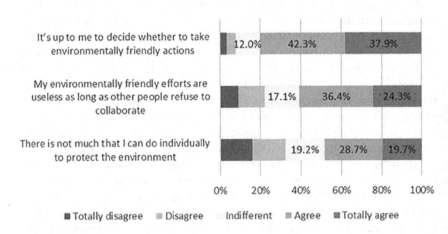

Figure 8.20 Fans' perception of the contribution that they can give to the sustainability of football events – part 1 (n. 1,352)

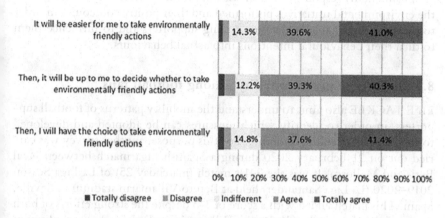

Figure 8.21 Fans' perception of the contribution that they can give to the sustainability of football events – part 2 (n. 1,348)

the perceived effectiveness of individual actions taken by supporters may fill the attitude-behaviour gap.

Also, more than 60% of supporters agree or strongly agree with the fact that their "*environmentally friendly efforts are useless as long as other people refuse to collaborate*". The power of taking collective action in solving environmental issues is perceived by many respondents as crucial, highlighting the social dimension of these problems.

As seen in the previous paragraph among the various actors that can trigger positive change, supporters' favourite football clubs are certainly the most appropriate for two reasons. Firstly, their visibility in newspapers, TVs and social media is very high, allowing them to reach most supporters in different ways. Secondly, the emotional connection and the identification of supporters with their favourite team can facilitate a process of acceptance and emulation of environmentally friendly behaviours. Figure 8.21 illustrates the results of assessing the supporters' perception of the contribution that they can give to the sustainability of football events if their favourite football club implements sustainable initiatives.

If combined with the findings of Figure 8.20, these results may signal that the difficulties of supporters in acting in an environmentally responsible way during sport events may be associated with a lack of commitment by their favourite football clubs towards sustainable initiatives. The results are similar for all the questions that have roughly the same meaning. More than 80% of supporters believe that "*it will be easier for me to take environmentally friendly actions*" if their favourite football club implements sustainable initiatives, as well as to have the choice to take environmentally friendly actions and to decide whether to take environmentally friendly actions. Implications for football clubs and sports organisations are straightforward. Implementing sustainable initiatives is in itself positive for those organisations who want to be environmentally responsible. Also, it is important to effectively communicate the environmental initiatives performed and their positive outcomes in order to promote sustainable behaviours among supporters and to influence them to turn their behavioural intentions into actual behaviours.

8.3 Incentivise green mobility among football fans

LIFE TACKLE also aims to understand the mobility patterns of football supporters, in order to identify which measures can be adopted and developed to support eco-friendlier mobility. For this purpose, another survey was carried out on 21 February 2020 during a Spanish Liga match between Real Betis and Mallorca. It was the 241st match (matchday 25) of La Liga Season 2019–2020 (La Liga Santander) held at Benito Villamarín stadium in Seville, Spain. This match ended with a score of 3-3 despite the strong efforts of both teams to win the match. The Benito Villamarín stadium is a home stadium of Real Betis and has a capacity for 60,720 supporters. However, this particular match was attended by 47,231 supporters.

Real Betis Balompié, one of the oldest football clubs in Spain, was founded in 1907. The club was granted an honorary title "Real" in 1914 by King Alfonso XIII. This club not only enjoys its rich history but also has been focusing on sustainability, installing sustainable solutions in their home stadium. Real Betis Balompié has more than 50,000 active members.

This survey was organised by Real Betis Balompié and a total of 208 football supporters participated in it. As in the other survey, the sample is mainly composed of young male adults, around 68% of respondents are male, while 32% are female (Figure 8.22). It is worth noting that over 62% of respondents are under the age of 34, of which 33.2% are between the age of 15 to 24, while 29.3% are between the age of 25 to 34. After these two age groups, 19.2% of respondents are between the age of 35 to 44 while 12% of respondents are between the age of 45 to 54. Only 6.3% of respondents are over 55. (Figure 8.23).

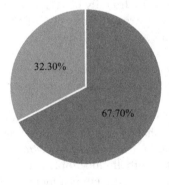

■ Male ■ Female

Figure 8.22 Gender of Real Betis' respondents (n. 195)

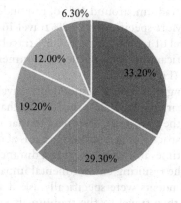

Figure 8.23 Age of Real Betis' respondents (n. 208)

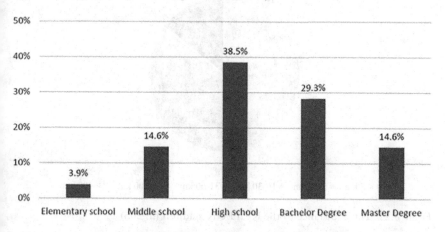

Figure 8.24 Level of education of Real Betis' respondents (n. 205)

With regard to the level of education, most of the respondents are well-educated. Indeed, around 43% of respondents have completed university education, of which 28.3% hold a bachelor's degree and 14.6% hold a master's degree. Also, over 38% of respondents have completed their high school education. In contrast, around 15% have completed middle school while 4% have just completed their elementary school education (Figure 8.24). In short, most respondents are well-educated youngsters who might be more sensitive to environmental issues. Thus, the obtained results (perceptions of supporters) of this survey could be really valuable in designing effective measures regarding the mobility of supporters.

Most of the respondents come to the stadium from nearby locations. Indeed, 54% of respondents travel the distance around 0–15 km to reach the stadium, of which 14.6% are residents from a distance of less than 5 km while

39.5% are residents from a distance between 5 to 15 km from the stadium. However, to reach the stadium, around 46% of respondents travel between 16 km to above 100 km. More specifically, 27.3% travel 16 to 30 km, 8.8% travel 31 to 60 km, 3.4% travel 61 to 100 km, and 6.3% travel above 100 km. These figures are surely significant in terms of the environmental impact due to the mobility of supporters (Figure 8.25).

It is also worth noting that 85% of respondents travel to the stadium more than five times in a year (Figure 8.26): this means that the results are more generalisable because they are related to people that often attend matches. Suppose that half the capacity of this stadium, that is about 30,000 supporters, go to the stadium five times in a year covering a distance between 16 and 100 km, it is evident that the resulting environmental impact is significant.

In this survey, respondents were specifically asked about how they travel in daily life and how they travel to the stadium. It emerged that the most

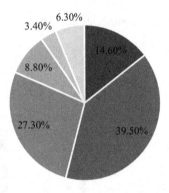

■ < 5 km   ■ 5-15 km   ■ 16-30 km   ■ 31-60 km   ■ 61-100 km   ■ > 100 km

Figure 8.25 Travel distance to the Real Betis' stadium (n. 205)

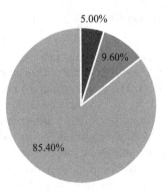

■ 1-2 times a year   ■ 3-5 times a year   ■ >5 times a year

Figure 8.26 Frequency of attending matches at the Real Betis' stadium (n. 198)

frequent means of mobility are private cars and public transport irrespective of the occasion. In daily life, over 65% of respondents often use cars and around 34% of respondents often use public transport. Over 25% of respondents often prefer walking, around 14% of respondents often use car-sharing, and only 8% of respondents often use bicycles (Figure 8.27).

When they travel to the stadium, over 65% of respondents often use cars and around 30% of respondents often use public transport. Over 19% of respondents often use car-sharing and around 13% of respondents often prefer walking. However, only 3% of respondents always use bicycles when they travel to the stadium (Figure 8.28).

It is worth noting that Seville city has around 160 km (100 miles) of separated bike lanes which are often protected from cars by a kerb and fence (Figure 8.29).

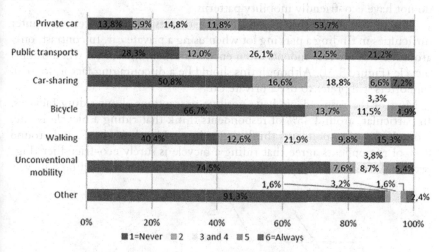

Figure 8.27 Mobility patterns in the daily life of Real Betis' respondents (n. 203)

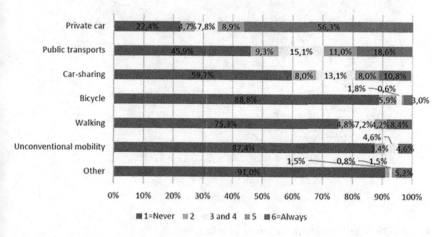

Figure 8.28 Mobility patterns to reach the Real Betis' stadium (n. 192)

Most of the respondents never use bicycles when they travel to the stadium to attend a football match, although the stadium is just 14 km from Seville Airport and 5 km from Santa Justa Station (Figure 8.30).

The more frequent use of private cars or the less frequent use of bicycles implies a higher environmental impact. As a matter of fact, respondents use private cars to reach the stadium most often in comparison to their daily life mobility patterns (+2.6%). Indeed, 56.3% of respondents always use private cars when they travel to the stadium. This is a bit higher compared to the case in daily life. Even though a significant number of football supporters come from nearby locations, only 3% of respondents (football supporters) always use bicycles when they travel to the stadium. This is a bit lower compared to the case in daily life (-1.9%). Also, public transport or walking is considerably less preferred to reach the stadium. In short, most of the football supporters do not have eco-friendly mobility patterns.

This survey shows that around 55% of the respondents often encounter difficulties in finding a parking lot when using a private car. In contrast, only around 6% of the respondents often encounter such difficulties when using a bicycle (Figure 8.31). Although this should be a discouraging factor, football supporters still prefer to use a private car.

Most of the respondents have positive perceptions about riding bicycles. In particular, around 45% of respondents think that riding a bicycle is safe, around 66% of respondents think that riding a bicycle is cheap, and around 80% of respondents agree that riding a bicycle is surely eco-friendlier (Figure 8.32). However, only 40% of respondents consider that riding a bicycle

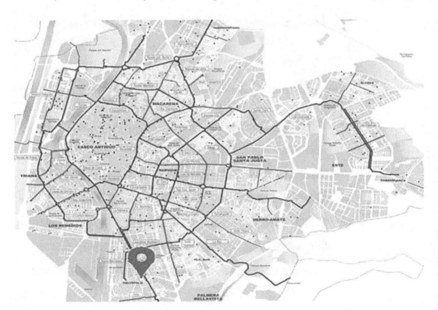

Figure 8.29 Seville city infrastructure of bike lanes

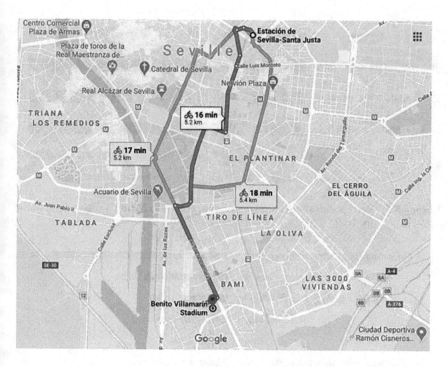

Figure 8.30 Cycling route from Santa Justa Station to Benito Villamarín Stadium

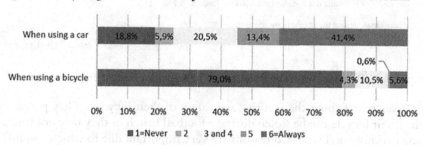

Figure 8.31 Difficulties in finding a parking lot near the Benito Villamarín Stadium (n. 186)

is comfortable. In other words, a significant number of football supporters perceive that riding a bicycle to reach the stadium is uncomfortable.

This survey revealed that most football supporters are youngsters who believe that riding bicycles is eco-friendlier. Yet they do not usually use bicycles to reach the stadium. Therefore, it is important to know what hinders football supporters from using bicycles to reach the stadium. In this regard, this survey highlights some factors. Around 55% of respondents indicated that they do not use bicycles because the stadium is located very far from their homes. It is worth noting that around 39% of respondents indicated that they

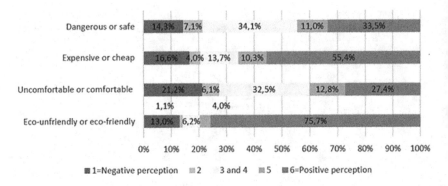

Figure 8.32 Perceptions about riding bicycles to reach the Benito Villamarín Stadium (n. 182)

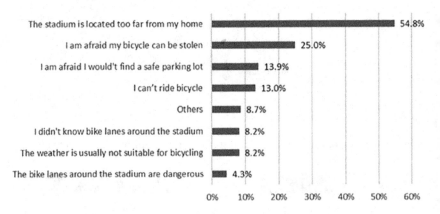

Figure 8.33 Barriers to using bicycling to reach the Benito Villamarín Stadium (n. 208)

are concerned about the security and safety of their bicycles. They perceive that their bicycle can be stolen during a football match or they may not find a safe parking lot. These two reasons are very important due to which a significant number of football supporters do not prefer to use bicycles when traveling to the stadium. There are also other reasons, though not prominent, due to which football supporters are often reluctant to use bicycles (Figure 8.33).

This survey revealed that if appropriate measures are taken then football supporters may use bicycles to travel to the stadium. In short, some measures such as installing bike racks, installing video surveillance cameras and paving safe bike lanes from the city centre to the stadium may promote riding bicycles which will consequently help to alleviate the environmental impacts of football matches (Figure 8.34).

To sum all the information collected thanks to these two surveys, we can prove that supporters have a biased perception of what are the most relevant impacts on the environment due to a football match. In fact, the most relevant issue is identified with waste and plastic usage. The indirect impact of CO_2

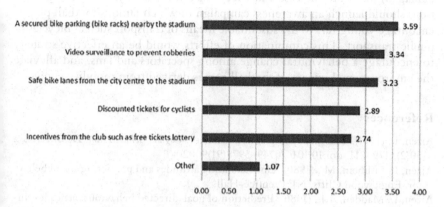

Figure 8.34 Potential solutions to promote bicycling to reach the Benito Villamarín
Stadium (n. 208)

emissions produced by supporters' mobility is perceived as only the fourth
most impactful issue and energy and water consumption are the less important in supporters' perception. There is a clear misalignment between the real
impacts of football matches, that are huge especially in relation to energy and
water consumption and to CO_2 emissions derived from supporters' mobility,
and supporters' perception about it. This interpretation might partially explain
why, when asked about the which actions they would be willing take during
matches to reduce their own environmental impacts, they enlist waste prevention and separate waste collection as the most relevant ones whereas the usage
of public transport or bikes is the least chosen option. Finally, supporters believe
they have the possibility to adopt individual environmentally friendly actions,
but they do not perceive that those individual actions can strongly benefit the
environment. Thus, there is the need to communicate and explain the contribution that each supporter can individually make to tackle environmental
issues during matches to encourage their pro-environmental behaviour.

If we look more specifically at supporters' mobility patterns, the results of
the second survey show that they usually opt for the use of private cars instead
of more sustainable means of transport. The more frequent use of private cars
and the less frequent use of bicycles among football supporters surely implies a
greater environmental impact. Benito Villamarín, the fourth largest stadium
in Spain, is fully equipped with modern facilities. Seville city has sufficient
infrastructure to support the use of bicycles, and there are bike lanes that
reach Benito Villamarín stadium from various locations within the city, such
as the city centre, the train station and the airport, as well as from the out-
skirts of Seville city. With all of this, it is surprising that football supporters
who reside in nearby areas often prefer the use of private cars over bicycles.

To encourage football supporters to use bicycles, we recommend the installation of bike racks and video surveillance cameras on the stadium premises
to ensure the security and safety of bicycles. In addition, the local government should improve bike lanes (or improve maintenance if bike lanes are

damaged) to ensure the ease and safety of cyclists. Finally, football organisations should launch an awareness campaign in which famous football players encourage youngsters to use sustainable means of transport such as bicycles or public transport. This combination of efforts would be an effective strategy to encourage a behavioural change among spectators and fans, and alleviate the environmental impact of football games derived from mobility choices.

References

Ajzen, I., (1991). The theory of planned behavior. *Organ. Behav. Hum. Decis. Process.*, 50(2), 179–211. doi:10.1016/0749–5978(91)90020-T

Ajzen, I., Fishbein, M., (1980). Understanding attitudes and predicting social behavior. Englewood Cliffs, NJ: Prentice-Hall.

Ajzen, I., Madden, T.J., (1986). Prediction of goal-directed behaviour: attitudes, intentions, and perceived behavioural control. *J. Exp. Soc. Psychol.*, 22 (5), 453–474. doi:10.1016/0022–1031(86)90045-4

Bandura, A., (1977). Self-efficacy: toward a unifying theory of behavioral change. *Psychol. Rev.*, 84, 191–215. doi:10.1037/0033–295X.84.2.191

Belk, R., (1975). Situational Variables and Consumer Behavior. *J. Consum. Res.*, 2, 157–164. https://www.jstor.org/stable/2489050

Bray, J., Johns, N., Kilburn, D., (2011). An Exploratory Study into the Factors Impeding Ethical Consumption. *J. Bus. Ethics*, 98, 597–608. doi:10.1007/s10551-010-0640-9

Carrington, M.J., Neville, B.A., Whitwell, G.J., (2010). Why Ethical Consumers Don't Walk Their Talk: Towards a Framework for Understanding the Gap Between the Ethical Purchase Intentions and Actual Buying Behaviour of Ethically Minded Consumers. *J.J. Bus. Ethics*, 97, 139–158. doi:10.1007/s10551-010-0501-6

Chaihanchanchai, P., Anantachart, S., (2022). Encouraging green product purchase: Green value and environmental knowledge as moderators of attitude and behavior relationship. *Bus. Strategy Environ.*, article in press. doi:10.1002/bse.3130

Chung, J., Monroe, G.S., (2003). Exploring Social Desirability Bias. *J. Bus. Ethics*, 44, 291–302. doi:10.1023/A:1023648703356

Fishbein, M., Ajzen, I., (1975). Belief, Attitude, Intention, and Behavior: An Introduction to Theory and Research. Reading, MA: Addison-Wesley.

Krumpal, I., (2013). Determinants of social desirability bias in sensitive surveys: a literature review. *Qual. Quant.*, 47, 2025–2047. doi:10.1007/s11135-011-9640-9

Larson, R.B., (2019). Controlling social desirability bias. *Int. J. Mark. Res.*, 61(5), 534–547. doi:10.1177%2F1470785318805305

Mezger, A., Cabanelas, P., Cabiddu, F., Rudiger, K., (2020). What does it matter for trust of green consumers? An application to German electricity market. *J. Clean. Prod.*, 242, 118484. doi:10.1016/j.jclepro.2019.118484

Padel, S., Foster, C., (2005). Exploring the gap between attitudes and behaviour: Understanding why consumers buy or do not buy organic food. *Br. Food J.*, 107(8), 606–625. doi:10.1108/00070700510611002

Rotter, J.B., (1966). Generalized expectancies for internal versus external control of reinforcement. *Psychol. Monogr.*, 80 (1), 1–28. doi:10.1037/h0092976

Testa, F., Pretner, G., Iovino, R., Bianchi, G., Tessitore, S., Iraldo, F., (2021). Drivers to green consumption: A systematic review. *Environ. Dev. Sustain.*, 23 (4), 4826–4880. doi:10.1007/s10668-020-00844-5

Index

Printed in the United States
by Baker & Taylor Publisher Services

Printed in the United States
by Baker & Taylor Publisher Services